D1522383

Metamorphic Readings

Metamorphic Readings

*Transformation, Language, and
Gender in the Interpretation
of Ovid's* Metamorphoses

Edited by

ALISON SHARROCK,
DANIEL MÖLLER,
and
MATS MALM

OXFORD
UNIVERSITY PRESS

OXFORD

UNIVERSITY PRESS

Great Clarendon Street, Oxford, OX2 6DP,
United Kingdom

Oxford University Press is a department of the University of Oxford.
It furthers the University's objective of excellence in research, scholarship,
and education by publishing worldwide. Oxford is a registered trade mark of
Oxford University Press in the UK and in certain other countries

© Oxford University Press 2020

The moral rights of the authors have been asserted

First Edition published in 2020

Impression: 1

Published in the United States of America by Oxford University Press
198 Madison Avenue, New York, NY 10016, United States of America

British Library Cataloguing in Publication Data

Data available

Library of Congress Control Number: 2020935104

ISBN 978-0-19-886406-6

Printed and bound by
CPI Group (UK) Ltd, Croydon, CR0 4YY

Preface

Ovid closed his fifteen-book epic of transformation with the metamorphosis of the poet into his work and his work into its own reception, summed up in the final word: *uiuam* ('I shall live'). The prophecy has been self-fulfilling, in that the *Metamorphoses* has entertained readers and inspired artists in different media for two millennia since the poet's death in AD 17. Loved for its vast repository of mythic material as well as its sophisticated manipulation of story-telling, the poem can be, and is, appreciated on many different levels and by audiences of very different backgrounds and educational experiences, whether it is for the tale of Pyramus and Thisbe or the endless but endlessly fascinating debate over the generic status of this epic which breaks all the rules and yet somehow must be included in any canon of Roman epics.

The present volume began life in a 2016 international meeting of *Metamorphoses* scholars in Stockholm, funded by the Royal Swedish Academy of Letters, History, and Antiquities, in conjunction with the publication of Ingvar Björkeson's new translation of the poem into Swedish. It is designed not as a handbook to the poem or a comprehensive introduction to the critical debates surrounding it, but as a collection of original scholarly articles addressing issues in the poem, articles which are united by interest in metamorphosis of and in language, gender, and theme. While all contributions are written for scholars, they seek also to be accessible to undergraduate students and to non-specialists (all Latin and Greek is translated).

AS, DM, MM

University of Manchester
Lund University
University of Gothenburg

Acknowledgements

The editors acknowledge with gratitude the support of the Royal Swedish Academy of Letters, History, and Antiquities. On behalf of all the contributors, Alison Sharrock would like to thank Mats Malm and Daniel Möller for organizing the Stockholm conference which was the initial driver for this volume. We are grateful also to Karen Raith and the team at OUP, especially our copy-editor Christine Ranft, for all their work in the production of this book, and to Julene Abad Del Vecchio for her work especially on the indices.

Contents

List of Contributors

Monika Asztalos is Professor Emerita of Latin at the University of Oslo. She has written on, and published critical editions of, Medieval Latin texts and is about to complete a critical edition, with a commentary and translation into English, of Boethius's *Commentary on Aristotle's Categories* for the Brill series *Philosophia antiqua*. Her interest in textual criticism in a historical perspective as an interpretative tool in the study of Roman poetry, manifested in the present contribution, has resulted in an online *Repertory of Conjectures on Horace* and an article on *Carmen* 4.10 in *HSCP* 93.

Alessandro Barchiesi is Professor of Classics at New York University. His work on Ovid includes a commentary on books 1–3 of *Metamorphoses*, in a multi-author commentary issued by the Fondazione Valla, and a general introduction to the poem.

Andrew Feldherr is Professor of Classics at Princeton University. He has published widely on Latin Literature, particularly in historiography and the poetry of the Augustan period. His books include *Spectacle and Society in Livy's History* (1998) and *Playing Gods: Ovid's Metamorphoses and the Politics of Fiction* (2010). Articles include studies on Ovid, Virgil, Sallust, Catullus, and Livy.

Mathias Hanses is Assistant Professor of Classics and Ancient Mediterranean Studies at Penn State University. His main research interests lie in Roman comedy and its reception in Latin literature; acrostics, telestichs, and related forms of wordplay; and Black Classicism.

Philip Hardie is a Fellow of Trinity College, Cambridge, and Emeritus Honorary Professor of Latin Literature in the University of Cambridge. His interests are chiefly in Latin literature and its Renaissance reception. His books include *Ovid's Poetics of Illusion* (2002) and *Classicism and Christianity in Late Antique Latin Poetry* (2019).

Niclas Johansson is Senior Lecturer in Literature at Mälardalen University. His research has focused on decadent, symbolist, and modernist literature in French, German, English, and Swedish. He is the author of *The Narcissus Theme from Fin de Siècle to Psychoanalysis: Crisis of the Modern Self* (2017).

Aaron Joseph Kachuck is Junior Research Fellow in Latin and Neo-Latin Literature at Trinity College, Cambridge. He works on the development of political and religious symbolism and their literary form in the early Principate, as well as on their intertwined reception in later periods, especially Early Modern Europe.

Mats Malm is Professor of Comparative Literature at the University of Gothenburg. He has published monographs on Early Modern Scandinavian historiography, the first Swedish novels, on Swedish Baroque and on the voice in poetry (*Poesins röster*, 2011). His monographs in English treat the Swedish Baroque from the perspective of history of literature, ideas, and media, and the reception of Aristotle's *Poetics*, following the definition of the soul of poetry up to Romanticism.

Daniel Möller is Associate Professor of Comparative Literature at Lund University. He has published two monographs on seventeenth- and eighteenth-century Swedish literature, *Dumb Beasts in Hallowed Tombs: Swedish Funerary Poetry for Animals 1670–1760*, trans. Alan Crozier (2015) and *Rolldiktningens poetik. Olof von Dalins experimentella tillfällesdiktning* (*The Poetics of Role-playing Poetry: Olof von Dalin's Experimental Occasional Verse*, 2019). Möller has also co-edited an anthology on Swedish verse *c.* 500–2016, *Svensk poesi* (*Swedish Poetry*, 2016) and written several articles on Swedish and European Baroque and the Classical tradition.

Eleni Ntanou is Lecturer in Classics at the National and Kapodistrian University of Athens. She is mainly interested in pastoral and epic poetry and, generally, the study of genre as well as gender in Augustan and Flavian literature. Alongside these interests, she works with migration narratives, literary geographies, and identity.

Alison Sharrock is Professor of Classics and Head of Department of Classics, Ancient History, Archaeology, and Egyptology at the University of Manchester. She has published extensively on Latin poetry, especially Ovid and Roman comedy, and has particular interests in literary theory and feminist approaches to classical literature. She is the author of *Reading Roman Comedy: Poetics and Playfulness in Plautus and Terence* (2009), and of *Seduction and Repetition in Ovid's Ars Amatoria 2* (1994). She is co-editor, with David Konstan, of the series *Oxford Studies in Classical Literature and Gender Theory*.

Louise Vinge is Professor Emerita of Comparative Literature at Lund University. She is the author of many books and articles on comparative literature, including *The Narcissus Theme in Western European Literature up to the Early 19th Century* (1967) and *The Five Senses: Studies in a Literary Tradition* (1975).

Robin Wahlsten Böckerman is a Swedish Research Council postdoctoral researcher at the Department of Romance Studies and Classics, Stockholm University, and visiting researcher at the Centre for Medieval Literature, University of Southern Denmark. His research is focused on the medieval commentary tradition on Ovid.

Introduction

Unity in Transformation

Alison Sharrock, Daniel Möller, and Mats Malm

At the end of the extended account of Phaethon's disastrous celestial journey (*Met.* 1.750–2.400), the hapless charioteer's family and friends give way to wildly expressive grief. Phaethon's father, the Sun, refuses to shine (2.329–32); his mother, Clymene, wanders over the world looking for his scattered bones until she finds his tomb (made by some helpful nymphs, 2.325–8) at which to mourn *in extremis* (2.333–9); his friend and cousin Cycnus turns into a swan (2.367–80), the first of three metamorphic characters of this name in the poem;[1] and the boy's sisters, also children of Helios, turn into trees (2.340–66). These metamorphic mini-narratives might seem like a token metamorphosis as a coda to the long and somewhat baroque account of Phaethon's attempt to drive the chariot of the sun across the heavens, tacked on in order to justify the presence of the whole extended episode within the *Metamorphoses*.[2] Although the Heliades, including their metamorphosis into trees, are a well-attested part of the myth of Phaethon in Roman and especially Greek literature,[3] such an interpretation of them as a tokenist add-on would not be entirely out of keeping with Ovid's sometimes outrageous mechanisms for creating a form of poetic unity in his playfully problematic epic. What makes their moment in the spotlight more than just tokenism, however, and thus a useful symbol for this volume, is that they can both reflect back on their brother's ordeal and also stand programmatically for significant aspects of the poem as a whole and for how it has met its readers over the last two millennia. It is as a symbol of the present volume and its relationship with Ovidian transformative mechanisms that we offer this brief reflection on the episode, drawing out its implicit metamorphic unity.

[1] A Cycnus who becomes a swan (*olor*) is mentioned also at 7.371–2, while the extended account of the invulnerable opponent of Achilles (12.72–145) ends with Cycnus' transformation into a white bird who keeps his name (12.144–5).

[2] See for example Galinsky (1975) 49: '[t]he metamorphosis theme is tacked on only perfunctorily at the end of the story, when Ovid mentions the transformations of the Heliades and Cycnus'. See also Sharrock (2018) 128 for discussion of such 'tokenism' with regard to the death of Orpheus.

[3] It is a well attested part of the myth, for which see Barchiesi (2005) 230–1, 264. Tragedies by both Euripides, whose *Phaethon* seems to have been well known, and Aeschylus refer to the Heliades, as does a scholion to Homer *Odyssey* 17.208, which includes the weeping of amber tears. See also Norton (2013) 145–8.

Alison Sharrock, Daniel Möller, and Mats Malm, *Introduction: Unity in Transformation* In: *Metamorphic Readings: Transformation, Language, and Gender in the Interpretation of Ovid's* Metamorphoses. Edited by: Alison Sharrock, Daniel Möller, and Mats Malm, Oxford University Press (2020). © Oxford University Press.
DOI: 10.1093/oso/9780198864066.003.0001

The metamorphic climax provided by the Heliades draws attention to the subtler or even negated transformations within the Phaethon story, perhaps the greatest of which is the near-return to primaeval chaos—a kind of anti-transformation perhaps—and thus to the very beginning of the poem. More explicitly, the cataclysm caused by Phaethon's failure to control the chariot of the sun is responsible for the darkened skin of the Ethiopian people (2. 235–6), for the creation of the Libyan desert (2.237–8), and for the famous riddle regarding the source of the Nile (2.254–5).[4] More nebulously, on the other hand, but potentially significantly, we might note that the (catasterized) Heliades play an important role in the prologue to Parmenides' fragmentary philosophical poem on the nature of the universe, where they act as guides to the charioteer who seeks the path of enquiry and wisdom. Whether Phaethon's own chariot-ride had a place in Parmenides' proem is disputed,[5] but the exploration of their story by Ovid may create an additional link between the Heliadic family and the poetic-philosophical tradition of cosmology, which Ovid remythologizes through his account and throughout his poem, after Lucretius had told the story (5.396–406) then determinedly demythologized it as the irrational story of Greek poets.

> scilicet ut ueteres Graium cecinere poetae.
> quod procul a uera nimis est ratione repulsum.
>
> Lucretius 5.405–6

Thus indeed the ancient poets of the Greeks sang, a story which is excessively far removed from true reason.

The fact that the Heliades, called by their brother's name rather than their standard patronymic, appear also in the Song of Silenus in Virgil's sixth *Eclogue* is another link to the philosophical-cosmological tradition, with Virgil leading the way on remythologization.

> tum Phaethontiadas musco circumdat amarae
> corticis atque solo proceras erigit alnos.
>
> Virg. *Ecl.* 6.62–3

Then he surrounds the sisters of Phaethon with the moss of bitter bark and raises up from the ground tall alders.

---

[4] See, for example, Loos (2008) 282. Loos argues that the story may also hint at a catasterism for Phaethon into the constellation Auriga, an aspect well known elsewhere (for example in both Nonnus and Claudian) but not explicit in our passage. On the relationship with Nonnus, see Knox (1988). Likewise, Ahl (1985) 178–81 suggests that the reference to Aurora at 2.113 may constitute a nod towards the alternative parentage for Phaethon given by Hesiod (*Theog.* 984–91), from Eos and Cephalus, on which see Ziogas (2013) 69–70.
[5] Granger (2008) 6 and his note 15.

The daughters of the Sun, then, enhance the cosmic significance of Phaethon's cataclysm and the poem's place in the philosophical-scientific tradition of Greek and Roman literature and thought.

The Heliades are among the many women in the poem whose metamorphosis is explored not only in detail,[6] but also with a high level of emotive identification with the victim.[7] The reader has already met one woman-tree in Daphne's story, itself highly programmatic as the first erotic tale of the poem.[8] Now, however, the emphasis on the suffering involved in metamorphosis is much developed, with words of complaint (2.347, 352, 355) and finally with the violence of the bleeding tree which epitomizes the horror of metamorphosis, when their mother attempts to pull off the tree-elements which appear to cover but are in fact part of her daughters.

> truncis auellere corpora temptat
> et teneros manibus ramos abrumpit; at inde
> sanguineae manant tamquam de uulnere guttae.
> 'parce, precor, mater,' quaecumque est saucia clamat,
> 'parce, precor; nostrum laceratur in arbore corpus.
> iamque uale'—cortex in uerba nouissima uenit.
>
> *Met.* 2.358–63

She tries to pull off the bodies from the trunks and breaks the tender branches with her hands; but from there bloody drops ooze as if from a wound. 'Spare me, I beg you, mother' each one shouts as she is wounded, 'spare me, I beg; our body is being lacerated in the tree. And now farewell'—the bark came over the final words.

This moment looks forward to future suffering trees in the poem, including the bleeding Lotus-tree (*Met.* 9.334–93), and especially the most extreme example of anthropomorphic pain in a supposedly stable changed form, which actually maintains its human feeling—the Myrrha-tree straining to give birth. The Heliades and Myrrha are more obviously linked, in addition, by the precious substance which exudes from them/their trees right down to Ovid's own times.

> inde fluunt lacrimae stillataque sole rigescunt
> de ramis electra nouis, quae lucidus amnis
> excipit et nuribus mittit gestanda Latinis.
>
> *Met.* 2.364–6

---

[6] Barchiesi (2005) 264 describes Ovid's innovation here as consisting in the extraordinary virtuosity of the metamorphosis itself.

[7] See Sharrock in this volume.   [8] See Hanses in this volume.

From there tears flow and amber, dripping from the new branches, grows hard in the sun. A clear stream receives the drops and sends them to be admired by Latin brides.

> flet tamen, et tepidae manant ex arbore guttae.
> est honor et lacrimis, stillataque cortice murra
> nomen erile tenet nulloque tacebitur aeuo.

Met. 10.500–2

But still she weeps, and warm drops ooze from the tree. There is honour also to these tears, and the myrrh which drips from the wood retains the name of its mistress and will be spoken of forever.

Both episodes, then, end with a reference to future time. For the Heliades, this reference explicitly links deep mythic time with contemporary Rome, thus crystallizing the issues of dynastic succession which scholars have seen as informing Ovid's Phaethon and his interaction with his father.[9]

We suggest that the Heliades' story is emblematic of the way in which metamorphosis in the poem is not just a matter of stories of people (especially women) becoming trees, spiders, lizards, horses, birds, rocks, water, gods, and poems, etc., but also a pervasive transformative force explored in the metamorphic manifestations of identity, imagery, narrative, intertextuality, intratextual structure, and interpretation, throughout the epic and its reception. Just as this transformative force, working with the reader's intratextual desire for order and the strong figure of the poet, acts to pull the poem together, so too are the ten chapters in this book drawn together by their focus on metamorphosis in the extended sense described above, together with the strong figure of the poem.

Ovid's remarkable and endlessly fascinating epic is one of the best known and most popular works of classical literature, and, with the possible exception of Virgil's *Aeneid*, perhaps the most influential of all on later European literature and culture. It has been the subject of a number of important monographs recently,[10] while individual articles and chapters are liberally scattered around a range of publication venues. What is surprising, however, is the relatively small number of multi-authored volumes dedicated to the poem, despite the popularity of this form of publishing and despite the advantages in visibility and impact that can be gained from a collection focused on an individual work which is widely studied in Classical scholarship at all levels across the world. The most frequently cited collection, and deservedly so, is *Ovidian Transformations: Essays on Ovid's Metamorphoses and its Reception,* edited by Hardie, Barchiesi, and Hinds (1999). The current collection may, we hope, be seen in the tradition of this volume, while being perhaps somewhat more thematically focused than was

---

[9] Barchiesi (2005) 230, 231. On Phaethon as a (failed) repetition of his father, see Feldherr (2016).
[10] For example, Feldherr (2010), von Glinksi (2012), Ziogas (2013), Curley (2013).

appropriate for that seminal work of contemporary of Ovidian studies. More recently, Fulkerson and Stover's volume, *Repeat Performances: Ovidian Repetition and the Metamorphoses* (2016), constitutes a rare thematic volume on the poem, its focal point being 'repetition' in a fruitfully broad range of senses.[11]

Our volume takes metamorphosis as its underlying theme: the explicitness of this theme ranges from Barchiesi's highly focussed discussion regarding the poem's role in shaping our sense of ancient myths of metamorphosis, through the poem's own transformations of genre, language, gender, and the physical world, as well as entities within it, to discussions of the poem's reception in mediaeval and modern literature and scholarship, in which we can see the continued transformation of the text and its meaning. Despite the widely held view that Ovidian transformation is stable once completed, many of the papers are witness to the traces of change which survive the moment of metamorphosis, whether that is in the ongoing self-awareness of Io, Callisto, or Actaeon, or the bleeding trees explored above. Likewise, the poem itself can never be wholly fixed in shape, but retains some sort of identity whatever its permutations. That identity, ultimately, is what gives unity to this collection—and ongoing life to the poem.

The book is divided into three parts: Part I 'Transformations into the *Metamorphoses*', a short but essential section which sheds new light on the tradition leading up to Ovid's work; Part II 'Transformations in the *Metamorphoses*', which offers a number of new readings of the poem, with a particular interest in gender and the transformative, but also transformed, power of language; and Part III 'Transformations of the *Metamorphoses*', presenting new insights in the exceptionally rich reception of this seminal text.

Transformations into the *Metamorphoses*

The influence of the *Metamorphoses* on Western culture is of such magnitude that the preceding tradition is at risk of vanishing from sight. Nonetheless, Ovid's poem obviously stems from the Greek tradition. On many points, Ovid's sources have been mapped and precursors pointed out. In his introductory chapter, 'Reading Metamorphosis in Ovid's *Metamorphoses*', Alessandro Barchiesi turns the perspective in a most illuminating way: instead of looking for similarities, he uses the conclusions of previous research to define more closely what actually makes Ovid different from his precursors. In this way, Barchiesi is able to define a

---

[11] Between these two volumes have come two multi-authored collections wholly concerned with reception, Keith and Rupp (2007) and Clark, Coulson, and McKinley (2011) (in Ginsberg 2011). There have also been some excellent examples of essays on *Metamorphoses* in the Companion/Handbook format, including Hardie (2002a), Boyd (2002), Knox (2009), plus, as regards reception, Miller and Newlands (2014).

number of instances where Ovid on the one hand utilizes tradition, but on the other hand also transforms it and approaches metamorphosis in new ways. The instances Barchiesi maps span a wide register: state of origin and destination of the transformation, kinds, causes and reversibility of metamorphosis, aetiological and genealogical functions, issues of continuity and communication, and so on. Applying this perspective, Barchiesi paves the way for a number of future studies.

Transformations in the *Metamorphoses*

Part II begins with a study of the significance of metamorphosis for gender, and gender for metamorphosis. Alison Sharrock's chapter 'Gender and Transformation: Reading, Women, and Gender in Ovid's *Metamorphoses*' ties together previous approaches to a general discussion of the underlying notions of gender in the *Metamorphoses* and their aesthetic staging. Ovid often displays a remarkable attention to the psychology of female actors, but the question is to what extent this attention can be regarded as truly sympathetic and empathetic, and to what extent it is objectifying. Rather than treating this question in one or a few passages, Sharrock approaches the problem systematically. The chapter explores the rules which seem to apply to gender through transformation, including those instances that are actually metamorphoses of gender. Thus, not only a well-known example like Tiresias but a number of others are summoned to detail how Ovid does in a variety of ways sensitively represent female subjectivity—but only in negative contexts. Metamorphosis of gender goes almost exclusively in one direction. Sharrock suggests the possibility of holding in tension both sympathy and objectification, arguing that there is a disproportionate emphasis on women's (as opposed to men's) experience of metamorphosis and that this is combined with the power relations which make certain kinds of metamorphosis a negatively feminizing process. The chapter thus proposes new ways of laying bare the entangled notions of gender which run through the *Metamorphoses*.

In 'Between a Rock and a Hard Race: Gender and Text in Ovid's Deucalion and Pyrrha Episode (*Met.* 1.313–415)', Andrew Feldherr discusses Deucalion and Pyrrha's regeneration of the human race after the destruction of the flood. Feldherr links the hermeneutic 'transformation' of stones to bones both to a thematic interest within the narrative in the relationship of the new future to its Iron Age past, and to the readers' experience of the text before them. The key, he argues, to perceiving the connections between the content and the real-world presence of Ovid's text is the phenomenon of sexual difference. Within the narrative, the opposition between male and female encodes the difference between an ordered, stable future and a rebellious past. But this tension also involves the relationship between the new forms imposed on the world and the subsistence of a material stratum that implies sameness. New transformations, like Deucalion's of bones to stones, struggle to reconfigure reality, while the readings of Pyrrha threaten to erase this difference. Feldherr suggests that Ovid's foregrounding of gender as a formal aspect of his text helps to create a parallelism between the experience of the reader and the hermeneutic challenges that play out within the story. Against a narrative of remaking that correlates Ovid's translation of reality to representation with the Augustan escape from the disordered past, a gendered alternative emerges of blurring difference that pulls the text back to the world, and the ordered cosmos back to the eternal sameness of chaos.

Arethusa is a symbol (originally linked to Greek colonialization) who in Ovid's *Metamorphoses* is transferred from Elis to Sicily and transformed into a Romanized figure. In her article '*HAC Arethusa TENUS* (*Met.* 5.642): Geography and Poetics in Ovid's Arethusa', Eleni Ntanou demonstrates how Ovid uses Arethusa's geographical transition to thematize her transposition into a different cultural context—that of Italy, as well as a new generic frame, that of epic. Ntanou explores how the delineation of space in the Arethusa story and the altering of her identity contribute to the narrative of Ovid's *Metamorphoses* 5, as well as to the broader poetic mapping of the ever-changing world in the *Metamorphoses*. Ovid, Ntanou argues, activates in the spatial context of Arethusa's story the possibilities offered by Arethusa's past in colonial myths and in pastoral poetry in order to renew the poetics of epic. Arethusa's tale is enclosed in the narrative of Ceres' search for the abducted Proserpina. Arethusa presents herself to the goddess and narrates how she migrated from the Peloponnese to the Syracusan Ortygia in an effort to escape the river god Alpheus. The story of Arethusa's and Alpheus' travel was traditionally deployed in ancient geographical treatises and in the mapping of the world stemming from colonialism. Ovid picks up Arethusa's association with migration and her meta-poetic symbolism to renew the epic genre, by systematically mapping out Arethusa's travel.

Aaron Joseph Kachuck's chapter, 'Ovid's Dream, or, Byblis and the Circle of *Metamorphoses*', explores the role played by the Byblis episode in Ovid's *Metamorphoses* as a form of authorial self-portrait. Byblis, placed at what this paper shows to be the poem's chronological centre, is both the work's first long-form writer and its first, and only, dreamer of fully human dreams. Where Morpheus in the *Metamorphoses*' House of Sleep may serve as model for the poet as shape-shifter and creator, Byblis represents the intimate connection between creativity and self-deception in Ovid's poetic programme. Through Byblis, this paper argues, Ovid comes to recapitulate Latin literature's 'primal scene of instruction', the Hesiodic and Callimachean dream of Homer that opens Ennius' *Annales*. This paper unfolds in three parts: first, a review of the place of metamorphosis in dreams, of dreams in Ovid's *Metamorphoses*, and of the dreamlike qualities of the poem as a whole; second, a close reading of Ovid's account of Byblis (*Met.* 9.454–665) that focuses on the connection between her dream, her metamorphosis, and her status in the poem as *prima inventrix* of literature; and, finally, an exploration of Byblis' exemplary role in Ovidian self-fashioning by reading her story into, and against, the poem's narrative frame (*Met.* 1.1–4; 15.871–9). The metempsychotic dimension of Ovid's representation of his own poetic project, this paper concludes, has important affinities with the circular form of the self-perpetuating fountain into which Byblis is transformed, and with the anthropocentric dreams that make possible Byblis' metamorphosis, and the circle of Ovid's *Metamorphoses* as a whole.

In Mathias Hanses' chapter, '*Naso deus*: Ovid's Hidden Signature in the *Metamorphoses*', the author makes observations on the presence of a thus-far undiscovered telestich at *Met.* 1.452–5, spelling out the noun Naso. Hanses posits that it ought to be connected to the acrostic *deus*, noted by Isidor Hilberg at 1.29–32. Together, the two so-named intexts form the authorial signature *Naso deus*, which resembles Ovid's references to himself elsewhere in his poetry and invites a number of playful interpretations ranging from the metapoetic to the political. By including intexts in his poetry, Ovid inserts himself into a tradition of literary sophistication that reaches back ultimately to the Hellenistic era. Yet Ovid's signature also highlights the poet's role as the demiurge who created the cosmos of the *Metamorphoses*. The *deus* acrostic occurs in a passage describing the formation of the universe, and the *Naso* telestich marks the famous *Primus amor Phoebi* episode, which narrates the world's transformation into a truly Ovidian realm of illicit sexual affairs between humans and gods. For this literary creation, the signature suggests, Ovid can claim divine status, and the title of *Naso deus*. Since it constitutes a claim to immortality, Ovid's signature also invites comparison to another individual then declaring himself divine, i.e., the emperor Augustus. If we regard the signature from this perspective—and realize its similarity to such paratexts as the sphragis at the end of the *Metamorphoses* (15.871–9)—we notice that the intext engages the *princeps* in a battle of competitive self-memorialization. Not unlike an epitaph, Ovid's signature has been inscribed on a monument that will ensure his survival.

Transformations of the *Metamorphoses*

Our studies of the metamorphoses of Ovid's poem in reception start out with the seminal question as to whose text we actually meet in scholarly editions. The literary complexity of Ovid's *Metamorphoses* is what has made the work survive and reach so many readers. This literary complexity has also been a tool for deciding which passages to consider authentic, and which to discard. That is, the work has been defined and edited from certain understandings of its meaning and aesthetic standard. In that respect, the work as well as its author metamorphose through different editions and interpretations. In 'Latent Transformations: Reshaping the *Metamorphoses*', Monika Asztalos argues that the reverse can occasionally be detected in the poetic language: when an expression is repeated, the appearance (word) is the same while the inner being (meaning) is not. Three cases are discussed: (1) *latet siluis* at 3.393 and 400 in the Echo-episode, (2) *ars adeo latet arte* at 10.252 in the Pygmalion-story, and (3) *latebat causa/causa latet* at 7.525–6/7.576 in the story about the plague in Aegina. It is shown that in all three cases the hidden transformations are subtly signalled by the poet. In the first and third cases the poet's hints to the readers have been overlooked; as a result, lines containing one or both of the expressions have been considered interpolations by some critics and bracketed in the most recent OCT-edition. Arguments are presented in support of their authenticity, and it is suggested that in the first and second case textual problems, that may have arisen as a result of early readers' and copyists' failure to catch a hint by the poet, can be eliminated by means of conjectures rather than by bracketing entire lines. In the third case—the most intricate—it is shown that the meaning of a repeated expression is undergoing a transformation by reappearing in a different generic surrounding.

After this introductory chapter on the foundations of textual criticism, Part III continues with cases of text transformation in the long history of Ovidian reception. In 'The Bavarian Commentary and the Beginning of the Medieval Reception of the *Metamorphoses*', Robin Wahlsten Böckerman explores the earliest material witnesses to the medieval reception of Ovid's *Metamorphoses* and shows what they can tell us about what attracted the medieval reader to Ovid's great work. The earliest witnesses consist of two families of freestanding commentaries, both of which seem to stem from Bavaria around the year 1100. Wahlsten Böckerman demonstrates how the commentaries make use of several different interpretative strategies. These include, of course, explanations focused on the mythological background, but also comments on the grammar and vocabulary of the *Metamorphoses*, as well as explanations focusing on neoplatonic cosmography and Euhemeristic interpretations of Ovid's work. As this is the first documented stage of adapting, and in that sense transforming, Ovid's *Metamorphoses* for later readers, the categories of commentary discerned also lay the foundation for relating and understanding later stages of the tradition.

An entirely different type of material, and a different approach, is employed by Philip Hardie in 'The Metamorphoses of Sin: Prudentius, Dante, Milton'. While the transformations of Ovid have regularly served to introduce him into the Christian frame of reference, Hardie shows how three Christian poets—Prudentius, Dante, and John Milton—reworked metamorphosis into a snake, each in his own very specific way. The central text is *Metamorphoses* 4.569–603, where Cadmus and his wife Harmonia are transformed into snakes in fulfilment of a supernatural prophecy, the ultimate consequence of Cadmus' slaying of the serpent of Mars on the site of Thebes. While the metamorphosed Cadmus falls physically to the ground, in the Christian authors serpentine metamorphosis signifies a theological and spiritual fall. In the late fourth century, Prudentius projects the transformation on to Satan, while Dante in the early fourteenth century exploits Ovidian metamorphosis into snakes for the punishment of sinners in Inferno. Coming to the seventeenth century, Milton, a reader of both Prudentius and Dante, applies the metamorphosis to Satan, but in a very different way from Prudentius. Each of these Christian poets explores the motif of serpentine metamorphosis in their own language, and within their own culture. The demonic repetition of falls into serpentine metamorphosis also figures the repetitive migration of the Ovidian motif through the Christian centuries.

Finally, Louise Vinge's and Niclas Johansson's jointly written piece, 'Narcissus Revisited: Scholarly Approaches to the Narcissus Theme', brings the transforming force of reading Ovid's epic up to the present, by offering a view of the differences in the scholarly situation encountered by two researchers investigating the Narcissus theme at the distance of half-a-century—one in the 1960s, the other in the 2010s. In the first part, Vinge gives a view of the scholarly conditions under which she prepared her celebrated work on the Narcissus theme in the mid-1960s. Vinge describes how she collected her material, from Greek and Latin literature and onwards, up to the late seventeenth century—such as, for example, the twelfth-century lai *Narcisus*, Calderón's drama *Eco y Narciso*, and Sor Juana Ines de la Cruz's *El divino Narciso*. In the second (and longer) part, Johansson presents an overview of scholarly investigations of the Narcissus theme over the fifty years since the publication of Vinge's study. The expansion of theory in literary studies since the end of the 1960s has produced a wide range of different approaches to Narcissus. The theoretical advances as well as the growth of research on the Narcissus tradition has made it difficult to grasp the entire history of the theme. In the resulting divergence of perspectives, there arises an implicit disagreement not only about the meaning of Narcissus, but also about how Narcissus is conceptualized in the first place. The dispersion of the unified object matter is highlighted in particular by the transition from Narcissus to narcissism. By being generalized as a psychological concept, Narcissus ceases to be a well-defined mythological figure and the scholarly field devoted to him is ever more vaguely defined. What nonetheless remains as a common ground for this field is the thematological foundation laid by Vinge, which, perhaps in virtue of its relatively small theoretical load, has been able to stand the test of time.

These ten chapters are all linked not only by their focus on a single, albeit highly varied, poem, but also by the authors' explorations of change—in the world, in the poem, in the meaning of metamorphosis, in the effects of language, change which exists as much in the process of reading as it does in the simple transference from human to vegetable or mineral state. Perhaps the best symbol for the volume is Byblis, transformed to water but more significantly also to book.

PART I

TRANSFORMATIONS INTO THE *METAMORPHOSES*

1

Reading Metamorphosis in Ovid's
Metamorphoses

Alessandro Barchiesi

Introduction

Change and the suffering for change (what we might call the underlying theme of the *Aeneid*) becomes a spectacle in Ovid's poem, and undergoes a process of aestheticization which has controversial moral implications.[1] Ovid rejects the structure of Homer and Virgil, a main story that is open to digressions, and instead proposes an open-ended collective poem, where it is up to the reader to judge the links between the stories and introduce order to the chaos of the narrated world.[2]

Metamorphosis is not a 'major' or primary category in Greek thought or myth or religion: it is the strength of Ovid as a narrator of the inexplicable, and then the later tradition, which also includes Kafka, that creates a sort of retrospective illusion. We might even state that our current general idea of Greek myth[3] has been conditioned by Ovid's *Metamorphoses* and the spectacular transposition of myth implemented in a Roman setting. The task of examining the entire Greek tradition has already been performed many times (e.g. Otis 1966, 346–94), but according to a preconceived idea: it is the search for a 'pre-Ovidian metamorphosis', entirely focussed on the interpretation of Ovid's poem. The Greek material has been thought of either as a 'source' of Ovid, or as a background that allows us better understanding of the continuities and even innovations in his work. However, it is useful radically to reassess the matter of metamorphosis. It is in fact necessary to ask ourselves if the strong presence of Ovid's work, which stands

---

[1] On 'reading metamorphosis' and 'reading Ovid's rapes' see the fundamental insights of Richlin (1992).

[2] For different overviews of the research see: Galinsky (1975); Hardie (2002a); Hardie (2002b); the essays of Segal and Barchiesi in Barchiesi (2005). Fundamental on the poetics of the spectacle are Rosati (1983), with an essay by Antonio La Penna, and Hinds (1987b). Among the commentaries to the poem, other than the series of volumes from the Fondazione Valla (completed in 2015 with the sixth volume edited by Philip Hardie, Books 13–15: Hardie (2015b)), those of Hopkinson (2000) to Book 13 and Myers (2009) to 14 have particularly useful introductions. As a short overview of Ovidian metamorphosis Feldherr (2002) is invaluable; a useful longer treatment is Solodow (1988), esp. 168–202. Good information also in the endnotes to the English edition by Michael Simpson (2001).

[3] Cf. Feeney, introduction to Feeney (2004); Barchiesi (2005).

Alessandro Barchiesi, *Reading Metamorphosis in Ovid's* Metamorphoses In: *Metamorphic Readings: Transformation, Language, and Gender in the Interpretation of Ovid's* Metamorphoses. Edited by: Alison Sharrock, Daniel Möller, and Mats Malm, Oxford University Press (2020). © Oxford University Press.
DOI: 10.1093/oso/9780198864066.003.0002

between ancient tradition and Medieval and modern European culture, has the power to falsify our perspective. Perhaps it is precisely Ovid's poem (with the whole history of its reception, at least until Kafka) which creates our preconception that there is a sort of stable category, mythical, psychological, and even cognitive, that should be called 'metamorphosis'. But the ancient Greek attestations themselves—if we look at them from a stand-alone perspective, freeing them from the Ovidian revision—resist this unifying reading. If we look at the Greek tradition, there is no terminological base or definition of metamorphosis that can act as a connective tool for all the different myths, or images, that we evaluate in the same framework because Ovid has collected and then arranged them in a unifying narrative structure.[4]

The aim of this paper is to emphasize distinctions between Ovidian metamorphosis and the Greek tradition, with an eye on the development of reception studies. I have used my experience as an editor of a commentary on Ovid's poem as a starting point, but I cannot record all of my debts to previous scholarship: the references in the footnotes are very selective and sometimes reductive.[5] Let us therefore try to give an overview of some recurrent aspects of the visual and textual materials to which reference is normally made while speaking about metamorphosis in Greece. For each initial statement, which defines the Greek situation, I look at differences and continuities with respect to Ovid.

Ovid and Greek Metamorphosis: a List of Differences in Approach

The Human and the Divine

In the Greek context, stories of metamorphoses that are popular enough to be illustrated (on vases, and to some degree on other types of decoration preserved to us), or attested in genres such as epic, lyric, and tragedy, principally have to do with the encounter between the human and the divine. The encounters are exceptional and critical moments, beyond the channels of socially accepted contact between humans and gods (cult and prayer). Most of them are moments of insecurity and danger: transitions in the life of an adolescent, solitude in nature, transgressions, or being exposed to the desire of the gods. At these times of crisis

---

[4] Useful with this in mind are Forbes-Irving (1990); Frontisi-Ducroux (2003); Buxton (2009), rich in perspectives, but often in debt to Forbes Irving and Frontisi-Ducroux; for a systematic vision of the more than 250 stories and micro-stories of metamorphosis in Ovid, Tronchet (1998).

[5] In general, in terms of variety of approaches, historical and comparative, to metamorphosis, Gildenhard and Zissos (2013) can be helpful as a first orientation. See also Warner (2002); Citti-Pasetti-Pellacani (2014) (my paper here complements and develops my contribution to that volume).

or dangerous intensification of the contact between men and gods, it is possible for the other border that defines the human—the one between the human and the animal—suddenly to collapse.

Ovid does not of course downplay this aspect: the poem opens by invoking the gods as authors of the metamorphoses, and in a certain sense co-authors of the poem. The presence of divine characters is recurrent, the sense of danger[6] is intense and almost physical for the reader. At the same time, there are also discontinuities. The presence of the gods as agents is in many cases invisible or enigmatic; the motivation may consequently be left in the dark, with a shift of interest towards the victim, the mutating subject. In any case, Ovid puts together stories where the gods are agents of bodily change and stories where the gods are impersonators and shape-shifters: this second approach has the important consequence of highlighting that basic paradox we all know about gods in ancient polytheism—for humans, gods are only accessible through incarnations anyway, and their natural essence remains a matter of speculation, so that the difference between their nature, their image, and their metamorphic adventures is always open to deconstruction.[7]

Therefore Ovid, while affected by the archaic Greek conception, did not wish to apply it consistently and systematically, while—as we will see shortly, and as the programmatic insertion of Pythagoras' message at the end of the poem shows[8]— in many other ways he gave greater consistency to a realm of the fantastic that is not unified and regulated by Greek culture.

Kinds of Metamorphosis

In Classical Greece, the transformation is usually from human to animal, more rarely into a mineral substance, while stories of 'phyto-metamorphosis' and aquatic metamorphosis tend to occur later,[9] in the Hellenistic age, and accounts of catasterism, transformations into stars and heavenly bodies, are notoriously later. There is no stable connection with the idea of apotheosis or heroization.

---

[6] Segal (1969).   [7] Cf. Feeney (1991) and von Glinski (2012), ch. 2.

[8] The didactic speech of Pythagoras reveals that the operations of metamorphosis constantly imputed to the gods in the epic narrative are in fact part of a natural law of change, since all of nature is about change, decay, death, and rebirth: there are interesting controversies regarding the seriousness of this message, and its degree of compatibility with the surrounding epic narrative, but what matters for us is that its level of systematic approach to natural knowledge transcends the typical contexts of Greek metamorphosis myths. What those two levels have in common (as a major difference from the representation of nature in Lucretius, where 'do not marvel' is the goal of the physiological argument) is the focus on 'wonder', a dimension of knowledge that includes curiosity and amazement.

[9] Much later for total transformations of people into streams and watersources, if indeed Forbes Irving (1990) 307 is correct that the earliest example is Parthenius, fr. 28 Lightfoot; see also Lightfoot (1999) 178.

Ovid treats animal metamorphoses and other kinds with equal interest, so much that his landscapes also include 'plant bodies' and even petrified *corpora*; however, he considers catasterisms a category in their own right, to the extent that he almost invariably includes them in his parallel work, the *Fasti*, and excludes them from the *Metamorphoses*. He does, however, include apotheosis in the plan of his epic poem, and does so with a special agenda. While the main corpus of the stories set in Greece and depending from Greek tradition registers divinization as a problematic, often catastrophic theme, the books set in Italy, which in general show a marked tendency to upbeat developments and improvements,[10] culminate with the divinization-catasterism of Caesar, which is no less than the announcement of the metamorphosis of Rome from republic to global empire and autocracy.[11] Both in the Greek tradition and in Ovid, there are certain restrictions that offer insights into the association between kinds of metamorphosis and shapeshifting subjects: for example, it is hardly a fluke that divine beings never change into a 'botanical body',[12] and that the humans that turn into water are almost exclusively women or boys, not virile characters. These restrictions are so fundamental that they occur in both Ovid and the Hellenic tradition.

Causes of Metamorphosis

In the great majority of cases, the myth or image incorporates an explanation of the mutation in terms of punishment or revenge, or at least divine intervention (next to punishment, the most common motive has to do with the lust of the gods for nymphs, young men, or mortal women).

As seen in section 'The Human and the Divine' these categories also recur in Ovid,[13] but there are also many others, such as pity, the impossibility of resolving a crisis, shame, or the action of an irrational and unexplained force.

Reversibility of the Transformation

The transformation is not always stable, but in several cases, as befits a punishment, it is reversible and limited in time.

In Ovid, the transformation regularly has conclusive and irreversible results, produces lasting forms, and the moment of a final aetiology is often stressed (but see also section 'Aetiology: Local Versus Global Metamorphosis').

[10] In this respect note the approach of Porte (1985) to Roman-style metamorphoses.
[11] Barchiesi (1997a); Hardie (1997); Feeney (1991).   [12] Cf. Forbes Irving (1990) 263.
[13] Indeed, according to Solodow (1988) 169, only on fifteen occasions (out of around 250 metamorphic tales) is punishment explicitly detailed, and in this group only four cases are expounded by the voice of the author.

Nature is in perennial flux, everything transforms, but metamorphosis tends to produce a new 'state of nature' that no longer changes. 'Metamorphosis is final'.[14] The reader can feel safe and reassured—unless he or she adopts the point of view of a potential victim (see section 'Causes of Metamorphosis').

Anthropocentrism (Partial)

Stories of metamorphosis are isolated crises, inserted into contexts that denote their exceptionality, and therefore are ultimately connected to a vision of the world that is anthropocentric and has a strong anchorage in the 'normality' of the relationships between bodies and identities.

Ovid's vision of the world is also powerfully anthropocentric, but metamorphosis tends to discover zones of ambiguity in nature's hierarchy: Ovid presupposes the natural knowledge typical in works such as Aristotle's biological writings, so he has a vision of the world that is much more cohesive, organized, and classificatory with respect to archaic Greece, but then he introduces a series of transgressions to this framework, such as plants and animals that not only hear but try to communicate across species barriers. The detailed cross-references between human and non-human bodies in the context of transformation are a triumph of the fantastic, but they also imply a good deal of systematic knowledge, a structural and comparative inter-species approach to nature. The repetition of these homologies (arms as branches, branches as arms, hands as fins, and so on) creates a narrative world where we do not need to be reminded every time: once we learn the analogies, they are always there for us, every time we experience a tree or a fish leaping in the sea, every time we touch the bark of a tree.[15] The repetition also promotes the centrality of the human body as a parameter for the knowledge of nature, just as it foregrounds the importance of human language in plotting those analogies and links in the realm of nature.

[14] Habinek (2002) 52.
[15] To list only a few examples, since space forbids a full analysis: arms and branches (a leading connection since *bracchia* is a regular word when talking about trees in Latin) 1.567, 2.352, 9.363, 375, 11.83–4 etc.; fingers and twigs 10.494; tears and sap, 2.364–5; arms and front legs, 2.669, 9.319; (fore) arms and wings, 2.580–1, 5.548, 14.501; hands and fins, 3.678; legs and tail, 13.963; skin and bark, 10.494; mouth and beak, 11.738; nails and claws, 10.699; hair and feathers, 14.498–9; arms and paws, 2.487; *umeri* and *armi*, 10.700; hair and leaves, *passim*; hair and mane, 2.673–4, 10.698–9; marrow and core of a tree, 10.497. Interestingly the process, once initiated, tends to include human artefacts and not only human bodies in the web of associations with the other species, so, e.g., train of a dress and tail, 2.672–3; human bodies and ships, 14.550–5.

Origin of Species

Metamorphosis does not usually have the role of explaining the aetiology[16] of the first specimen of a species: Io is not the first cow, nor is Actaeon the first stag.

Ovid also tends to avoid this kind of function of metamorphosis, but there are exceptions in the world of birds that may be significant. Some bird metamorphoses actually work as 'first sightings' of some new type of bird: this may have 'realistic' implications (in the avian world the appearance of 'new species' from the perspective of the human observer is a common experience) or sacred motivations (the ancient observer is more of an haruspex than a bird-watcher), or be connected to the sources used by the Roman poet (cf. the suggestively titled *Ornithogonia* of Boio or Boios, revived in Latin by a poet respected by Ovid, Aemilius Macer).[17]

Genealogy

Metamorphosis does not have the role of explaining the origins of human lineage, as happens in what is known as totemism: it does not involve families and groups of humans who may descend from weasels or apes, from falcons or dolphins.

Ovid also avoids this approach, with the sole exceptions of the genesis of postdiluvian humanity from stones and the famous legend of the Myrmidons, the 'anthumans'. The poem's relationship with genealogy and procreation is generally unsettled or perverted: 'The poem is an extraordinarily tense mixture of the generative and the perverse. And Ovid is not interested in reconciling them.'[18] The myth of Daphne, so prominently positioned in the structure of the poem as the first story about desire (1.452–567), is significant in this respect: it is the first erotic narrative, the main characters are a rapist god and a nymph from old times, and the episode acts as a model for many later situations in the epic. It looks as if the universal history of the *Metamorphoses* will adopt Hesiod's *Catalogue of Women* as its initial reference, since we know that in that Greek epic stories of mortal women or nymphs persecuted by the gods were a central topic.[19] However, Daphne also represents a surprise in this respect: her resistance to Apollo brings about a metamorphosis, and so prevents the story from reaching the ending typical of the *Catalogue*: unlike the heroines of Hesiod, Daphne will not be the mother of a hero, someone who will be a demigod or a king and the origin of some

---

[16] On other 'aetiological' aspects of metamorphosis, the production of new cults and institutions, see below, section 'Aetiology: Local Versus Global Metamorphosis'.
[17] See Magnelli (2014) 41–62. [18] Burrow (1988) 99–100.
[19] This kind of intertextuality is systematically researched by Ziogas (2013).

important Greek genealogy. With intentional irony, the narrator thematizes this surprise from the very beginning of his version of the tale, where Peneus is asking for grandchildren, but the story will not end up in childbirth. This approach to ancient traditions about gods and mortal women has the important consequence of focalizing the heroine and the rape in itself, not the origin of a genealogy, as the true interest of the stories, with the serious consequences examined by Richlin (1992).

Continuity and Gradualness

In the conventions for representing what we would call metamorphosis,[20] the treatment of time is never gradual and progressive.[21] We rather witness a series of abrupt 'leaps' that may naturally be inherent in poetics and the style of various forms of representation (for example narrative epic style, the typical mythological references of lyric poetry, the special treatment of time typical of figurative art in that period), but that as a whole still give an impression of consistency. Narrative texts tend to treat the transformation as an instant in time, an abrupt, clear shift from one form to another; the figurative examples, as we shall see in the following section, oscillate between two opposite solutions, neither of them suitable for suggesting a gradual and continuous dynamic. In Greek, the basic styleme for the narrative representation of metamorphosis is something like *egeneto* ('became', a verb that also means 'was born'), or some other aorist. The Greek aorist is a verbal aspect (rather than tense) which has the precise function of representing verbal action as a point in time, as opposed to a gradual development or a result of previous action. Aorists typically convey the simple idea that, at a certain point, an event took place, without any specific implication of process or resultative product. In any case, mentions of metamorphosis tend to recur as a simple change, encapsulated in a single verbal element of the narrative. It would be silly to offer a long list of examples, so let me just quote a few typical moments from various epochs and literary genres (but always from mythological tales): 'they became dolphins' (*H.Hom.Dion.* 53); 'until Kypris made her a spring' (Parthen. 28.4 Lightfoot); 'they say she became the tree that is called "daphne" after her name' (Parthen. 15.27 Lightfoot); 'you shall become a bitch' (Eur. *Hec.* 1265); 'he turned his body' (Mosch. *Eur.* 79).

Ovid develops an innovative style of representation that focuses entirely on the continuity and the gradualness of the transformation, combining fantastical

---

[20] The word is not attested in Greek before the Roman occupation period, and Frontisi-Ducroux (2003) can be used to suggest that metamorphosis is not a unified field in Greek culture. Her claim that the word itself is not pre-Ovidian is, however, excessive: cf. Diod. Sic. 4.81.5; Strab. 1.2.11.

[21] The fundamental insight of Frontisi-Ducroux (2003) 91.

transgression and visual power (a choice to which Dante will be sensitive). At the level of poetic diction, he valorizes expressions like inchoative verbs (the forms in -*sco* that highlight the start of an action and its evolution), or certain kinds of adjectives and participles indicating change and dynamics (e.g. *subitus, nouus, modo factus*, etc.). Important are also figures of thought exploring grey areas, indecisions, in-between states, 'not quite but almost', 'not the real thing yet an imitation of it': so e.g. 1.405–6, 2.667–8, 3.237–9, 4.378–9, 8.512, 12.203–4, 13.607–8, 14.508–9.[22] This whole strategy of his becomes a leading influence on the figurative art of later eras (cf. section 'The Implicit and the Hybrid'), although it is not in turn directly conditioned by well-defined figurative models in Greco-Roman painting or statuary. He may have had poetic predecessors, but they are unlikely to be from the Greek sphere. Some conjecture (see below, section 'First Conclusions and Possible Developments') is possible with regard to the Neoteric poems that we label epyllia, such as Cinna's *Smyrna* or Calvus' *Io*, which were in any case short texts, not works of epic proportions.

The Implicit and the Hybrid

In figurative art,[23] the way of representing metamorphosis is divided into two strategies: the implicit and the hybrid. In the implicit approach, what we see is animal, and so the viewer must rely on his or her expertise to supplement the story of the transformation (Io represented throughout as a heifer, but in a setting that indicates her exceptional biography), or what we see is human, and in the same way the viewer must proceed according to the image's implication (Actaeon, perfectly human, torn apart by his dogs; or Actaeon hidden under a deerskin). In the hybrid approach, the figure appears established but dimorphic, as if a Centaur or a Triton, not in transition from one form to another; Io can be a girl with horns, or a heifer with a human face; Actaeon, a human with a stag's antlers, or a stag with a human face.

Ovid, as was seen in the preceding section, establishes a new trend, which in figurative art will bear fruit only later on, such as with Bernini's *Apollo and Daphne*. If we start from the dual approach typical of ancient figurative art, we might want to speak of 'momentary hybrids', but this would still be reductive

---

[22] See the brilliant discussion and more examples in Solodow (1988) 186–8; note however that when he points out, as an exception, one specific precedent in Greek poetry, Ap. Rh. 4.672–3, the passage is not actually a good fit for the Ovidian dynamic approach: the sentence 'beasts, but not similar to wild beasts nor to humans in their bodies, a combination of heterogeneous limbs' is an Empedoclean fantasy of hybridization, not the representation of a transitional state.

[23] See the important discussion by Sharrock (1996); for a renewed attention to similes in the poem note also von Glinski (2012), which complements Sharrock's approach. On the interactions between text and image in Ovidian studies, see Colpo, Ghedini, and Tondo (2011).

vis-à-vis the dynamism of Ovid's representational strategy: 'transient hybrids' would be a more adequate definition.

Communication and Emotions

Finally, and this is a crucial difference, in the Greek sphere there does not appear to be any special interest in the theme of communication and emotions during the process of transformation. Ovid, however, has placed communication and the emotions of the character undergoing a transition or crisis of identity at the centre of his work. It is important to note how these aspects are practically absent when we consider Greek stories of transformation and loss of identity: in particular, voice[24] and gesture seem almost to be the 'author's signature' that Ovid imposes on the Greek material he readapts and Romanizes in his poem.[25] Ovidian metamorphosis is phonocentric and uses voice to familiarize and defamiliarize metamorphosis.[26]

Aetiology: Local Versus Global Metamorphosis

I will finally single out a theme to which the critical literature may not have given the attention it deserves.[27] I have already mentioned ideas of origin, of species and of human groups, but more important is the tradition of specific aetiologies, of names, cults, places, traditions and landscapes.[28] In the Hellenistic period, metamorphosis receives greater attention than in the past, with the works of authors such as Apollonius Rhodius, Euphorion, Parthenius, and especially Nicander, and

---

[24] I cannot offer a full discussion but here is a partial list of examples where voice and its transformation and loss becomes the focus of a myth (often as a conclusion or a climax): 1.233 Lycaon; 1.552, 567 Daphne; 1.637, 647–50 Io; 1.706–8 Syrinx; 2.355 Heliades; 2.373 Cygnus; 2.482–4 Callisto; 2.665–9, 675 Ocyrhoe; 2.829–30 Aglauros; 3.200–3, 229–31 Actaeon; 3.400–1 Echo; 4.239 Clytie; 5.192–4 Nileus; 5.561–3 Sirens; 5.677–8 Pierides; 6.374–7 Lycian farmers; 6.556–60 Philomela; 7.645–6 Myrmidons; 8.512–14 Meleager; 8.717–19 Baucis and Philemon; 9.369–70, 392 Dryope; 10.513 Adonis; 10.702 Hippomenes and Atalanta; 11.52–4 Orpheus; 11.192–3 Midas; 11.325–7 Chione; 11.734–5 Alcyone and Ceyx; 12.203–5 Caeneus; 13.567–9 Hecuba; 13.608–11 Memnonides; 14.60 Scylla; 14.99–100 Cercopes; 14.153 Sibyl; 14.280, 306–7 Macareus; 14.497–8 Diomedes' companions; 14.523 Apulian shepherd; 14.578–80 the city of Ardea. Again, detailed comparison with Greek models and parallels for the individual passages help to point out that there is no comparable tradition for representing 'vocal' metamorphosis in the pre-Ovidian tradition.

[25] This crucial point is emphasized by Forbes Irving (1990) 37; see also Buxton (2009) 112. A comprehensive monograph on Ovid and music/music in Ovid has been another important desideratum of Ovidian studies: the gap is now filled by the idiosyncratic but formidable historical excursus by Isotta (2018).

[26] There are a number of links in this area with the important study of 'absent presences' in Ovid's work by Hardie (2002b).

[27] But on Nicander and Ovid, Forbes Irving (1990) 29–30 is particularly important. Useful observations in Ducci (2013). For the authors of the Hellenistic age, cf. Magnelli (2014).

[28] A complex territory, well surveyed by Myers (1994).

this systematic interest is linked to the concept of aetiology. This idea obviously unites the Hellenistic poets with their Roman followers and interlocutors, the Neoterics and the Augustans, and is of fundamental importance to Ovid's poem. But the metamorphic aetiology of the Ovidian poem—here is the difference that should be clearly highlighted—functions in a very different way from that of its Hellenistic predecessors, who are Ovid's models and can be compared with him whenever the state of the tradition permits it. In a number of cases, as duly noted by Forbes Irving (1990) 29, the Roman poet omits cult *aitia* that were important enough to Nicander to form the conclusion of the individual stories.[29] Yet it is even more interesting to observe what happens when some form of *aition* is being adapted to the Ovidian narrative. Ovid systematically distorts, selects, manipulates, generalizes, and sometimes treats ironically local and localistic Greek aetiologies: origins of cults, rites, monuments, landscapes, natural elements, place and *polis* names, and all that has been established and made memorable through metamorphosis. His aetiologies are global and not local, rejecting scholarly scruple and precise identification with the continuity of the Greek world to which they belong. Ovidian metamorphosis is regularly the aetiology of something that is shifted, diverted, and appropriated in the great world of the Roman Empire; it produces *exempla* and, even more importantly, memorable and transferable emotions, instead of grounding and identification with the Greek territory and its mythology.

A good way to exemplify this difference is to look briefly at the scholarly dossier about one impressive discovery of epigraphic poetry, the so-called 'Pride of Halicarnassus'. This elegiac text[30] provides us with a Greek testimony about the cultural importance of the story of Hermaphroditus, not simply as a literary tradition, but as a vital part of the cultural heritage of the Greek city of Halicarnassus, an important settlement in the history of Greek colonization in Asia Minor. What happens if we compare this new text with the story of Hermaphroditus at *Met.* 4.285–388? As there is not space within the confines of this chapter to explore the exciting details of this text in their relationship to Ovid, I limit myself to one aspect. This is in fact about the role of aetiology in the two narratives. The Greek text, an epigraphic poem with a very significant location, is completely embedded, materially and intellectually, in the setting of a cult area at the periphery of Halicarnassus: besides its main topic, which is ostensibly the celebration of the origins of the Greek colony and its glorious history and traditions, the poem even offers the myth of Hermaphroditus as the

---

[29] The 'origins' and causes (*aitia*) of particular and local forms of cult are already a central concern in the *Aitia* of Callimachus, but metamorphosis is rarely mentioned in his work, and even more uncommon is a physical and visual description of those phenomena.

[30] See Isager (1998). On the transformation of Greek aetiology in *Metamorphoses*, Barchiesi (2005) CXXXVIII–IX, and above.

aetiology of the human institution of marriage.[31] The Ovidian text pointedly refuses to engage with those concerns in their original Greek context: far from being a story about the invention of marriage, this becomes a story about transgression and gender hybridity. The story is offered to a Latin-speaking audience where there is a limited interest for Hellenic traditions and aetiologies, and a strong curiosity for the extremes and the breaking points of human sexuality. This severing of the myth from its local setting amounts to the creation of a theme park of human desire and transgression: Hermaphroditus will take his/her place in a global arena of Romanized Greek mythology.

Although schematic, the difference between 'global' and 'local' aetiology could be helpful here. Some such difference seems to be operative wherever we know something substantial about a Greek metamorphosis story in its local and original setting.[32] The passion of the nymph Dryope (*Met.* 9.329–93) is in Ovid a study of transspecies suffering: according to Antoninus Liberalis (32, from Nicander), the metamorphosis is not only the origin of a tree in a specific sanctuary setting, but of an entire sanctuary, and of athletic games near Mount Oeta. The young hero Cyparissus (10.107–42) is the aition of a tree, and that looks like a hint of a Greek poetic tradition that we cannot access anymore: however, the specific funerary function of the cypress tree is more evident and relevant to a Roman than to a Greek audience (cf. Tissol 1997, 192). Byblis, the girl who melts into tears and water (9.450–665), is famous for the pathetic narrative of incest: she should be the origin, as the Greek texts attest (Ant. Lib. 30 etc.), of a well-known fountain in the Greek colonial metropolis of Miletos. This location gets lost in the Ovidian narrative of displacement and annihilation into nature:[33] once again, a triumph of emotional display and transgression over the idea of aetiological 'recuperation' to a locale and a Greek tradition. The story of Iphis, the culmination of gender-bending and trans-sexuality in Ovidian epic, does have a precise setting for its final coup, a sanctuary of Isis at Phaistos in Crete (9.773–6). Yet this location, precise as it seems, and capped by the aetiology of a memorable votive inscription (9.794), is no match for the Greek sources (Ant. Lib. 17.6), where the account is that from Iphis derives a religious name for Leto at Phaistos, plus the intriguing name of Ekdysia ('Strip-tease') for the name of the Leto festival in the same spot, plus the origin of a bizarre pre-nuptial rite. All the emphases in the Ovidian version lead elsewhere,[34] and there is no focus on the destiny of Iphis as the origin of permanent local traditions. Even the cult of Isis, not attested in the Greek sources for this anecdote, looks definitely more 'global' and attuned to the gender trouble that dominates the Ovidian version. One might compare here the situation for

---

[31] The difference with Ovid is discussed by Romano (2009), with other references.
[32] The discussion of Ducci (2013) ch. 5 is important here.   [33] See Kenney (2011) 468.
[34] For this 'elsewhere', see the memorable discussion of Kamen (2012), combining precise close reading with the impact of queer theory.

some major characters of *Metamorphoses*, such as Daphne or Orpheus, characters who claim a significant role in the reception of the poem: in all these examples, it becomes evident that the Ovidian signature is the focus on pathos, extreme situations, loss, displacement, and bodily change, versus a traditional Greek emphasis on aetiology and permanence of the myth *in situ* and inside Greek culture.

First Conclusions and Possible Developments

From here onwards, the argument of this paper could ramify in different directions. First of all, we could consider the idea of going into further detail about the history of metamorphosis in terms of verbal representation. We have already mentioned (above, section 'Continuity and Gradualness') that a continuous, visually oriented, and at the same time paradoxical and transgressive style of representation is the most visible trademark of Ovid's reinvention of the metamorphosis tradition. This point is so important that it connects with a number of other observations one could make about the poetics of *Metamorphoses*, for example the poetics of spectacle and entertainment, the ambivalent fixation on sexual violence, the lack of commitment to Greek aetiological tradition. Can we aim at a more fine-grained analysis of this tradition? It would be helpful to be able to locate this descriptive strategy in the wider context of Hellenistic literary history.

The most likely area of comparanda for Ovid's poetics of metamorphosis as regards literary system is the tradition of poetry that is often labelled as Alexandrian/Hellenistic and Neoteric. One would not be surprised if certain forms and stylemes of metamorphic narrative/description had been pioneered before Ovid, but not as early as classical Greek poetry. This leaves open possibilities for a section of Greek literary history that goes roughly from Callimachus to the Augustans. All critics agree that in this phase the interest in metamorphic myths was rising. Is it possible to be a bit more precise? First of all, metamorphosis is not a main concern in the most influential Greek aetiological poem, Callimachus' *Aitia*:[35] we should remember the caveat expressed at section 'Aetiology: Local Versus Global Metamorphosis' about the difference between Ovidian aetiology and Greek traditions of aetiology. But even authors who are known to engage with the theme of metamorphosis more systematically do not offer a true parallel for the Ovidian attention to somatic change. In Moschus, the author of the influential epyllion *Europa*, an author demonstrably familiar to Ovid, one would expect a particular attention to the dynamics of transformation.

---

[35] Note the paucity of reference to metamorphosis in the thematic index of Harder (2012).

The story of Zeus who 'becomes' a bull, carries Europa away from Asia, and manifests himself again as predatory male, seems to invite attention to its paradoxical transitions: the bovine identity of the god finds an interesting mirror in the story of Io in the inserted ecphrasis,[36] another story of divine rape and bovine metamorphosis but with an exchange in metamorphic roles (cf. *Eur.* 45 'still being a heifer, not yet having the nature of a woman'; 52 'from a horned cow she transitioned back to woman'); in view of the subtle collusion of the narrator with the predator god Zeus, it is intriguing that the poet's name means 'Calf' in Greek. However, when it comes to emphasis on the physical nature of metamorphosis, even this poet who clearly has a talent for sensual representation and malicious innuendo does not offer anything detailed: 'Zeus removed the god, modified his body, and became a bull' (79); 'Zeus recuperated his shape again, and loosened her girdle: the Hours prepared her bed: the one who was formerly a girl became the bride of Zeus, and she bore children...' (163–5).

Emphasis on the 'durative' aspect of transformation and on transformation as spectacle is also not important to Nicander, at least to judge from the scanty and indirect fragments, and there is no evidence connecting this style to other poets influential in Rome, such as Euphorion and Parthenius.[37] Among the Hellenistic poets, the only promising exception appears to be Lycophron, whose *Alexandra* has been unjustly neglected in many studies of Augustan poetry until recently.[38] Lycophron promises indeed more than other Hellenistic poems in terms of attention to the act of change in itself. To list quite briefly his connections to a metamorphic poetics, he has a recurring interest in animals as metaphors and symbols for humans and human endeavour, a style that frequently crosses over from human to animal reference, and a crucial interest for violent transformations in myth, landscape, and history: he is fascinated by hybridity, ethnic mixing, humiliation, and desperate voices of suffering women. All of this would seem to promote him easily to fellow-Ovidian, but there is one difference. Unlike Ovid, Lycophron does not tackle the mutation in terms of visual, sensual, and vocal features: he specializes in compressed and paradoxical intimations of metamorphosis: 'the dove, the Pephnaian bitch, to which the aquatic vulture gave birth' (87–8); 'he turned into male humans the army of six-footed ants' (176); 'wolf-shaped, who divided the flesh of Nyktimos' (481) 'the arboreal branch released her

[36] Perutelli (1978) on what he elegantly terms 'l'inversione speculare' between narrative and ecphrasis in the epyllia tradition.
[37] Lightfoot (1999) 39–40, 241–2, in her discussion of Parthenius offers very useful references to earlier poets such as Nicander and Euphorion, and deals with many stories that include (even potentially) metamorphic episodes or developments; on the new elegiac text (POxy 4711) that includes examples of metamorphosis see Henry (2005) and Hutchinson (2006). I am not convinced by the attribution to Parthenius of Nicaea and it is hard to be sure that the text is pre-Ovidian: in any case, the fragmentary poem does not include any representation of the act of bodily change.
[38] Hornblower (2015) brings new life to the study of this poem; note also McNelis-Sens (2016) and Hornblower (2018).

from the birth-pains' (829–30). My point is, therefore, about similarity but also difference. Similarity: it is not just that those myths are typically shared with Ovid and feature a prominent moment of change (unlike what happens in Callimachus): what is close to Ovid is also the delight in hybridity and physical transformation. However, the typical style for transformation in Lycophron is epigrammatic, not cinematic. To this end, he exploits the anomalous format of three-word trimeters, where the line is typically occupied by long words, especially creative compounds, and a certain tendency to brevity and mystery: metamorphosis tends to be alluded to, rather than described or narrated *in extenso*, by allusive strategies such as hybrid neologisms and learned kenningar. Those choices are of course all motivated by the overarching concern with prophecy and oracle that is fundamental to the poem, an extended speech by Cassandra.

In Rome, the Neoteric tradition, although very fragmentary and speculative for us, offers some promising hints. It is already customary to focus on the catalogue of mythical tableaux in Virgil, *Ecl.* 6.45–81,[39] where in particular the treatment of the Pasiphae, Phaethon, Scylla, and Philomela stories is suggestive of some prior tradition; but if we apply some pressure on the fragmentary evidence, at least two earlier epyllia, the *Smyrna* by Cinna and the *Io* by Calvus are worthy of mention here. Again, what matters to me is not so much that the mythical narratives are relevant to Ovid's epic poem (and they are, see Ov. *Met.* 1.568–750 and 10.398–513) but whether the representation of metamorphosis as a process and a situation of paradoxical hybridisation was a sort of 'money shot' in which the poet invested energy and sophisticated verbal art. The argument may be partly circular, but in his penetrating analysis of Calvus and Cinna Adrian Hollis moves precisely in this direction.[40] Dealing with Calvus, he notices that in the story of Io Ovid has an unusual emphasis on the process of reverse transformation from animal to human (*Met.* 1.738–46) and makes the attractive suggestion that this is *imitatio cum uariatione* since Calvus had already offered a detailed account of the transformation from human into heifer, and quotes Virg. *Aen.* 7.790 as a possible allusion to that Neoteric model. About the story of Myrrha and its treatment in Cinna, Hollis goes even further and remarks that if one compares Calvus, the *Ciris* with its (presumable) Neoteric models, and some passages in Virgil, Propertius, and even Lucretius, it becomes likely that the detailed account of transformation was actually 'standard in Neoteric epyllia'.[41] In short, the fragments of Cinna's well-known and much admired Zmyrna epyllion in their relationship to the Ovidian account of Myrrha warrant the speculation that the Neoteric poet did

[39] *Eclogue* 6 is crucial to well-known discussions such as Otis (1970) 48 'the nearest thing to the *Metamorphoses*' and Knox (1986), but they focus respectively on the structure of a collective poem, *perpetuum carmen*, and on the importation of elegiac sensibility and diction into epic narrative, while my interest is on the history of the 'durative', continuative, and spectacular approach to metamorphosis.
[40] See Hollis (2007) 51.   [41] Hollis (2007) 60–6.

have a pathetic and transgressive depiction of how the girl turns into a plant and continues to bear a child, in what may have been a poster example of interspecies metamorphosis. We can conclude that in the area of Neoteric experimentalism, in a strain of Latin literature that presents itself as strongly Hellenizing, the poetics of durative, physical, and pathetic metamorphosis took shape. It was a paradoxical birth, like the birth of Adonis from the myrrh tree, and it was mostly a specific Roman development, in spite of the huge claims of Hellenism displayed by the Neoteric poets. However, the danger of this approach is some kind of nativist, ethnic essentialism: far from claiming the existence of a 'Roman' and a 'Greek' metamorphosis as distinct entities, we should caution that the distribution of our evidence may be conditioned by some kind of implicit social difference, or even a class-based difference. The closest we get in the Greek tradition to an Ovidian style representation of bodily change is in fact a low-key text, a prose narrative that experiments with some kind of humble realism: it is the well-known transmutation of Loukios in pseudo-Lucian's *The Ass* ([13] '...but alas I did not become a bird. Instead, a tail sprang out from my behind, and all my fingers and toes vanished I know not where. I kept four nails in all and these were unmistakably hooves, while my hands and feet had become the feet of a beast, my ears had grown long and my face become enormous. When I looked myself over, I could see that I was an ass, but I no longer had a human voice with which to abuse Palaestra...'). If we do not want to restrict the analysis to the difference between Greek poetry and Roman poetry, we should remind ourselves that there is *diffidence* about metamorphosis in a number of important strands of the higher Hellenic poetic tradition (e.g. in the *Iliad*, in lyric, in mainstream tragedy, and in Callimachus) and that detailed bodily representation of change may well be a matter of literary and genre-based hierarchy, not just of language-based traditions. In this perspective, the point is rather that Ovid has opened up epic to a 'lower' style in the visualization of metamorphosis.

Once we locate the style in its tradition, however, we have not exhausted the interest of the topic. If we look at Ovidian metamorphosis, the problem of literary influence is far from being the most important. We should take into account the other main factors that emerge from our survey: the emphasis on visuality, on the voice, and on emotions. These factors have a strong link with the 'durative' strategy of representation, and it is not necessary to pinpoint any of them as cause or effect: together, they define whatever distinctive originality will be perceived in Ovidian metamorphosis by future readers such as Dante and Kafka; they create the conditions for the resistant readings of feminist criticism.[42] The aestheticization of the body and the importance of the voice are rightly emphasized in this critical tradition.

---

[42] See Richlin (1992); Liveley (2005); Sharrock in this volume. For influential work on the Renaissance rhetoric of the body Enterline (2000) and Stanivukovic (2001).

Can we say something to historicize the formation of this style? Here the research should refuse to accept a purely textual vision of the issues. First of all, it is important to focus on the visual arts and on material culture. Many studies have already suggested specific analogies between the poem and the practices of Roman visual culture: on the *Metamorphoses* as a 'sculpture garden' note for example Barchiesi (2005) CLIII-IV.[43] In this area the most important guideline has been offered by Andrew Feldherr (2010): in his discussion of metamorphosis as spectacle and as artwork, he cautions that no matter how many specific analogies we can discover between textual details and particular works of art or monuments, the really important connection is the one linking the entire poem with the 'culture of viewing' of Augustan Rome. Building on important arguments in Sharrock (1996)[44] and on the work of Jas Elsner (2007), Feldherr goes beyond the 'material turn' in Roman studies, and situates the representation of metamorphosis within the politics, not just the poetics, of vision and display.

If this is true, and I endorse his formulation, we should be busy more with ways of viewing and displaying than with single artefacts or places or monuments, no matter how important. In this context, perhaps the really important addition in recent years has been the impressive research by Ismene Lada-Richards[45] on the importance of pantomime as a context for the Ovidian manipulation of Greek myth. This perspective is of clear importance for our analysis: the distinctive impressions of bodily fluidity, gradual and spectacular transformation, and emotional representation of change, are all aspects that connect the Ovidian epic to the world of pantomime. We do not need to rehearse the many intriguing interactions suggested by Lada-Richards: our discussion up to now is a good preparation for her coup de theatre. The rapprochement between *Metamorphoses* and pantomime is so effective, that we should conclude by emphasizing a lingering difference. This difference signals one important aspect of the Ovidian project: the inexhaustible appropriation of visual spectacles into the text is empowering for the poet, but there is also an element of competition and resistance. We should remember that the other crucial figure of late-Augustan culture, Horace, had framed his opus as an alternative to the visual arts and to material culture, as if resisting the dominating politics of images and their power.[46] Now we can fully appreciate

---

[43] In that paper I quote the research by the art historian Ann Kuttner as my main inspiration. The approach has been somewhat revived by the chance discovery of the so-called 'Villa of Messalla' with its sculptures of dying Niobids in what was presumably a suburban park with *natatio*: see e.g. Calandra, Betori, and Lupi (2016). The Niobids were shot down during athletic exercise in the open air (cf. Ov. *Met*. 6.218 *planus erat lateque patens prope moenia campus*...), and their tragic death was represented in a famous play by Sophocles, the *Niobe*, a text that was perceived by some as scandalous and nicknamed *Paiderastria*, cf. Plut. *Mor*. 760d; Athen. 13, 601a; Easterling (2006) 12–5.

[44] Sharrock's emphasis on metamorphosis as metaphor is preceded by an interesting strain of Russian formalist theory, see the important paper by Pianezzola (1999, first published 1979).

[45] Lada-Richards (2013), a programmatic paper followed by other soundings (2016), (2018). Cf. also Barchiesi (2005) CLIV.

[46] See Hardie (1993).

the other crucial aspect of difference between Greek and Ovidian metamorphosis representation, the one succinctly evoked at my section 'Communication and Emotions': the primacy of voice (or its suppression and alienation) in the act of transmutation. The most eloquent vindication of this aspect is the work of Lynn Enterline, an essay focussed chiefly on early modern literature that represents (for now) perhaps the zenith of feminist criticism in the study of Ovid.[47] Precisely because the spectacle can be imagined as a matrix of the entire poem, the importance of voice operates as a corrective and a supplementary Ovidian signature: as a poet of voice and sound, Ovid guarantees to his text a space that cannot be entirely taken over by the many visual competitors that provide context and inspiration to his work, such as monuments, gardens, pantomime performances, sacrifice, the circus, and the arena.[48] Perhaps even our insistence on the visual in the poem is reductive: we need a more globally 'embodied' approach, like the one taken by Calvino (1979), who speaks about the 'percorso delle parole attraverso la persona del lettore'. Calvino, I suppose, was simply pointing out that this poem is a revelation that reading is an activity that involves the entire body, not just the mind.[49]

A Brief Epilogue About Reception

Beginning with these innovations, several events in the history of the *Metamorphoses*' reception appear more understandable. The narrative structure based on metamorphosis poses a continuous challenge to the reader: the saturation of the text in an allegorical setting may be arbitrary, but it cannot be denied that metamorphosis unleashes a continuous request for supplementation, precisely due to its violent rupturing of the categories of predictability and physical naturalness (after all, Ovid is the only Latin author to be a direct provider of images for psychoanalysis). At least two different trends branch off from here in the medieval age: the use of the poem as a sort of great book of nature—magical and scientific—and the development of allegoresis (anticipated, as we know, by important Ovidian experiments with allegorical ecphrasis, inserted into epic

---

[47] Enterline (2000). See also the helpful monograph by Natoli (2017) on voice and silenced voice throughout Ovid's work.

[48] Ovid, one must add, was an important theatrical author, at least with his influential tragedy *Medea*: the importance of tragic voices in his vision of myth should not be underrated (and note the important monograph by Curley (2013)). It is striking, however, that in the foundational text of Augustan classicism, Horace's *Ars Poetica*, the crucial examples for bad taste in theatrical representations of myths are all potentially metamorphic situations, such as the vision of Cadmus and Harmonia turning into snakes, something that in Ovid's *Metamorphoses* is pointedly described as metamorphosis *with spectators* (cf. *Met.* 4.598); cf. also the passages quoted in Barchiesi (1997b) 252 with n. 26. Ovid's vocal metamorphoses are in pointed contrast with Horatian prescriptions on what to avoid on the tragic stage.

[49] Cf. also Barchiesi (2005) CXXI.

action in a way that develops Virgil and anticipates Statius, Claudian, and the medieval epic). The loss of context due to the end of polytheism does not prove particularly serious for the poem's fortune, while Virgil has had to undergo deeper re-adaptations: the Ovidian spirit triumphs in Renaissance, Baroque, and Classicist painting. Fortune fluctuates, but if we had to venture an overall interpretation, we might say that while Virgil's *Aeneid* seems sensitive to political changes and great ideological crises, Ovid's text (which has often offered itself up as an alternative and counterweight to Virgilianism) entrusts its fortunes to changes of 'somatic economies',[50] to times at which a new sense of the corporeality and materiality of life is asserted.[51] In this way, we might explain that 'Ovidian' moments in European culture are in particular the late medieval period,[52] the first modern age,[53] and the twentieth to twenty-first centuries. In the case of our era, the contexts most likely to explain the unexpected return of the fortune of the *Metamorphoses*[54] have to do with the new relationship between nature and artifice (a great Ovidian theme)[55] and with ideas of 'correcting' physicality and consciousness: plastic surgery, genetic engineering, cloning, psychopharmaceuticals, virtual worlds, modification of digital images, cyborgs, or sciences such as bioethics, ecology, and artificial intelligence. Ovid's poem is becoming relevant again, no less than it was in the Rome of the first modern age, with its rediscovery of the marble bodies from the classical past.

---

[50] For the expression note Zissos and Gildenhard (1999).   [51] See also Kilgour (1991).
[52] Simpson (1995).   [53] Barkan (1986).
[54] For an alternative analysis see Ziolkowski (2005).
[55] Cf. in particular Hinds (2002) 122–49 and Italo Calvino's *Gli indistinti confini* (Calvino 1979), a sort of manifesto of postmodern Ovid. Magical realism, frequently influenced by Ovid (e.g. Rushdie, Garcia Marquez), has been a fundamental influence on recent readings of Ovid, and it is now time to evaluate new-wave Ovidian imaginations, often based on post-human visions and ecological crises.

PART II
TRANSFORMATIONS IN THE *METAMORPHOSES*

2

Gender and Transformation

Reading, Women, and Gender in Ovid's *Metamorphoses*

Alison Sharrock

Readers and Reading

Ovid's poetry has had, over the centuries, a remarkable ability to elicit and encompass different responses.[1] The *Metamorphoses*, with its self-referential instability and its extraordinary generic innovation, has so many 'further voices' that it may seem to lack any fixed centre to which those voices can be 'further'.[2] Inevitably, it being in the nature of reading, scholars have sought such fixity in many aspects of the poem, both thematic (love, art, metamorphosis itself) and structural (Otis' triadic structure, chronological movement *ab origine mundi ad mea tempora*), but it is in the poem's nature also to resist such drives.[3] Its very multiplicity, in characters, narrators, generic interactions, and even tone, together with infection from the poet's wider elegiac context, has meant that women in the *Metamorphoses* have received more attention than in other epics, while 'Ovid' has been regarded as 'sympathetic to women' even when such an attitude was an act of chivalry rather than a sign of heightened sensitivity and gender-consciousness.[4] Such is the material I seek to explore in this chapter: what are the possibilities

---

[1] It is customary to refer, disparagingly, to the tradition of 'Ovide moralisé' to illustrate the extent of this range. I would suggest, rather, that such readings are perfectly valid appropriations of the text for the purposes of the interpreters' context—just as I hope is mine to its.

[2] On this wide-ranging subject, Segal (2005) xxii–iii says (in my re-translation): 'the Ovidian body in the *Metamorphoses* can be compared to the carnivalesque body of Mikhail Bakhtin, because it is characterised by fluidity more than by stability, by porosity and the presence of cracks rather than by impenetrable barriers'. At the furthest extreme, Solodow (1988) 38: 'there is basically a single narrator throughout, who is Ovid himself', although this does not undermine his appreciation of the fluidity of the poem. Barchiesi (2001) chapter 3 is an important contribution to the peculiar type of polyphony in epic singularity presented by the *Metamorphoses*. See for example page 49: 'the polyphony of the *Metamorphoses* does not consist in the separation of narrative voices, but in an alternation among registers directly controlled by the single narrator's voice, according to an exhibitionary logic'. See also Barchiesi (2002).

[3] Ludwig (1965), Otis (1966) chapter 3, Galinsky (1975) chapter 2, Wheeler (2000).

[4] Keith (2000) is unusual in the extent of attention she gives to epic women. An example of reading Ovid as sympathetic to women is Curran (1978).

Alison Sharrock, *Gender and Transformation: Reading, Women, and Gender in Ovid's* Metamorphoses In: *Metamorphic Readings: Transformation, Language, and Gender in the Interpretation of Ovid's* Metamorphoses.
Edited by: Alison Sharrock, Daniel Möller, and Mats Malm, Oxford University Press (2020). © Oxford University Press.
DOI: 10.1093/oso/9780198864066.003.0003

when we read the poem with the benefit of modern ideals of reformed masculinity, contemporary gender theory, and the very recent far greater visibility of trans-gender identities and behaviours? This paper will look at the stability or otherwise of gender-categories in the poem, at some of its female characters and the processes of responding to them, and thereby at the extent of flexibility available to the (modern) reader in her, or his, interpretation.

'Gender' and 'women' are my subject matter, while my argument relates to the nature of reading. A simplistic expression of my case would be that there are many valid readings. This hardly surprising or innovative argument masks a difficult but important issue in what I would like to call the ethics of interpretation. Many readings might be valid, but not all are helpful.[5] Indeed, it is an inevitable consequence of the doctrine of multiplicity and situatedness in reading that it is not possible to claim, for example, that the fascist appropriation of Virgil is simply invalid: rather, I suggest, it is morally wrong. Reading—that is, literary interpretation—has a moral aspect in the same way as does all communication. While I ascribe to the view that the 'author's intention' should not (and for good theoretical reasons cannot) be the limit of the meaning of a text, a risk in anti-intentionalist criticism is that it might exonerate the author from all responsibility for what he or she says.[6] This, indeed, is a sleight of hand Ovid himself attempts in exile, when he develops the trope of disconnection between literature and life—in the face, be it noted, of a crash between the two—into a full-scale denial of responsibility for what he writes.[7] Ovid's claims that it isn't his fault if Roman women read what isn't meant for them, that he had offered trigger warnings, and that it's all made up anyway,[8] are part of a complex game—though perhaps it is Russian roulette—about literature, reading, crime and punishment throughout the exile. It is, in essence, the same argument as that which would deny any negative effect from violent videogames and Internet pornography.[9] What does it mean to claim that your poetry or other production has no effect? Is it possible to deny all responsibility for it? Although an author cannot have total control of the meaning of his/her work, the latter tenet should not be allowed to function as a get-out clause for the former.

I would suggest that this same point applies to what we do as modern scholars of ancient texts, since critics are writers as well as readers, both in the sense that

---

[5] By the claim in this sentence, I intend a cryptic allusion to St Paul, 1 Corinthians 10.23.

[6] I develop thoughts about the nature of authorship and readership, particularly as regards Classics, in Sharrock (forthcoming). Derrida's (1988) deconstructive defence of De Man is a classic instance of the problem.

[7] Catullus offers nice instantiations of the trope, for example in poem 16, where the contention that *castum esse decet pium poetam/ipsum*, [but] *uersiculos nihil necesse est* (4–6) is surrounded by threats of very physical (but metaphorical?) aggression against naive readers unable to appreciate the point, on which see Fitzgerald (1995) 49–53.

[8] See *Tristia* 2.243–56, 353–6.

[9] On this topic with regard to ancient texts, see O'Rourke (2018) 111 and his n. 4.

they create new (critical) texts and in that their critical writing is crucial in
constructing the ancient text for the modern reader. There is, therefore, also a
question of responsibility in interpretation. I do not intend to imply that only
those interpretations with which I agree are morally responsible, but rather to set
my discussion of multiple readings in a context which takes the process of
interpretation as a serious endeavour. Indeed, a critical move which I have already
made in this piece is itself an example of this problem in the ethics of interpretation and the control of meaning. In order to think about women, in order to
avoid the simple equation between human and male, the modern world has found
it necessary to use the abstract notion of gender. This paper, like many others in its
field of feminist approaches to classical literature, takes it as axiomatic that one
can slip comfortably between the categories of 'women' and 'gender', because the
two seem to belong to the same general semantic area. In doing so, however, we
arc inevitably (and I use the word advisedly) supporting the idea that men are 'just
people', whereas women are 'gendered', to the extent that female characters seem
to have more to do with the abstract notion of gender than do male characters—
which is a problem.[10] As I do not see any way out of this bind, I am obliged to
continue with the feminization of gender, but I hope the reader will bear in mind
the possibility—still at some remove from contemporary reality—of an academic
discourse in which gender is no more connected with women than it is with men.

My thinking about how (modern) readers respond to gender in the
Metamorphoses is informed by two dichotomies in feminist reading: resisting
versus releasing approaches and what I propose to call optimistic versus pessimistic assessments of the ancient authorial position. The first, the distinction
between 'resisting' and 'releasing' strategies in feminist interpretation, is a relatively well-known critical practice. In brief, a resisting reading, originally popu-
larized by Judith Fetterley's eponymous book, is one which identifies the
chauvinist, sexist, or other ideology of the text but refuses to play along with
it.[11] A releasing or recuperative reading, by contrast, opens up possibilities for
women's voices which exist in the text, but which have traditionally been downplayed or ignored by the critical establishment. Much of the important feminist
reading of Ovid's *Heroides* in recent years has come in this category.[12] My second
distinction, between 'optimistic' and 'pessimistic' readings, has not been widely
theorized in feminist literary criticism, but is widely observable in practice.[13] What

[10] I do not intend here to undermine the importance of the excellent work that has been done in the
last twenty-five years on Roman masculinity and on the gendering of the male, such as Gleason (1995),
Keith (1999), and Gunderson (2000), but to note that even such cases are liable to be classed alongside
feminist readings that are concerned only with female characters. 'Gender', even male gender, still tends
to go along with women, and risks being sidelined as such.
[11] Fetterley (1978). Good classical examples include Liveley (1999) and Salzman-Mitchell (2005).
[12] See especially Spentzou (2003), Fulkerson (2005), Fabre-Serris (2009).
[13] It has, for example, taken the form of wondering whether Ovid or Euripides 'is a feminist or a
misogynist'. Readers will notice my adoption of terminology which has considerable baggage in the

I am calling an 'optimistic' reading is when the author, whom for convenience I call Ovid, is regarded as 'sympathetic to women', and/or shown to be exposing fluidity of gender against the rigidity of Roman norms, in a way that looks remarkably modern. 'Pessimistic' readings, on the other hand, are those which regard Ovid as rather more compromised to his chauvinist social milieu and see him as reifying women and playing out Roman anxieties about masculinity.[14]

Such distinctions are susceptible to deconstruction: a common critical move in which the resisting reading is appropriated as optimistic is by presentation of the ancient author as exposing and/or parodying the positions being resisted, rather than being himself responsible for them, while a variation on this strategy is the description of a 'persona' who expresses the views resisted, rather than the 'author' himself. Such was the move I took in Sharrock (1991), an article which tends towards the optimistic, in that it constructs Ovid as delineating rather than enacting the elegiac objectification of the female as work of art. I read Pygmalion's creation of the statue as a misogynistic act to be resisted, but I presented Ovid as exposing this process on the part not only of Pygmalion himself but also of the elegiac norm. In contrast to Sharrock (1991), I would regard Sharrock (2015) as a much more pessimistic reading of Ovid: I argue that Virgil gives warrior-women the opportunity to escape from the objectifying and sexualizing Amazon image, while Ovid puts them firmly back into place, and the rest of the Roman epic tradition follows suit from him. Reading Ovid pessimistically in this way is a critical move that is made easier for the modern critic by the fact that another ancient poet (it happens to be Virgil) is lauded as the outstanding precursor of modern feminism.

An example of a strongly pessimistic reading is Richlin's famous 1992 piece on 'Reading Ovid's rapes', which lacerates the poet for his prurient and objectifying depiction of victims of sexual violence. While most readers do not feel able to go quite so far in principled vituperation, it is partly because of articles like this that it is no longer possible entirely to skate over or explain away the cruelty of the beautiful but disturbing world of the *Metamorphoses*. Many readers will soften the

interpretation of Virgil over the last sixty years. While what I am proposing for Ovid in the sphere of gender does not map simply onto the 'further voices' which have been identified for Virgil in (mostly) the political sphere, I feel that there is some value in the comparison, at least as regards the capacity of great works to encompass different readings.

[14] It is entirely possible for both pessimistic and optimistic readings to be feminist. It is no doubt also possible for optimistic and pessimistic readings, in my terms, to be anti-feminist, but I think it would be difficult for them to be uninterested in matters of gender. On the other hand, it might turn out to be useful to expand the terminology into other areas. Obvious candidates would be other matters of what I call 'situated' readings, such as those concerned with race or class, but in principle I think the categorization could apply usefully to any reading which is conscious of itself as something more than a paraphrase of the text. It would, moreover, be possible to characterize my 'pessimistic' reading as a form of 'resistance', while an 'optimistic' strategy would be a form of 'recuperation', not so much of female voices but of the poet himself.

blow for themselves by presenting Ovid himself as critical of the vices of his world. In addition, there has also been a strand in Ovidian criticism, especially around the turn of the millennium, of a much more extreme optimistic reading, produced partly by using the power of the releasing reader to draw out elements in the text which work against its own master-narrative. Liveley offers a good example of this extreme optimistic reading.[15] She presents her reading as a resisting one, which it certainly is, but it is also a releasing reading in that it gives a voice, metaphorically, to Eburna, the Ivory Woman herself, in the form of an implied agency to control as well as to interpret the world. The suggestion is that (the) Eburna might be manipulating Pygmalion by using the advice in Ovid's *Ars* 3. Although I cannot see it as entirely liberating to become the woman of *Ars* 3, I present (and admire) this interpretation as a strong form of the optimistic reading. Different in detail but similar in optimistic approach is the reading of Salzman-Mitchell on the statue, whom she calls 'Galatea',[16] of whom she says (188): 'Galatea is, then, symbolically the landscape and surface of the poem, into which the narrator and reader intrude. But the gaze of Galatea rejects this reading of *Metamorphoses* and its fixation of women. Galatea can be seen as a critical reader of the gender stereotypes that *Metamorphoses* proposes.'

Both the optimistic and the pessimistic responses to the *Metamorphoses* are valid readings of the poem. Often, however, our readings need to acknowledge both possibilities at once and to accept that the coexistence of objectification and empathy should make it impossible for us either to convict or to exonerate the poet.[17] In the remainder of this chapter, I shall be exploring the disproportionate sympathetic identification with the female victim undergoing metamorphosis, but showing how when the metamorphosis is precisely of gender the masculine is strongly prioritized, to the extent that male characters stand a much better chance than female of escaping from the potentially victimizing and objectifying power of involuntary metamorphosis. My reading will thus be—not on the fence between optimism and pessimism—but displaying both at once. As such, it could be regarded as a classic deconstruction of binaries. But is that morally good enough?

---

[15] Liveley (1999), especially 207.

[16] Salzman-Mitchell (2005) 184–93. Ovid himself never uses the name Galatea to apply to Pygmalion's statue, but it is indeed widely used in the tradition. See also Salzman-Mitchell (2005) 161 for a reading of Alcithoe as displaying 'a certain irreverence toward and independence from the overarching author'.

[17] An important recent contribution to consideration of aesthetics and violence in Ovid is Newlands (2018), where she describes the tension between these two as 'vital to the dynamic power of Ovid's poetry' (177).

Gender and (Lack of) Metamorphosis

It is remarkable, given its historical period, how much Ovid's epic poem is concerned with this important but problematic categorization that we call 'gender'. As is well known, the *Metamorphoses* is a poem in flux, where change extends far beyond the literal moments of direct corporeal metamorphosis. Indeed, the very concept of metamorphosis itself is highly fluid within the poem, in the degree of ongoing consciousness, the nature and extent of trans-formation, the symbolism and meaning of acts of metamorphosis, and the inter-plays between continuity and change.[18] In such a context, and given the prominent stories of sex-change, it strikes me as particularly surprising that, alongside its predictable preference for male gender, the poem in fact displays considerable *stability* in gender. I shall argue that although gender is foregrounded in this poem of flux, and is subject to metamorphosis itself, it nonetheless remains as a remarkably stable conceptual bedrock.

If a person is undergoing a major ontological change, such as that between human and vegetable, is it really necessary that the characteristics of human sexual dimorphism should be implicitly carried through to the new form? I suggest that this is, in most cases, exactly what happens in the *Metamorphoses*. From the beginning (so to speak) it was so: when Deucalion and Pyrrha repopulate the world after the flood by throwing stones over their shoulders, Deucalion's stones produce men and Pyrrha's produce women.[19] Most metamorphosed characters maintain their original gender as part of their ongoing consciousness, even though the latter varies in the extent of its continuity.[20] Io becomes a cow, not a bull—and a beautiful one at that: *inque nitentem / Inachidos uultus mutauerat ille iuuencam / (bos quoque formosa est)* ('he had changed the face of the daughter of Inachus into a shining heifer (and the cow was also beautiful)', *Met.* 1.610–12). Actaeon becomes a *ceruus* (3.194), not a *cerua*. Lycaon is a *lupus* (1.237), not a *lupa*. These examples are cases where Latin has distinct words for the male and the female of the species. Ovid, however, draws attention to the ongoing femininity of the Io-*iuuenca*, not only with the juxtaposed alternative designation *bos*, which, unusually for animal nomenclature, can be either masculine or feminine, but also with the adjective *formosa*, a programmatic term in the poem but also here an anthropomorphizing epithet for the pretty cow. The Lycaon-wolf also *ueteris seruat uestigia formae* ('keeps the traces of his old form'), including grey-white

---

[18] These issues are widely discussed in the literature. See especially Feldherr (2002).

[19] See Feldherr in this volume for an extensive discussion of the role of gender in this crucial new beginning.

[20] I hope to explore in more detail, in a separate publication, the gendered nature of metamorphic destination. For example, almost all metamorphosed trees were once women, whereas the greatest gender equality is with birds. I suggest that what is surprising is not so much that women become trees, but that comparatively speaking so many men become birds. I suspect it may be connected with the capacity for movement.

hair, the violence of his face, his shining eyes, and the same *feritatis imago* ('appearance of wildness', 1.238–9). It is implied, if again not explicitly stated, that he also maintains his masculinity, in however undesirable a form. He remains Callisto's father, if not approachable as such, at 2.495.[21]

To explore further my contention that gender remains stable in most cases of metamorphosis, we will consider a number of examples. When Daphne is 'saved' from Apollo's intended rape by her father helpfully turning her into a tree (thus fixing her to the ground and making it easy for Apollo to catch up), we follow closely the intricate process of transformation, which has been so extraordinarily fertile in visual art thereafter. We are told that once every part of her has been taken over by the tree, *nitor unus* ('only / one brightness / beauty', 1.552) is all that is left of what had previously been Daphne.[22] Although the narrator says that the only aspect of continuity between the nymph and the tree is this non-specific *nitor*, I propose that the narrator is unreliable. Daphne's feminine gender also remains *in illa*. Both the generic term *arbor* and most names for tree-species are grammatically feminine, but there is no noun with which the ablative feminine singular *illa* (1.552) directly agrees here, so the phrase has no option but to be translated 'in her', while the *hanc* which opens the next line and is the continuing object of Apollo's love likewise maintains a strong sense of its biological as well as grammatical gender.[23] More importantly, not only does Apollo continue to treat the Daphne-tree as female, not only does the semantic connection (so often played out in metamorphosis) between parts of the tree and parts of the human body continue after the claim that only one thing remained, but also the consciousness of Daphne appears unchanged. As a tree, she still behaves like a young woman attempting to resist unwelcome sexual advances. There is a deep irony that what she asked her father to do was *qua nimium placui, mutando perde figuram* ('destroy the appearance / shape by which I have excessively pleased, by changing it', *Met.* 1.545). She did ask for metamorphosis, a dangerous thing to do in this poem, but she did not get what she asked for, as the continuity in her *figura* was

---

[21] Interactions between grammatical and biological gender will be considered further below.

[22] The passage is one of the best known in the poem and has been studied extensively. See especially Hardie (2002b) 45–50. Wheeler (2000) 59–60 glosses *nitor* (rightly linking it with Io as *nitentem ... iuuencam*) with the comment that 'each nymph retains her attractiveness after she is transformed'. Gender is not mentioned explicitly, but seems to be implied exactly as it is by Ovid.

[23] Corbeill (2015) makes a strong case for an ancient Roman fascination with grammatical gender, including its connection with biological sex. On trees, see especially pages 36, 44, 68 ('we have already seen several instances of such nouns, as demonstrated most clearly perhaps by tree names, where native speakers attributed the production of their feminine grammatical gender to a perceived "female" aspect of trees, despite the strictly masculine morphology of the nouns that describe them'), and 89–92 on 'masculine trees'.

exactly what continued to be excessively pleasing to Apollo.[24] So she does not escape.

This is the first such story in the *Metamorphoses* (by the time we reach Caenis in book 12, the poem's rape victims have learnt that a safer request is for a change of biological sex). As with Daphne, so Io's metamorphosis also leaves her mind unchanged and her behaviour that of a woman whose voice has been cruelly suppressed. There are many other examples of women who undergo a metamorphosis in which they clearly keep their gender—usually with its associated suffering. Callisto the bear, Galanthis the weasel, and the trees Myrrha and Dryope all continue to be defined by their motherhood even when they have lost the physical shape of humanity. Callisto (2.409–530), having been impregnated by Jupiter, is punished for giving birth by Juno, with a torturous metamorphosis into a bear (2.468–84) in which the goddess is vindictively determined to take away from her 'rival' the *figura* (again) which so pleased her own husband (2.474–5). Juno attempts to close down the ambivalence of *figura* by the metamorphic destination of a horrible bear with its *ora ... deformia* (2.481), but is thwarted by the outcome: Callisto's resultant mental state is one of the most explicitly continuous in the poem, as she continues to behave and think exactly like a deeply troubled and abused human woman (2.485–95). Years later, on seeing her fifteen-year-old son out hunting, she (*quae*, feminine) *restitit Arcade uiso / et cognoscenti similis fuit* ('stopped at the sight of Arcas and was like one recognising', 2.500–1). The mixed focalization is interesting here: with *Arcade uiso* we seem to be still inside Callisto's mind, but with *cognoscenti similis* it feels more as if we are a sympathetic observer, unless perhaps, after all these years, this one element of human contact is, even to herself, only a shadow of recognition. The other focalizing possibility is Arcas himself, the only actual observer, who might seem for a moment to be thinking 'that bear is looking at me as if it recognises me', but if so it is only a fleeting moment, for he immediately runs away and is even about to commit unknowing matricide, until this possibility is forestalled by Jupiter's catasterization of mother and son (2.505–7). Not only gender, then, but all human relationships have been maintained in Callisto's metamorphosis.

Myrrha's motherhood survives her metamorphosis to the extent that she gives birth, in a way which is remarkably human compared with the tradition of her myth, as a tree.[25] Dryope's particularly distressing metamorphosis also leaves her still a mother (9.324–93). It is important to note the maternal, indeed puerperal, context of this tale: it is told by the pregnant Iole, in response to Alcumena's account of her traumatic birthing of Hercules, including the story of the maid-

---

[24] As ever in the *Metamorphoses*, continuity and change are bound up in each other: Daphne's *figura*, in the sense of 'shape' (*OLD* 1), has changed, while her *figura*, in the sense of 'looks' (*OLD* 3c, cf. *Met.* 10.69), has not changed.

[25] See Reed's excellent commentary (2013) on the passage, including other versions of the story in which the birth of Adonis is enabled by a man wielding an axe.

attendant Galanthis who is punished for her cleverness in tricking Lucina into allowing the birth, by being turned into a weasel that gives birth through its mouth (9.280–323).[26] Dryope, the half-sister of Iole (9.330), is unusual among the rape-victims of the poem in overcoming the trauma of abuse by Apollo to the extent of managing to establish and maintain a happy marriage-relationship (9.331–3).[27] One day, she is walking the countryside to take garlands to the nymphs; she is not alone (good move—solitude is a major risk), being accompanied by her sister the narrator, and is carrying her nursing baby (9.334–9). Dryope plucks a lotus flower (342) to give to her son (mistake). Although plucking flowers is a risky activity for women in the *Metamorphoses*, as indeed elsewhere in literature, this example is embedded in the maternal relationship and surrounded by protective sisterhood. But the damage of rape runs deep. Drops of blood fall from the flower and the Lotus tree itself shudders (9.344–5).

At this point, the eyewitness-narrator fills in the back-story of which the participants were ignorant at the time: the nymph Lotis had been turned into this tree when trying to escape from Priapus' attempts to rape her (9.346–8). We are told that the resultant tree kept the name of the nymph (348), but what we are not explicitly told is nonetheless also clear: she keeps her female gender and the psychological damage from her experience. Tragically, she also passes it on, causing the innocent Dryope to be turned also into—most unusually—the same kind of tree.[28] The blood dripping from the lotus flower seems to suggest a

---

[26] Here is another example of continuity which includes not just gender but the highly sex-specific action of giving birth. Although the story claims that Galanthis is punished in her mouth because it was by means of her deceitful mouth that she tricked the goddess (and, the reader might note, laughed at her), it is no accident that the result is a perversion of birth, not a direct perversion of speech (though it is implicitly that also). On mothers in the *Metamorphoses*, see Lateiner (2006).

[27] Kenney (2011) 431 says that the brief, parenthetical allusion to the earlier rape is made only to indicate that Dryope's baby is the son of Apollo, not of Andraemon, but I would say that Ovid is deliberately playing down any question of offspring arising from the rape. In Antoninus Liberalis' account (AL 32), although there is mention of the marriage to Andraemon after the rape and before the birth, the marital relationship plays no further role in the story. Dryope's metamorphosis (if so it is) does not take place until her son Amphissus is old enough to be king and to have founded a sanctuary to Apollo. Then, in Celoria's translation of Antoninus (1992) 91: 'as Dryope was approaching that temple, the hamadryad nymphs gathered her up affectionately and hid her in the woods. In her place they caused a poplar to appear out of the ground. Beside it they made a spring to gush forth. Dryope was changed from mortal to nymph.' Amphissus then set up a shrine to the nymphs, 'in honour of the favour shown to his mother'. There follows an aetion for women not being present at the associated foot-race, which is that 'two maidens told local people that Dryope had been snatched away by the nymphs. The nymphs were angry at this and turned the maidens into pines.' Antoninus states Nicander as his source. We can see, then, that Ovid's tale is quite different as regards the relationships involved. On the other hand, Ovid has downplayed the problem of the baby's parentage to a remarkable degree, for example by not including any complaint on that score to the god on the very vocal Dryope's part, and by not allowing the issue to do any harm to the relationship between Dryope and Andraemon. This, I suggest, has the effect of creating a story in which family love and a good relationship manages, at least until a further disaster occurs, to overcome the trauma of abuse.

[28] That is, if we read *loton* at 365, in keeping with manuscripts, when Iole points to the tree in response to Dryope's husband and father looking for her. Kenney (2011) 434 (following Tarrant in the OCT (2004), who obelizes and comments *uix sanum*) says that this reading is impossible, because the Lotus is the one type of tree which Dryope certainly cannot become. On the problem of the type of tree,

bizarrely incomplete metamorphosis, rather than a continuation of the common trope linking human and dendrological body parts.[29] Perhaps it also alludes to the physical wound of rape. Despite the fact that this wound was narrowly avoided in Lotis' case, and seems to have been healed by family love in Dryope's, nonetheless it breaks out again at this moment of stress. Dryope's metamorphosis is set in the context of that continuing family love: son (356–8), sister (359–62), and husband and father together[30] (363–6), are present but they are helpless to help her. What these relationships do offer her, however, is an unusual opportunity, even as the bark is growing over her, to speak—for a full twenty lines (371–91). She asks her family to enable her to continue in her role as mother, by bringing the child to visit his mother-tree and teaching him to be aware of her imprisoned identity. She also wants to ensure that he never plucks any flowers (380–1). I am tempted to suggest that the mother is begging her family to ensure that the child does not grow up to be a rapist.[31] This is followed by words of loving farewell, in which that to the man called *care... coniunx* comes first (9.382). As such, then, Dryope has maintained both female gender and feminine roles after metamorphosis.

Sympathy and Empathy in Moments of Transformation

Such emotive narratives of transformation are a hallmark of the poem. My argument in this section is that it is predominantly the female characters with whom the reader is invited to empathize strongly during the process of metamorphosis. I would suggest that the poem empathizes more with women than with men in all its aspects (for example, in the well-known psychological soliloquies of Medea and of Scylla, daughter of Nisus), but the point I am aiming to make here is more specific: it is particularly the connection between the process of metamorphosis and empathy with the victim's perspective which I argue correlates significantly with female gender. While there are indeed male characters whose point of view is explored by the narrative, there are relatively few such characters

see also Bömer (1977) 375–6, who also regards transformation into a second Lotus as very unlikely. It seems to me, however, that this might be a place to apply the textual 'law' of *difficilior lectio potior*, and accept that not only has Lotis infected Dryope with treeness, but specifically with her type of tree. Anderson (1972) 440 accepts the resulting tree as a lotus without further discussion, but suggests that Ovid invented Dryope's connection with Lotis.

[29] See Gowers (2005) esp. 335–7 on the connection between humans and trees in Roman thought. The line cannot, however, avoid a reference also to Polydorus, as noted by the commentators: Kenney (2011) 432, Bömer (1977) 382 and Anderson (1972) 440.
[30] Line 363 hints at Lucretia, as Bömer (1977) 386 notes. For my purposes, crucial is the construction of Dryope within a loving and functional family.
[31] Plucking flowers notoriously prefigures potential rape, as for example for Proserpina (*Met.* 5.392), but that itself is, at least in part, because the action of picking flowers acts metaphorically for defloration, as in Catullus 62.39–47.

with whom the reader is encouraged to identify during the actual process of metamorphosis. For this reason, for example, Hippolytus/Virbius does not fit into the category of those whose point of view is explored in transformation, because the extended description is of his death, rather than his revivification and metamorphosis into a minor deity, the narrative of which at 15.533–44 barely constitutes a metamorphosis.[32]

This argument about the predominantly female focalization of transformation applies not only to the obvious cases of Daphne, Dryope, the Heliades, Io, Callisto, Myrrha, Ocyroe, and so on, but even to negatively-portrayed women such as Aglauros. This unlovely character was one of three daughters of Cecrops, the loveliest of whom, Herse, caught the eye of Mercury in Book 2. As he approached the girls' bedrooms, Aglauros intercepted the god, who asked for her support in his courtship. She, however, demanded gold of great weight for her services (2.570). The situation annoyed Minerva, who was already angry with Aglauros and remembered that the girl had disobeyed the goddess' instruction not to look at the contents of the sacred basket which she had entrusted to the three daughters of Cecrops (the baby Erichthonius). Minerva decided to enlist the help of one of Ovid's magnificent personifications, Envy, to torture Aglauros with thoughts of her sister's fortune (2.760–86).[33] This is horribly successful. When Aglauros tries to block Mercury from entering her sister's bedroom, she makes the (risky) threat that she will not move from that spot until she has repulsed him (2.817), which Mercury promptly literalizes by turning her to stone. Despite the fact that Aglauros is an unpleasant character and partakes also in the supreme nastiness of the personified Invidia, nonetheless we enter into the horror of her transformation (2.819–32). This is a remarkable representation of a woman's subjectivity, offered to us in the case of a character with whom we might not inherently want to sympathize. The situation, reinforced by the example in the next paragraph, seems to me to suggest that there is something markedly gendered about metamorphosis.

Similar is the case of the Thracian women who witnessed[34] the murder of Orpheus being turned into trees by Bacchus. The account of the metamorphosis (11.67–84) has the hallmarks of an Ovidian tree-transformation, with its strong focalization through the victim, but in place of the semantic slippage between body-parts and tree-parts which is the main focus elsewhere, in this case stress is placed on the victims being painfully bound (ironically instigated by Bacchus

---

[32] Actaeon will be considered briefly later.   [33] Hardie (2002b) 231–8, esp. 236.
[34] Reed (2013) 315 says that the phrase *quae uidere nefas* (11.70) is not restrictive and refers to all the women. He suggests that seeing here implies 'being guilty of' in the sense that all those who were present and saw the action participated in it at different levels. I would suggest, however, that the phrase adds to the vindictiveness of Bacchus in this passage, identified by Reed. It might also pick up again on another group of rampant Bacchants who committed sparagmos on a man, in that *uidere nefas* was what Pentheus was seeking to do (*nefas* from his point of view) when they caught him.

Lyaeus, the loosener, 11.67). The passage has a number of marked features: metamorphosis of the murderers of Orpheus is not attested elsewhere;[35] the metamorphic destination is generic trees, rather than specific species;[36] the account contains a simile within the metamorphic description, thus drawing on the connection between imagery and metamorphosis almost to the extent of implying a secondary conceptual metamorphosis into birds—trapped ones (72–5).[37] The crucial point for me is the extent to which this description of transformation is extended and sympathetically presented *from the point of view of the women*, for fifteen lines through their eyes (*quae uidere nefas*, 'those who saw the crime', 70, thus taking on new significance). Only at its end does the point of view move from verbs in which the women are the agents (*quaerit, aspicit, conata ... plangere, percussit*), through 'impersonal' verbs in which the body-parts and tree-substance become subjects and complements (*fiunt, sunt*—note also the chiasmatic arrangement of *pectus ... robora / robora ... umeri*), and finally to an intrusive appeal to the reader to observe the semantic slippage of trees and humans as it stabilizes on trees (11.83–4).[38]

What does it mean for Ovid to give so much space and attention to the transformation of women? I hope that the 'meaning' received by my readers is appreciation for the sensitivity of the accounts and the remarkable foregrounding of women's subjective experience. That would be the optimistic reading which I do indeed aim to share. On the other hand, these highly developed accounts of the moment of metamorphosis also *enact* the loss of voice, personality, identity, often movement, and capacity for deliberate action which the transformation entails. The extraordinary stress on the loss of voice in metamorphosis is epitomized by the severed tongue of Philomela, which Enterline insightfully takes as the controlling image of her study.[39] Similar (if less pornographically violent) struggles with communication are encountered by the metamorphosed Daphne (whose

---

[35] See Reed (2013) 314. For the interactions between Orphic, Apollonian, and Bacchic traditions in this passage, see also his page 304.

[36] It is thereby particularly far removed from any aetion, although there is presumably some additional irony in the women-trees adding to the forest which listened to Orpheus' song. On the connection between metamorphosis and aetia see Barchiesi in this volume.

[37] On similes and metamorphosis see Barkan (1986) esp. 20–2 and Schmidt (1991). On similes in the *Metamorphoses* see von Glinski (2012), who gives a good account of the history of the question (2–9). She discusses the death of Orpheus at 21–5. As she rightly points out, the simile of the trapped birds alludes to that used for the killing of the maids in *Odyssey* 22.468–72, thus (I suggest) enhancing the viciousness of Bacchus' punishment of the women (although at least Odysseus distinguished different levels of guilt).

[38] The final word, *putando*, as noted by Wheeler (1999) 153, meaning 'in/by thinking' also hints at a term uncomfortably appropriate for trees—'in/by pruning'. This rather gruesome joke extends to the whole phrase as a warning on interaction with trees in this poem: not just 'be deceived if you thought so' but also 'and you wouldn't [would you?] make the mistake of pruning them'. Be careful how you treat trees in this poem.

[39] Enterline (2000). Salzman-Mitchell (2005) also makes extensive use of Philomela's tongue, as does Segal (1994) and (1998). See also Natoli (2017) chapter 2 for careful accounts of the loss of voice in the *Metamorphoses*.

nod Apollo appropriates but we cannot interpret, 1.566–7), Myrrha (who cannot call upon Lucina to aid her parturition, 10.506–7), Ocyroe metamorphosed as she speaks (2.655–75), while the voice of Echo, forever unable to initiate any communication (3.359–61), offers a more comfortably aestheticized but equally telling representation of female lack—to the extent that she has become a feminist icon.[40] The other power which women lose disproportionately is movement, from the moment when Daphne's prayed-for metamorphosis has the effect of stopping her running and enabling Apollo to catch up to the trapped-bird simile discussed above.[41] All these representations could be taken as sympathetic exposure of the damage done to women—but the problem is that they could equally well be enactment and even fetishization of it. The extent of the emphasis on victimhood may perhaps suggest the latter.

But what about men? Men do indeed also lose the powers of speech and movement, so what is my justification for saying that metamorphosis is a form of victimization gendered female? My argument depends on three things: preponderance rather than absolute numbers, emotive identification, and (most problematically) a certain negative feminization which I shall suggest occurs in core categories of metamorphosis. In brief, the argument is that while there are indeed men who are victimized by metamorphosis, they are disproportionately few, disproportionately lacking in subjective identification, and finally some of the cases that do exist also involve certain other power-relations which are effectively (and negatively) 'feminizing'. I want to suggest, then, that there is a kind of metamorphosis which is damagingly feminizing. There may be a circularity to this argument, but it is a circle from which, I suggest, it is hard to escape.

One of the few examples of a male character whose loss of voice is narrated is Lycaon, who *frustra . . . loqui conatur* ('tries in vain to speak', 1. 233), in a description of metamorphosis (1.233–9) dispassionately—or perhaps vindictively— narrated by the tyrannical Jupiter. Cadmus likewise *uult plura loqui* ('wants to say more', 4.586), but is prevented by the forking of his tongue as he becomes a snake. Silenced victim of an outraged deity also is Actaeon, a rare example of a male whose metamorphosis invites close empathy. His story, unusually for a man, includes extensive focalization during the process of metamorphosis itself (3.195–248), a forestalled attempt to bewail his lot (3.201–2), and an equally unsuccessful effort to impose his status as human and master (3.230).[42] My first and most important point about the emotive focalization of the Actaeon story is that it is rare. I would note in addition, however, that as a young huntsman who

---

[40] See Spivak (1993), Berger (1996).

[41] Segal (2005), in a valuable discussion of the female body in the *Metamorphoses* (31–49), draws attention to the immobilization and imprisonment of women, including via metamorphosis (see especially 36).

[42] There is some doubt about the text here, but the issue is not significant for my current argument.

falls foul of Diana/Artemis through inadvertent voyeurism, his position is negatively sexualized.

As regards movement, in absolute terms there may be as many men immobilized by metamorphosis as there are women, if one includes all the victims of Perseus' use of Medusa's severed head (two hundred, according to 5.209), but rarely do we engage with them subjectively. The brief account (5.205–6) of the amazement of Astyages at the lithification of Aconteus is a case in point: it is captured forever in the ecphrastic topos of astonishment as Astyages suffers the same fate.[43] Phineus himself is turned to stone in an account (5.210–35) which takes his point of view, briefly, but also condemns him from the viewer's perspective (Perseus' and, probably, the reader's) as a cowardly parody of the Turnus of *Aen.* 12.[44] Similar to this controlling victimization (deserved or otherwise) are a number of other cases of petrification: the luckless bearer of the poisoned cloak to Hercules, Lichas (9.214–29); the yokel Battus, who makes the mistake of promising silence to Mercury by saying that a stone will speak first (2.696), with a predictable result (2.705–7); and the shepherd who is unlucky enough to be asked to resolve a dispute among the gods regarding Ambracia and is turned to stone by one of the losers (13.713–15). All these male human–stones—be it noted—are socially lowly.

In the light of the arguments above, I propose a mechanism for categorizing types of metamorphosis according to the extent to which the transformation is an imposition which more or less painfully limits the activity of its victim: this mechanism forms the basis of the argument for feminization. Excluded from my category of victimized, feminized metamorphoses are apotheoses, shape-changing, and 'near-misses' (explained below), all of which are predominantly male, and either actively powerful or at least distanced from victimhood.

Becoming a god is almost entirely reserved for males, ranging from relatively weak characters like Acis or Hippolytus/Virbius through Glaucus to the great heroes of Roman politics (Hercules, Aeneas, Romulus, Aesculapius, Caesar, Augustus—and Ovid), while on the female side Hersilia is allowed to join her husband Romulus among the gods (14.829–51), and victims like Io, Callisto, and Leucothoe eventually gain some form of (relatively passive) divinity. Shape-changing is mostly the province of the gods but includes also Mestra (8.848–74), who is constrained by filial duty, and Periclymenus (12.555–76), the voluntary shape-changer introduced only at his death at the hands of Hercules.[45] 'Near-miss' transformation is indirect, implied, or distanced metamorphoses such

---

[43] See Rosati (2009) 157.

[44] This is the judgement also of Rosati (2009) 159, who describes it as a melodramatic parody.

[45] See Reed (2013) 436–7 on the myth of Periclymenus in classical literature. He rightly draws attention to the connection with Mestra and the role of Neptune in both cases. Both these (rare) mortal shape-changers share in the metamorphic qualities of the sea. On shape-changers, see Forbes Irving (1990) 171–94.

as the flower which symbolizes/replaces Narcissus (3.509–10), the mulberry tree which changes colour when touched by the blood of Pyramus (4.125–7), the stream which flows from the tears of those mourning Marsyas (6.392–400), Ariadne's crown (8.178–82), the block of wood which is coextensive with and in control of the life of Meleager (8.451–7), the blood of Adonis (10.728–39), the snake which is turned to stone to stop it attacking Orpheus' severed head (11.56–60), the flower that commemorates Ajax (13.394–8), the birds in honour of Memnon (13.600–16).[46] It will be noted that, except for Ariadne's crown, all the examples of near-misses which I have given are of or related to male characters. The most obvious further female examples are secondary to the primary tree-metamorphosis in the case of the tears of the Heliades (2.364–6) and Myrrha (10.500–2). So near-misses, apotheoses, and shape-changers are predominantly male.

Transformations that do not fall into the categories just mentioned are overwhelmingly those in which the metamorphosed being is most forcefully constructed as a victim. Many cases are punishment (deserved or otherwise), but even when these transformations are rescue or even reward, nonetheless they fix the transformed person in a passive, subordinate, and actually or potentially abused position. And they are predominantly female. I suggest, therefore, that metamorphosis thus construed is an instantiation of abusive power, of which women are predominantly the victims. In addition to these women, there are also certain categories of male victims who are 'feminized' by the process. Actaeon belongs to that category, as do Lichas and Phineus, but the vast majority of the victims with whom the reader is encouraged to identify are female. Pessimistically, I am inclined to suspect that if there is any way of telling such stories without disempowering and negatively feminizing the victims, Ovid's *Metamorphoses* has not found it.

Metamorphosis of Gender (One-way Only)

In the second section of this paper, I argued that gender is remarkably stable in the process of metamorphosis, while the third suggested that the poem both encourages empathy with female victims and also victimizes them. But what happens when the transformation is precisely in the matter of gender? My claim regarding stability of gender needs to be considered against the directly transsexual stories, while the outcome of this consideration may throw further light on the issue of empathy and victimization.[47] On a maximalist view, there are six accounts of sex

---

[46] *See Buxton (2009) 214–28 on metamorphosis of tears, blood, and related.

[47] Important in discussion of sex-changes and related phenomena in the ancient world is Brisson (2002), but see Corbeill (2015) 151 for careful nuancing of the significance of hermaphrodites in

change in the poem, but two of these are unenlightening for my purposes. First, Mestra is a shape-changer who takes on multiple guises, including some play about gender, as well as a horse and other animals, but her brief moment as a fisherman is not really significant as a sex change, despite her clever wordplay at 8.867–8 (quoted in the footnote at the end of this sentence), while the defensive power granted by her shape-shifting is one of general unrecognizability rather than gendered invulnerability.[48] Second is Sithon, whose story is among those rejected by the Minyad Alcithoe as too common for her to sing. According to Lateiner's account of mimetic syntax, the description *modo uir modo femina* (4.280) implies repeated action,[49] but the absence of any further development by Ovid means that this character cannot contribute very much to a reading of transsexuality in the poem.[50] Of the remaining four, Hermaphroditus is distressed to change from (very young) man to intersex person, Tiresias claims that women enjoy sex more than men but nonetheless clearly prefers to be a man, while Caenis and Iphis are both people born as women whose lives are immeasurably improved by the divine gift of transsexuality. A point to note about these stories is a very strong preference for male gender on the part of characters.[51] It seems that for all Ovid's sensitivity to matters of gender, in ways that can be read as remarkably modern, nonetheless masculinity always trumps femininity in the poem.

To put a little more flesh on this claim, we will need to examine each of these stories briefly. The case is particularly clear, although suppressed by the poet, for Hermaphroditus. It is a story, as is well known, shot through with interplays and complexities of gender, even before the fateful embrace in Salmacis' pool.[52] Once

Roman culture. See also Forbes Irving (1990) chapter 7. Regarding *Metamorphoses*, see also Lateiner (2009).

[48] I am grateful for this formulation to the anonymous reader, who helpfully points out that Mestra is in a sense a doublet for Caenis, as rape victim of Neptune. In both cases, the god responds to the woman's request for deliverance from further victimization through the loss of her female form. On the Mestra myth, see Forbes Irving (1990) 149. Mestra-the-fisherman plays explicitly with gender when claiming that *nemo...litore in isto / me tamen excepto nec femina constitit ulla*. At 8.873, Mestra becomes *equa* (feminine, where there would have been a choice), *ales* (grammatically feminine), *bos* (masculine or feminine), and then *ceruus* (masculine where there would have been a choice). I am generally averse to arguments from meter, in that other words are available, but this would be the easiest explanation for *equa* and *ceruus*.

[49] Lateiner (1990) 226. He comments: 'The pattern of repeated words produces a continuity of identity on the verbal level reporting the metamorphic action, a parallelism that adds meaning, not merely rhetorical emphasis.' I am not sure whether the claim is relevant to the character's underlying identity separate from her/his gender.

[50] One further case of sex-change in the poem occurs in Pythagoras' list of examples of 'natural' changes: the hyena *quae modo femina tergo / passa marem est, nunc esse marem miremur* (15.409–10).

[51] Fantham (2004) 61 also notes the preference for male gender in the stories of transsexuality. See also Keith (1999), Segal (2005) 49–54.

[52] Nugent (1990), Labate (1993), Keith (1999) 216–19, Robinson (1999) 217–18. Recent work on the Halicarnassus inscription and the wider history of the myth, such as Romano (2009) and Groves (2016), give valuable insights into what Ovid chose not to do. See further Barchiesi in this volume. Zajko (2009) is unusual in explicitly relating the story of Hermaphroditus to modern intersex experiences.

the nymph's ill-judged prayer is granted and the two become one flesh (in not at all the way she meant[53]), the female element disappears completely. The Hermaphroditus who leaves the pool is deeply angry about the effect on his body, but there seems to have been no effect at all on his mind, personality, or sense of self. The 'one' that the two have become is all him.[54] Indeed, the story leaves the grotesque impression that the only remaining traces of Salmacis are in the female sexual organs which now form part of Hermaphroditus. It is true that his *membra* are also *mollita* and he speaks *uoce* no longer *uirili* (4.381–2), but given his youthful, ephebic status at the beginning of the passage and the extreme infectiousness of any one aspect of damage to masculinity, these elements are hardly traces of the individual person who was Salmacis.[55] While agreeing with Romano that the opposition between 'Hermaphroditus the inventor of marriage and Hermaphroditus the victim of rape' shows 'the nature of Ovid's appropriation', I am uncomfortable with the suggestion that 'Hermaphroditus' rape stands out both for its reversing of roles, making the nymph the aggressor, and for the simple fact that it is at last a rape that ends, in a manner of speaking, with a 'successful coupling'.[56] Even with the qualification, surely there is nothing successful about Salmacis' total loss of identity. By comparison, many male rapes are 'successful couplings' in that intercourse happens and produces pregnancy. It causes trauma to the victim, but not the annihilation which Salmacis suffers. I would suggest that at the end of this story it is no longer Hermaphroditus but Salmacis who is the victim.

Regarding Tiresias (3.322–31), I am not the first to note that during the female years Tiresias behaves in exactly the same way as in the male years. In her important article on the story, Liveley is particularly interested in Juno's response to the 'jokey argument', but she also describes the way in which Tiresias is a man even when he is a woman.[57] It is not difficult to see that the staff with which Tiresias twice violates a pair of copulating stakes (3.325) is a phallic symbol, while there is no feminine adjective applied to Tiresias during his period as a woman. In

---

[53] Keith (1999) 220 takes the outcome of the embrace as the female narrator Alcithoe's gift to Salmacis, but I would read her prayer at 4.371–2 as nothing but a wish for a permanent relationship and the kind of metaphorical 'oneness' of sexual intercourse, a wish that is cruelly interpreted by the gods who fuse the two bodies.

[54] Keith (1999): 'paradigmatic of the erasure of female subjectivity' (though this is only one of her possible readings).

[55] See Robinson (1999) 213 on the spread of emasculation-by-implication.

[56] Romano (2009) 560.

[57] Liveley (2003) 157. She suggests that Juno's anger could be at Tiresias daring to speak for women, and at Jupiter's expectation that she, Juno, is Woman rather than expressing her own, subjective, experience (for which Jupiter should bear a lot of responsibility). Balsley (2010) makes a similar suggestion, that Juno's anger is because 'her attitude towards the pleasures of sex is being debated and determined by two men, one of whom has no business being involved in the matter whatsoever, and the other of whom has permitted this man to render such an opinion'. I am grateful to Elena Giusti for giving me advance sight of her article (2018), which powerfully exposes not only the chauvinism of Tiresias but also its implications for Ovid throughout the corpus.

other accounts of the tale, Tiresias undergoes multiple (six) sex changes, including also changes of life-stage and gendered experiences such as motherhood, but Ovid has not chosen to explore these.[58] The effect of this, I suggest, is to give us a Tiresias who has no experience of female subjectivity, despite his claims to be able to adjudicate on the matter. The most generous interpretation would be to regard the female Tiresias as an un-transitioned transman, who sees the only way out of his uncomfortable female body to be violence. Be that as it may, he wants to get back to being a man.

The cases of the two straightforward transmen are easier. Iphis, biologically a girl but brought up as a boy, and therefore culturally gendered male, becomes biologically male on her/his wedding day in a rare piece of 'happy ever after' in the poem. The story of Iphis and Ianthe could be read as a literalization of ancient maturation-rituals, as an early account of gender dysphoria, or as a lesbian story.[59] Iphis could be regarded, in modern terms, as a 'man caught in a woman's body', since he lives as (and has been raised as) a man. Her long lament at 9.726–63, however, displays the psychology of a woman, no more masculine than other women who grieve at their erotic situation.[60] There is nothing in the speech to suggest male subjectivity, so to describe her as 'psychologically transgendered' is not, I think, accurate. She wants to be a boy, she is reared as a boy, but as constructed by Ovid she is not a boy caught in a girl's body. It would be more accurate to call her a girl dressed up as a boy. Ormand rightly draws attention to the remarkable degree of similarity and mutuality between the two lovers, which takes a standard trope of erotic discourse to destructive extremes (as for Narcissus), making any kind of love relationship impossible. He argues that 'what Iphis finds unthinkable is not the typical Roman category of tribadism (to say nothing of "lesbianism"), but a romance of equal partners'.[61] So, is Ovid pointing out a problem in Roman sexuality that it is so extremely dependent on inequality? Or is he overwhelmingly privileging conformist relationships and male gender? I am inclined to suspect the latter, though both readings are available.

In the story of Caenis, the privileging of male gender is extreme, but comprehensible from a psychological point of view and given the realities of masculinist society. Caenis chooses wisely when offered a gift in recompense for the rape of her virginity by Neptune—she asks to be a man (12.201–3). One might object that

[58] See Barchiesi and Rosati (2007) 171–3, and O'Hara (1996). If O'Hara's reconstruction of 'Sostratus' poem' is right, the stories available to Ovid regarding both Hermaphroditus and Tiresias show the extent to which he has chosen to focus on disruptions to male subjectivity in his accounts.

[59] See Pintabone (2002), Ormand (2005). Kenney (2011) ad loc., makes no mention of either transsexuality or lesbianism in his commentary on the story, apart from twice remarking (477 and 479) on Iphis' charmingly naive ignorance of the poetry of Sappho.

[60] She even knows that she must use feminine adjectives of herself (745–8), which, if this were a realist text, would be odd. Ovidian grammar usually maintains the underlying gender (or skirts the issue), but an exception is *mirata est* of Vertumnus disguised as an old woman, *Met.* 14.657.

[61] Ormand (2005) 92.

her prayer is *femina ne sim* 'not to be a woman' rather than 'to be a man', but the implications of *femina* stress gender rather than humanity. Moreover, in the circumstances her prayer *tale pati... posse nihil* ('not to be able to suffer such a thing') must remind the reader of the notorious phrase for undergoing sexual penetration, *muliebria pati*. Neptune makes clear his and Ovid's understanding of the implications of the wish, not only by immediately granting her the external signs of masculinity, but also by making her invulnerable to weapons (12.203–7).

The context for the story within the poem is another invulnerable warrior, Cycnus, who caused Achilles considerable annoyance by refusing to die in the normal way before Troy. Once he had finally been strangled with his own helmet-straps and battered to death by the irate superhero (12.132–43), Cycnus was turned into his eponymous bird, the swan. In a break in the war, Nestor comforts the confused Achilles with the account of an earlier impermeable warrior, Caeneus, whose inviolability was all the more remarkable because *femina natus erat* ('he was born a woman', 12.175).[62] Invulnerable warriors are a known phenomenon in early Greek and Indo-European mythology, but rarely are they so explicitly linked to gender and sexual penetration.[63] The new man Caeneus rejoices in the gift and happily pursues a career as a male warrior (12.208–9). His death finally comes about during the battle of Centaurs and Lapiths, expansively narrated by Nestor. Caeneus has been taunted by the centaur Latreus with his female origins (12.470–6), followed by the inevitable failure of the centaur's spear to have any effect, when the Lapith replies with a particularly violent and unpleasant version of pleasure in penetration (12.490–3). This display of masculine prowess calls the attention of all the centaurs onto Caeneus. They uproot trees from the surrounding mountains and pile them on top of him until he is finally suffocated (12.510–21).

What happens next is uncertain (12.522). Some say that Caeneus was pushed right down to the underworld by the weight of trees, but his companions see a bird flying out from the woodpile, a bird which Nestor has never seen before or since (12.526). It is hailed by Mopsus as the metamorphosed form of Caeneus (12.530–1). Does this outcome mean that Caeneus reverts to his birth gender (once *uir*, now *auis... unica*)? Virgil certainly had him become female again, in order to join other dead heroines surrounding Dido in the underworld

---

[62] The mix of genders between the subject and predicate is amusing here. It is amusing also, in the Ovidian way, that everyone is immediately amazed at the *monstri nouitate* (175). Although there may be good reasons, including metapoetic ones, to regard the story as novel, Caenis/Caeneus is nonetheless a repeat of Cycnus, down to the metamorphosis into a bird. On the play with novelty in Caeneus, see Ziogas (2013) esp. 182–3, n.9.

[63] On invulnerable warriors in Indo-European tradition, see West (2007) 444–5. On the connection between masculinity and penetration in these stories, see Papaioannou (2007) 72–83. On the role of Caeneus as an embodiment of masculinity, including in the *Iliad*, see Ziogas (2013) 184–8, as part of a major discussion of the Caenis/Caeneus story. Important also is Keith (1999) 233–9.

(*Aen.* 6.448–9).[64] Reed argues that the bird is in continuity with Caeneus (flying around his camp) but also with Caenis, in that she has reverted to female gender.[65] He rightly notes, however, that Mopsus does not see it that way, with his masculine vocative *Caeneu*. I would add that the masculine vocative *maxime* implies even more strongly that Mopsus regards the bird-Lapith as still male, still greatest. A bird, after all, is grammatically feminine, just as *proles* takes a feminine adjective, even when referring in patronymic style to a (heroic) male offspring, as frequently in Ovid and Virgil.[66] Perhaps the best explanation would be that from Mopsus' point of view Caeneus is still Caeneus, but for the author/ reader the grammatically feminine *auis unica* draws attention to the interplays of gender. If, as seems likely, the feminization is designed to remind us of the *Aeneid* passage, we might well think that the Lapith would be much better off as Caeneus-bird than as Caenis among the suffering underworld heroines. The lines are also pleasing and satisfying to the reader, especially if it is remembered that Nestor began by describing Cycnus as *unicus* (12.169). The story tells us that it is much better to be a man. Is that true even if it makes you push weapons up to the hilt into other people's bodies and twist them round to cause maximum damage? Both 'yes' and 'no' are answers which the poem makes open to the reader. Nonetheless, the optimist in me regards the story as remarkable in exposing the psychological as well as physical damage done to the victim.

Ovid provides what seem to be some highly sensitive and empathetic representations of women's subjectivity, but only in negative contexts. This is in part because adversity makes better stories, but the joy in the poem is not evenly distributed. No one in the poem rejoices in the new-found experience of being a woman. The nearest we see to a male being who plays out a female role is when a god disguises himself as an old woman or a goddess in order to gain nefarious access to a young woman. As Raval says: 'Ovidian tales of male-to-female cross-dressing reassert the masculine power of the transvestite hero or god and thus reinforce a gender binary.'[67] Moreover, they also impose a hierarchy. Most if not all non-fictional accounts of transsexuality in antiquity are also of female-to-male transition, for example Pliny *NH* 7.34, Phlegon of Tralles *Mirabilia* 5. One might want to say that Ovid is exposing this tendency in his society, but unfortunately that there is nothing to suggest that it might be an exposure rather than enactment. Be that as it may, the privileging of male gender in the poem plays out

---

[64] Ziogas (2013) 188–9 reads the reversion as a Virgilian invention.   [65] Reed (2013) 436.

[66] There are many examples, including in the Book 12 version of Cycnus (and the first version of Cycnus, though with a different nomenclature for the adjective, 2.367) as *Neptunia proles*, echoing examples of that phrasing in the *Aeneid*, on which see Reed (2013) 391. *proles* plus feminine adjective is also used of Caenis herself in the opening of her story, *Clara decore fuit proles Elateia Caenis*, 12.189.

[67] Raval (2002) 151. She also points out that in the poem men-as-women do not actually perform the female gender, but rather parody it. Much of her argument is what I would describe as pessimistic, although she may (consciously or not) be making use of the comforting trope whereby the ancient author is said to be 'comment[ing] explicitly on the constructed nature of gender identities' (152).

masculine superiority even more deeply than more obviously masculinist stories, by making it seem natural.

Conclusion

Although it is only in recent years that readers, including readers of Latin poetry, have become acutely sensitive to gender-difference and gender-fluidity, the *Metamorphoses* provides an extraordinary wealth of material for a reader who is so sensitized, such that it seems hard to imagine that these things are not in some sense intentionally seeded in the poem. Among my goals in reading Ovid's poetry is to draw out the female consciousness, subjectivity, and experiences in the texts, which have been suppressed by forces also in the texts, and to explore the power dynamics and gendered dynamics of Ovid's fictional world. Whether or not we are happy to fix the blame for violence, fetishization, and oppression on a persona or a fictional character, thus exonerating 'the poet himself', releasing these elements out into the open is a reading, at once both pessimistic and optimistic.

3

Between a Rock and a Hard Race

Gender and Text in Ovid's Deucalion and Pyrrha Episode (*Met.* 1.313–415)

Andrew Feldherr

Ovid's Deucalion and Pyrrha episode highlights both sexual difference and the nature of language. Indeed, it seems to complicate the relationship between these themes: on the one hand the metamorphosis which produces a new human race, divided from their origins into men and women, results from a new awareness of how language represents. Yet within the poem's narrative, the debate about what the words of the oracle mean already associates different attitudes to language with characters who are emphatically husband and wife. My aim here is to describe how this problematic correlation between gender difference and representation informs its audience's understanding of both the world and the nature of Ovid's text.

My claim will not be that Deucalion and Pyrrha mark the creation of gender difference within the poem.[1] This is self-evidently false since they are themselves presented as already male and female. But the episode nevertheless seems to provide a mythical explanation for gender difference in the contemporary world. Of the multiple creations of the human race in Ovid's poem, only here is gender explained as an enduring effect of that creation.[2] I shall use the paradoxical double vision of gender that results, as something always there and something specifically created, as an element of my argument. Gender difference within the poem, as in other mythical cosmogonies, bears a symbolic meaning in Ovid's account of creation even before the moment when it receives emphasis as a feature within the represented world of the narrative. An important element of that symbolism involves the contrast between progress, moving forward to a stable world, and a return to earlier beginnings, which are in Ovid's poem associated with a lack of order and hierarchy. This sense of temporal directionality in turn

---

[1] See Schmidt (1991) 35.
[2] I draw here on the formulation suggested by Alison Sharrock, *per litteras.*

Andrew Feldherr, *Between a Rock and a Hard Race: Gender and Text in Ovid's Deucalion and Pyrrha Episode* (Met. *1.313–415*) In: *Metamorphic Readings: Transformation, Language, and Gender in the Interpretation of Ovid's* Metamorphoses. Edited by: Alison Sharrock, Daniel Möller, and Mats Malm, Oxford University Press (2020).
© Oxford University Press.
DOI: 10.1093/oso/9780198864066.003.0004

helps shape an understanding of the responses to language formulated by man and wife. The woman, by referring words to nature, to what was already there before, sees no way to escape the past, while the man's sense of how representations change an understanding of reality, by seeing stones as bones, make it possible for the words of the oracle to construct the future Ovid's audience inhabits. In the final two sections of my paper, I argue that the alternative approaches to language associated with Deucalion and Pyrrha, privileging reality as the referent that explains words versus language as the basis for our understanding of reality, together generate the world. By that I mean that they illustrate two contrasting moments of reading *Metamorphoses*, which can be construed as themselves hierarchized or as working inevitably in tandem to make sense of the poem and decide whether it creates a new world or must always be understood in terms of what already is. Gender thus provides a complex and unstable model for the relationships between these two approaches to the text. Yet gender is also, crucially, something that words describe. As much as understanding attitudes to language as male and female helps articulate alternative strategies for interpreting Ovid's poetic creation, so the models of reading developed within that poem can also help readers think about whether representation constructs gender in the real world.

*

From its first word (*separat*, *Met.* 1.313)[3] the episode thematizes separation and immediately superimposes a temporal distinction onto a geographic border.[4] Phocis, where Deucalion and Pyrrha come ashore on Parnassos, separates Boeotia from Thessaly, but its relegation to the sea at that time (*illo tempore*, *Met.* 1.314) contrasts with its being land before (and now).[5] The juxtaposition of spatial boundaries with temporal ones, however, has two further consequences for a reading of the poem. First, since the separation of elements was the crucial process for the creation of the cosmos out of chaos in the poem's opening, the emphasis on the new divisions of land and sea and earth and sky here raises the question of whether this newly redefined landscape in fact does mark a new temporal epoch or points simply to timelessly recurring natural cycles. Second, the problem of the likeness between before and after within the text forms a mirror for Ovid's audience's relationship to the cosmos his poem represents. One way in which the receding of the flood does differ from the first creation is that it takes place in a landscape both viewed by humans and that can be mapped via human geography. The first creation was a matter of elements precipitating out in

---

[3] The poem is cited throughout from Tarrant (2004).
[4] Stressed especially in Wheeler's treatment of this episode, which he places under the rubric 'New Beginnings' (2000) 32–9.
[5] Ahl (1985) 102–3 brilliantly notes how the new landscape recalls the seals (*phocae*, *Met.* 1.300) and dolphins (*delphines, Met.* 1.302) who frolicked there during the flood.

the universe. There is no earth from which to watch the creation of the earth. Indeed, our world seems created from its edges inward since the first named places are the cardinal extremes where the winds are banished to prevent fraternal discord (*Met.* 1.61–6). We see this second ordering, however, from the very navel of the world, Delphi. And while this is not quite the first use of geographic place names in the poem—Jupiter maps Lycaon in Arcadia[6]—the shift to a terrestrial view of the flood in this episode makes their prominence here more marked. Phocis may separate Boeotia from Thessaly now, but even if we assume that the places on a map are older than the human history that establishes them, the division creates difference between how Ovid's reader views the world and the world within the narrative: during the flood, after all, there was no Boeotia, or Thessaly, simply water. Within the plot of the poem, the problem is whether this new present will be like or different from the past. From outside the frame of the poem, the audience uses its own present sense of the world to imagine the uncanny sight that met Deucalion's eyes and locate it in our conception of space.

The crucial presence of a human perspective within the narrative relates to another dimension of the separation that constitutes the new order, the distinction of high and low. During the flood there are no gradations of the landscape, simply the uniform surface of the water (*aequor*, *Met.* 1.318).[7] Verticality too becomes a temporal marker, since the only way to survive the flood is to be above it (*superesse*, *Met.* 1.326–7~*superant*, *Met.* 1.317). And this reference to height also recalls the initial creation of mankind at *Met.* 1.76–87. Humans are different from the other animals both because they are more receptive of the/a 'high' mind (*mentisque capacius altae*, *Met.* 1.76) and because they raise up their countenance while other animals are prone (*Met.* 1.85). But man's upright physique immediately creates a new form of confusion in that he comes to resemble the gods themselves, and this confusion was itself a matter of perspective. Man both looks like the gods, and looks as the gods do on the world, from above. Precisely this overlap re-emerges after the flood. Jupiter looks down on man from above and sees that they are above the flood (*Met.* 1.327). Later on, Deucalion will mimic that action, looking down from the intermediate height of a mountain onto the plain below (*Met.* 1.348–9) and recapitulating Jupiter's conclusion, though with the difference that no longer are 'they' alone, but 'we' are. Height in the episode thus not only enables temporal comparisons by looking back to deep time, and forward to the survivor's descendants, it also models different ways of understanding this temporal change. Absolute height can impose a stable hierarchy of gods, who in Ovid's poem live in the sky and emphatically not on Olympus, man, perfectly positioned on Parnassos to see the plain and the sky, and the earth below. But it

---

[6] 1.216–7. The gods' upward mobility from Olympus at 1.154–5 will be discussed below.
[7] The word itself conflates present land with past sea since it most commonly designates the latter but can mean 'terrestrial plain' as an archaism.

can also highlight the relative sameness of men and gods as well as suggesting a path to divinity if the gods' rivals can only raise themselves high enough.[8] It was when the Giants tried to do this earlier in the poem that Jupiter apparently destroyed the gods' traditional mountain home (*Met.* 1.154).

This hierarchical dimension of semantic confusion also plays an important role in the plot of Ovid's poem so far and thus also highlights the differentiation of past and present within the work. Both the absolute separation of gods and men at the end of the Iron Age when Astraea, last of the 'heavenly ones' leaves the earth (*ultima caelestum terras Astraea reliquit, Met.* 1.150), and the descent of Jupiter to Lycaon, which goes wrong when the king cannot recognize the god in his anthropomorphic form, suggest that the proper separation of the divine and the human would be the prerequisite for a new world. The showing of the earth to the sky, which results from the god's sight of men and presumably allows men to predict the end of the deluge, thus at once highlights a temporal separation by seeming to stabilize a spatial one and relates this to a political hierarchy: after all the confusing traffic between gods coming down to earth dressed as men, who themselves were really wolves in human disguise, the human and divine realm will see one another, from a distance, for what they are. And there is no more appropriate geographical place to unfold this vision for the reader than Delphi, a boundary both horizontally between Thessaly and Boeotia and vertically, between earth and sky, whose twin peaks themselves manifest difference,[9] and where men receive the ultimate lesson of the gods, to know their own difference.

When Deucalion begins to speak, the likenesses between man and god again come to the fore through an intertextual echo. As Schmitzer suggests, Deucalion's address to his wife begins with a reminiscence of the first speech in the *Aeneid*, where Juno describes herself as 'both wife and sister' of Jupiter (*et soror et coniunx,* Virg. *Aen.* 1.45).[10] In addressing Pyrrha this way, he indeed makes their relationship resemble the divine marriage of Jupiter and Juno. Even if *soror* can mean simply 'close relative',[11] the intertext itself encourages seeing her as his sister. Deucalion and Pyrrha's genealogical position, as descendants of Titans and ancestors of men, makes their own ambiguous identity figure both the ambiguities of temporal separation in the narrative and the distance between the narrated time and its historical audience. Looking back creates a fundamental confusion

---

[8] Varro provides a rationalized vision of gigantomachy set after not before the flood (fr. 6 Fraccaro=Serv. *Aen.* 3.578). According to him, after the flood, those who had survived on the mountains were challenged by other survivors attacking them from below. This is the origin of the gods' being called *superiores*, while the giants are the *terrigenae*. See Cole (2008) 67. Reading Ovid's episode through this intertext suggests that the situation of Deucalion and Pyrrha recalls the etymological origins of the gods themselves.

[9] Ahl (1985) 110–1.

[10] Schmitzer (1990) 75. That this speech marks the end of a flood, while Juno's provokes the beginning of the storm that starts the plot of Virgil's poem, the point of Schmitzer's comparison, provides another strong link between the passages. See also Hardie (2006) 39 n. 76.

[11] Bömer (1969) *ad loc.*

between men and gods, recalling the moral confusions of the Iron Age and the political ones of the Titanomachy. Looking forward predicts the fundamental difference of men from gods, established here by the lack of a genealogical link between Deucalion and Pyrrha and their human 'offspring'. The flood itself, of course, served as one of the ultimate demarcations of human, historical time; it was as far back as genealogies could be traced.[12]

And as if to signal this shift in epochs, the final member of the tricolon whose beginning, *O soror, o coniunx*, aligns Deucalion with Virgil's Juno, addresses Pyrrha as *femina*, a word making its first appearance in the poem. Juno's was a soliloquy emphasizing her own high status among the gods when human actions seemed to have challenged it; for Deucalion, the same nouns begin an act of commiseration. Juno's self-description as Jupiter's *coniunx* highlights the indignity of her defeat by 'one race' (*una cum gente, Aen.* 1.47). Deucalion's speech stresses the connection between *coniunx* and 'joining' by repeating other forms of that verb (*Met.* 1.353) and in place of one hostile race asserts that they two constitute a crowd (*nos duo turba sumus, Met.* 1.355). The recognition that Deucalion is speaking to a human audience rather than about them complements other narratological effects of the speech. This is the first directly reported speech of a human character (as he may appear in retrospect). Only Jupiter, and Lycaon in Jupiter's tendentious report, have previously addressed the reader. And the possibility of a new focalizing figure within the narrative correlates with the shift from Jupiter to Deucalion as subjects of verbs of seeing (*Met.* 1.326; 1.348).

The presence of these two divine models for Deucalion, Juno outside the poem and Jupiter within it, help to clarify the semantic effects of gender in the passage. Zeitlin observes of the Pandora narrative in Hesiod, whose portrayal of the relationship between the sexes as anything but cooperative and 'like-minded' makes it an important foil to Ovid's portrayal of this couple, that a central effect of the creation of woman is to emphasize the split between men and gods.[13] Here too, while gender imposes a new problem of likeness and difference in relation to the husband and wife, it also functions to open the separation between the couple's human future and divine past. This new axis of difference, male against female as opposed to human against divine, complicates an understanding of both alternatives. Deucalion's alliance with Pyrrha as a human creates a new 'us' in which the reader participates. Yet the divine paradigm may conversely suggest a model of gender difference that implies the hierarchy of male over female rather than their cooperation: Juno in the *Aeneid* defines her status by relation to

---

[12] On the flood as a dividing point between epochs in the poem, see Feeney (1999) 15, with Cole (2008) 63–6. And as Ziogas (2013) 63–7 points out, this genealogical break was also an intertextual one. In the Hesiodic corpus, Deucalion stands at the bridge between the *Theogony* and the *Catalogue of Women*; he thus emphasizes the continuity, but also the potential separation, between human and divine ancestry.

[13] Zeitlin (1996) esp. 83–6, and, on the atypical 'bleakness' of Hesiod's view of women, 59–61.

Jupiter's, and in the Hesiodic model the relationship between male and female divinities begins in struggle and conflict. So too within this passage, Deucalion reports his quasi-divine gaze over the landscape: 'of whatever lands the setting and rising sun behold,[14] we are the population,' (*terrarum, quascumque vident occasus et ortus / nos duo turba sumus, Met.* 1.354–5). When in place of looking down, as the sky (note that a celestial body is the one whose perspective on the world he presents), he looks up at it, describing the terror the clouds create, he becomes both sympathetic and identifies his fate with Pyrrha's. The divine perspective had made them different (*unum~unam, Met.* 1.325–6) yet the terrestrial perspective joins them, and the echo between *terra* (*Met.* 1.349, 1.354, 1.364) and *terrent* (*Met.* 1.357) relates this to a shared fear. However, the Jovian model may remind us that even when Deucalion equates their two experiences, in a line whose structure repeats the account of what Jupiter saw (1.325–6), Pyrrha herself has not gained a voice and her husband can only conjecture her feelings by analogy with his own:

> quo sola timorem
> ferre modo posses? quo consolante doleres?
> namque ego (crede mihi), si te quoque pontus haberet,
> te sequerer, coniunx, et me quoque pontus haberet.
>
> *Met.* 1.359–62

If you survived alone, how would you be able to endure your fear? Who would console you grieving? For truly, trust me, if the sea held you as well, I would follow you, wife, and the sea would hold me as well.

Before going on to consider further how the advent of gender in the post-flood world affects the reader's understanding of the poem, I want to close this section

---

[14] Interpretation of this phrase proves somewhat more contested than any commentary I have found suggests. The most straightforward reading would be to take *ortus* and *occasus* as verbal nouns describing the east and the west, a common usage for each (*OLD* s.v. *occasus* §3, *ortus* §2). However, the tautology of lands seeing themselves creates an awkwardness that some have resolved by assuming that the words refer to the rising and setting sun, not *occasus* [*solis*] but [*sol*] *occasus* (so the Loeb translation of Miller and the Oxford of Melville). Sixteen lines earlier, Ovid's description of how far the sound of Triton's signal extends diabolically anticipates both readings: *litora uoce replet sub utroque iacentia Phoebo, Met.* 1.338. The division into east and west will return in Deucalion's description of the whole world, but the expression 'each Phoebus', glossed precisely by *ortus* and *occasus*, also introduces the sun as a presence in the later line. Seneca echoes the line frequently, three times in the scope of a single play. At *HF* 871, *quod occasus videt et quod ortus*, describing the whole scope of the world, 'east' and 'west' would be suitable translations, and the tautology that derives from *terras* as object of *vident* is removed. At *HF* 443, *quodcumque Titan ortus et labens videt*, the missing sun is explicitly returned as a viewer and *labens* are participles. Then in 1060–2, *obitus pariter tecum* [sc. *Titan*] *Alcides uidit et ortus / nouitque tuas utrasque domos*, *ortus* and its opposite appear unambiguously as terrestrial regions, but the viewing subject sees them from the position of the sun (and the boundary between human and god is challenged by this change in perspective). If this pattern of Senecan imitation points to the same alternative understandings of the Ovidian expression reflected in modern English translations, then the flickering ambiguity about whether the viewer implied by *uident* is located on the earth or above it would complement my reading of the speech.

by anchoring the phenomenon more fully in Ovid's thematization of spatial and temporal distinction. Whether the new creation seems to repeat the first cosmogony or to rewrite it will largely be decided by references to gender. That earlier creation whose chaotic consequences this one replaces was, in its Hesiodic version especially, heavily gendered. Female figures like Chaos and Gaia have the power to create chthonic divinities spontaneously until they are supplanted by the male generations of Zeus.[15] Ovid's earlier superimposition of a generalized masculine *deus*, in confusing tandem with a *melior natura*, seems at once a new and improved way of excluding those figures, adding a male to make a better nature, and so to fulfil the trajectory of the *Theogony* on the meta-literary plane (*Met.* 1.21).

It is not only through the divine presence of Earth that gender becomes a feature in the landscape where the episode takes place, for the Parnassos of Deucalion and Pyrrha is in itself poised for a gender revolution. Its summit is the haunt of generalized 'mountain divinities' but also of Corycidian nymphs, and Themis, the giver of oracles (*Met.* 1.320–1). Of course, in historical times the oracle at Delphi belonged to the male god Apollo, now waiting in the wings to make his first appearance in Ovid's poem as the slayer of Python, and then as the pursuer of Daphne. The idea that Apollo displaced a previous female owner of the oracle, whether Gaia or Themis, occurs in many forms and has been powerfully related to the gendered hierarchization of order in the cosmos that symbolically aligns the victory of the male Zeus over his chthonic female ancestors with the victory of Apollo over similarly female and chthonic forces.[16] Within human history as well, both the previous human generations within the poem and the recent periods of Roman history to which the Ovidian Iron Age alludes, the relations of male to female emphatically differentiate past and present. The good couple of Deucalion and Pyrrha present a model of gender harmony among humans that differentiates the Iron Age from the new as much as the physical separation of the divine virgin Astraea. The crimes of the humans destroyed by the flood conclude with stereotypical paradigms of marital disharmony. Women look forward to the deaths of their husbands, and husbands do the same, a unity in dysfunctional hatred to counter the New Age couple's shared superiority in piety (*Met.* 1.146). And if Pyrrha fears the gods and therefore becomes a kind of mother, Iron Age women are themselves fearsome, *terribiles*, as false mothers to children who are not their own, *nouercae*. Sexual difference, then, not only alerts us to the familiar background noise of gender rivalry as a theme in Greek cosmic myth or its Hesiodic literary manifestation, it also becomes precisely the bridge, or the boundary, that unites all of these levels of the past,

---

[15] See the classic treatment by Arthur [Katz] (1982).

[16] Sourvinou-Inwood (1987). On Ovid's uses of this theme in the subsequent narrative, see Ahl (1985) 124–8.

from creation of the world, to the Iron Age, to the present in which Ovid's text replaces a Hesiodic model. Against the background of such an Iron Age, knitting men and women in wedlock seems to compete with the triumph of the male as a marker of this new beginning, which in turn invites us to see the episode as a replay of cosmic origins, asking which of the Empedoclean opposites we ought to emphasize, love or strife?

*

The first part of my discussion has demonstrated both the range of differences thematized in the episode's emphasis on separation and change and the special importance of gender both in signalling and interpreting change. In this section I add two new points. First I will show that gender provides not just a further binary on which to map other oppositions like before or after. Rather, our understanding of the meaning of the category 'woman' and the relationship between the sexes will itself be influenced by whether it was there before. Second, I will correlate the problem of whether woman's creation marks a new and different world within the narrative with the invention of a new distinction, that between representation and reality, for this is what I understand to be the import of Deucalion and Pyrrha's divergent readings of the oracle.

This new discovery about language manifests itself in a new level of self-consciousness about the text that confronts the reader with a sense of its potential difference from the world of experience. It would be impossible to argue that there are no signs depicted in the poem, or no self-consciousness about its own artifice, before this moment.[17] It also turns out to be strictly false that there are no women before Pyrrha and her descendants. But by presenting aetiologies for both phenomena, and especially by linking them together, Ovid goes beyond giving them a turn in the thematic spotlight. The relationship between reality and representation will itself be interpreted according to gender. This is demonstrated within the myth by attributing the discovery of this possibility about language to the man. We are provoked to see as male the idea of language as making something new. And yet it would have been impossible to read the poem before gender difference, both because of the structural importance of grammatical gender within the Latin language but also because metaphors of sexual difference emerge in all preceding accounts of creation. At the same time this recognition reveals a deep question about gender, if it was there all along, then language's representation of it makes language seem truer to reality. But if it was not, then simultaneously gender itself is revealed as a construct and the poem's claim to offer an authoritative view of the world called into question. Could we really imagine a world without women? In one sense, then, this very problem is structured by an association of reality with the woman and artificial creation with the man.[18] Here too it becomes difficult to

---

[17] See Wheeler (1995).   [18] See Lev Kenaan's (2008) 187–8 discussion of the episode.

formulate an idea of representation without a pre-existing idea of male and female difference. But the consciousness of the possibility of artifice, that language is different from things, makes it imaginable that it has not described the world (woman) as it is. The reading of the episode to follow will show how the conundrum of the priority of sexual difference or words, which the myth of the invention of both highlights, becomes at once a prompt to ask whether gender is a matter of words or things and whether texts are produced by reality or refashion it. Finally, by presenting the text before the reader as a manifestation of the very polarities of likeness and difference it represents, Ovid most dramatically extends the chronological border between before and after up to the very moment of reading. He makes clear that his audience do not necessarily stand outside the narrative as Jupiter stands above the earth and apart from its pressures of isolation and temporality. He allows, rather, the possible relationships between the ban-ished past and the future coming into being to model how the real conditions of the text's reception change or are changed by what it represents. To see the new future as different from the past within the text correlates with the possibility of seeing texts transform perceptions of the world rather than always being shaped by reality.

In beginning this stage of the argument, I want to return to the textual figure that aligns Jupiter's view of the earth after the flood and Deucalion's reiteration of it to Pyrrha. This figure is called epiphora (Lausberg § 631-2), and takes the form of a backwards anaphora, where the endings rather than the beginnings of a unit provide the point of similarity that defines repetition:

> et superesse uirum de tot modo milibus unum,
> et superesse uidet de tot modo milibus unam,
>
> *Met.* 1.325–6

And [Jupiter] saw that one man survived from so many thousands once, and from so many thousands once one woman.

In this context, the construction echoes other emphases on the symmetry and equivalence of the couple, such as the repetition of *ambo* in the line that follows and the elaborately patterned earlier claim, initially similar in substance, that 'no man was better than he nor more loving of justice or was any woman more fearful of the gods than she' (*non illo melior quisquam nec amantior aequi / uir fuit aut illa metuentior ulla deorum, Met.* 1.322–3). As Barchiesi (2005) 195 notes, the parallelisms highlight the 'perfetta corrispondenza' of this 'coppia perfetta'. But Bömer (1969) 117 also adds an important observation: Ovid tends to use this schema to highlight contrasting binaries, in this case gender. This qualification again raises the question of whether to put the emphasis in interpreting this formula on likeness or difference. *Unus* plus *una* do not inevitably add up to *ambo*, and this perfect couple now seems to embody rather an Empedoclean *discors concordia* (cf. *Met.* 1.433) that reflects their natural associations with water and fire. We remember too that the first equivalence between Deucalion and Pyrrha was based on a similarly striking Empedoclean opposition. He was superior because of his love of what was same, while she excelled because of her fear of what was different, the gods. Thus beyond simply linking the two perspectives on the human couple, this figure of speech highlights the larger problem raised by the creation of men and women, whether to emphasize likenesses or differences, and relates them to a change in textual form that signifies the same difference, the switch from the masculine *unum* to the feminine *unam*, directly subordinated to it in the text of the poem.

To press the symbolism of the formal structure that depicts Jupiter's perception of human survival, we might specify that the pattern that begins in sameness ends in difference. The initial word that establishes the resemblance between the two lines, *superesse*, conveys at once a likeness between past and present (man survives from then to now) and between gods and man, both of whom are 'above'; while the ending makes a distinction through gender, and correlates the change within the text with a perception of change in the world it represents. In this way the marked artificiality of the construction reproduces an interpretative question raised precisely by the highlighting of male and female difference within the story: is it really new? It has been observed that Hesiod's narrative of Pandora signals contradictions and ellipses in the myths of human origin he presents: the moulding of Pandora and her endowment with divine gifts seems a doublet for the way Prometheus creates man himself, yet not only is that scene never described but the human partner of Pandora is not Prometheus' creation but his brother, so that the moment when humans become a different race from Titans is blurred. Correspondingly, Hesiod describes Pandora as the likeness of a 'modest maiden' (*Th.* 572, *WD* 71), yet, as Loraux describes, here the imitation seems to come before the model that inspires it: Pandora is a copy without an original.[19] By his own symmetrical elision of the creation of woman, while he describes in detail the moulding of man that Hesiod leaves out, Ovid signals how his account of human origins raises questions similar to Hesiod's about the natural inevitability of sexual difference.[20] By presenting his only account of the creation of women as though it were a recreation, he alludes back to the prior model, as Hesiod may have done in the *Catalogue of Women*, his 'sequel' to the *Theogony* and the *Works and Days*, and so perpetuates through literary history the Pandoran enigma of how a creation can be an imitation.[21] More simply, he also forces his audience to ask

[19] Loraux (1993) 82.
[20] For further discussion of how Ovid signals the absence of Pandora in the account of the Myth of the Ages and elsewhere in the poem, see Van Noorden (2015) 248–51.
[21] For the arguments about whether Deucalion and Pyrrha's myth was presented in the *Catalogue*, see Ziogas (2013) 63 and Hirschberger (2008) 113–14.

precisely whether or not women have been there all along, and whether we can imagine the human race apart from its division into men and women.

As the last point makes clear, however, the distinction between men and women is not just something conjured up by texts through the pointing of morphological differences or through intertextual allusions it is a phenomenon that, seemingly, exists in the world as a component of humanity that can appear as natural as grammatical gender. When Deucalion seems at a loss to imagine how he and his wife could possibly reproduce in any other way than as potters, the humour comes precisely from the shock of thinking away what we take to be the inevitable consequence of men and women's being different. What is involved in imagining the creation of women, or more precisely in asking whether such a creation is even possible, is therefore a hermeneutic approach to the text, a decision to use reality as a criterion for interpreting Ovid's narrative, but at a point when the text claims to locate the origin of that reality, of what we are (*sumus*, 1.414), in unbelievable stories. Gender difference therefore functions as Parnassos does within the geography that initially figures separation in the episode. It implies a rocklike superimposition of the way things really are now that allows us to escape from the fluid confusions that would come from experiencing the mythical past from a truly internal perspective.

To see how this relationship between the audience's now and the text's then might be modelled within the narrative, and how it relates to some of the other issues bound up in questions of continuity and difference, let us examine briefly those passages that contradict the notion that Pyrrha is the first woman and the origin of women. Ovid's description of the first three human ages makes no reference to gender difference or any form of human reproduction. The suggestion is that each new metallic race simply replaces the one before.[22] If the Golden Age hints at the absence of reproduction, the Iron Age suggests another paradox. It is only at the very end of the description of this epoch that specific gender roles within the family are first ascribed to human society, and that individual humans are marked by grammatical gender. Yet if the problem of reproduction seems solved by the suggestion that children and family relations exist in a recognizable form, those roles are there unnaturally adapted not to create new life but to

---

[22] Indeed, Ovid seems playfully to raise the question of where these races come from near the end of the account of the Golden Age when he describes how 'zephyrs caress the flowers born without seed,' *mulcebant zephyri natos sine semine flores (Met. 1.108).* The word order makes it fleetingly possible to take *natos* as a substantive before construing it as a participle modifying *flores.* In such a sense it is a virtual synonym for *proles,* which Ovid uses as the term for every race henceforth (*argentea proles, Met.* 1.114; *aenea proles, Met.* 1.125: *ultima* (sc. *proles*), *Met.* 1.127. (For the glosses that identify *proles* with sons and daughters, see *TLL* s.v. 10.2.1819.67–71.) The first race (*aetas*) which do not seem to be the 'offspring' of anyone, are by contrast described as 'sown', *sata (Met.* 1.89). Thus the line by simultaneously pointing forward to the new 'sons' of the Golden Age, born seemingly without seed, and backward to the originary race that was, paradoxically, 'sown' invites speculation on the precise mechanisms at work in these successive generations. On the role of sowing imagery in the account of the Golden Age, see Ahl (1985) 114–16.

destroy it. Jupiter's flood seems superfluous as stepmothers kill their offspring and husbands and wives plot one another's death. The prior existence of men and women as different in the narrative therefore comes specifically in a context that suggests the stereotypical vices of the Roman present were already present in the past and assigns women only the unnatural role of ending life through strife rather than creating it through love. The *uirgo*, who, 'last of the heavenly beings,' (*ultima caelestum*, *Met.* 1.149–50), departs from an earth men have already drenched in blood, as if rationalizing in advance the divine miracle of the flood, thus has a complex function even beyond marking the separation of earth and sky that the ending of the flood narrative will, potentially, reverse. She is at once the antitype to all those deadly human females, the maiden who must logically have existed before there were stepmothers. But she also raises the question of the ontological status of women in the poem. From one perspective, the disappearance of the *uirgo* may suggest the unreality of any female model other than those suggested by the hyperrealistic satiric modes the passage recalls, or indeed by Ovid's predecessor Hesiod, where human women simply are an 'evil' (*Th.* 570). But if we see a true separation between our race and the Iron Age, and insist that the destroyed world does not figure contemporary vices, Ovid's absent *uirgo* highlights the mysterious creation of women by appearing as an avatar of that Hesiodic *parthenos aidoiê*, the absent original for Pandora herself.[23] The idea that women were always there, then, links a commonsensical assumption that things in the poem must be measured by the way they are in the real world with a strongly negative judgement about both women themselves, who were murderers before they were maidens or mothers, and about all human nature.

The other strong indication that the category of women was already present before the new creation comes in the very words of the oracle itself with the reference to a feminine *magna parens*, whose bones the couple are instructed to cast behind them (*Met.* 1.383). Yet whether that *magna parens* should be understood as a human mother or as the raw material for the original 'fiction' of man (*Met.* 1.80) is precisely the question set for the male and female readers within the episode. Pyrrha's understanding of the oracle is only imaginable on the presumption she had a mother. Beyond the overlap between actual and internal audiences that results from the direct incorporation of the oracle into the text, what Deucalion and Pyrrha are trying to figure out turns out to be but a specific instance of the same thematically charged problem raised for Ovid's readers: were women always there, and was natural generation, with all its confusions of creation and destruction, the inevitable source of the human race?

With that new consciousness of the relationship between the reader and the internal audience in mind, I turn to the much discussed issue of Deucalion and

---

[23] For linguistic and structural connections between Dikê and Pandora in Hesiod's *Works and Days*, see Olstein (1980) esp. 306–7.

Pyrrha's strategies for interpreting the oracle, but from a somewhat different angle by taking precisely the new entity of representation itself, manifested also in the comparison of internal and external audiences, as the focus of the passage. The opposition between Pyrrha's approach to the oracle and her husband's has often been described as that between literal and metaphorical or figurative reading.[24] For Pyrrha, a stone is always only a stone, but for Deucalion the likenesses between things make it possible to use the same words to denote different objects. By this interpretation, stones can become bones, and the female great parent may be not the mother but the mother-like earth. Yet we can also place the emphasis not on what words mean but on the fundamental difference between representation and reality. Pyrrha does not recognize that the word is anything other than what it denotes. Deucalion's capacity for metaphorical reading, however, demands not only prizing apart words from a one-to-one dependence on things, but looking on things themselves from without so that he can perceive the likenesses between objects that can then be expressed in language. He is in essence working as much with the pair *ossa* and 'bones', as with *ossa* and *lapides*. This way of understanding the origins of metaphor suggests some important parallels with other themes of the episode. If 'seeing' was a point at which man resembles divinities, both looking out over the desolate post-flood scene beneath them, it is precisely his perception from outside that allows him to see the earth as mother. Indeed, the object of his vision at that point '*terras*', is precisely what he recognizes as '*parens*' (*Met.* 1.349; 1.393, where the word *terra* is repeated twice, at the caesura and line end); recall that only Deucalion was described as seeing (*uidit*).

This idea that recognizing that language exists in its own right results from the distance that separates viewers from the objects of their gaze is intensified by the application of a complementary pattern of visual imagery to the *uerba* of the oracle, which, like the earth, are 'dark with unseen hiding places' (*caecisque obscura latebris*, *Met.* 1.388). At the same time looking into things makes it possible for words themselves to be seen, metaphor conveys their new materiality, and the reification of language through metaphor becomes insistent in this passage.[25] When the couple 'roll the words about among and between themselves' (*uerba ... secum inter seque uolutant*, 1.389), the specificity of the prepositions gives a particular physicality to an expression that is more unusual than has sometimes been noted. Both *uolutare* and its simple form *uoluo* frequently occur metaphorically to describe intellectual activity, but it is strictly speaking

---

[24] Lev Kennan (2008) 187.

[25] Within this progression, when Deucalion first solicits aid for *mersis ... rebus* (*Met.* 1.380) it seems a sort of pre-metaphor. On the one hand it is unclear whether it is in fact a metaphor since all things really have been submerged. But if we hear it as one, we are likely to take it as a kind of bad joke on Ovid's part. The two perspectives on the expression, that of the contemporary author who sees it as figurative, and of the internal speaker, who sees it as literal, tend to pull apart before Deucalion's own discovery of how likenesses between things create a new kind of language different from what it represents.

unprecedented for their object to be the words themselves and not some idea that they contain.[26] The words seem already to be stones, but also present as the physical text available to the reader to unroll.[27] And the words in the line just before Deucalion discloses his new reading stand out for their elaborate visual patterning reminiscent of the epiphoric patterns through which I have suggested that gender itself was called into being by the text: *inde Promethides placidis Epimethida dictis / mulcet* (*Met.* 1.390-1). Here it is interlocked word order that creates an effect of symmetry and balance, accentuated by the repetition of the two central syllables of each name, which itself connotes the couple's shared origins as the children of Titans, while the gender difference emerges from the slightest of morphological clues: *Epimethida*, as direct object, could be masculine or feminine, but the nominative *Promethides* could only be a masculine patronymic.

This very attention to verbal texture suggests another aspect to the teleology and futurity of Deucalion's discovery of language as different from its object. Beyond making possible the future within which we read the account of our origins, there is a directionality to the hermeneutic process itself that makes us come after Deucalion. As Deucalion sees the fundamental similarity between unlike things, stones and bones, that allows the same word, *ossa*, to designate both, so the reader of Ovid's text, confronted by phrases like *Promethides placidis Epimethida dictis*, perceives similarities in unlike words suggesting analogies based on form that themselves challenge differences in meaning, and also subtle differences, like that between *unam* and *unum*, in forms whose meaning is, precisely, one. Pyrrha does not distinguish words and things, nor perhaps does she look on things from outside; Deucalion suggests with great uncertainty that different things with similar properties can be named with similar words; finally, the Ovidian readers stand in relationship to words as Deucalion does to things. And this addition of a hierarchical process of reading constitutes a distinctively Ovidian take on an analogy between letters and matter familiar from the materialist poetics of Lucretius, an emphasis on the mutability of texts through processes of allusion and reference and an opening for suggesting resemblances that do not exist in the things they describe.[28]

---

[26] *OLD*, s.v. §11 (*uoluo*) and §9 (*uolutare*). There is one parallel for this idiom later in the description of the house of Fama (*Met.* 12.55), where again attention to the issue of words' materiality also suits the context; the closest extant model for Ovid's use here may be *Aen.* 3.102, where Anchises, also about to propose the interpretation of an oracle concerning an ancient mother (*antiquam matrem*, *Aen.* 3.96, as an anonymous referee observed), contemplates what men of old recalled to him (*ueterum uoluens monimenta uirorum*). Conversely Cicero (*Brut.* 246) does speak of 'rolling out words', but he is describing a speaker's rhetorical fluency, not an audience's consideration of meaning.

[27] I owe this observation to Alison Sharrock, *per litteras*.

[28] In this sense the passage could also be a programmatic invitation to the interpretative innovations of Ahl (1985).

We see a little sample of this at work, importantly, not in Deucalion's interpretation of the oracle, but in the representation of that interpretation in Ovid's text. Here are the words of the oracle as 'given' by the goddess:

> 'discedite templo
> et uelate caput cinctasque resoluite uestes
> ossaque post tergum magnae iactate parentis!'

Met. 1.381–3

'depart from the temple; veil your head; loosen your girded clothing and cast the bones of your great parent behind your back!'

Deucalion's reinterpretation of *ossa* similarly involves a repetition of the last line of the oracle that can also be viewed as a recombination of its words:

> 'lapides in corpore terrae
> ossa reor dici; iacere hos post terga iubemur.'

Met. 1.394–5

'I think that stones in the body of the earth are being called bones; we are ordered to cast those stones behind our backs.'

The miracle itself, when it happens, literally combines the hard words of the goddess with his softened reading:

> discedunt uelantque caput tunicasque recingunt
> et iussos lapides sua post uestigia mittunt.

Met. 1.398–9

They depart; veil their heads; unbind their tunics, and cast the ordered stones behind in their tracks.

The first line reproduces not only the substance but much of the language of the oracle itself. But the following line already anticipates the miracle by substituting the 'soft' option developed by Deucalion. For bones, he already reads stones, and the participle *iussos* from his own verb *iubemur* not only completes the allusion to this new reading, but it makes it seem as though this is a return to an original command. That's what the gods ordered all along. So this emended, mixed formulation itself can seem to recover the original mildness of the divinities, or to decompose into a blending of hard words softened by the eye of the beholder that then miraculously model reality.[29]

---

[29] Concomitantly, what his statement does anticipates the metamorphosis for which it prepares. The verb of which *Promethides* is the subject and *Epimethida* the object is *mulcet*: The son of Prometheus

To conclude this section, the audience's challenge to imagine a world before gender difference appears synchronized to Deucalion and Pyrrha's challenge of imagining words themselves as something different from the world. Within the narrative, the idea of gender as a new creation can seem impossible given the pre-existence both of the caricature stepmothers of the Iron Age and of the inevitable gendering of divine and natural processes represented through language. What may be new, then, is the representation of gender that raises the audience's consciousness of those presences within the text. Whether the pious Pyrrha and her likenesses in the present can be differentiated from the murderous mothers of the past illuminates, and is determined by, the question of whether the word *femina*, when it first appears in the text, can be separated both from the pre-existing females, and the pre-existing cultural notions of women that inform Ovid's portrayal of them. The emphasis on grammatical gender as a textual phenomenon, through devices like epiphora, intensifies that question by seeming at once a necessary precondition for reading Ovid's poem and a present manifestation of a division of the world precipitated by Deucalion and Pyrrha's actions.

I suggested that the patterned line juxtaposing Prometheus' son and Epimetheus' daughter provides another case where the role of grammatical gender in interpreting the text seems highlighted. As we sort these two Titanic offspring into male and female, we also note the differences implied by the prefixes pro- (before) and epi- (after). Prometheus was famously the one who exercised forethought, and Epimetheus the one who gains wisdom only after the fact. Doblhofer (1968) has rightly argued that in context these become 'speaking names', but his interpretation of their point, that Deucalion thinks before speaking while Pyrrha speaks before thinking, is too limited. While Deucalion's forethought suggests a view to the future, Pyrrha appears as Epimetheus' daughter because her hermeneutic strategy of looking only to things would itself make the casting of stones a throwback to the moral situation before the flood and would condemn her to take on the impiety of that time by desecrating a real mother's real bones.[30] (Thus despite the character's own intentions, her place in the larger pattern of the text potentially recasts her efforts to be pious as impious.) But thanks to Deucalion's insight, an action that would have been completely at home in the social conditions of the Iron Age, profiting from the death of near relations, will now be made

'soothes' the daughter of Epimetheus. But the word can also mean 'sculpt' and as such is embedded in the name Mulciber, Vulcan, who in Hesiod moulds (*sumplasse / plasse*, *Th.* 570; *WD* 70) the first woman. In this way too the conversion of words to things parallels the creation of gender difference.

[30] And if *ossa* just are *ossa* and, like Parnassos, suggest a fixed reality that never changes, another transgressive element in her reading may emerge if we remember *ossa* would also therefore become identical with that other Greek mountain that the Giants used as a weapon against the gods (*Met.* 1.155).

comprehensible in the context of the new world of piety even though it is described in the same words.

*

> saxa (quis hoc credat nisi sit pro teste uetustas?)
> ponere duritiam coepere suumque rigorem
> mollirique mora mollitaque ducere formam.
> mox ubi creuerunt naturaque mitior illis
> contigit, ut quaedam, sic non manifesta, uideri
> forma potest hominis, sed uti de marmore coepta,
> non exacta satis rudibusque simillima signis.
> quae tamen ex illis aliquo pars umida suco
> et terrena fuit, uersa est in corporis usum;
> quod solidum est flectique nequit, mutatur in ossa;
> quae modo uena fuit, sub eodem nomine mansit;
> inque breui spatio superorum numine saxa
> missa uiri manibus faciem traxere uirorum
> et de femineo reparata est femina iactu.
> inde genus durum sumus experiensque laborum,
> et documenta damus qua simus origine nati.

Met. 1.400–15

The stones (who would believe this without the testimony of antiquity?) began to put aside their hardness and their stiffness and to soften gradually, then, having grown soft, to take on a shape. Soon when they had grown and a softer nature had come upon them, the shape of a human can be seen, a sort of shape, though not apprehensible, but as if begun and not yet sufficiently expressed from the marble, and most like to crude sculptures. The part of the stones that had been damp with some liquid and earthy was transformed into the function of a body, what is solid and inflexible, is turned into bones, what was just now a vein, has remained in the same name. And in a short space by the power of the gods above the stones sent from the hands of the male took on the appearance of men, and woman is restored by the woman's toss. From thence we are a hard race and knowing of labors, and we give proofs from what origin we are born.

The last section argued that the interpretation of the oracle highlights the discovery of verbal representation as something potentially different from what it shows[31] and suggested how gender both structures different responses to this discovery and is itself defined by them. The second half of this paper will explore the consequences of this argument for an understanding of Ovid's poem. It will

[31] Cf. Barkan's observation (1986) 30 that the episode, together with Phaethon's ride, marks a shift toward narrative explanations of origins away from the non-'mythological' account of cosmic beginnings.

begin with a discussion of the narrative linking then and now: the metamorphosis of the stones to men that allows Ovid's poem to continue by not having the human race exterminated and shows how mythical transformations might or might not create reality. The creation of man in the past as a real element in the world turns out to coincide with the formation of the reader as a self-conscious interpreter of himself/herself, in a geographically appropriate realization of the Delphic motto. And the metamorphosis in turn possesses a Janus-like status as a proof (cf. *temptare*, *Met.* 1.397) within the story of the correctness of Deucalion's reading by giving it an effect in the world and as a challenge to the reader to assess the truth of the story itself. Looking forward, Deucalion and Pyrrha impose form on matter, like the original creator, making stones into men, but from the perspective of the present audience, the effect of the story, once it is seen as story, is to give substance to a form—at once to fill our form with the legacy of its stony origins and to establish the reality of representation.

I start with Barkan's inspiringly optimistic understanding of the episode as a use of metamorphosis to demonstrate the power of Ovid's art:

> When Deucalion realises the *parens* is to be taken metaphorically... he turns the destructive form of confusion among elements into a creative one.... A whole series of parallels is implicit in Deucalion's interpretation: literal mothers and mother earth, bones and stones, stones as the recreated human race. These parallels are the very basis of which Ovid's poem is made, for when we accept—so early in Book I—the metaphoric flow among separate categories of existence, we are prepared to understand how metamorphosis defines the multiple nature of things.... the transformation itself tells us that we are what we are because of the flow from gods to giants to men to bones to stones.[32]

While earlier he makes an important distinction between the cosmic confusions of the original creation and the moral confusions resolved by Deucalion's reading of the oracle, Barkan's emphasis here lies on continuities. In particular, his final image of metamorphic flow bridges at once the distinction between past and present ('us') and also between Ovid's poem and the characters within it. The poet becomes a Deucalion making poetry out of natural variety and thereby showing us ourselves. This remains a striking formulation of a powerful reading of the metamorphosis, one that aptly reveals how the creative process described continues in the work not only of the poet but also the reader/critic. But I would like to complement it here with another approach that takes its starting point from a transition within the text that Barkan quite literally leaves out of his citation of the

---

[32] Barkan (1986) 31, the middle section is also quoted and discussed in McAuley (2015) 122, whose own interpretation stresses the consequences of the gender difference, somewhat left aside in Barkan's analysis.

passage, and which emphasizes the divisions between then and now and between the story and its reception. Just when the metamorphosis narrative begins, with the *saxa*, so to speak, hanging in the air, Ovid interrupts it with an aside: 'who would believe this without the testimony of antiquity?' (*quis hoc credat nisi pro teste uetustas?*, *Met.* 1.400).

Beyond fracturing the narrative illusion with this effect, Ovid here puts the relationship between his text and the story in a very different light. He draws attention to the temporal position of his text as contemporary with its reading by differentiating it from 'antiquity', but in place of the coalescence between crafted word and crafted matter, this interruption pulls them apart. One way of appropriating this interruption to a progressive reading of the metamorphosis like Barkan's might be to stress its position at the beginning of the change: like the coming together of form and matter, the creations of the text and in the text merge until the (possibly very dubious) testimony of antiquity is replaced by the material and inescapable proof of our own bodies in the here and now, so that 'we', author and audience combined, become authorities that grant reality to the narrative and make it the validation Deucalion sought for his reading. But the aside also sets up a less easily bridged limit to the effective presence of the text, one that in turn suggests a different view of temporal progression. This newly invented mode of representation, or as Barkan stresses this first myth of creation, remains just that, a story and simultaneously a verbal construct that for that very reason conveys no truth. Far from the forward-looking view of and on the new creation as at once a correction of the past and proof of the authority of Ovid's art, we can imagine the miracle as continually awaiting a validation that is endlessly deferred. The very question, on either end of the metamorphosis, of whether truth comes from the past and from words, from the authority of an old story, or from the present and reality, the proof we give, mobilizes this contrast in perspectives. What is worse, the possibility of reading Ovid's aside about the testimony of the past ironically undermines in advance the happy ending of the text's realization in the present, and the present's affirmation of the text. For after all, if that proof is our 'hard' nature, a metaphor that has slipped back into seeming literal, is that not in itself simply a matter of words? One could equally well say of the present Romans, and many contemporaries did, that they were 'soft' or 'avaricious' or condemned to an endless cycle of violent strife. And merely by making that claim, such a speaker would with as much force as Ovid disprove that we were born from stone and prove that we were formed from the same giant blood as the race destroyed in the flood. If Deucalion's creation of man takes its beginnings not only from the recognition of variety in the world and its translation into language, as Barkan suggests, but from the separation between words and things, as I have read his conversation with Pyrrha, then for all its claims to the contrary, it remains trapped in its 'real' reality as mere representation, just words.

This deferral of the final moment of truth for the creation narrative goes together with another fragmentation of temporal boundaries that affects its origins. For as we shall see, a corresponding contrast in perspectives emerges within the metamorphosis between the impression that the transformation was something sudden and that it happened gradually so that it is able to be broken down into multiple stages. We should not underestimate the originality of Ovid's representational strategy here. As Frontisi-Ducroux has suggested, Greek metamorphoses tend to be presented in the aorist, as mere occurrences that have no temporal depth.[33] This approach results precisely in the juxtaposition of the earlier and later form and tends to mystify how the one became the other. Ovid at once suggests this perspective in his final resumé of the transformation at lines *Met.* 1.411–13, where he insists that it happens 'in a short time' (*breui spatio*) and employs the perfect tense, which provided the Latin equivalent to the aorist. The perfect at the beginnings of the story, however, refers to the inception of a process, *coepere*, which is immediately broken down into its component parts. One result of this slowing down of the metamorphosis is precisely to blur the lines between present and past, to make the reader seem specifically to be witness to the change as it unfolds, and so to blend, as I will argue shortly, a view of the text and of the event. But it also replicates in miniature an aspect of Book I as a whole, its multiplication of beginnings. If this new creation of man is the really decisive one, both overwriting the alternative narratives and specifically beginning history rather than becoming just another in a series of creations each of which retains some explanatory power, then the question of precisely when and how that change happens gains a special force. But the fragmentation of the process of metamorphosis, together with the alternative kinds of creation that it can resemble, from the 'male' alternative of imposing form on matter through art to the 'female' moulding of offspring through emphatically natural processes, raises the question of when the decisive change happens. Indeed, the division of the narrative into its inchoative portion and its aorist resumé constitutes one such division in addition to making the audience, for all their ability to witness the process, wonder whether they may have blinked at the decisive moment.

In terms of substance too, the fragmentation of the qualities of the stone seems to pull against Deucalion's use of a single word to draw together very different entities in the human and natural worlds. Stones, as it turns out, already possess multiple components: they have their own hard bits, but also unexpected signs of dampness. The fundamental shift from hardness to softness seems initially simply reiterated but is in fact very precisely broken down by words that can casually seem to be mere synonyms. For instance, line 401 may seem pleonastic, and yet there is also a distinction to be made between the surface 'hardness' evoked by

---

[33] Frontisi-Ducroux (2003) 91–2, cf. Barchiesi in this volume, 19–20.

duritia, and the inflexibility suggested by *rigor*. And this difference itself appears repeated in the next line. *Mollita* answers *duritia*, but it is only once the stones have lost this quality that they lose their *rigor* by becoming plastic.[34] The doublet *solidum flectique nequit*, may seem just another repetition of the theme, and indeed inflexibility comes pretty close in meaning to *rigor*. But *solidum* connotes something rather different from either *duritia* or *rigor* here thanks to the contrast with *umida*, suggesting not just a hard external surface or unbendability but a dense and impenetrable fabric that shuts out water. Thus, like the parts of which it is made, the qualities of stone appear capable of infinite differentiation. The particularization of the points of similarity between humans and stones may seem to affirm Deucalion's comparison of human to terrestrial bodies, to make it even more true in its realization than it was before by pointing out the many aspects of human nature that both resemble stones and can be named with the same sign (*uena*, 1.410). But Ovid's insistent renaming of the very property that stones must lose so that we can become stones, their hardness, offers a metonymic riposte to the principle by which he solves the oracle. Like names highlight only similarities between things, but Ovid's profusion of vocabulary finds multiple distinctive aspects within a single quality. As the simple statement that the 'stones took on the form of men' seems no longer adequate to convey the variety of either entity or the infinite refraction the metamorphosis can accommodate, so the multiplication of names and parts suggests the fundamental inadequacy of language to represent the world since every summary description could presumably be further anatomized. There are, as it turns out, bones within bones. And the equation of different parts at the level of language (*ossa* for stones and earth) comes at the cost of moving representation farther from reality because it makes things that are alike the same.

Together with this attention to representation as something different from reality and its distinguishing of new stages in the change from stones to men, Ovid's metamorphosis narrative highlights its own representational capacities and offers a kind of taxonomy of the different ways that texts can depict reality. But these multiple aspects of how Ovid's poem can show us what happened do not necessarily add up to a unified image of art harmonizing differences by including them all in its own capacious form so that it can constitute itself as at once a complete mimesis and the generative point for a new reality. The first of these representational strategies, and the one that most clearly articulates the shift from then to now, is focalization, the construction of an audience within the narrative whose perspective becomes available as a way of seeing for the work's audience. We approach the metamorphosis with the inner focalization of the couple in the past strongly demarcated. They wonder whether the procedure will

---

[34] This distinction has also been noted by Lee (1953) 114.

work, but we of course know that it will. And although Ovid's reference to *vetustas* in the aside immediately makes it clear that we will not be seeing the metamorphosis from their anxious perspective, it is striking how completely Deucalion and Pyrrha vanish from the text.[35] Even their names are replaced by mere indications of their gender in lines 412–13, redirecting our attention from their presence as characters to the traces they have left in the real objects directly present not just in the now of the poem's composition but also of its reception. Every reader has a body.

The two other ways in which Ovid's text represents the metamorphosis are themselves polarized by this progression away from the perspective of the past. First is *enargeia*, the property of a narrative that makes us seem to see directly what it describes. The passage begins with generalities and with qualities that cannot be seen because they are tactile and are in any case presented as abstract nouns: *duritia, rigorem*. The first visualizable quality of the stone is *forma*, though again we are not at first told what *forma* the stones are taking on. But Ovid is tracking the process of the stones into visibility, and it is precisely as they take on a form that he makes it possible for the reader to see it not only by the attention he draws to the action of sight (*uideri*) but also through the use of a simile, the figure that according to Quintilian (*IO* 8.3.72), was 'a luminous invention for shedding light on things'. By making the vehicle of that simile itself an image, and one progressing into visibility, Ovid not only throws attention on the power of art as at once a verisimilar source for the miracle and the means by which we can begin to apprehend it, he also, conversely, draws attention to his own verbal art by evoking the analogy between word and image as ways of making the reader see.[36]

And as the statue is precisely not the thing it allows one to see, so at the very same time Ovid foregrounds his visual representation of the past, he makes the audience aware of his own text's changing form, not as a means of showing us directly what happened but of imitating it for the reader. And this requires not looking through the text but looking at it. We have already seen an example of this iconic textual presence in the way Ovid correlates the increasing formal distinctness of the stones themselves with the increasing vividness of his description. But as Deucalion's reading of the oracle has invited the reader to look for likenesses and differences in words as well as things, so here Ovid will convey the differences between before and after through verbal patterns of repetition and variation. An early example of this comes in the line *mollirique mora mollitaque ducere formam*. While, as Barkan (1986) 32 observes, the sonant, liquid sounds with which it

---

[35] A point also stressed by Meinrath (2014) 63–4.

[36] Ovid's introduction of his text as a representation to compete with the simile features in different ways in the analysis of von Glinski (2012) 37–8 ('As if caught in the act of writing ekphrasis, Ovid shows how his words literally build the artifact diachronically, and do not merely replicate it mimetically') and Barchiesi (2005) 199. My debt throughout these pages to von Glinski's reading of the simile goes beyond this specific quotation.

begins might be described as soft, graphically too the replication of syllables with slight variations conveys the passing from one stage in the process to another. Beyond the way these subtle variations in form convey changes in things, Ovid's syntax also reproduces the phases of transformation, recalling the first lines of the poem where he advertises the metamorphic character of his work by making his readers realign the syntactic structures of his Latin.[37] And appropriately the word central to this transformation is *forma* itself, the noun that also stood at the hinge of the transformation from the poem's first to second line. As opposed to the first sentence of the description, where *saxa* emerge as the immediate object of our attention, the linear presentation of the simile initially makes it impossible to recognize *forma* as the subject because it is deferred to the beginning of line 405, and this goes together with another ambiguity resulting from the formal similarity between *ut*, which might seem to introduce a simile, but here is a correlative with *sic*, and *uti* in the next line, so that the object of comparison and the act of comparison come into view at the same time. Thus at the moment when Ovid brings his account closest to visual transparency he is simultaneously making the reader notice the material shape of the words themselves, making it difficult to know whether we are seeing the form, or simply reading *forma*.

This moment of representational ambiguity, occurring precisely between now and then, between the changing rocks of the past and the human form of the present, signals the incompletion of the form also by the genitive that describes it, *hominis*. While the images as described in the final summary have the property of gender, this description looks back, as it were, to the time before Deucalion and Pyrrha, when man, *homo*, was created without specified gender (1.78). And the iconic image of metamorphosis in Ovid's language replicates this moment in its own use of gendered forms. As I have suggested, the precise syntax of the simile is made difficult to grasp by the feint of a correlative *ut* and the deferral of the noun that allows us to identify the gender of the adjectives, *quaedam* and *manifesta*, which could be either feminine singular or neuter plural. And these options point to another, retrospective, uncertainty about what the simile is really describing; is it the singular form (*forma*) or the plural stones (*saxa*)? When *forma* appears it seems to settle the issue, but the meaning of the actual simile could raise doubts even when the same ending recurs in *coepta*, *exacta*, and *simillima*. For one can use the verb *exigere* to mean something like 'express' to describe what a work of art represents; it can also mean 'bring to completion' and seems to take as its object the material work itself: *opus exegi*, as Ovid will put it at the poem's conclusion (*Met.* 15.871). And in addition to the verb's making it possible to compare the stones themselves to incipient statues rather than comparing the *forma* to what those statues themselves represent, so too the vehicle of the simile, the *rudibus signis* are themselves plural. Thus while the readers can always look backward to the form (*forma*) as what they are able to see, the language also allows them to

---

[37] Excellently described in Barchiesi (2005) 133–7.

look forward to real images compared to stones. And at the very moment when the images themselves are imperfectly visualizable to the audience because the feminine gender has not yet come into being, we see on the textual surface a female *forma* uncertainly emerging among the stones.

*

As we have seen, the transitions that the metamorphosis narrative presents are themselves multiple. The shift from stones to men opposes also the perspectives of the present and the past, the world within the narrative and the world outside it, and leaves the poem itself open for construction as the present manifestation of legendary events, or as the verbal artistry that alone summons those myths into being. But this inbetween status of the text, as transparent to past forms or obscuring them with its present matter, mirrors the very nature of its subject: mankind itself, poised halfway between chaos and order, nature and gods, and already bearing the double aspect of form and matter. So reading the text, in this sense as well, becomes a way of knowing one's self. Yet at the centre of these exchanges, within the mythical world described by the text, within the cultural present when it was composed, and, as the last section has suggested, on its own linguistic surface, the signs of gender difference act as the prompts for reflecting on these alternatives, and in so doing stand on the boundaries between the kinds of reality in which the text could be said to partake. In this final section, I conclude the argument by considering more fully how the different views of creation that emerge from the metamorphosis episode point to alternative understandings not just of gender, or of Ovid's poem, but of human nature itself.

As I argued, Deucalion and Pyrrha can be recognized as the first human characters in the poem with whom the audience can identify, both because of the ability to see what they see, and because of the couple's place at the beginning of the story that leads to man's final creation. This recognition, however, requires distinguishing the couple both from the gods and from earlier instaurations of humans, among them Lycaon, conveniently rebranded as a beast, whom they resemble in form. When, as I argued in my second section, the couple's interpretation of the oracle makes possible the differentiation between representation and reality, it thus articulates a distinction between form and substance that turns out already to be crucial for understanding the relationship between them and their antecedents. It will be equally important for making sense of the metamorphosis to follow. For that metamorphosis turns stones at once to flesh and to form. As opposed to Greek accounts that made the couple biological parents of all the tribes of Hellenes, Ovid's creates the conundrum that we are not the descendants of our parents but resemble them only in form.[38]

---

[38] Barchiesi (2005) 195 emphasizes the importance of this change. For an illuminating account of how Ovid uses the nature of Deucalion and Pyrrha's parentage to address contemporary concerns about cultural and social reproduction, see Meinrath (2014) 26–66.

From the first, man is either a divine product linked by nature and manufacture to the gods, or a material consequence of the imperfection of divine artistry. The 'maker of man' is himself divine (*ille opifex rerum*, *Met.* 1.79), and the seed of which man is made at once becomes a divine substance (*diuino semine*, *Met.* 1.78) and also as 'seed' assimilates this originary creative act to natural processes of generation. We are made like the gods *and* we are born like the gods. But this unity is immediately fractured by a second story that not only competes with the first, but splits the two models of creation it had run together (*Met.* 1.80–4). In this story, the matter of humanity comes from the earth itself, and its very persistence after the sorting of elements that turns Chaos into the created world seems a regressive challenge to the divine ordering that had reached its ultimate goal in man. The natural origins of man in mixed and discordant matter are now juxtaposed with an act of artistic creation that imposes a temporal separation between the newly transformed earth and the matter that had created it:

> sic modo quae fuerat rudis et sine imagine tellus
> induit ignotas hominum conuersa figuras.
>
> *Met.* 1.87–8

So what was just now earth unformed and without an image, transformed, put on the unknown figures of men.

Again the coming into being of the human form creates a break with a chaotic and disordered past, like that between the new human era and the Iron Age, or between the flooded landscape and the one after the flood. The positing of a continuous human identity based on form thus locates the reader at the end of this highly directional process, but a focus on the continuity of matter stresses a connection with the time before the beginning. Once more a question of continuity within the narrative of the poem demands a calibration of the reader's own responses, whether they privilege the ending points or the very stories that reconnect endings to beginnings. A recognition of human form threads together all of these temporal differences by connecting a divine origin to its present manifestation in the shape of man and subsumes all change, the processes of birth and nature, within this teleological design. An emphasis on matter necessarily focuses on difference, on the various substances this sign can contain, and rather than making each human creation, so to speak, look the same, imposes different readings on the end by making the human form refer back to earth, or blood, or hard stones.

These alternatives are restated immediately before and after the metamorphosis of the stones in ways that seem to clarify the gendered divergence between a female process which focuses on matter, and so highlights a changeability in who we are that resists temporal distinctions and teleology, and a male process that emphasizes how form controls matter.³⁹ However, as in the first creation, the seemingly final male ordering appears first and the female creation, by coming after, threatens to erase difference. Another point that emerges from these passages is the very separability of the gods themselves from matter. For each contrasts a very different way of placing the gods in the world. From one perspective, the divinities stand apart from nature, as causes creating change. In this way the separability of form from matter is conveyed by the idea that the divine form is imposed on the world. But the female creation begins precisely from a loss of this essential difference between eternal divine causes and matter itself. The first description of man's origins came after the rest of creation, described as we saw as a final 'clothing of the earth' in forms. Here though the process works backwards, and it is only after man that 'the earth bears the other animals in their diverse forms, on her own' (*cetera diuersis tellus animalia formis / sponte sua peperit*, Met. 1.416–17). Editors interestingly unite in not personifying the earth at this point, despite that creation's being compared explicitly to human pregnancy, and so they unwittingly abet Deucalion's translation of a *magna parens* into the earth itself, simultaneously revealing and eliding a female presence implicit in the very idea of 'nature'.

An equivalent temporal chaos emerges from the simile that compares these new creations to the many half-formed creatures farmers find in the Nile mud (*Met.* 1.422–9). Ovid's account of the metamorphosis of the stones may question continuities and differences between beginnings and endings, but this comes after they have been strongly differentiated by a linear account of change. As we have seen, a gradual process characterized by delay evolves into a before and after snapshot. Here not only is delay the essential time frame for creation (*creverunt... morando*, Met. 1.421), but the different phases of formation seem to co-exist together in the creative mud. And if the 'now' from which we look back to find an origin for our hard form seems at the end the real proof of myth, here the effect is to confound the primordial and the immanent. We are back again at the edges of the earth, where the beginning of the world seems to be endlessly recurring in the cyclical floods of the Nile.⁴⁰ What appears the fresh mud from *the* Flood (*recens*, Met. 1.424) turns out to be a feature of our own present. Thus the 'natural' interpretation of creation assimilates both man and god to material principles, while also characteristically associating the dominance of nature with the dominance of the female, and linking both with a cycle of returns and recurrences.

The contrasting passage does seem to accomplish and represent a change in epochs. When Neptune calms the waves, he employs Triton as an auxiliary in a passage that may look gratuitously decorative (*Met.* 1.330–42). The image of

³⁹ On these gendered alternatives for figuring creation, see McAuley (2015) 120–1.
⁴⁰ A point also noted by Ahl (1985) 121.

Triton, like the humans Deucalion and Pyrrha, appears at a cusp between elements, at the surface of the sea, and the aural signal he gives for the waves literally forms a pre-echo of the imagery of human creation. The sign arises if not from 'animation' then from the 'inspiration' of a hard trumpet, which 'conceives air in the middle of the sea' (*inspirare*, *Met.* 1.334; *medio concepit ubi aera ponto*, *Met.* 1.337). Not only is this mixed Triton himself the sort of highly artificial creation we might see in statuary, and indeed the next time Triton appears it will be as a sculpture on the doors of the Palace of the Sun (*Met.* 2.8), but the signal he gives is itself indistinguishable from a statue, *signum* (*Met.* 1.334). Thus by contrast to formless matter spontaneously taking on diverse *formae*, here we see the form or sign itself as the generator of order, a process that prioritizes art over nature and is presided over by a hierarchical sequence of exclusively male figures, Jupiter, Neptune, and Triton. And yet the recognition of Triton as already a sculpture, rather than seeing the human emerge from the material waves, so to speak, opens the door to another kind of confusion precisely by relying on human art to figure the existence of the gods, who therefore, as a Xenophanes would insist, can never reveal anything but their human makers.[41]

This last qualification reveals the essential ambiguity of Ovid's juxtaposition of gender difference with the distinction between representation and reality. Gender seems to stand on both sides of the border. On the one hand, like grammatical gender in the text, it helps us essentialize and compare past and present, nature and artifice, human and divine, and yet it violates all of those boundaries since it was present among gods and man and as a component of creation as well as its result. More essentially, gender emerges from the problem of reading, of matching image to reality and form to matter and helps to structure and destabilize interpretation itself. The very differences that make form apprehensible are the results of form, or to be less Delphic, we cannot read a narrative of human creation without gender, and yet that very narrative reveals it to be anything other than natural. One example of such *ex post facto* normalization of gender roles in the narrative is the figure of Deucalion himself. His resemblance to Jupiter and the way his difference from Pyrrha in the matter of the oracle allows the plot of the poem to continue may encourage us to see him as emblematic of a male 'line' of artists with their eyes on the higher forms. Yet in his initial address to Pyrrha, for

---

[41]   DK 11 B 15–16, see the discussion in Feeney (1991) 6–7.
   Another of the shimmering verbal veils in the metamorphosis narrative by which Ovid's text can seem to mirror nature or obscure it comes when the strongest claim about the cause of the human transformation, that the stones take on a human shape by the will of the gods, *superorum numine*, is either confirmed or undone by the visual and aural echo between *numine* and *nomine*, which occupies the same position in the line directly before or above. The idea that the names of body parts prove the connection between man and stone affirms the miraculous story of divine agency: *nomina* can be signs of *numina*. But it also suggests the opposite metamorphosis, where *numina* become merely words.

all the ways he seems to be playing Jupiter, teleology is the last thing on his mind. Rather his thoughts are temporally bounded by the mortality he shares with his wife. The two are not like the gods because their death seems certain, and it is the very fact of death that makes them want to reproduce. The image of both Deucalion and Pyrrha being held by the sea similarly contrasts poignantly with the divine figure of Triton emerging from it. And the result of his speech will be the opposite of the stiffening moral that the narrative's conclusion foists back on us: 'He spoke and they wept' (Met. 1.367).

The way that Ovid makes the constructedness of gender emerge from the aetiological narrative that seems to naturalize it has, of course, important immediate political significance: Ovid's describes how gender oppositions structure a new order that, however, also defines itself as promoting a harmony between genders in the form of a stable family structure wherein, for example, spouses no longer plot one another's deaths and women do not threaten destruction for others wives' offspring. The iconography of Actium, of Antony and Cleopatra as an example of how the lack of distinction between male and female threatens to lower the Capitoline to the level, we might say, of the Nilotic ooze, highlights the normative aspects of Octavian's side, and yet that side would in turn give new prominence to the imagery of women as instantiators of the imperial order. The holes and discontinuities in the way women and men are related between the imagery of the regime as it was coming to be and in its finished form stand out more clearly thanks to Ovid's articulation of the *discordia concors* between concord and discord themselves.

As one of the main emphases of this discussion has been the way reading the world and reading the text go together, it is appropriate to conclude with a backward glance not to what Ovid contributes to an understanding of gender but how a new recognition of gender changes one's understanding of Ovid's poem and especially its effect on the audience. We have found several ways in which the polarities of gender reveal a complex mixture in Ovid's text that mirrors both the finished statues and their generation. Its final focus on a hard race gestures towards didactic rigidity but must be balanced by both the plurality of perspectives it contains and the many generic and intertextual strands which have contributed to its formation. The suturing up of before and after in that hard conclusion seems to excise both these aspects of variety. The text's status as a material product, shaped at the level of its own verbal elements by the nature of things, competes with an emphasis on the shaping of matter which puts art's ultimate subject, the human form, the artist, and the reader outside of the flow of time and suggests their affinity to the divine. In that sense my claim that Ovid's poem matches its Delphic setting by teaching its audience to know themselves implies more than waking them to the power of verbal constructions in the Augustan present or even the originality and power of Ovid's forward-looking aesthetic achievement. In it, Ovid continues the work of the original *opifex* in moulding humanity itself.

Even apart from its potential opposition to natural matter, the form the *opifex* bestows turns out to be a deeply ambiguous sign. It can guarantee a resemblance to the gods that subsists across every change, or it is the first thing lost when men become the god's victims. It allows humans to look up; which can mean a continual awareness of celestial affinity or a confusing, counterfeit resemblance. (This posture we recall is not specifically given to man by the divine *opifex*, but by the alternative *opifex*—already 'sown' as the son of Iapetus and the father of Deucalion. And it shows not man's kinship to the gods but merely Prometheus' imitation of their likeness, *finxit in effigiem, Met.* 1.83.) Their intermediate upright position, however, also allows humans to look down, again to see like the gods as well as looking like them. Yet what this shows us is our alternative origins in the earth. For Deucalion, to look down reveals mankind's aloneness and the image of his own and Pyrrha's death.

I imagine the discovery of representation in the Deucalion and Pyrrha episode as an accentuation of man's trajectory upward in space and forward in time. It provides another level of distance above matter, and it allows Ovid's reader in the present to look on the poem as the gods look on the world. As I suggested, Deucalion's insight does not make him a full-fledged Ovidian reader; it merely points him in that direction: it is left to the poet's audience to read the text as he looked at nature. It is striking that after the couple's attempts to 'conquer' and 'soften' Themis (*uicta remollescunt, Met.* 1.378), her commands have the effect of changing their own form in a way that seems to undo this movement above the earth. The pious posture demanded requires them to veil their heads, and throw- ing stones means bending back to the earth to get them: Deucalion's rephrasing of the divine command turns *iactate* to *iacere* (*Met.* 1.393), so that in Ovid's text throwing becomes lying down (*iacêre*). But Ovid allows his audience to see not only the transformations in words, but the metamorphosis of the stones, which the divine command makes it impossible for Deucalion and Pyrrha to observe because it happens behind them. In this sense too he gives his audience a godlike perspective in relation to his text, the world, and themselves, just when divine Themis takes it away. Such divine restriction of vision recurs at another crucially self-reflexive moment in the poem that also locates a human artist at the surface of the earth trying to overcome mortality. When Orpheus 'bends' his eyes (*flexit, Met.* 10.57), he violates the same command and simultaneously seems to undo the metamorphosis of the stones, which had grown first soft then hard. And instead of these new creations raising themselves from the surface of the earth, Eurydice slips back beneath it (*relapsa*).

What would these characters have seen and how far does Ovid's text exempt his readers from the blindness the gods impose on them? Perhaps the secret is the power of art itself not just to perpetuate man's divine form through time, but in Ovid's narrative representation of visual *signa*, to let them speak as well and so create the effect of a living cosmos for its audience. Perhaps, however, we do share the couple's gaze after all in that, for all its descriptive power, Ovid's text can never show us the true quality of our origins. Or perhaps what he does show us is precisely what the mutual consolation of the human couple requires, the ultimate inability of art ever to break free of mortal nature, while the eternal figures who guide our steps may be no more than what human art has made them.

4

HAC Arethusa TENUS (Met. 5.642)

Geography and Poetics in Ovid's Arethusa

Eleni Ntanou

When we reach the fifth book of the *Metamorphoses*, we find ourselves for quite a few lines resting on Ortygia, a little island attached to Sicily and forming the most ancient and most well-known quarter of the city of Syracuse.[1] Characterized as the 'resting place' of the river Alpheus at the opening of Pindar's *Nemean* 1 (ἄμπνευμα ... Ἀλφεοῦ, 1), Ortygia turns in Ovid into an extensive 'resting place' in the narrative of the rape of Proserpina and the wanderings of her mother, Ceres (*Met.* 5.346–661). The story creating this pause in the rape of Proserpina is that of Arethusa's flight from Greece to Ortygia in an effort to escape her aspiring rapist, the river-god Alpheus, a story narrated by Arethusa herself to Ceres and markedly broken up into two different places in the narrative (*Met.* 5.486–508, 5.572–641).[2] The myth of Arethusa's and Alpheus' travel was traditionally deployed in ancient geographical and paradoxographical treatises and in the mapping of the world stemming from colonization. I will suggest that the *Metamorphoses* inverts gender and genre in the story of Arethusa by playing out the nymph's traditional journey to arrestingly cast her in a role similar to that of epic migrating heroes.

In recent years, there has been growing interest across different disciplines in the study of space, a trend typically designated as 'geographical or spatial turn'.[3] The appearance of four collected volumes on space, De Jong (2012), Skempis and Ziogas (2014), Rimell and Asper (2017), and Fitzgerald and Spentzou (2018), has promoted the theorizing of the field in Classics and has brought literary geography into sharp focus.[4] Building on these studies, the present discussion offers a novel approach to Arethusa, exploring how the delineation of space in her story contributes to the narrative of *Metamorphoses* 5, as well as to the broader poetic mapping of the world in the Ovidian epic.[5] Space stands at the epicentre of

---

[1] See Braswell (1992) 32.
[2] On the broken-up nature of Arethusa's narrative see my discussion below. See also Johnson (2008) 69.
[3] See Skempis and Ziogas (2014) 1, De Jong (2012) 2.
[4] For a recent study on space in Latin literature see also Rimell (2015).
[5] As Nicolet (1991) 4–14 argues, cartography and geography were almost inextricably linked in antiquity. Johnson (2016) 1 points out that 'texts from Late Antiquity often display what I call "cartographical thinking": the world becomes a symbolic container of many types of knowledge, and the-world-as-symbol is thus made equivalent to the author's chosen literary form'.

Eleni Ntanou, HAC Arethusa TENUS (Met. 5.642): *Geography and Poetics in Ovid's Arethusa* In: *Metamorphic Readings: Transformation, Language, and Gender in the Interpretation of Ovid's* Metamorphoses. Edited by: Alison Sharrock, Daniel Möller, and Mats Malm, Oxford University Press (2020). © Oxford University Press.
DOI: 10.1093/oso/9780198864066.003.0005

Ovid's Arethusa as we follow her first running and then, transformed into a spring, flowing away from Alpheus in both Greece and Sicily, and in the upper and the underworld.[6] I will argue that in the *Metamorphoses*, the migration of Arethusa acts out and renews the traditional epic thematics of colonizing travels. Ovid uses Arethusa's geographical transition to thematize her transposition into a different cultural context, that of Rome, as well as a new generic frame, as she 'migrates' from pastoral to epic poetry. Moreover, it will be argued that the geography of Arethusa's journey mirrors the narrative structure of her speech in the *Metamorphoses*.

The Arethusa story features in an episode of outstanding narrative complexity.[7] Arethusa, embedded as already mentioned in the rape of Proserpina, forms part of the competing song of the Muse Calliope against the Pierides, the mortals who challenge the Muses to a singing *agon*.[8] The singing competition is enclosed in yet another episode, that of the encounter between the Muses and the goddess Pallas, who listens to the song-contest as retold by an unnamed Muse.

Arethusa's story in the *Metamorphoses* goes as follows: Like Daphne and several other female characters from the Ovidian epic, Arethusa is a beautiful huntress nymph opting for a life of virginity (5.577–84).[9] One day, returning exhausted from hunting, she spots a crystal-clear river in the middle of a deep Arcadian forest and enters it to bathe. Aroused by the sight of the naked nymph, Alpheus, who is the river enfolding Arethusa's body, takes on an anthropomorphic guise

---

[6] See Skempis and Ziogas (2014) 3: 'spatial visualizations of epic story telling are not always compatible with the confinements of human existence, but occasionally become figurative enough to sketch out transcendent topographies pertinent to the divine or the dead'.

[7] See Wheeler (1999) 81–3, Rosati (2002) 272, Barchiesi (2002) 188–95, Johnson (2008) 41. See also Sharrock (2002a), esp. 223–5, for the Muses as narrators in *Metamorphoses* 5.

[8] Books 5 (featuring the contest between Muses and Pierides, part of which belongs to Arethusa), 10 (featuring Orpheus but also the Pygmalion story) and 15 (featuring Pythagoras), are of outmost significance in terms of poetics and metapoetics alike, about which see Hardie (1995), Galinsky (1997), Nagle (1988).

[9] The story of Alpheus' attempted rape of Arethusa finds a significant intratextual counterpart in Apollo's attempted rape of Daphne in *Metamorphoses* 1, see Stirrup (1977), Curran (1978) 234–5, Hinds (1987b) 158 n. 46, James (2016) 156–7, Fantham (2004) 63. After Daphne, the motif of the huntress who enters a distant, bordered, and ostensibly idyllic landscape and turns into the victim of sexual violence is multiply repeated in the Ovidian epic, which, as Curran (1978) 214 notes, encompasses approximately fifty stories of rapes and attempted rapes. See also James (2016) 155–8. The repeated rape narratives of the *Metamorphoses* have rightfully received considerable scholarly attention: see Segal (1969), Heath (1991), Stirrup (1977), Parry (1964), Curran (1978) Richlin (1992) 158–79, Salzman-Mitchell (2005) 177–83, Fantham (2004) 63–6, James (2016), Hinds (2002) 131. See also Miller (2012) 181 for the occasional victimization of male-hunters in the *Metamorphoses*. Aside from the Daphne story, Alpheus' attempt to rape Arethusa ostensibly parallels the rape of Proserpina, which forms the framing of Arethusa's story, and the *quasi*-rape of Cyane, a story also embedded in the narrative of the rape of Proserpina and closely preceding the story of Arethusa in the poem, see Zissos (1999). As Hinds (1987b) 92–3 rightly suggests, the attempted rape of Proserpina substitutes what in the *Homeric Hymn to Demeter* was an 'epic repetition' of Persephone's abduction. The mention of the geographical proximity between Cyane and Arethusa (*Met.* 5.409–10) also suggests the parallelism of their stories as regards the violence suffered by the two nymphs by male deities, see Zissos (1999) 98–103, Segal (1969) 56.

and tries to rape the nymph (5.597–617).[10] Arethusa flees for a long distance around various locations in the Peloponnese (5.600–9). When she cannot keep running any longer, in answer to her prayers, the goddess Diana envelops her with a mist to conceal her from the river-god (5.618–31). But as Alpheus approaches the mist, Arethusa terrified starts melting, until she turns gradually into water (5.632–6). Despite Arethusa's liquefaction—a transformation, in fact, facilitating her erotic mingling with a river-god[11]—Alpheus recognizes her new form and reverts to his river-shape to mingle his waters with those of Arethusa (5.635–6). Taking pity on Arethusa, Diana opens an undersea passage for her to escape (5.639). After her movement, Arethusa is received by a new place, Ortygia (5.640–1), where she remains as a spring nymph, encompassing the twin identities of water and anthropomorphic deity so common in the poem.[12]

In the markedly spatial aspects of the story, Ovid picks up and activates the possibilities offered by Arethusa's past in Greek colonial myths. As I will argue, the *Metamorphoses'* re-enactment of Arethusa's traditional association with Greek colonization is strikingly employed to reconstruct her as a Romanized figure. Geography and colonization lie at the core of Arethusa's myth; ancient geographical treatises comprised the story of Arethusa's and/or Alpheus' travel, often in conjunction with colonization.[13] In his *Geography*, after narrating the foundation of Syracuse (Strab. *Geog.* 6.2.4.1–48), Strabo comments on the belief that the stream of Arethusa is Alpheus flowing from Greece and gushing out in Sicily from the Syracusan spring (Strab. *Geog.* 6.2.4.50–5). He reports a tale that was thought to give proof to this mingling according to which a cup which had been thrown into Alpheus' stream in Olympia and got stained by an ox-sacrifice occurring near the waters of Alpheus re-emerged in Arethusa's spring (Strab. *Geog.* 6.2.4.55–61). Strabo rejects the possibility of such a blending ever taking place and rejects the story of the Olympic cup as 'utterly mythical' (παντελῶς μυθῶδες, Strab. *Geog.* 6.2.4.74–5); he explains that it would be impossible for Alpheus to retain his waters unmixed with those of the sea during his maritime crossing, as there is no visible channel where the river pours out to the sea, and that Arethusa's sweet waters are evidence to the falsity of her mingling with Alpheus. In offering the story of the link between the Peloponnesian Alpheus and the Sicilian Ortygia immediately after the narrative of the Peloponnesian colonization of Syracuse, Strabo possibly suggests Arethusa's symbolic role in the mythologization of Greek colonialism.

---

[10]   For the dual identity of Ovid's Alpheus, see below, footnote 12.

[11]   Repeatedly in the *Metamorphoses*, the transformation impedes the escape rather than helping the potential victims, see Feldherr (2002) 172, Davis (2016) 184. The running Daphne gets transformed into an immobile part of the landscape in the midst of her effort to escape her pursuer, a transformation which has been read as a *quasi*-marriage with Apollo, see Salzman-Mitchell (2005) 91–2. See also James (2016) 172 n. 11, Levine (1995) 84.

[12]   For twin identities in the *Metamorphoses* see Hardie (2002b) 8. As discussed above, Alpheus also alternates between two forms, featuring both as the river and the river-god. On Alpheus' double identity see also Segal (1969) 9, Barchiesi (2002) 188.

[13]   For Arethusa's migration under 'colonial terms' see also Jones (2005) 43–4, Dougherty (1993) 68–9.

The association between the geography of Arethusa's spring and colonization is explicit in the geographical treatise of Pausanias (2nd c. AD). Pausanias claims that the story of Alpheus' love for Arethusa originates from the physical mingling of their waters, which he does not dispute. He provides as testimony to the mingling an oracle that Archias was thought to have received from Delphi when the Achaeans were first setting out to colonize Sicily,[14] instructing him to found Syracuse in Ortygia, at the very spot where Alpheus mingles his waters with those of the spring of the broad Arethusa (Paus. 1.7.3.2–10). As Dougherty points out, 'the Greek river's (Alpheus) transoceanic travel from the Peloponnesus to Sicily prefigures the colonists' own westward movement from Corinth; erotic conquest symbolises a new political foundation, and the intermingling of the two streams becomes an emblem for Greek and native interaction'.[15] Hence Arethusa had developed and for long retained a strong affiliation with the ktistic origin of Syracuse.[16] Although Pausanias postdates Ovid, the story of the oracle is much older than Pausanias,[17] in all probability predating even Alpheus' appearance in Ortygia in Pindar's *Nemean* 1.[18] This oracle served to anticipate and preserve the link between the metropolis (the Peloponnesian Elis) and the colony (Syracuse) through the water of the Ortygian spring Arethusa, which was thought to be directly linked with the Peloponnesian Alpheus. The ample attestation of Arethusa's head on Syracusan coins, especially tetradrachms from the 6th to 4th c. BC,[19] was also a means for advertising the bond between Syracuse and the metropolis.[20]

But by the time Ovid composed his epic, Sicily, although still retaining much of its Greek affiliations and character, had developed strong bonds with Rome.[21] Sicily had become Rome's first province as early as 241 BC after the end of the first Punic War.[22] As has been noted, the Roman presence and character of Sicily were reinforced during the Augustan era. As Finley points out, under Augustus, Syracuse and five other Sicilian cities acquired the 'status of a Roman *colonia* [...] all citizens of a *colonia* were full Roman citizens'.[23] Moreover, the strong affiliation between Sicily and Rome was already acted out in another, far more serious migration than Arethusa's, that of Aeneas and his comrades forcibly leaving Troy and migrating to Italy in Virgil. The extensive narrative of Sicily in the *Aeneid*, where Aeneas lands twice, stresses the ties between Sicily and Rome.[24]

---

[14] On Delphic oracles and colonization see Bradley and Wilson (2006) 48–51.
[15] Dougherty (1993) 69.   [16] See also *LIMC* s.v. 'Arethusa' pp. 582–3.
[17] The story of the Olympic cup is attested already in Ibycus *PMG* 323. It has been suggested that there might have originally been a spring with the name Arethusa in the Peloponnesian Elis that triggered this myth, see Braswell (1992) 34.
[18] See Braswell (1992) 33.   [19] See Metcalf (2012) 145–52, Kraay (1976) 209–15.
[20] Cf. Jones (2005) 43–4.   [21] See Hutchinson (2013) 77–81.
[22] Dufallo (2013) 24, Galinsky (1999) 199, Hutchinson (2013) 77–81.
[23] See Finley (1979) 152, Hutchinson (2013) 77. See also Bradley (2006) 161–2 for the importance of colonization for Rome's expansion and dominion.
[24] Galinsky (1999) 199. See also Lomas (2000). The interplay among space, politics, and poetics is, of course, not unprecedented before the *Aeneid*. For a relevant study in Callimachean poetry, see Asper (2011).

Galinsky notes that 'the *periplous* of Sicily forms the last part of Book III. Since this was not part of the traditional Aeneas legend, Virgil no doubt intended it as a tribute to Sicily, or as R.D. Williams has put it so well, 'he associates the destiny of Italy with its nearest neighbour'.[25] Galinsky also points out that 'the second landing in Sicily anticipates the Trojans' arrival in rustic Italy'.[26] The significance of Sicily for Rome and the connection between the two, as had been established in the *Aeneid*, are redeployed in the *Metamorphoses*.

As Ovid programmatically announces in the prologue of his epic, the *Metamorphoses* encompasses a history of the world from its creation down to his own times (1.1–4). In this unfolding of the world, Sicily stands as both a temporal and a spatial threshold to Rome, which will become the epicentre of the poem in the so-called 'little *Aeneid*'[27] (13.623–14.582) and especially when entering into the Roman space and history in the last two books.[28] But the *Metamorphoses* first brings into sharp focus the links between Sicily and Italy in the Arethusa story. Arethusa's transference to the Sicilian Ortygia provides the first extensive story of a westward movement in the Ovidian epic, a theme that becomes a pattern in the last books, where several migrations from Greece towards Italy take place including, most prominently, that of Aeneas.[29]

Ovid picks up Arethusa's traditional links to colonization and fashions Arethusa herself as a colonist. In her speech to Ceres, Arethusa presents herself as a foreign nymph who has, however, developed firm bonds with the new place she has landed:

> Pisa mihi patria est et ab Elide ducimus ortus,
> Sicaniam peregrina colo, sed gratior omni
> haec mihi terra solo est: hos nunc Arethusa penates,
> hanc habeo sedem.
>
> *Met.* 5.494–7

My native land is Pisa, and I derive my origin from Elis, I live in Sicily as a foreigner. But this land is dearer to me than all: I, Arethusa, now have this home, this is my dwelling-place.

Arethusa deploys the rhetoric of colonization, and indeed as Jones has pointed out, she uses the Roman legal terminology of migration. Jones notes that 'like a colonist, she came as a foreigner, but has made this new place her permanent home. Such terms as *patria* (5.494) and *peregrina* (5.495) evoke the legal status one such as Arethusa would have. The term *penates*, however, places her

---

[25] Galinsky (1999) 187.   [26] Galinsky (1999) 199.
[27] For an extensive study of Ovid's 'little *Aeneid*' against the backdrop of Virgil's *Aeneid*, see Papaioannou (2005).
[28] Rome is thus projected as the *telos* of Ovid's epic, about which see Fulkerson (2016) 82.
[29] See Wheeler (2000) 130–1, 152.

squarely in a Roman context.'[30] Thus Ovid has Arethusa, the landmark of Greek colonization in Syracuse, become Romanized once she reaches Ortygia.[31] Despite the fact that Arethusa is a stranger (*peregrina*) to Sicily[32], in highlighting her affection for her new settlement (*Met.* 5.493–4), she presents herself as an 'adopted patriot'.

Arethusa has arrived in a Sicily, whose character as a near-Italy, spatially and symbolically, is already well explored in the *Aeneid* and revisited here by Ovid. The new setting of Arethusa is recast in the *Metamorphoses* as a Roman *oikos* entailing its own *penates,* the Roman household gods.[33] The reference to the *penates,* standing for Arethusa's new (Roman) house, also gestures towards the *Aeneid*, where these deities guide Aeneas during his colonizing travel (*Aen.* 3.147–71). As has been pointed out, Aeneas' transference of the *penates* from Troy to Latium has a 'ktistic function and [...] is set up as a symbol of continuity'.[34] Thus the reference to Arethusa's *penates* suggests the parallelism between hers and Aeneas' travels and serves to load her migration with colonizing connotations. The shift of Arethusa's identity after her migration from her homeland parallels the shift of the identity of Aeneas and his comrades during their journey, from Trojans to proto-Romans, an idea that is central in Virgil's epic.[35] Nonetheless, the fact that Arethusa has *now* acquired these *penates* (*hos nunc Arethusa penates*, *Met.* 5.496), rather than transferring them from her homeland like Aeneas, points to the more forceful alteration of her identity after her migration and her Romanization in the *Metamorphoses*.[36]

Arethusa, who is very briefly mentioned in the epic *periplous* of Aeneas in Virgil as the Sicilian fountain, from which Alpheus is thought to gush out (*Aen.* 3.694–6), acquires a voice of her own and an extensive narrative of her journey in the *Metamorphoses*. In her passage from Greece to Sicily and her role as a colonizer, Ovid's Arethusa anticipates and becomes a counterpart to Aeneas, whose role as a migrant founder has been considerably discussed in scholarship.[37] Moreover, Arethusa significantly replays the role of Virgil's Evander, himself constructed as a double of Aeneas in Virgil.[38] In *Aeneid* 8, Aeneas meets

[30] Jones (2005) 44. In light of the migration crisis, the problematization of identity after migration is perhaps more current than ever over the last years, to which the Arethusa story offers a significant parallel from antiquity, but I am not going to pursue the issue in the current article.

[31] Cf. Skempis' (2014) remarks on colonization in the *Aeneid*.

[32] Through this claim, Arethusa suggests that she is not biased in her effort to save Sicily, see Rosati (2009) 216.

[33] Cf. Anderson (1997) 548.   [34] See Gransden (1976) 20.

[35] See Quint (1989), Fletcher (2014).

[36] Moreover, as usually in the *Metamorphoses*, Arethusa's altered identity is accompanied by her physical transformation into a spring. The fact that Arethusa has the same name as the Roman *matrona* of Propertius 4.3 might also be at play in the Romanization of Arethusa in the *Metamorphoses*, especially in light of their common role as narrators. On Propertius' Arethusa as a narrator see Wyke (2002) 85–93.

[37] See Lee-Stecum (2008) 73–5, Fletcher (2014), Dench (2005) 102–3.

[38] For Evander as a double of Aeneas see Papaioannou (2003), Lee-Stecum (2008).

Evander, the Arcadian king of Pallanteum, who becomes his ally in the wars within Italy. In migrating from his homeland and settling in Italy, Evander prefigures Aeneas' own role as a city-founder and a leader.[39] Ovid's Arethusa thus plays a similar role to Virgil's Evander in anticipating and doubling Aeneas' travel. The fact that both Virgil's Evander and Ovid's Arethusa are of Arcadian origin migrating westward links the two figures closer together.[40]

In the *Metamorphoses*, Arethusa takes on a role traditionally held in the epic genre by male heroes, that of the migrating hero.[41] The typical epithet of Odysseus as *polutropos* denotes him being 'very-wily' as well as 'much-wandering'.[42] As De Jong notes, Odysseus' travel to strange places in the West 'reflects the expanding world of the Greeks in the eighth and seventh century BC'.[43] Malkin suggests that Odysseus is a 'protocolonial hero'.[44] Malkin also points out that 'many *nostoi*—the term denoting both the action and the person[45]—had to leave home altogether and migrate elsewhere, siring royal genealogies and establishing new settlements'.[46] Set into epic, Arethusa's transposition from East to West and her settlement in Sicily are recast as a story of an epic journey, creating a female counterpart to male epic colonizers.

The extensive topographical details of the Arethusa story are aligned with the epic genre's fascination with geography, as strongly displayed in epic's thematization of *nostoi* and colonizing travels.[47] Alongside the traditional centrality of geography in epic poetry, the interest in geography was particularly renewed during the expansion of the Roman *imperium* under Augustus.[48] As Feldherr has pointed out, the *Aeneid* employed the renewed curiosity over geography during the Augustan era to innovate in epic's concern with geography.[49] I will suggest that in introducing the mapping of Arethusa's itinerary into his epic in rich topographical detail, Ovid arrestingly presents the Arethusa story as suitable material for epic poetry and, indeed, for Augustan epic poetry.

The introduction of Arethusa's travel into epic, however, is not unproblematic: by the time Ovid composed the *Metamorphoses*, Arethusa's figure, migration, and her new homeland, Sicily, had become emblematic of a genre typically considered

---

[39] Ibid.

[40] Moreover, unlike the typical pattern of the visitor narrating his/her stories, both Virgil's Evander and Ovid's Arethusa are the ones recounting stories to the travellers arriving at their settlements, Aeneas and Ceres respectively.

[41] See Malkin (1998) *passim*.   [42] See Frame (1978) ix.

[43] De Jong (2014) 123. Furthermore, Homeric epics were typically thought by ancients as the beginning of literary geography, see Dueck (2012) 20–1.

[44] See Malkin (1998) 3–5.   [45] See Malkin (1998) 2–3.   [46] Malkin (1998) 3.

[47] On the primacy of space and geography in epic see Ziogas and Skempis (2014) *passim*, esp. pp. 3–4. See also Purves (2010) 65–117.

[48] Nicolet (1991) *passim*, Dueck (2012) 18, 32–5. Dueck argues that the 'atmosphere of unprecedented political and geographical achievement' (p. 34) is depicted in Augustan poetry.

[49] Feldherr (1999). See also Skempis and Ziogas (2014) 6: 'For precisely the spatial dynamics of the *imperium* spring from the Roman aspiration to "globalization" and thus generate narratives about the mediation of space and its integration.'

as 'lower' than epic in the hierarchy of genres, that of pastoral poetry.[50] Arethusa
has had a long tradition with the topography and poetics of the pastoral world
appearing already in Theocritus' *Idyll* 1, in which the archetypal pastoral hero
Daphnis bids farewell to the Syracusan spring of Arethusa during his death hour
(Theoc. *Id.* 1.116–18).[51] In post-Theocritean poetry, both Sicily—the death-place
of Daphnis and Theocritus' self-claimed homeland[52]—and its fountain, Arethusa,
become markers of the pastoral genre. In his *Eclogues*, Virgil repeatedly charac-
terizes his pastoral poetry as 'Sicilian', *Sicelides Musae, paulo maiora canamus,*
('Sicilian Muses, let us sing things a little greater', Virg. *Ecl.* 4.1,), *prima Syracosio
dignata est ludere uersu / nostra neque erubuit siluas habitare Thalea* ('My Thalia
first deigned to play with the Syracusan verse nor did she blush to dwell in the
woods', Virg. *Ecl.* 6.1–2).[53]

Arethusa's inextricable relationship with the pastoral genre is displayed in a post-
Theocritean pastoral poem, pseudo-Moschus' *Lament for Bion*, in which she is
presented as inspiring pastoral poetry. Pseudo-Moschus itemized the relation
between springs and specific types of poetry: he presented Arethusa as a source of
pastoral inspiration and a foil to the spring Hippocrene, from which Homer (i.e. epic)
used to drink,[54] ἀμφότεροι παγαῖς πεφιλημένοι· ὃς μὲν ἔπινε/Παγασίδος κράνας, ὃ δ'
ἔχεν πόμα τᾶς Ἀρεθοίσας ('Both were beloved of water-springs, for the one drank at
Pegasus' fountain and the other had his drink from Arethusa' [Mosch.] *EB* 75–6).

Arethusa is recast in a similar role in the final poem of Virgil's pastoral
collection, the *Eclogues*. Enacting Arethusa's transoceanic journey from Greece
to Sicily, Virgil asks the fountain-nymph to grant him inspiration to sing of
Gallus' erotic sufferings, with the prayer that she does not have her waters mingle
with those of the bitter sea:

> Extremum hunc, Arethusa, mihi concede laborem:
> pauca meo Gallo, sed quae legat ipsa Lycoris,
> carmina sunt dicenda; neget quis carmina Gallo?
> sic tibi, cum fluctus subterlabere Sicanos,
> Doris amara suam non intermisceat undam,
> incipe: sollicitos Galli dicamus amores
>
> Virg. *Ecl.* 10.1–6

---

[50] For pastoral as a 'low-genre' see Hardie (1998) 61, Barchiesi (2006) 403.

[51] For Daphnis as the legendary pastoral herdsman see Hunter (1999) 7–8.

[52] See Id. 11.7, 28.16. See also Hunter (1999) 64.

[53] Already in pseudo-Moschus, the line ἄρχετε Σικελικαί, τῷ πένθεος ἄρχετε, Μοῖσαι ('Begin Sicilian
Muses, begin the grief', *EB*. 8), occurring first in line 8 and repeated as a refrain throughout the *Lament
for Bion*, shows the meta-literary notions of the term 'Sicilian' in post-Theocritean pastoral.

[54] In *Metamorphoses* 5, Pallas visits the Muses to examine the recently formed Hippocrene (*Met.*
5.254–63). By creating a story where Hippocrene and Arethusa appear together—albeit in different
narrative levels—Ovid gestures towards the interplay between epic and pastoral in the episode of the
encounter between the Pierides and the Muses as well as the embedded story of Arethusa.

Grant me this last toil, Arethusa: a few songs I must tell for my Gallus, yet such as Lycoris herself may read. Who would refuse songs to Gallus? Begin, thus may the bitter sea not mingle her stream with yours, when you flow under the Sicilian waves: let us tell the troubled loves of Gallus.

Virgil deployed Arethusa's strong connection to pastoral poetry, as was particularly established in the *Lament for Bion*,[55] as well as thematizing Arethusa's migration from East to West. As Saunders notes, '*Eclogue* 10 is a prime example of a poem that uses geographical markers as a way of defining its own nature and place within literary history'.[56] While before the *Eclogues* Arethusa features in pastoral as a *fixed* landmark of Sicily, Virgil throws her transposition into sharp relief and emphatically sets her migration at the opening of the last poem of the *Eclogues*. Arethusa's appearance in the very last poem of *Eclogues* marks the end of Virgil's pastoral collection as the end of pastoral poetry, closing the circle which began with Arethusa's appearance in Theocritus' *Idyll* 1.[57] In her travel in *Eclogue* 10, Arethusa links two pastoral settings together: Sicily, a traditional symbol of pastoral poetry, and Arcadia, which is established as a significant pastoral setting from Virgil onwards.[58] Arcadia was reworked as a place with significant pastoral connotations in Virgil's epic, in the Arcadian origin of Evander in *Aeneid* 8, a book where there is significant intertextuality between pastoral and epic.[59] More than that, the mobile geography of Arethusa, which had previously been fundamental in ktistic myths, becomes in Virgilian pastoral a metaphor for the 'transference' of the pastoral genre from Greek to Latin literature. As Hutchinson and Dufallo have suggested, Virgil creates a complex of spatial references in the *Eclogues*, wavering between Greece and Rome, alluding thereby to the Greek precedent of the pastoral genre, which is now transposed into Latin literature.[60]

---

[55]   For Arethusa as a pastoral Muse see also Davis (2012) 142–3.

[56]   Saunders (2008) 65. See also Hutchinson (2013), Breed (2006) 118–19.

[57]   Cf. Harrison (2007a) 60–1.

[58]   Cf. Hubbard (1998) 129. For references to Arcadia see *Ecl.* 4.58, 7.4, 8.21, 10.26, 10.31. On Arcadia's connection to pastoral in Virgil see Hardie (1998) 25, 60–1. On the establishment of Arcadia from Virgil onwards see Volk (2008) 18–47, Lee (1989) 33–8. For the reworking of a pastoralized Arcadia in Ovid see Hinds (2002) 128. See contra Kennedy (1987) and Harrison (2007a) 62 who suggest that Arcadia is associated in the *Eclogues* with Gallus' poetry rather than the pastoral genre, and Jenkyns (1989) who argues against the reading of Virgil's Arcadia as a spiritual land of pastoral poetry. See also Heslin (2018) 57–8, who reads Arcadia and Sicily as symbolizing elegy and pastoral respectively and suggests that these two refined genres are linked through the waters of Arethusa. Heslin (pp. 56–7), however, points out that we cannot know whether the association between Arcadia and Gallus should be traced back to Gallan poetry or if it is a Virgilian invention in honour of Gallus and Parthenius.

[59]   See Hardie (1998) 60–1. See also Wimmel (1973).

[60]   Cf. Hutchinson (2013) 178: 'The last poem of the book forms part of a frame with the first in stressing the reader's spatial perspective; at the same time it marks the culmination of the spatial confusion which plays with the literary and ethnic identity of the transposed genre.' See also Davis (2012) 142, Dufallo (2013) 79–92.

Arethusa's undersea crossing acquires strong metapoetic symbolism in the *Eclogues*.[61] The implied threat of the mingling of Arethusa's waters with those of the sea looks at Callimachus and suggests the problematization of generic purity.[62] At the end of Callimachus' *Hymn to Apollo*, the personified Envy murmurs secretly that the poet should not be admired if he does not sing as much as the open sea (105–6).[63] The idea is rejected by Apollo, who famously declares his hatred for the muddy and big stream of the Assyrian river[64] and his predilection for the choicest crown of a tiny drop, ὀλίγη λιβὰς ἄκρον ἄωτον ('This little stream the choicest crown', 112) brought from the stream which springs up pure and undefiled from a sacred fountain (108–12). The vast and muddy body of water becomes in Callimachean poetics a metaphor for the lengthy poetry and is associated particularly with epic poetry.[65]

Eclogue 10 brings the question of genre to centre-stage and the poem's intricate interplay between pastoral, elegy and, possibly, epic are still hotly debated in scholarship.[66] Virgil appears to attempt a definition of pastoral poetics by exploring them primarily against elegy. Elegiac poetry is constantly in the background of *Eclogue* 10, as Virgil has the elegiac poet Gallus play the role of the pastoral hero Daphnis of Theocritus' *Idyll* 1.[67] Moreover, as Ross points out, the elegiac poetry of Gallus should be considered as a significant intertext for this poem.[68] The strong sense of an interplay between Virgilian pastoral and Gallan elegy in the *Eclogues* led Skutsch to attempt to 'retrieve' and 'restore' entire passages from the (lost) poetry of Gallus, all of which were supposed to be found in the Virgilian poem.[69] This approach was later criticized by Conte, who notes the critic's deception involved in traditional approaches, such as this of Skutsch.[70] Epic may also be at work in the poem's exploration of pastoral boundaries, a reading particularly intriguing in the reference to the open sea (10.4–5), a metaphor commonly used for epic poetry.[71] Despite the scholarly debate as to whether the threat of the mingling with the sea in *Eclogue* 10 refers to a generic mingling with

---

[61] See also Van Sickle (1978) 189–91 who suggests that in presenting us Arethusa's travel from Greece to Sicily, Virgil sets the dramatic time in a pre-Sicilian and, hence, pre-Theocritean time.

[62] See Saunders (2008) 70–1. For water and poetry in Hesiod and Callimachus see also Jones (2005) 55–7. For the reworking of the Callimachean metaphor of water in Augustan poetry see Hunter (2006) *passim*.

[63] For the interpretative problem of these lines see Williams (1978) 85–9, Cameron (1995) 403–7.

[64] Probably meaning 'Euphrates,' see Williams (1978) 91–2.

[65] Harrison (2007b) suggests that the metaphor of the 'ocean of *epos*' starts from Callimachus and is repeatedly used in Latin poetry.

[66] For the interplay between pastoral and elegy in *Eclogue* 10, see Harrison (2007a) 59–74, Heslin (2018) 57–9, Conte (1986) 100–29, Perkell (1996), Ross (1975) 85–106, Whitaker (1988). See also Hardie (2002b) 59–61, Gagliardi (2003) 15–38, Skutch (1901).

[67] For the 'Daphnidization' of Gallus see especially Conte (1986) 100–29, Gagliardi (2011), Perkell (1996).

[68] Ross (1975) 85–106. See also Heslin (2018) 56–7, who notes that the representation of Gallus in similar fashion in Propertius should be read as a complex intertextual game, which strongly gestures towards the *Eclogues*, rather than as an 'independent testimony about Gallus' (p. 56).

[69] Skutsch (1901).   [70] Conte (1986) 100–1.   [71] See Harrison (2007b).

elegy or with epic, scholars seem to agree that the contemplated danger suggests an over-the-top generic mixing that Arethusa should avoid.[72] I will argue that unlike her Virgilian counterpart, Ovid's Arethusa will cross the generic divide and, cast into epic, will not avoid the generic blending with which Virgil had threatened her in the *Eclogues*.

In encompassing an iconic pastoral figure within his epic and giving her an extensive narrative of her own, Ovid pushes further the boundaries of epic poetics. The whole episode where Arethusa features systematically gestures towards Arethusa's association both with pastoral poetry and the problematizing of generic boundaries. As mentioned above, the Arethusa story is enclosed within the story of the Muses' competition against the Pierides, which is, in turn, told in replay by an unnamed Muse to Pallas. The singing competition between the Muses and the Pierides, enacted against an idyllic natural landscape,[73] firmly alludes to pastoral poetry,[74] where this form of encounter is a *topos* of the pastoral genre. The occurrence of the daughters of Pieros in the episode further presses the allusion to pastoral poetry. Although the term *Pierides* is often used in Greek and Latin literature as an epithet for the Muses themselves, the greatest attestation of the Pierides in Latin poetry before Ovid is in Virgil's *Eclogues*, where there is reference to the Pierides in exactly half of the poems.[75] Virgil had confined the use of the epithet Pierides to his pastoral poetry and never mentioned Pierides again in the *Georgics* or the *Aeneid*. In singing about Arethusa's travel, Calliope, a Muse typically associated with the *genus sublime*, the epic genre,[76] is strikingly presented in the *Metamorphoses* as weaving a pastoral story into her song.

Gesturing towards Virgilian pastoral, the *Metamorphoses* restages the passage of Arethusa from Arcadia to the Syracusan Ortygia. By repeating Arethusa's transfer, Ovid acts out anew Arethusa's affiliation with generic mixing as well as with shifting cultural frameworks, as had been established in the *Eclogues*. But the introduction of Arethusa's migration into poetry is much more systematic in the

---

[72] Harrison (2007a) and Thorsen (2014) 89–91 suggest that the phrase *Doris amara* signifies the genre of love elegy and the bitterness of elegiac love. Hubbard (1998) 130 reads the mention of seawater in its common use as a metaphor for the epic genre. Kennedy (1987) 48–9 argues that the Sicilian sea may symbolize Theocritean pastoral, an idea refuted by both Harrison (2007a) 61 and Hubbard (1998) 130.

[73] And indeed Helicon, an iconic *locus amoenus*. On Helicon's symbolism see Hinds (1987b) *passim*, Hinds (2002) 124.

[74] Cf. Johnson (2008) 41–7 who also notes the allusions to pastoral poetry in the encounter between the Pierides and the Muses.

[75] See *Ecl.* 3.85, 6.13, 8.63, 9.33, 10.72.

[76] Even though the association of each Muse to a specific type of poetry was not yet fixed in Ovid's time, the process of specialization as to their spheres had begun much earlier, see Morrison (2011). Calliope, representing the Muses in the contest, was often related to what is paramount in poetry: already in Hesiod, Calliope is mentioned as the greatest of the Muses, Καλλιόπη θ᾽· ἡ δὲ προφερεστάτη ἐστὶν ἁπασέων ('and Calliope, who is the greatest of them all' Hes. *Theog.* 79). Calliope's association to epic poetry in the *Metamorphoses* is suggested in her characterization as 'the greatest' (*maxima, Met.* 5.662) denoting that Calliope is the eldest of the Muses as well as the greatest, see Hinds (1987b) 125–6.

Ovidian epic, where the outline of the itinerary of Arethusa's flight is described in great geographical detail. As I have already suggested, the extensive narrative of the topography shaping Arethusa's transmigration reinforces her epicization, as it ties in with the pronounced role of geography in epic, where the nymph's journey is now replayed. In his study of Roman geography, Nicolet underlines the significance of travel for the conceptualization of space in the ancient world: 'travel (by land or sea), whose practical importance is evident, can also be expressed graphically. The route becomes a linear network with distances and intersections carefully noted in one dimension'.[77] Arethusa's travel, albeit far from linear, leads to a complex mapping of the setting in the *Metamorphoses*, which will be transferred westward.[78]

Arethusa's first occurrence in the narrative of the *Metamorphoses* as a speaking character takes place after the goddess Ceres has arrived in Sicily in search for her daughter Proserpina.[79] After finding Proserpina's girdle in Sicily, Ceres decides to punish the island where her daughter was abducted by depriving it of grain (*Met.* 5.470–80).[80] It is then that Arethusa lifts her head from her Syracusan pool and tries to dissuade the goddess from her plan, out of affection for her new homeland. Arethusa is linked with multiple geographical markers at once: the *Syracusan* spring is described as being 'of Elis' in the Peloponnese and 'of Alpheus', *tum caput Eleis Alpheias extulit undis* ('Then the girl of Alpheus lifted her head from the Elean waters', *Met.* 5.487). In referring to Arethusa's connection with Alpheus, Ovid reprises Alpheus' attempted rape of the nymph, a story conspicuously absent from the journey of the nymph in *Eclogue* 10,[81] and correlates it anew with the passage of Arethusa. Although the two figures are presented together in *Aeneid* 3.694–5, contrary to the *Metamorphoses*, Virgil places emphasis on Alpheus' migration, while Arethusa features as already being a Sicilian spring.

The myth of Arethusa's arrival in Sicily had two different versions, one according to which Arethusa escaped rape and one attesting that in spite of her transmigration she was still raped by Alpheus.[82] Cicero in his *Verrine Orations* provides both explanations for Arethusa's waters as being either native or fed from Alpheus' waters (Cic. *Ver.* 6.17.3.3–5). In the story that Arethusa narrates in the *Metamorphoses*, she does not explicitly clarify whether Alpheus managed to unite

---

[77] Nicolet (1991) 4.   [78] On the non-linear route of Arethusa, cf. Rosati (2009) 234.

[79] For the Sicilian locale of Proserpina's abduction in the *Metamorphoses* replacing the Eleusinian setting of the *Homeric Hymn to Demeter* see Hinds (1987b) 39–42.

[80] Sicily had for a long time after the first Punic War been the larger supplier of grain to Rome (see Montarese (2012) 222) thus making this detail all the more shocking to Ovid's contemporaries.

[81] The love of Alpheus for Arethusa is, however, at the background of *Eclogue* 10 tying with the elegiac features of this poem and Gallus' passionate love, see Hubbard (1998) 129–30, Davis (2012) 142–3. Alpheus is an 'absent presence' in the narrative of *Eclogue* 10. For 'absent presences' see Hardie (2002b) *passim*.

[82] See also Coleman (1977) 275.

his waters with hers or not, rather implying that she was saved from rape.[83] However, the epithet *Alpheias* (*Met.* 5.487) with which Arethusa is introduced in the Ovidian narrative problematizes Arethusa's escape[84] hinting at the more common version of the erotic mixing of her waters with those of Alpheus.[85] This suggestion of Arethusa's rape by Alpheus associates Arethusa with the multiple other rape-victims of the *Metamorphoses* and, especially, with its own narrative frame, the story of the rape of Proserpina.[86] Moreover, the victimization of Arethusa gestures towards the typical occurrence of acts of murder and rape in the mythology of city-foundations and, in particular, in the foundation of Rome.[87] Although the notion of sexual violence reprises the thematics of foundations, the fact that Arethusa's migration results from her effort to escape rape differentiates her from the migration-stories of male epic colonizers.

The geographical details of Arethusa's speech not only underscore the connection of her travel with the amatory attempts of Alpheus, but also stand in contrast to her urge for separation from Alpheus. The topography of Arethusa's origin and route act out, to a great extent, the geography of Alpheus as a river. Arethusa mentions Pisa as her native land (*Pisa mihi patria est*, 'My native land is Pisa', *Met.* 5.494), a region spatially demarcated by Alpheus, διαβήσῃ [. . .] ἀπὸ τούτου τὸν Ἀλφειὸν καὶ ἐντὸς γῆς ἔσῃ τῆς Πισαίας ('And if you cross Alpheus after this, you will be in the land of Pisa', Paus. 6.21.5.4–5). Arethusa's identification with Alpheus is also strongly suggested in Arethusa's Elean origin, *et ab Elide ducimus ortus* ('I derive my origin from Elis', *Met.* 5.494).[88] The double meaning of *ortus*, denoting both the origin of a person and the source of a river,[89] invites two contrasting interpretations, at once following and diverting from the version of her story that Arethusa offers in the *Metamorphoses*. Even though Arethusa pointedly refrains from any association with Alpheus, the mention of her Elean *ortus* hints at the version according to which the source of Arethusa is in the Elean Alpheus, Ἀρέθουσαν δὲ τὴν ἐν Συρακούσαις [. . .] τὴν πηγὴν ἔχειν ἐκ τοῦ κατὰ τὴν Ἠλείαν Ἀλφειοῦ, ('And Arethusa, the one in Syracuse [. . .] springs from the Elean Alpheus', Call. *Paradoxa* fr.407.45–7 Pfeiffer). Intratextually, in the very lines preceding Arethusa's speech, Alpheus is defined as the 'river of Elis' (*fluminis Elei*, *Met.* 5.576), a characterization also alluding to the *Aeneid*, *Alpheum*

---

[83] Zissos (1999) 104 and Hinds (1987b) 157 n. 46 suggest that Ovid's Arethusa seems to have escaped rape. See contra Johnson (2008) 69 and Barchiesi (2002) 191 n. 22, who, like the approach suggested here, argue that the enclosing narrative implies that Arethusa was indeed raped by Alpheus.

[84] Cf. Barchiesi (2002) 191 n. 22.

[85] For an extensive account of attestations of Arethusa's and Alpheus' myth see *LIMC* s.v. 'Arethusa' p. 583.

[86] See above, footnote 9.

[87] For violence as a motif in the foundation of cities see Dougherty (1993) 41. See also James (2016).

[88] Pisa was often used as a metonymy for Elis, see Rosati (2009) 217.

[89] See *TLL* 9.2.1069.7–32 for *ortus* denoting the origin of people and *TLL* 9.2.1068.20–30 for the word used for riverine sources. Cf. Rosati (2009) 217. An etymological wordplay between *orior* and *Ortygia* might also be at work, about which see Kyriakidis' (2014) 278 interesting discussion.

fama est huc Elidis amnem ('There is a rumour that Alpheus, the river of Elis, here', *Aen.* 3.694).

Furthermore, Arethusa enlists herself among the Achaean nymphs, *pars ego nympharum, quae sunt in Achaide,* ('I was part of the nymphs, who are in Achaia' *Met.* 5.577).[90] Although *Achais* is used as a substitute for Greece,[91] pointing to Arethusa's Greek origin, which is redeployed in Ovid, it should also be perceived here specifically against the backdrop of Peloponnese, where Arethusa pinpoints several locations during her flight. Read as such, Ovid presents Arethusa as associated with one more district in the Peloponnese, in addition to Elis and Pisa, that of Achaia. As Morgan argues 'the ambiguity of the adjective *Achaios* was particularly finely exploited in the west [...], but mainland Achaeans also drew on it in establishing their migratory ancestry'.[92] This use would make the ambiguity of *Achais* all the more effective for Ovid's Arethusa as a colonist. In the *Natural Questions*, Seneca the Younger attests the region of Achaia as the location from which Alpheus dives under the earth before re-emerging in Sicily in the spring of Arethusa, *quid? cum uides Alpheon, celebratum poetis, in Achaia mergi et in Sicilia rursus traiecto mari effundere amoenissimum fontem Arethusam?* ('And what [will you say] when you see Alpheus, celebrated by poets sink in Achaia and again in Sicily, having crossed through the sea, to pour in the fountain of Arethusa?', Sen. *Nat. Quest.* 6.8.2.7–9). In bringing together different sites in the Peloponnese through her origin and course, Arethusa is more strongly identified with Alpheus, the great river of the Peloponnese.

The most prominent Peloponnesian region for the Arethusa story is Arcadia. Pausanias had underlined that Arcadia, and not Elis, should be considered as Alpheus' source (Paus. 5.7.1). The Arcadian location of Alpheus is explored in Ovid, when Arethusa recalls coming back from hunting at the Stymphalian grove, situated in Arcadia, *lassa reuertebar (memini) Stymphalide silua* ('Tired, I was coming back (I remember) from the Stymphalian forest', *Met.* 5.585). As has been pointed out, *memini* often functions as an intertextual marker in Latin texts, and the references to 'personal memory' strongly allude to the 'poetic memory' of literary precedents.[93]

---

[90] In the *Georgics* 4.344, Arethusa is mentioned as the climax of a catalogue of nymphs listening to the nymph Cyrene's love story. As Thomas (1986) 190–3 points out, Arethusa is a new addition to the traditional catalogue of the Nereids recorded in the *Theogony* and the *Iliad*. Hence, Arethusa, who is narrating here her own story, has a past in love stories, as an object of love (in her traditional myth), as well as an audience (as in the *Georgics* 4) and an inspirer of love-stories (as in *Eclogue* 10).

[91] Thus read by Bömer (1976) 374 and Anderson (1997) 558. See *TLL* 1.0.384.57 for *Achais* as an adjective of 'Achaia', Greece and *TLL* 1.0.384.60 for the term used as a substitute for Greece.

[92] Morgan (2003) 35.

[93] See Hinds (1998) 4. For 'personal' and 'poetic memory' in Ovid's Pythagoras, see Hardie (1997) 188. Aside from its pastoral precedent, the reminiscence of the Arcadian origin of Arethusa also looks at Ovid's *Amores* 3.6.29–30, where in a catalogue of rivers in love, Ovid calls Arethusa the 'Arcadian maiden' (*Arcadis virgo, Am.* 3.6.30) who was loved by the river Alpheus. Unlike all the attested treatments of the myth before Ovid, Alpheus' love and pursuit is focalized in the *Metamorphoses* through Arethusa herself. As Salzman-Mitchell (2005) 180 points out in her account 'Arethusa switches from the male gazer to the experience of the young virgin'.

Arethusa's mention of Arcadia particularly looks at her pastoral past and thus her crossing of multiple borders between locations and regions parallels her transgression of yet another boundary in the *Metamorphoses*, that of genre. Having been already set up as a place with significant pastoral connotations within epic in Evander's Arcadian origin in the *Aeneid* 8,[94] Arcadia is brought into sharp focus in the *Metamorphoses* in the geography of Arethusa's flight.[95]

Arcadia becomes the centre of attention when, being still a woman and not yet a spring, Arethusa starts running away from Alpheus:

> usque sub Orchomenon Psophidaque Cyllenenque
> Maenaliosque sinus gelidumque Erymanthon et Elin
> currere sustinui, nec me uelocior ille;

Met. 5.607–9

As far as under Orchomenus and Psophis and Cyllene and the Maenalian valleys and the cold Erymanthus and Elis I endured to run, nor was he quicker than me.

As has been pointed out, the route that Arethusa describes is astonishing in terms of length, as it has been estimated to be more than 150 miles.[96] The numerous locations she traces are all in Arcadia apart from the last two, Erymanthus and Elis. Erymanthus was the name of a chain of mountains that stood as a border between Arcadia and Elis, as well as the name of a river originating in these mountains.[97] Erymanthus is also spatially linked with Alpheus, for it joined Alpheus by flowing into it (Paus. 5.7.1.10–4). Arethusa's incredibly long flight replicates the movement of a river and, in particular, Alpheus, as she describes how she ran through plains (*per tamen et campos, Met.* 5.612), over mountains (*per opertos arbore montes, Met.* 5.612); rocks and hills (*saxa quoque et rupes, Met.* 5.613) and in dead-end locations (*qua uia nulla, cucurri. Met.* 5.613). Ovid deploys the ambiguity of *curro* used for both people running and for the flowing of rivers and springs to anticipate Arethusa's aquatic transformation, but also to identify the nymph with her riverine pursuer.[98] Alpheus was the 'territorial marker' of the Peloponnese,[99] presented in Ovid through the perspective of the geography of Arethusa's flight. During her flight,

---

[94] Hardie (1998) 60–1.

[95] Arcadia, whose terrain is explored in great detail in the Arethusa story, is first introduced into the Ovidian epic in the Lycaon episode (*Met.* 1.163–252), a story setting up the diversion of pastoral in the *Metamorphoses*.

[96] See Anderson (1997) 561.

[97] In *Metamorphoses* 2.244, Erymanthus is one of the rivers drying up from the fires of Phaethon's chariot.

[98] See *TLL* 4.0.1514.10ff.

[99] See Campbell (2012) 423 n. 139. For aquatic boundaries and particular rivers functioning as borders see Campbell (2012) 98–100, 106–9. See also Jones (2005) *passim* for rivers forming but also destroying borders.

Arethusa enters Alpheus' domain either following his riverine topography without realizing it or even giving an additional aetiological twist to the story by shaping the course of Alpheus' stream not only from Greece to Sicily—as widely believed—but also within the Peloponnese.

Not only does Arethusa's itinerary to a great extent perform and act as a substitute for Alpheus' riverine geography, but also she takes on wider poetic significance, in that she stands in place of male epic heroes as well as male narrators. During her passage from Greece to Sicily, Arethusa performs a *katabasis*, a descent to the underworld where she catches sight of Proserpina (*Met.* 5.504–5). The interjection of Arethusa's *katabasis* in Ovid's epic presses further her resemblance to epic heroes. Like Aeneas, Arethusa's westward journey includes a descent to the Underworld, before she reaches her final destination.[100]

In addition to her heroic role, Arethusa also develops a narrative role. In informing Ceres about the fate of her daughter, Arethusa takes on the mantle of Helios, the Sun, as a narrator in the *Homeric Hymn to Demeter*.[101] As Zissos points out, this 'active participation of Arethusa seems to be an Ovidian invention'.[102] The exchange of Helios' speech to Ceres for the speech of Arethusa is even more marked when the version of the *Metamorphoses* is read against the narrative of the rape of Proserpina in the *Fasti*, where, following the version of the *Hymn* (*Fast.* 4.583–4), Ovid presents Sol, the Latin equivalent of Helios, and not Arethusa as the narrator of Proserpina's abduction.[103] The substitution of Arethusa for Helios/Sol in the *Metamorphoses* becomes all the more forceful if Arethusa is identified, as has been suggested by scholars of ancient epic, with *Hesperethusa,* one of the *Hesperides,* the daughters of Night.[104] In that case, Ovid could also be pointing to the firm links to the West through the epithet *hesperios,* denoting the 'nocturnal' as well as the 'western'.[105]

In the *Hymn*, Helios vigorously features as the single eyewitness of Persephone's abduction by Hades (*hCer.* 56–80), and thus suggestively as the only reliable narrator of the girl's wanderings.[106] This version is overturned in the

---

[100] As mentioned above, in the *Aeneid*, the Underworld is not only described extensively but also becomes a place of almost geographical interest during Aeneas' *katabasis*. See Feldherr (1999) who suggests that the difficulties in the clear mapping of the Underworld parallel the complexity of the epic genre and the narrative of the *Aeneid*. Of course, her descent also parallels Proserpina's story and descent to the Underworld, about which see Rosati (2009) 236.

[101] See Hinds (1987b) 87, Zissos (1999) 103. For Arethusa as a female narrator see also Salzman-Mitchell (2005) 8, 179–82.

[102] Zissos (1999) 98. Zissos stresses the 'feminization of the myth' of Proserpina (107) and suggests that the extensive narrative presence of Arethusa in the story should be read in light of Calliope's effort to please the female audience of nymphs judging the competing songs.

[103] The *Fasti*, written contemporaneously and sharing several stories with the *Metamorphoses*, invites multiple comparisons with the Ovidian epic. For the multiple differences between the rape of Proserpina in the *Fasti* and the *Metamorphoses* see Hinds' (1987b) excellent discussion. See also Barchiesi (1999).

[104] See Malkin (1998) 193.   [105] Ibid.

[106] On eyewitnesses and reliability in ancient texts see Marincola (2013) 112. See also Hunter (1982) 57 who rightly suggests that eyewitnesses may, however, still alter the truth and manipulate their narratives.

Metamorphoses, where, constructed as a double of the Sun, Arethusa highlights the fact that she also saw Proserpina in the Underworld with her own eyes, *uisa tua est oculis illic Proserpina nostris* ('I saw there your Proserpina with my own eyes', *Met.* 5.505),[107] thereby featuring as an additional eyewitness narrator of Proserpina's abduction. Her speech to Ceres replays as well as continues the Sun's narrative: if Sol saw Proserpina up until Pluto abducted her and headed with the girl towards the Underworld (*Fast.* 4.583–4), Arethusa sees and narrates Proserpina's fate in the Underworld, where the Sun cannot reach.[108] In effect, in encompassing Proserpina's underground adventures, Arethusa's speech and sight are strikingly projected as being fuller than that of her male counterpart, the all-seeing (?) Sun. The fact that the substitution of the Sun's voice and vision for that of Arethusa take place within epic, the male genre par excellence, gestures towards Ovid's bold innovation of epic poetics.[109]

Aside from informing Ceres about Proserpina's fate in the Underworld, Arethusa also tries to comfort the goddess, saying that Proserpina has become the queen of Hades (*Met.* 5.506–8). By highlighting the distinguished status of Proserpina's groom, Arethusa repeats the Sun's speech in the *Hymn* (83–7) and the *Fasti* 4.584,[110] where he also notes Pluto's greatness, as well as anticipating Jupiter's speech to Ceres in the *Metamorphoses*: *neque erit nobis gener ille pudori, / tu modo, diua, uelis. ut desint cetera, quantum est / esse Iouis fratrem!* ('Nor will he as a son-in-law be shame for us, goddess, if you only consent. Even if all the rest were missing, how great thing it is to be the brother of Jupiter', *Met.* 5.526–8).[111] In featuring as a counterpart to the Sun as well as to Jupiter, the most prominent and authoritative male epic figure, Arethusa's narrative turns into a 'dangerous voice' threatening the typically male agenda of epic poetry.[112]

Arethusa is presented as remarkably self-aware of her role as a narrator throughout her appearance in *Metamorphoses* 5. She refers to her own story and even controls its time in the narrative, by defining the order of events and the circumstances when her story should be fully narrated, which is when Ceres is free from care: *mota loco cur sim tantique per aequoris undas / aduehar Ortygiam, ueniet narratibus hora / tempestiua meis* ('As to why I have moved from my place and, through the waves of such a long sea, I am brought to the Sicilian Ortygia, there will come a proper time for my narrative', *Met.* 5.498–500).[113] Arethusa

---

[107] Salzman-Mitzell (2005) 175 comments on the passive *uisa* and suggests that 'Arethusa's gaze poses the same implications as other female gazes [...] in an indirect and oblique way, she can act upon her gaze by telling the story and stimulating others'.

[108] See also Anderson (1997) 549.

[109] On male gender and the epic genre see Sharrock (2002b), Keith (1999).

[110] Cf. Hinds (1987b) 87.

[111] Hinds (1987b) 59 notes that Jupiter's speech to Ceres in the *Fasti* draws from Helios' speech in the *Hymn*.

[112] On the dangerous female voices in epic, see Holst-Warhaft (1992) *passim*.

[113] As Rosati (2009) 217 points out, the neologism *narratus* underlines the meta-narrative concerns of the episode. See also Anderson (1997) 549, Barchiesi (2002) 189.

gives full account of her miraculous movement later in the narrative of *Metamorphoses* 5, when, having found her daughter Proserpina, Ceres returns to the spring and asks her for the *aetion* (*causa*, *Met.* 5.573) of her relocation and transformation into a sacred fountain. Arethusa's control over narrative and poetry is also displayed when she invites Ceres to 'cease her toils', *siste labores* (*Met.* 5.490). The term *labor*, on a first level, refers to Ceres' wanderings and her decision to punish the people of Sicily,[114] from which Arethusa tries to dissuade the goddess. But more than that, Arethusa's reference to *labor* strongly gestures towards the opening of *Eclogue* 10, *Extremum hunc, Arethusa, mihi concede laborem* ('Grant me this last toil, Arethusa', Virg. *Ecl.* 10.1), where *labor* defined Virgil's pastoral poetry as serious and well-refined, according to the Alexandrian style.[115] Ovid thus points to the role of Arethusa as a pastoral Muse inspiring serious poetic works, as she featured in Virgilian pastoral. In dissuading Ceres from the destruction of Sicily, Ovid's Arethusa intervenes in the plot of Proserpina's rape but also pauses her own story, transposing it to a later time.

The division of Arethusa's narrative into two parts (*Met.* 5.487–508, 5.572–642) pointedly recreates her mobile geography and her physical breaking into two different locations.[116] Accounts of springs and rivers disappearing at one spot of their course and re-emerging elsewhere were contained in geographies, albeit as seen in Strabo not always indisputably, and in paradoxography, a genre concerned with *mirabilia*, incredible things, customs and marvellous phenomena of the natural world.[117] The miraculous geography of Arethusa's stream was part of Callimachus' prose work on *mirabilia*, the *Paradoxa* (fr. 407.45–50 Pfeiffer).[118] Moreover, as discussed above, Seneca the Younger refers to Alpheus' course towards Arethusa in his *Natural Questions*, a work including *paradoxa*.[119] Pliny encompasses the wondrous course of Alpheus in his paradoxography, the *Natural History* (Pliny *NH* 2.225.1–7).[120] Such *mirabilia* are endorsed in the *Metamorphoses* most prominently in Pythagoras' speech, where the philosopher includes bodies of water with astonishing qualities among the wonders of a world

[114] Anderson (1997) 548.
[115] Cf. Hubbard (1998) 129, who notes that this notion of work, contrasting with the leisure of pastoral life, might be also looking forward to the *Georgics*.
[116] Campbell (2012) 150 suggests that 'this kind of story was just as relevant in Italy as in Greece, because of the fear of local people that seasonal rivers that dried up during the hot summer months would not reappear'. For Arethusa's and Alpheus' disappearance and reappearance see also Rosati (2009) 229.
[117] On paradoxography in Augustan literature see Hardie (2009) *passim*.
[118] See Myers (1994) 149. Callimachus' works *On the Rivers of Europe* and *On the Rivers of the Inhabited World*, although known to us by title alone, display similar interests, see Nichols (2018) 8.
[119] On Seneca the Younger and paradoxography see Myers (1994) 148.
[120] For Pliny and paradoxography see Hardie (2009) 11–12, 15. For the disappearance and reappearance of Alpheus and other rivers in different places see also Seneca *Natural Questions* 6.8.1.1–6.8.3.2. The same theme was quite possibly included in the now lost treatise *On the Wondrous Rivers of Sicily*, attributed to Polemon.

constantly changing (*Met.* 15.273–334).[121] The narrative and geography of Ovid's Arethusa unfold in tandem: Ovid replicates Alpheus' and Arethusa's marvellous course in the structure of Arethusa's narrative, which pauses briefly only to reappear after Ceres has found Proserpina.

The end of Arethusa's narrative coincides with the geographical end of her migration by arriving in Ortygia:

> 'aduehor Ortygiam, quae me cognomine diuae
> grata meae superas eduxit prima sub auras.'
> Hac Arethusa tenus

Met. 5.640–2

'I am brought to Ortygia, which is dear to me for it has the epithet of my goddess,[122] and first raised me to the upper air.' No further than this, Arethusa.

In stark contrast with the majority of the stories in the *Metamorphoses*, the end of the Arethusa story is demarcated explicitly, *Hac Arethusa tenus* (*Met.* 5.642). The *tmesis*, separation of parts, of the compound term *hactenus*, which means 'no further than this', inside which Ovid places the name of Arethusa, visually marks the new borders set for the spring, *HAC Arethusa TENUS*. Arethusa, who crossed the boundaries from Greece to Sicily, from the upper to the underworld, and even from nymph to a body of water (although she seems to retain a twin identity in Ovid), is now spatially confined in Sicily and comes to be a boundary herself. Besides, this is the way that Ovid originally introduces Arethusa as a *fixed* part of the setting, forming a boundary together with the spring of Cyane and enclosing the Great Harbour: *Est medium Cyanes et Pisaeae Arethusae / quod coit angustis inclusum cornibus aequor* ('There is in the middle of Cyane and the Pisaean Arethusa a harbour, formed by the union of the narrow arms of the shore', *Met.* 5.409–10). Ovid deploys physical borders to reflect on poetic boundaries and narrative frames. The end of Arethusa's destination and story in the *Metamorphoses* conjures up her association with endings of songs and books. Arethusa's transference, which in *Eclogue* 10 signalled the end of Virgil's pastoral poetry, is here set near the end of Calliope's song as well as the end of the fifth book of the *Metamorphoses*.

But more than that, the abrupt and explicit ending of Arethusa's speech signals the return to the typical power-dynamics between genres and genders. Arethusa, the emblematic pastoral Muse, acquires an extensive role and a substantial

---

[121] On paradoxography in Ovid's Pythagoras see Myers (1994) 133–66, Beagon (2009).

[122] The name of the island Ortygia points to another story moving from mobility to fixation, that of Delos. Ortygia looks at the birth of Diana (the patron-deity of the huntress Arethusa) and Apollo in Delos, whose old name was Ortygia, see Anderson (1997) 564. Ovid attests the name 'Ortygia' for Delos in the *Metamorphoses* and mentions the end of the island's mobile geography, see *Met.* 6.191, 6.333, 15.337.

narrative of her own within the realm of epic. Her geographical transference to a place out of her native borders, to which she is foreign, as she explicitly underlines (*peregrina*, *Met.* 5.495), goes hand in hand with her generic displacement in the *Metamorphoses*. Breaking the narrow borders of pastoral poetry, Arethusa's transposition in the Ovidian epic functions as an almost palpable intertextual metaphor. In reprising a figure from Virgilian pastoral, and, indeed, one strongly linked with the problematizing of generic mingling, Ovid expands and challenges the borders of the epic genre, as had been established in the previous literary tradition and, in particular, in the *Aeneid*. Nevertheless, the end of Arethusa's journey sets a limit to the generic mingling between pastoral and epic as well as breaking the illusion of her narratorial control. We are here reminded that Arethusa's voice and narrative are controlled by multiple narrators (Calliope— the anonymous Muse—and, of course, Ovid). Becoming a double of male epic heroes, Arethusa' female voice and extensive narrative presence threatened to disturb the usual power-play of epic poetry. Nonetheless, the phrase *Hac Arethusa tenus* suggests the suppression of Arethusa's voice, which can be explored only up to a certain point.

Acknowledgements

I am grateful to the editors of the volume for their useful notes. Special thanks are due to Prof. Alison Sharrock, Dr Ruth Morello, Dr Sophia Papaioannou and Dr Andrew Morrison for their invaluable comments. I would also like to thank the audience of the University of Leeds, where an early version of this paper was given (7th Postgraduate Conference, 'Borders and Boundaries', June 2016).

5

Ovid's Dream, or, Byblis and the Circle of *Metamorphoses*

Aaron Joseph Kachuck

Introduction

At the centre of Ovid's *Metamorphoses*, one finds a self-portrait in the guise of Byblis, whose incestuous passion for her brother leads to her transformation into the spring of Byblos.[1] Byblis—'book' in Greek, whence Latin *bibliotheca* ('library') and English 'Bible'—is both the work's first long-form writer and, when her writing fails to achieve its aims, its first critic. Her final resting place, Byblos, on the west coast of modern Lebanon, underlines her connections to writing's invention: home to papyrus production ($\beta\iota\beta\lambda o s$='papyrus' inner bark'), Ovid's contemporary Philo of Byblos patriotically hailed the city as Phoenicia's first.[2]
By extension, her spring's location is also the origin of those 'Phoenician letters' (Herodotus, *Histories* 5.58) with which Greeks and Romans would come to write their own languages.[3]

Byblis thus resembles Ovid in her writing, but she resembles him, too, in her dreams: she is the poem's only dreamer to see dreams of her own fashioning.[4] Through Byblis, this paper argues, Ovid recapitulates Latin literature's 'primal scene of instruction',[5] the Hesiodic, Callimachean dream of Homer that opens Ennius' *Annales*. Scholarship has identified Ovid with his depiction of Byblis from a variety of angles: as a model of writerly failure to contrast with Ovid's success;[6] as *amator* doomed, à la Bovary, by her literary (especially elegiac) obsessions;[7] as 'sympathetic' incest case to contrast with that of Myrrha;[8] and as mirror for the

---

[1] On the various 'centres' of the *Metamorphoses*, see, below, section 'Byblis and the Circle of *Metamorphoses*'.

[2] On Byblos, see Dunand (1963) and Jidejian (1968).

[3] Cf. Lucan 3.220–2, of a time before which Phoenicians 'had learned how to weave riverine papyrus' (*flumineas…contexere biblos*).

[4] On ancient dream-literature, see Walde (2001); Harris (2009); Scioli (2015). Miller (1999) is a model for dream-approaches to diverse literary corpora.

[5] Cf. Barchiesi (2001) 133; Bloom (1975) 41–62 suggests 'primal scene of instruction' as literary correlate for *Urszene* ('Primal Scene'), the term Freud publicized in his 'Wolf Man' case of 1914, to describe the child's witnessing of parental intercourse; on the term's history and uses, see Lukacher (1986).

[6] Farrell (1998); Jenkins (2000).   [7] Raval (2001).   [8] Nagle (1983).

Aaron Joseph Kachuck, *Ovid's Dream, or, Byblis and the Circle of* Metamorphoses In: *Metamorphic Readings: Transformation, Language, and Gender in the Interpretation of Ovid's* Metamorphoses. Edited by: Alison Sharrock, Daniel Möller, and Mats Malm, Oxford University Press (2020). © Oxford University Press.
DOI: 10.1093/oso/9780198864066.003.0006

psychodynamics of Ovidian self-citation.[9] This paper builds on these approaches to show how considering Byblis holistically—as dreamer, writer, incestuous lover, and spring—helps illuminate the structural frame of the *Metamorphoses* that she metonymically models. With Byblis' help, Ovid takes up Ennius' mantle; with Byblis' help, we, too, may begin to detect, behind the changing figures of Ovid's *Metamorphoses*, hints of Ovid's own dream.[10]

This paper unfolds in three parts: first, a review of the place of metamorphosis in dreams, and of dreams in Ovid's *Metamorphoses*; second, a close reading of Ovid's account of Byblis (*Met.* 9.454–665) as the work's only dreamer of fully human dreams and as *prima inventrix* of literature; and, finally, an exploration of Byblis' exemplary role in Ovidian self-fashioning. If Byblis seems an odd candidate for Ovidian self-portraiture—more obscure than Myrrha (even in Ovid's own day), less psychologically emblematic than Narcissus or Pygmalion—this paper shows how her unique use of dreams and literature in the service of desire makes her a mirror for the poet and his 'poem without end' (1.4 *perpetuum ... carmen*).

Dreams and Metamorphosis

It is natural to look to dreams for self-representation in Ovid's tale 'of forms changed into new bodies' (*Met.* 1.1–2 *in noua ... mutatas ... formas / corpora*), for the ancient study of dreams tended to connect them to metamorphic visions and experiences. Aristotle, for one, thought dreams metamorphoses' natural home: sleeping people's sensory organs, he wrote, perceive shapes that 'possess verisimilitude in the way of cloud-shapes which in their rapid metamorphoses (μεταβάλλοντα) one likens now to a human being, now to a centaur' (*De Insomniis*, 461b16–21 ἔχουσαι ὁμοιότητα ὥσπερ τὰ ἐν τοῖς νέφεσιν, ἃ παρεικάζουσιν ἀνθρώποις καὶ κενταύροις ταχέως μεταβάλλοντα). Lucretius gave this notion an Epicurean spin: 'It sometimes happens again', he wrote, 'that the image that follows up is not of the same kind, but what was before a woman seems to be changed into a man in our grasp; or that different shapes and ages follow' (Lucr. 4.818–21 *fit quoque ut interdum non suppeditetur imago / eiusdem generis, sed femina quae fuit ante, / in manibus uir uti factus uideatur adesse / aut alia ex alia facies aetasque sequatur*).[11] Ovid's *Metamorphoses* turns such dreamed transformations real.

---

[9] Janan (1991). Pavlock (2009) 106 notes that Byblis represents 'a kind of self-absorption by the poet'; see *passim* on the broader theme of Ovid's poetic self-representation.

[10] Although I follow Zetzel (2002) in focussing on literary polemics rather than the subconscious, I use the term 'dream' instead of 'dream narrative' to preserve the term's ambiguities, and the ambivalences of the structure it helps lay bare.

[11] Cf. Aug. *De civ. D.* 18.18 (demons metamorphosing sleeping humans).

Secondly, and as both Aristotle and Lucretius' descriptions underline, not only dreams' content, but also their structure, renders them surreal. The prologue to Horace's *Ars Poetica* objected to hybrid concatenations, likening such monstrosities to 'the dreams of a fevered man', in whose mind 'empty appearances (*species*) are fashioned, so that neither the foot nor the head can be restored to a single form' (7–9 *velut aegri somnia, vanae / fingentur species, ut nec pes nec caput uni / reddatur formae*). Literary works built on this model turn such synchronic cross-breeding to diachronic variety.[12] Thus Quintilian seems to adapt Horace's monstrous figure to describe Ovid's rhetorical transitions: '[There are those who] seek applause for their magic acts, as Ovid is wont to be overly playful in his *Metamorphoses*, though he may be excused by the obligation to assemble the most diverse material into the semblance of a single body' (*Inst.* 4.1.77 *praestigiae plausum petat, ut Ovidius lasciuire in Metamorphosesin solet; quem tamen excusare necessitas potest, res diuersissimas in speciem unius corporis colligentem*).[13] Horace's characterization of such hybrids as 'the dreams of a fevered man' seems particularly well suited to the transitions Ovid conjures to connect the various episodes of the *Metamorphoses*, which, long ago, Frank J. Miller divided into eight categories: 1) Chronological, 2) Geographical, 3) Collective/Bracketing, 4) Story-by-the-way, 5) Coincidental/Contemporary Action, 6) Stepping-stone (i.e. creation-flood stories to Apollo–Daphne), 7) 'X only did not come' (i.a. 1.583 Inachus, 4.607–8 Acrisius, 6.421 Athens, 7.162 Aeson, 11.90 Silenus, 12.4 Paris), and 8) Linguistic/conceptual 'long leap' (15.552–621 'wonder', 15.745–6 'God in Y').[14]

If such freedom of movement caught Quintilian's critical attention, it also continues to provoke descriptions of the work's transitions as forms of 'dream logic' or 'free association'.[15] Both terms are Freudian, and although Freud objected to imposing narrative temporality on the unconscious, the censor's work described in Maury's dreams, the 'Dream of Irma's Injection', or the 'Dream of the Botanical Monograph',[16] would yield a list of transformative tropes similar to Miller's catalogue of Ovidian transitions. Further, the link between dreams and free association had wide ancient precedent, particularly vis-à-vis dreams that fall short of prophecy or revelation, i.e. the *insomnium/ἐνύπνιον*.[17] Cicero, for example, critiqued his brother Quintus' trust in dreams by demanding of him, sarcastically, '[Since] the orderly course of the stars has been discovered... tell me,

---

[12] On 'variety' in Roman aesthetics, see Fitzgerald (2016).

[13] As a reader for the Press underlined, Quintilian is using Ovid to illustrate how to connect a *Prooemium* with what follows; notably, the poet is faulted for habitually (*solet*) playing the desultor in his *Met.*

[14] Miller (1921); for a more recent treatment of narrative modes in Ovid's *Metamorphoses*, see Barchiesi (2002).

[15] 'Dream logic': Clarke (1995) 55; von Glinski (2012) 137. 'Free association': Galinsky (1975) 236; Janan (1988) 113; Wheeler (1999) 122; Schiesaro (2002) 66.

[16] Freud (2010) 87–8, 130–45, 193–9. On Freud and Latin literature, see Timpanaro (1976); Oliensis (2009).

[17] See Kenaan (2004) 255–61.

if you can, what is the orderly course of dreams and what the harmonious relation between them and subsequent events?' (*Div.* 2.146 *inuentus est enim ordo in eis stellis ... cedo tandem qui sit ordo aut quae concursatio somniorum*). Indeed, even a fateful dream (ὄνειρος, *somnium*) could be characterized by jarring transitions, as in Rome's foundational dream, that of Romulus and Remus' mother Ilia in Ennius' *Annales* (fr. 29 Sk.).[18]

Ovid's *Metamorphoses* is dream-like in both content and structure, in a way that Aristotle's description of cholerics' imaginative habits accommodates (*Div. Som.* 464a): 'Because of their liability to change (καὶ διὰ τὸ μεταβλητικὸν), the next image in a series comes rapidly before them (ταχὺ τὸ ἐχόμενον φαντάζεται αὐτοῖς); for just as the insane recite and recall to themselves the poems of Philaegides, such as the *Aphrodite*, in which the ideas are all associated, so they pursue their series of impulses (καὶ οὕτω συνείρουσιν εἰς τὸ πρόσω)'. Like Aristotle's maniacs (ἐμμανεῖς), the reader of Ovid's *Metamorphoses* must join together its episodes in their swift changes, and attempt to lead them along in what the poet calls, in the work's proem, his 'poem without end' (*Met.* 1.4 *perpetuum ... carmen*). Thus, the transitions between Ovid's episodes serve as associative tropes that, in their affinity to dreams, become a kind of meta-metamorphosis.

Dreamers in Ovid's *Metamorphoses* have a role to play as meta-metamorphic authors, but, Byblis excepted, they do so under the influence of external, divine force. Aeacus (*Met.* 7.614–60) falls asleep under Jupiter's oracular Dodonean oak, only to see in his prophetic dream that same oak tree give birth to his wished-for army of ant-men (Myrmidon < μύρμηξ = 'ant'). Erisychthon is visited by the dread goddess *Fames* (= 'Hunger') (8.823–4), a cruel contortion of dreams of *Fama* (= 'Fame'), and one that foretells his own self-consuming doom.[19] Telethusa, wife of ignoble Ligdus, dreams of the goddess Isis, who predicts that Telethusa will give birth to the gender-bending Iphis (9.682–703). Myscelus the Argive is guided by a dream of Hercules to leave his homeland and found Croton in Italy (15.19–59), while Aesculapius appears 'before your bed, O Roman (15.654 *ante tuum, Romane, torum*)' in Epidaurus, leading to the foundation of that god's healing cult at Rome (15.641–64).

Of the *Metamorphoses*' many dreams, that of Alcyone, which comes to her straight from Morpheus in the House of Sleep, has deservedly held pride of interpretive place. Taken as a whole, the episode of the House of Sleep is balanced by the later description of the House of Fame, itself a metapoetic symbol for literary labour.[20] Morpheus, 'artisan and simulator of appearance' (*artificem simulatorem-que figurae*, 11.634), was an apparently Ovidian addition to the mythological cosmos, and therefore mirrors the creative poet himself.[21] A 'master of mimesis',[22] his name, MORPHeus, personifies Ovid's MetaMORPHoses; it also suggests a

[18] See Krevans (1993).   [19] Hardie (2012) 172–3.   [20] Hardie (2012) 150–77.
[21] Tissol (1997) 79–81.   [22] Hardie (2002b) 277.

bilingual anagram of the poem's key-word *forma*.[23] Ovid's poem speaks of 'changed forms' (*mutatas...formas*, 1.1); the House of Sleep's dreams can 'equal true shapes through imitation (*ueras aequent imitamine formas*, 11.626).[24] Finally, Morpheus, like Ovid, fashions through self-fashioning: where Morpheus' close kin Icelos/ Phobetor and Phantasos 'become' (*fit*) animals and 'pass into' (*transit*) soulless objects, Morpheus becomes 'a kind of moving work of art'.[25] Morpheus' making constitutes self-making, prefiguring Ovid's retrospective representation of his *Metamorphoses* as self-portrait: 'My poems are my best likeness, those poems that tell of the changing forms of men' (*carmina maior imago / sunt mea...carmina mutatas hominum dicentia formas*, *Trist.* 1.7.11–13). For both Ovid and Morpheus, what best reveals the *persona* behind the mask is the multitude of masks they wear.

Yet, when compared with these other dreamers, and with Alcyone in particular, what makes Byblis uniquely fascinating as authorial self-portrait is that her dream is of her own making, and wholly human. True, Byblis does have semi-divine ancestry, as she is Apolline Byblis (*Phoebeia Byblis*, *Met.* 9.663), her brother Apolline Caunus (*Apollinei...fratris*, 9.455), because their father, Miletus, is the son of Apollo (*Phoeboque parente*, 9.444); if a god is involved, it is the divinity within. More crucially, where Morpheus crafts himself into a dream in order to deceive others, Byblis dreams to deceive, and please, herself, thereby exemplifying the logic of one of Virgil's dream theorists, the sorceress-lover of *Eclogue* 8 who sees, or believes she sees, her beloved approaching by dint of her magic: 'Do we believe it? Or do those who love fashion dreams for themselves (*credimus? an qui amant ipsi sibi somnia fingunt*, 108)?' Similarly, when Cicero wanted to convince his brother Quintus of the pointlessness of dreams, he averred that 'god is not the creator of dreams, nor is there any association of nature with what one dreams' (*neque deus est effector somniorum, neque naturae societas ulla cum somniis*, *Div.* 2.147). Byblis fits perfectly this mould: she, and no god, creates her dreams.

There is something divine in the circularity of this process, as Cicero's own refutation of dreams' truth-value paradoxically suggests: when Cicero claims that 'When [physical aid] is removed from the body and the soul is left alone by the languor of the body, the soul moves itself' (*cum autem haec subtracta sunt desertusque animus languore corporis, tum agitatur ipse per sese*, *Div.* 2.139), he makes the dreamer into the god-like soul described by his *Somnium Scipionis*, 'Which, if this is the only thing in the world that moves itself, is certainly not born but is eternal' (*quae si est una ex omnibus, quae sese moueat, neque nata certe est et aeterna est*, *Rep.* 6.28). Insofar as Byblis' desires fashion her own dreams, she serves as template for the self-portrait of Ovid's own poetic activities in the self-referential frame of the *Metamorphoses* as a whole. Virgil's *Aeneid* had shown Nisus asking of Euryalus, 'Whether the gods put this fire in our minds, Euryalus,

---

[23] Ahl (1985) 59–60.   [24] von Glinski (2012) 132.   [25] Hardie (2002b) 136.

or is it that each man's desire is his own god?' (*dine hunc ardorem mentibus addunt, / Euryale, an sua cuique deus fit dira cupido?, Aen.* 9.184–5). In the case of Byblis and Ovid, this paper shows, the answer is, emphatically, the latter.

Byblis in Exemplo Est

'Byblis is evidence that girls should love things permitted, Byblis, who was seized with desire for her Apolline brother' (*Byblis in exemplo est, ut ament concessa puellae / Byblis Apollinei correpta cupidine fratris, Met.* 9.454). Byblis' story is the first in a long series of women, narrated first by the poet and then by the arch-poet Orpheus, who suffer for their unfortunate object-choice.[26] She comes honestly to incestuous—paternal and Philadelphian—love. Our story begins with old Minos: due to Jove's recent interdiction of human rejuvenation (9.394–438), his age cannot now be made good. Consequently, Minos' senescent paranoia leads young Miletus to cross the Aegean Sea to establish on Asia's coast an eponymous city (9.450–3):

> Hic tibi, dum sequitur patriae curuamina ripae,
> filia Maeandri totiens redeuntis eodem
> cognita Cyanee praestanti corpora forma,
> Byblida cum Cauno, prolem est enixa gemellam.

Here, to you [sc. Miletus], while she follows the curves of her fatherly shore, the daughter of Maeander (who turns back so often on himself), Cyanee, was known, bodies with beautiful form, Byblis and Caunus, twin issue, she bore.

This sentence's sinuous syntax reflects the family's inward turns: Miletus has a child by Cyanee, having come upon her as she followed the banks of her father, the river-god Maeander, famous for turning in on himself (*totiens redeuntis eodem*). Endogamy is built into this human drama even before it gets started[27]—into its divine back-story, too: the first love of Byblis and Caunus' ancestor, Apollo, was Daphne (*Primus amor Phoebi Daphne Peneia, Met.* 1.452), whose beauty, Ovid notes, made her 'a rival of unwed Diana' (*innuptaeque aemula Phoebes*, 1.476). As Ovid's poem makes Apollo and Diana twins (*edidit... geminos Latona*, 6.336), Byblis' story thus re-enacts divine precedent.[28]

---

[26] On previous legends, see Otis (1970) 415–17; Bömer (1977 vol. IV) 411–12; Lightfoot (1999) 433–6; Classen (1981) compares Ovid's Biblis/Caunus with Virgil's Dido/Aeneas.

[27] Cf. *Met.* 8.162–6 [Maeander simile], for whose metapoetic qualities, see Boyd (2006) and Pavlock (2009) 63–4; my thanks to the Press's reader for this connection.

[28] Hardie (2006).

Byblis' story begins with her solitary reveries: 'Seized by desire for her brother' (*correpta cupidine fratris*, 9.455), Byblis long remains 'deceived by the shadow of piety' (*pietatis fallitur umbra*, 9.460), with her desire 'not yet clear to her' (*sed nondum manifesta sibi est*) even as it grows stronger and stronger. Soon, though, linguistic habits begin to reveal to us, if not yet to her, her affections' character and strength (9.466–71):

> iam dominum appellat, iam nomina sanguinis odit,
> Byblida iam mauult quam se uocet ille sororem.
> spes tamen obscenas animo demittere non est
> ausa suo uigilans; placida resoluta quiete
> saepe uidet quod amat; uisa est quoque iungere fratri
> corpus et erubuit, quamuis sopita iacebat.

For now she calls him 'Master', now hates their consanguine names, now prefers he call her 'Byblis' rather than 'Sister'. While awake, she did not dare to send obscene hopes down into her mind, but, loosened by peaceful quiet, she often sees what she loves, seems to join her body to her brother's, and blushed even as she lies sleeping.

Although Ovid only briefly describes her dream of 'joining body to her brother and blushing' (*uisa est quoque iungere fratri / corpus et erubuit*, Met. 9.470–1), we see her worrying this dream at great length (9.474–516), beginning with an exclamation (9.474–5):

> me miseram! tacitae quid uult sibi noctis imago?
> quam nolim rata sit! cur haec ego somnia uidi?

O miserable me! To what does it aspire, this image of silent night? Would that it not come true! Why did I see these dreams?

Even as Byblis querulously queries her dreams' source, she grasps that pleasure is somehow involved: 'In sleep a witness is missing, but not missing is the sense of pleasure' (*testis abest somno, nec abest imitata uoluptas*, 9.481). She continues (9.483–6):

> gaudia quanta tuli! quam me manifesta libido
> contigit! ut iacui totis resoluta medullis!
> ut meminisse iuuat! quamuis breuis illa uoluptas
> noxque fuit praeceps et coeptis inuida nostris.

How many joys did I take, how greatly manifest a pleasure touched me, how I lay there, unloosed in all of my marrow, how much it pleases to remember, even though pleasure was short, and night was headlong and envious of my undertakings.

At the centre of Virgil's *Aeneid*, it is through the Gates of Dreams that the spirits of the underworld 'send forth' (*mittunt, Aen.* 6.896) dreams unto men;[29] at a similarly marked structural point in Ovid's *Metamophorses*,[30] those 'hopes' that Byblis will not 'send down into her mind' (*demittere, Met.* 9.468) when playing the *songe-creux*, she will 'send forth' as she sleeps. Where Virgil saw dreams as coming from without, Byblis sends dreams to herself.[31] Where Virgil had to worry, with Homer's Penelope (*Od.* 19.560–9), about the truth or falsehood of dreams, Byblis' dreams break with ancient dream-science by ignoring considerations of truth: 'Sleep lacks a witness, but not the sense of pleasure' (*testis abest somno, nec abest imitata uoluptas! Met.* 9.481). Byblis' dreams, products of her own mimesis, are neither true nor false: they please her.

The problem, Byblis knows, is that such dreams cannot be shared: 'Just so long as, while awake, I attempt to commit no such act, sleep may return under similar guise' (*dummodo tale nihil vigilans committere temptem, / saepe licet simili redeat sub imagine somnus!* 9.479–80). Byblis' desire to realize her dreams socially turns her towards the written word, thus beginning her transformation into literary *mise en abyme*. Byblis' own 'undertakings' (*coeptis… nostris,* 9.486) specifically recall Ovid's own 'undertakings' (*coeptis… meis,* 1.2–3) at the beginning of the *Metamorphoses*, but also recall the poet's earlier works. Importantly, Ovid has Byblis justify her actions through divine precedent supplied by Ovid's own texts (9.507–8):[32]

> At non Aeolidae thalamos timuere sororum!
> unde sed hos noui? cur haec exempla paraui?

But Aeolus' sons did not fear their sisters' bedchambers! From where do I know this? Why do I proffer these precedents?

Byblis' soliloquy, as we have already seen, is a laundry-list of insistent questions—*quid* (9.474, 495), *cur* (9.475, 508), *quod* (495), *quo* (9.509). With this question, however, Byblis begins to see the interpretation of dreams as in need, itself, of interpretation. Why, Byblis wants to know, does she turn to the Aeolidae to justify her own dreams? The answer: Byblis' library. She might, of course, have read about the incestuous marriages of the sons and daughters of Aeolus in Homer's *Odyssey* (10.1–7), or perhaps in Euripides' *Aeolus* (*TGF* fr. 14–41), where Aeolus forces his daughter Canace to commit suicide for her having fallen in love with Macareus. More probably, however, she read this

---

[29] Barchiesi (2001) 133 sees Aeneas' underworld encounter with Anchises as yet a further 'primal scene'.

[30] On *Met.* 9 as centre, see below, section 'Byblis and the Circle of *Metamorphoses*'.

[31] Cf. Petr. *Sat.* fr. 30 Müller.

[32] On Byblis and self-citation (*Selbstzitat*), see Frings (2005) 180–94; cf. Barchiesi (2001) 58: 'The heroine behaves as if she were an ideal reader of the *Ars Amatoria*.'

Euripidean version in a source closer to home, in the eleventh of Ovid's *Heroides*.[33] Reading Canace's letter to her brother, of course, should have taught her that incest runs to ruin: Canace's baby dies at her father's order, and she is about to kill herself through the same. Hence, perhaps, the order of Byblis' question: first, she seeks to identify *where* she learned about this story (from Euripides via Ovid), then subsequently realizes the bad precedent: 'Why did I supply myself with *these* examples?' (*cur haec exampla paraui*, 9.501). We thus watch Byblis learning to read herself and her thoughts—for her, as for Ovid, autobiography can be autobibliography, an account of one's own reading.

Just as the *Divine Comedy*'s Francesca seduces pilgrim Dante by taking up the poet's own *dolce stil novo*,[34] so bookish Byblis' attachment to Ovid's own works helps explain what has surprised critics: 'despite Byblis' self-delusion, Ovid remains sympathetic to the end'.[35] From Byblis' three long discourses—she speaks or writes 122 of her episode's 212 lines in 'three erotic elegies composed in hexameter'[36]—we can guess that Byblis' bookshelf included at least Ovid's *Amores* (with 1.2 and 1.12 especially well-thumbed), *Ars Amatoria*, and *Heroides*. Byblis, proto-author, uses her own author, Ovid, to realize her love: writing, in the *Metamorphoses*, is born with an inward turn.[37] The reliance of Byblis' fraternal incest on Ovidian precedent causes her episode to shade into the paternal incest and 'narcissism' hinted at by the circumstances of her conception—her mother raped by Miletus as she 'follows the curves' of her self-involved father—as well as to foreshadow those Orphic tales of filial incest that we will treat in this paper's final section.

Byblis serves as unique aetiology of literature. Although Io's bovine foot traced 'letters in place of words in the dust' (*littera pro uerbis, quam pes in puluere duxit*, *Met.* 1.649), her 'text' was but a brief, onomatopoetic, onomastic cry: indeed, Inachus' response to Io's words (*me miserum...me miserum*, 'Oh miserable me, oh miserable me!', 1.651–3) translates into Latin the Greek lament ἰώ ἰώ (='Io'), thus emphasizing Io's own onomastics and anticipating Hyacinthus' *AI AI* (10.215)[38] and Ajax' hypostasized name (13.397–8).[39] Byblis' epistle is worlds away from Io's autograph and other writing that precedes her: the two-line

---

[33] The story was popular; see, for example, Nicander (*ap.* Antoninus Liberalis 30), Ov. *Tr.* 2.384; Aristophanes *PCG* III 2 fr. 1–16; Hyg. *Fab.* 238; for pantomime, see *Anth. Pal.* 11.254, with Nero's starring role (as Canace *parturiens*) at Suet. *Nero* 21, Cass. Dio. 63.10.2.

[34] Francesca's three *amor*-tercets (Dant. *Inf.* 5.100–8) open by citing a sonnet from *La Vita Nuova* (20.3) that in turn cites 'the wise poet', Guido Guinizelli; on this citational love-triangle, see Contini (1970) 343–8 and Kay (2016) 66–9.

[35] Nagle (1983) 314.   [36] Holzberg (1997) 141.

[37] Janan (1991) 245: '[Byblis is] an *altera* Ovid—the poet as he *might be* were he entirely self-referential.'

[38] Blanco Mayor (2017) 186.

[39] On Io as writer, see Ahl (1985) 147, connecting 'Io' to 'Isis', to whom Plutarch's *De Isid.* (3) ascribes the invention of writing; hence, Io's putative mythological journey to Byblos in her search for Epaphus (per Apoll. 2.1.3; Plut. *De Isid.* 15) makes Byblis an Io Redux.

epitaph of Phaethon (2.327–8) or the message (verbal or pictorial?) that Philomela had woven for Procne (6.576–82). Byblis absorbs these forebears: reflecting the oral fixation of Io's textual composition, she begins her *speech* with Inachus' translation of Io's text (*me miseram!*, 'Oh miserable me!', 9.474), but begins her letter with a sentence redolent of advanced (written) prose's periodic sophistication (9.530–1).[40]

Thus, while Morpheus may be Ovid's invention, Byblis a figure he inherited from tradition, the Byblis Ovid ends up showing us is wholly new—as her prose style shows, Ovid has reinvented her as a writer. Byblis points up her changed form by echoing her pre-literate instantiations, including Nicander's, where Caunus falls in love with her (cf. 9.511–2), and Parthenius', where Byblis orally confesses her love for Caunus.[41] It is purely coincidental that the longest surviving fragment of Parthenius' verse concerns Byblis, but it is suggestive that Byblis' is the only section of Parthenius' *Amat. Narr.* (11) to feature Parthenius' own poetry.[42] Finally, as Byblis is the *Metamorphoses*' first 'author', it might be possible to see an abecedarial acronym in her stage-entrance: 9.454 *Byblis in exemplo est, ut ament concessa puellae*, 9.455 *Byblis Apollinei correpta cupidine fratris*, with *Byblis* and *Caunus* both descended from *Apollo*.[43] When Ovid writes about Byblis, he is writing, too, about writing.

As writer, Byblis recalls Ovid's Canace (*Her.* 11), whose letter began by asking her brother Macareus to imagine her seated, her right hand with pen (*dextra tenet calamum*), left hand with dagger (*strictum ... ferrum*), and the writing parchment unrolled upon her lap (*charta soluta*): 'This is the image of Aeolus' daughter writing to her brother' (*haec est Aeolidos fratri scribentis imago, Her.* 11.5–6). In this, as in so many ways, Ovid makes Byblis Canace's double: 'Her right hand holds a metal stylus (*dextra tenet ferrum*), her left, the empty tablet' (*uacuam tenet altera ceram, Met.* 9.522). It does not bode well for Byblis that, for writing implement, she takes up, not Canace's 'reed-pen' (*calamum*), but her *ferrum*, which is to say, a metal stylus, doubling as dagger.[44]

---

[40] *hanc ... mittit* is typically epistolary; note that Byblis' salutation (*quam, nisi tu dederis, non est habitura salutem*) rehearses Phaedra's incestuous letter (*quam nisi tu dederis, caritura est ipsa, salutem, Her.* 4.1), on which connection, see Raval (2001) 300.

[41] Parth. Amat. Narr. 11.3 λόγους αὐτῷ προσφέρειν, '[They say she] carried proposals to him' > *Met.* 9.514 *ipsa petam! poterisne loqui? poterisne fateri?* ('I will see him out! Will you be able to speak? Will you be able to confess?'); cf. 9.519 *uiderit: insanos, inquit fateamur amores!* ('He will see: let me confess my crazy loves!'), in Ovid, through writing. For further variants, see White (1982).

[42] On Parthenius' Byblis, and potential relationships with Apollonius of Rhodes and with Nicander's *Heteroeumena,* see Lightfoot (1999) 67, 190–1.

[43] For alphabetic humour, see Dornseiff (1922) 148; compare the onomastic abecedary at Sen. *Apocol.* 3.4 *Augurini ... Babae ... Claudii.*

[44] Had Byblis taken up that 'reed-pen', local mythological associations would have augured ill, even as they pointed to a familial locus of writing-related myths: legend made Maeander father to Calamus (Nonnus, *Dion.* 11.464), who, having begged Zeus for death after the drowning of his lover Carpus, turned into a reed (Serv. ad *Ecl.* 5.48; Nonn. *Dion.* 11.370). Nonnus further makes Maeander father to Marsyas, thus associating the 'reed' (*calamus*) into which Calamus is transformed with the 'reed-flute' (*calamus*) with which Marsyas fatally challenges gods in song.

Byblis' claim to be the work's first writer is confirmed by her being the poem's first documented case of writer's block (*Met.* 9.522–7):

> incipit et dubitat; scribit damnatque tabellas;
> et notat et delet; mutat culpatque probatque,
> inque uicem sumptas ponit positasque resumit;
> quid uelit ignorat; quidquid factura uidetur
> displicet; in uultu est audacia mixta pudori.

She begins, doubts, writes, then curses the tablets, and scribbles and erases, changes and blames and approves and by turns puts them down having taken them up, takes them up having laid them down. What she wants, she does not know; what she seems about to do, displeases her; in her face, daring compounds with shame.

Byblis is the Every-Writer, suffering the poet's natural malady, and specifically recalling Horace's writer's-block (*Sat.* 2.3.1–8), and pre-empting Persius (*Sat.* 3.10–14). Her combination of 'boldness mixed with modesty' (*audacia mixta pudori, Met.* 9.527) recalls Virgil, who, known by the biographical tradition for his virginal modesty (*Vit. Verg.* 11), also marked himself out as the 'bold youth' (*audax iuuenta, G.* 4.565) willing to attempt in verse the previously unessayed.

Byblis, first to fail at writing, first whom writing fails, is also the first to critique, and thereby theorize, the problem of writing, and in terms that take up Plato's famous critique in the *Phaedrus* (274c–279c): if, instead of having written to her brother, she had *spoken* to him, she might have done rather more to seduce him effectively, for 'I would have been able to say more, than what the tablets themselves contained' (*plura loqui poteram, quam quae cepere tabellae, Met.* 9.604). This recapitulates Ovid's battle with the writing tablets that failed to seduce his beloved: 'Did I, a madman, entrust my loves to these [tablets], and give to my lady these words that were meant to bear to her gentle words ... Therefore I judge you two-faced by nature!' (*his ego commisi nostros insanus amores / molliaque ad dominam uerba ferenda dedi? ... ergo ego uos rebus duplices pro nomine sensi, Am.* 1.12.21–2, 27).[45] Once again, Byblis re-enacts Ovidian precedent.

Byblis' affinities with Ovid as writer are confirmed by their shared tendency towards what Cicero called 'the lucid, copious, and flowing style of speech' (*genus sermonis ... liquidum ... fusum ac profluens,* Cic. *De or.* 2.159), and consequently excessive *copia*: 'The filled tablet left the hand that had vainly scratched out so many words, and the last line clung to the very edge' (*Talia nequiquam perarantem plena reliquit / cera manum, summusque in margine uersus adhaesit, Met.* 9.564–5). One may forgive the world's first writer for inadequately layering out her tablets; besides, Byblis is following Ovid's own counsel, by way of 'scratched out

---

[45] Alison Sharrock *per litteras.*

tablets' (*peraratas ... tabellas, Am.* 1.11.7): 'Let her pack her lines together, that lines traced on the outermost margin should detain my eyes' (*comprimat ordinibus uersus, oculosque moretur / margine in extremo littera rasa meos, Am.* 1.11.21–2).[46] Quantity is only part of the story: if Byblis had spoken *with* her brother, instead of sending something written *to* him, she could have altered approaches when she alteration found. Fittingly, text as sign of vocal failure is somaticized by the dry mouth that leads Byblis to follow (and, historically, prompt) Phaedra's example (*Her.* 4.175–6) by using tears, not saliva, the eyes, not the mouth, to sprinkle authenticity on her sealed letter: 'Immediately, she seals her crimes with her signet ring, which she dampens with her tears—moisture had abandoned her tongue (*protinus inpressa signat sua crimina gemma, / quam tinxit lacrimis (linguam defecerat umor), Met.* 9.566–7). Normally, Latin speaks of 'speech / words failing you' (i.e. Cic. *Rep.* 1.37 *ne te ... deficiat oratio*): Ovid's liquid concretization of this metaphor has point, for, as we shall see, that moisture that abandons Byblis' tongue goes straight to her eyes, thus precipitating her eventual metamorphosis.

Writing's role in Byblis' fall is concretized in the omen of the tablets: as Byblis hands the crammed boards to her servant (just as Ovid does to servant Nape in *Am.* 1.11), along with a command phrased in such a way as to emphasize speech's lability (*Met.* 9.569–70), 'the tablets, slipping, fell out of her hands' (*elapsae manibus cecidere tabellae, Met.* 9.571). The failure of Byblis' writing is as fateful as the symbol of artistic failure at the heart of Virgil's *Aeneid*, where Aeneas gazes at Daedalus' doors: Icarus escapes representation, for 'twice, his father's hands fell' (*cecidere manus, Aen.* 6.33). Ovid thus follows Virgil in highlighting poetic failure, as well as in emphasizing the limits of reception, for Virgil follows his remarks on Daeadlus' fallen hands with the notice that Aeneas' viewing (*perlegerent oculis,* 34) was interrupted by the arrival of Achates and the Sibyl; just so, although Byblis' letter fails to persuade her brother, we cannot know to what extent this was due to his having hurled away the tablets 'with only part of it read' (*proicit acceptas lecta sibi parte tabellas, Met.* 9.575)—where, one would like to know, did he stop? In both the *Aeneid* and *Metamorphoses,* then, writing fails, but so does reading. In all events, Caunus' angry exclamation is as much an attack on Byblis and Ovid as it is on the servant: 'Flee while you can, criminal author of forbidden lust' (*dum licet, o uetitae scelerate libidinis auctor, / effuge!,* 9.577).[47] Caunus' implicit incrimination of Ovid as 'author' will further resonate with us, as readers of Ovid's *Remedia Amoris,* when Byblis begins her transformation: the Lelegean nymphs take Byblis in their arms (*teneris ... ulnis,* 9.652), as if she were *already* a book, 'so as to teach how to heal love' (*ut medeatur amori / praecipiunt,* 9.653–4).

But this is to anticipate the plot and its peculiar rhythm, as we approach Byblis' transformation into literary metonymy. As it turns out, Caunus' rejection of

---

[46] Raval (2001) 302; cf. Tissol (1997) 46.   [47] Cf. *Trist.* 5.1.65–8.

Byblis' letter, and her advances, leads to no immediate change in circumstances. Instead, it provokes a repetition complex quickly skated over by the text (*Met.* 9.630–4): 'While it shames her to have tried, it gives her pleasure to try' (*cum pigeat temptasse, libet temptare*, 9.631). Caunus, Maeander's grandson (9.574) ends this cycle (and forecloses one *particular* end to it) by fleeing to found his own city, which, in turns, incites Byblis, Maeandrus' granddaughter (*filia Maeandri*, 9.451) to flee, as she 'follows the footsteps of her fled brother' (*et profugi sequitur uestigia fratris*, 9.640). Byblis thus recapitulates the gesture with which this family romance had begun (*hic tibi, dum sequitur patriae cur-uamina ripae, / filia Maeandri totiens redeuntis eodem*, 9.450–1). Where Byblis' mother's course led her into matrimony and biological reproduction, Byblis' ends with her metamorphic removal from the social sphere. Her path leads her down Lycia's coast; it ends, tellingly for our tale of incestuous love, at Mount Chimera. According to legend, the Chimera was known to have mated with her own brother (Orthrus), thus producing the Sphinx, who would go on to play so central a role in the Oedipus-saga, an archetypical tale of incest.[48] The Chimera's end is particularly revealing: according to Hesiod's *Theogony* (319, 326), she was killed by Bellerophon, the son of Glaucus, the son of Sisyphus, the son, in turn, of Aeolus, the guardian of the winds who was famously incestuous for having given his six daughters to his sons to wife (θυγατέρας πόρεν υἱάσιν εἶναι ἀκοίτις, Hom. *Od.* 10.7). In the Chimera legend, as in Ovid's tale of Byblis, incest is a closed circle, destroyed, as it is born, from within.[49]

Mount Chimera is the ideal resting place for Ovid's inventor of writing, for it is found in the territory of Byblos, homophonic source of βύβλος/βίβλος, meaning 'papyrus' and, by extension, 'books'. Byblis' transformation into a bibulous 'spring' is thus a complex sign for the invention of literature (*Met.* 9.655–65):

> muta iacet uiridesque suis tenet unguibus herbas
> Byblis et umectat lacrimarum gramina riuo.
> Naidas his uenam, quae numquam arescere posset,
> supposuisse ferunt; quid enim dare maius habebant?
> protinus, ut secto piceae de cortice guttae
> utue tenax grauida manat tellure bitumen,
> utue sub aduentum spirantis lene Fauoni
> sole remollescit, quae frigore constitit, unda,
> sic lacrimis consumpta suis Phoebeia Byblis
> uertitur in fontem, qui nunc quoque uallibus illis
> nomen habet dominae nigraque sub ilice manat.

---

[48] On Chimera and incest, see Bettini (2013).
[49] On Hesiod's ambiguous pronouns, see Clay (2003) 159.

She lies silent, and grabs the green stems in her nails, our Byblis, and waters the grass with a river of tears; they say the naiads made from these tears a spring that never may run dry. For what more could they have done? Straightaway, just as drops of resin from cut pine, or like sticky bitumen from the heavy soil flows, or as at the arrival of the gently blowing west wind the water, that froze with cold, grows soft again with the sun, so she, consumed by her own tears, Apolline Byblis, turns into a spring, that even now in these valleys bears its mistress' name, and flows underneath the dark holm-oak tree.[50]

'She lies silent': even before her transformation, she has become like Canace's scroll (*et iacet in gremio charta soluta meo, Her.* 11.6), and has joined the ranks of what Latin proverbially called *muti magistri* ('silent teachers'), i.e. 'books',[51] taciturn as the tablets on which she wrote.[52] Byblis, who had naively cried onto her letter, now silently cries herself into metamorphosis. Her transformation is likened to an imagistic complex: first, to pitch dropping down from a cut tree (*ut secto piceae de cortice guttae, Met.* 9.659), then to bitumen seeping up (*manat,* 660), then, at the tricolon crescendo's close, to wintry ice melted by the arrival of the new season's sun, i.e. to water from above that has frozen into groundwater below.[53] The final synthetic similitude depicts Byblis as an infinity fountain, prefiguring in fiction the scientific invention of the 'Heron Fountain' in 1st century CE Alexandria (Heron, *Pneum.* 2.8). Byblis melts eternally into herself: she wells up into a fountain, which falls to replenish itself, the whole process miraculously wrought by naiads, 'Who, they say, made her into a water-course that never goes dry' (*quae numquam arescere posset, / supposuisse ferunt,* 9.657–8). In this transformation, Byblis more perfectly realizes the formula that had described her grandfather, the river Maeander, 'who turns back so often on himself' (*totiens redeuntis eodem,* 9.451). She becomes a spring whose self-orientation rivals that of the Ocean, that circular river that 'turns in on itself' (Hom. *Il.* 18.399b = *Od.* 20.65b ἀψορρόου Ὠκεανοῖο) in an eternal, liquid loop.[54]

---

[50] For an evocatively eroticized rewriting (and illustration) of this scene, see Louÿs (1898).

[51] Gell. *NA* 14.2.1.

[52] Ahl (1985) 212 glosses *muta iacet* with 'like an unread book', and, remarking that papyrus grows in water (as noted by Theophr., *Hist. pl.* 4.8.3–4), sees Byblis' transformation as ideally 'bookish' for Byblis, aka βύβλος/βίβλος = 'Papyrus'.

[53] Earlier, Byblis froze at her brother's reaction: *Met.* 9.582 *et pauet obsessum glaciali frigore corpus,* 'and her body trembles, gripped by frozen fear'; her transformation thus constitutes (paradoxically) a cure for fiery passions (9.457 *ignes*; 465 *igne . . . uerumtamen aestuat intus*; 516 *ignes*; [520 *ignem*]; 541 *igneus*; 647 *ignem* (of Chimera)).

[54] Cf. Hes. [*Sc.*] 314. Barchiesi (1994) 246 compares the temporal scheme of Ovid's *Metamorphoses* to the Maeander's course (*Met.* 8.162–6). Locally, a circular effect is achieved through Apollo's framed name (9.455, 9.663). Byblis connects herself to Ocean: had she experimented on safer waters (i.e. on an incremental scale), she might not now face oceanic disaster (9.593–4). Janan (1991) 243 notes that Maeander's form 'plays out a nightmare of artistic self-referentiality . . .', with implications for *Met.* 9's structure, as well as its relationship to Daedalus' labyrinth in *Met.* 8. On Homer, ocean, and epic, see Williams (1978) 98–9.

Byblis and the Circle of *Metamorphoses*

Having established the interrelationship of Byblis' various symbolic functions—as dreamer, lover, daughter, and writer—we turn, in this final section, to illuminate Byblis' role as mirror for the *Metamorphoses*; we will proceed through widening gyres, looking first as its local context and links to other incest stories, then at its place in the book as a whole, and, finally, conclude with its relationship to the poem's proem and epilogue. Byblis' only incestuous act transpired in mental solitude, and her transformation leaves her a stream that flows into itself. Byblis' tale thereby suggests a link between incest and self-love, and in such a way as prefigures the extended cautionary tale of Pygmalion and his descendants regarding the risks and rewards of creative self-love—a 'Narcissus' tale writ large (cf. *Met.* 3.339–510), and of Orpheus' own composition. Byblis' Orphic counterpart is Myrrha (*Met.* 10.298–502) who, thinly disguised as another girl of Myrrha's age (10.440–1), consummates her incestuous desire for her father—and her father's thinly disguised desires for her (10.467–8)—only to be chased out of town when the ruse is revealed.[55] As with Byblis, family matters: Myrrha is daughter to Cinyras, who is the son of Paphos, who is the daughter born to Pygmalion—the sculptor 'who 'fell in love with his own work' (*operisque sui concepit amorem, Met.* 10.249)—by that very sculpture. Like Pygmalion's statue, Myrrha falls for her maker. The downfall of Myrrha's son, Adonis, turns, too, on love's self-direction. Adonis is as beautiful as painted *Amores*, 'Love-Children' (10.516); when Venus falls in love with Adonis, having been bewitched by her son, Boy Cupid, the whole scene carries 'a strong whiff of the incestuous'.[56] Legend and ritual practice bring Byblis and Myrrha together: although Ovid expressed relief that Myrrha's story transpired in distant Cyprus (10.304–7), her transformation into a myrrh tree in exotic, independent, Sabaea,[57] the Adonis cult's metropolis was Byblos, city 'sacred to Adonis' (Strabo, *Geo.* 16.2.18 ἱερά ἐστι τοῦ Ἀδώνιδος).[58]

When Byblis is set alongside Myrrha's line, it is clear that, when it comes to Ovid and incest, 'we are dealing . . . with the psychology of the self-representation of creativity',[59] and so it is no wonder that Ovid has put this primal scene of writing and dreaming at one of the temporal centres of his *Metamorphoses*.[60] I say 'one of the temporal centres', because *Met.* 9 shares this accolade: in terms of

---

[55] Nagle (1983).   [56] Hardie (2006) 25.   [57] *RGDA* 26.5, with Cooley (2009) 227–8.

[58] On Adonis-worship at Byblos, see Lightfoot (2003) 305–19. Byblos is where Isis, 'Lady of Byblos', finds the chest containing her brother (and lover) Osiris; like Byblis, Isis 'sat down next to a spring, dejected and in tears' (Plutarch, *De Is. et Os.* 357a καθίσασαν ἐπὶ κρήνης ταπεινὴν καὶ δεδακρυμένην). On 'Lady of Byblos' identifications, see Zernecke (2013); on Isis and Byblos in Plutarch's *De Is. et. Os.*, Griffiths (1970) 137–43.

[59] Hardie (2006) 27–8 of incest and Narcissus. On Myrrha and the textual 'family romance', see Kachuck (2015) 264–5; on an epigram celebrating Lucius Crassicius' commentary; on C. Helvius Cinna's *Smyrna* (Suet. *Gramm. et rhet.* 18.1–2 Kaster (1995).

[60] On middles in Latin poetry, see Kyriakidis and De Martino (2004).

scrolls-on-the-shelf in the *bibliotheca*, *Met.* 8 is the fifteen-book poem's 'middle'. Though it has not, to my knowledge, been noticed, Ovid draws attention to *Met.* 8's centrality by having Daedalus kill his nephew Perdix (= 'partridge') for inventing the saw (linear motion) and the compass (circular motion): 'that one part may stand still, while the other might describe a circle' (*altera pars staret, pars altera duceret orbem*, *Met.* 8.249). Thus, Daedalus, jealous master-creator, together with Perdix's compass-and-saw, emblematizes the centre of what one might call, to alter George Poulet's title-phrase (1961), the circle of metamorphoses.[61]

Ovid's *Metamorphoses*, however, circles around several centres, and while the family romance in *Met.* 8 may serve as the poem's physical mid-point—and a marked one at that—the work's chronological fulcrum is found in *Met.* 9, where Ovid has clustered a nexus of 'beginnings of history' that set the stage for Byblis' role as *prima inventrix* of literature. Such markers of temporal watershed include the waning power of Minos, history's first thalassocrat, and the shift from the Pandionid to the Dardanid dynasties, a major genealogical shift in the poem.[62] Hercules' presence in *Met.* 9 represents yet another turning point in the work's genealogical scheme—this son of Jupiter, it has been shown, occupies the thirteenth/fourteenth generation of the thirty generations Ovid's *Metamorphoses* canvasses from Inachus to Numa, thus putting the next two generations (Miletus, and his child, Byblis) at the work's generational centre. Hercules' death also initiates what has been described as a 'movement away from metamorphosis', as Hercules sets a precedent for Romulus, Numa, Augustus, and Ovid himself in *Met.* 15, by metamorphosing into a divine version of his own self.[63]

Of all of the temporal markers of *Met.* 9, none so crucially sets the stage for Byblis' wholly human dreams, for her invention of writing, and for her usefulness as a model for Ovid himself, as the immediate prelude to Byblis' story, the promise of Hercules' heavenly consort Hebe (῞Hβη = 'youth') that her resurrection to youth of Ioläus will be the last such boon she will grant (9.401–2). Mortal human lifespans accord well with historical time, and, in this book, precede Byblis' important 'firsts'.[64] Once Byblis' story arrives, mortality means what it says: those who age will stay old, those who die will stay dead. Ovid capitalizes, here, on Virgilian mythological backstory: one of the gods to complain at Hebe's newfound restraint is Aurora, whose mortal consort Tithonus, prince of Troy and brother of the Trojan War's King Priam, will, although immortal, continue to

---

[61] See Crabbe (1981) on *Met.* 8 as centre.

[62] Minos: Feeney (2007) 125; Pandionid to Dardanid: Cole (2008) 37.

[63] Barkan (1986) 83. Compare *Met.* 9.269–70 with 15.875–6.

[64] Varro, after Panaetius (fr. 68 van Straaten), divided history into three periods (Censorinus *DN* 21.1): 1) the unknowable (ἄδηλον), 2) the mythical (μυθικόν), and 3) the historical (ἱστορικόν). Diodorus Siculus made use of a similar structure (Moatti (2015) 73–4). On Censorinus, see Broderson (2012).

grow older for all eternity. In his *Georgics*, Virgil had announced his ambitions 'to carry Caesar's name, through Fame, through as many years as Caesar is distant from the early origin of Tithonus' (*Caesaris et nomen fama tot ferre per annos, / Tithoni prima quot abest ab origine Caesar*, G. 3.47–8).[65] The proem of the *Metamorphoses* stands our poet on that giant's shoulders: Ovid will unspool his poem, he writes, 'from the initial origin of the world down to my own time (*Met.* 1.3–4 *primaque ab orgine mundi / ad mea... tempora*).[66] It is thus with a view to his own literary genealogy that Ovid alludes to Tithonus at one of the centres of his own poem—as harbinger of historical time, as prelude to Byblis' tale.[67]

As a centrepiece of this poem, Byblis—a bookish *fons lacrimarum*, self-regarding inaugurator of human dreams, human writing, and human time—is an ideal mirror for Ovid, poet of the *Metamorphoses*, who has asked her, her dreams, and her tears to instaurate, and in an especially Ovidian mode, Roman literature's 'primal scene of instruction', the opening of Ennius' *Annales*.[68] Like Ovid's *Metamorphoses*, Ennius' poem covers a wide sweep of time from the beginnings of Rome down to Ennius' own day. It opens with a variation on Callimachus' rewriting (*Aet.* fr. 2 Pfeiffer=2 Harder) of Hesiod's famous vision of the Muses on Helicon (*Theog.* 22–35), with Ennius dreaming of Homer (*uisus Homerus adesse poeta*, fr. 3 Skutsch 1985). Lucretius relates the vision: 'He [Ennius] recalls that the image of an ever-blooming Homer appeared to him, began to pour out salty tears, and unfolded the nature of the universe in his speech' (*unde sibi exortam semper florentis Homeri / commemorat speciem lacrimas effundere salsas / coepisse et rerum naturam expandere dictis*, Lucr. 1.124–6). Homer went on, it seems, to explain that his soul had passed into Ennius, a fact that dreamt paronomasia adumbrates: the 'ever-blooming Homer' (*semper florentis Homeri*, Lucr. 1.124) doubles as Ennius *perennis*, 'Ennius everlasting'.[69] Beyond verism, Homer's 'salty' (*salsas*) tears allude to the metonymic identification of Homer by the 'Ocean', a Hellenistic commonplace Romans put to frequent use.[70]

---

[65] As one of the readers for the Press notes, given Ovid's use of Ennius' Callimachus-inspired prelusive dream, it is relevant that the proem to the third of Virgil's *Georgics* alludes directly to the third book of Callimachus' *Aetia* (Thomas (1983) 92–101).

[66] Cf. *Trist.* 2.1.559–60 *pauca, quibus prima surgens ab origine mundi / in tua deduxi tempora, Caesar, opus.*

[67] Cole (2008) sees Ovid's poem covering ~1200 years from the giants' rebellion under Ogygus (~2400 BCE) to the era of the Trojan War in *Met.* 1–9 (~1200 BCE), then ~1200 years from Trojan War to Caesar in *Met.* 9–15. Barchiesi (1994) 247–8; Feeney (1999) 18; Holzberg (1997) 144–5 all place this transition in *Met.* 11, but the paronomastic reference to Tithonus (*Met.* 9.421) marks the arrival of the post-Herculean generation of the Trojan War.

[68] On Ennius' dream and Virgil's *Aeneid*, see Hardie (1986) 69–83, (1993) 103–5; Kofler (2003) 76–93; Goldschmidt (2013) 166–7.

[69] *Semper florentis=perennis*: TLL 10.1.1320.23–31. Lucretius emphasizes the connection through (frigid?) punning, introducing Ennius as 'the first who brought down from lovely Helicon a crown with perennial leaves' (1.117–8 *qui primus amoeno / detulit ex Helicone perenni fronde coronam*)'; cf. Bailey (1947) 158.

[70] Williams (1978) 88–9, 98–9.

Ovid alludes to Ennius' metempsychotic dream-tradition in his only two sorties from behind the *Metamorphoses'* curtain—its proem (*Met.* 1.1–4) and its envoi (15.871–9)—and in such a way as highlights Byblis' exemplarity, and underlines his own intimations of his (poem's) own poetic self-parentage. Byblis' spring that 'never may run dry' (*quae numquam arescere posset*, 9.657) is the kind of water-source the Romans would call 'perennial' (*perennis*: *TLL* 10.1.1319.34–5, 60–2), a word Latin grammarians used to gloss διηνεκής (*TLL* 10.1.1319.36), that poetic quality Callimachus had eschewed in his poetry (*Aet.* fr. 1.3 Pfeiffer=1.3 Harder), but that, in an act of polemical glossing, Ovid had applied to the *Metamorphoses*, his own 'poem without end' (*perpetuum... carmen*, *Met.* 1.4). When Ovid ends his perpetual poem, he pointedly turns more Ennian than Ennius: 'I shall be moved, perennial, above the high stars' (*super alta perennis / astra ferar*, 15.875–6).

Ennius dreamed of Homer, only to discover that dreaming of Homer meant dreaming of himself; Ovid borrows from Ennius, and from his tale of Byblis, to suggest that his *Metamorphoses* may be the poet's dream of his own apotheosis, or of an apotheosis achieved through poetic dreaming—as Africanus puts it in the *Somnium Scipionis* that concludes Cicero's *Republic*, although politicians have a ready-made 'path to heaven' (*uia... in caelum*, 6.16), it is poets themselves who, through literary efforts, 'have opened up their own return unto this place' (*aperuerunt sibi reditum in hunc locum*, 6.19).[71] Byblis well serves the poet's self-serving turn. Although Byblis' father Miletus was 'proud of his parentage' (*parente superbam*, *Met.* 9.444), the parents of Byblis' incest story, unlike those of Myrrha, remain the products of her, and her brother's, projection: both she and Caunus flee, as it were, from themselves. Ovid, similarly, takes up the role of *pater Ennius* as well as that of Ennius' Homeric parentage. At his poem's beginning, Ovid's spirit 'moves me to speak of forms transformed into new bodies' (*in noua fert animus mutatas dicere formas / corpora*, *Met.* 1.1–2); at its end, Ovid predicts of himself, that, based on his work's 'fame' (*fama*), and on his being read throughout Roman dominions, 'I will be moved... above the high stars' (*super alta.../ astra ferar*, 15.875–6).[72] Ovid's is not this work's only apotheosis, but his mode of conveyance is unique. Just before the Byblis story, Jupiter ferries Hercules' soul to the stars (*quadriiugo curru radiantibus intulit astris*, 9.272); just before the poem's close, Venus does the same for Caesar (*recentem animam caelestibus intulit astris*, 15.846). Ovid, however, appears to bear himself to his own highest heaven, and thus resembles the sleeper we have already seen characterized by Cicero: 'When [physical aid] is removed from the body and the soul is

---

[71] Ovid appropriately dreams his own apotheosis in the short story 'Sogno di Publio Ovidio Nasone' by Antonio Tabucchi (1992) 19–21, on which, see Miller (2001) and Ziolkowski (2005) 183–4; cf. Luc. *Somn.* 15.

[72] On *fama* and the *Met.*, see Hardie (2012) 150–77.

left alone by the languor of the body, the soul moves itself' (*Cum autem haec subtracta sunt desertusque animus languore corporis, tum agitatur ipse per sese*, *Div.* 2.139).

Ovid is the unmoved mover, the self-moving force, behind this poem's many changes. It is this quality that puts him, not 'among the stars' like Hercules or Caesars, but above them (*super alta ... astra*, *Met.* 15.875–6)—at least in his own eyes.[73] In this dream, Ovid plays all the roles, as though rewriting the climactic dictum of Cicero's *Somnium Scipionis*—'Know, then, that you are a god' (*deum te igitur scito esse*, *Rep.* 6.26)—not only *in propria persona*, but, as well, for himself: Ovid plays Cicero's Africanus and Aemilianus, the advisor and the advisee of Scipio's dream. But where Cicero's *Somnium* leaves its dreamer stationary, Ovid's *Metamorphoses* looks further back to Cicero's own source, Plato's *Republic*, whose visionary Er sees each soul's 'genius lead' it to new transmigrations (δαίμονα ... ἄγειν, *Rep.* 620d–e), much as Ovid's 'spirit moves' (*fert animus*, *Met.* 1.1) him, and his poem, into perpetual motion. The envoi's anticipation—'I will be carried higher than the high stars' (*super alta ... astra ferar*, 15.875–6)—puts him, in the terms of Cicero's *Somnium*, higher than the gods themselves, amid the sphere of the fixed stars where reigns 'that highest god, directing and containing all the rest' (*summus ipse deus arcens et continens ceteros*, *Rep.* 6.17), with Ovid turning heavens' wheel. Ovid, mover (*fert*) and moved (*ferar*), is that divine soul Cicero describes by adapting Plato's *Phaedrus* (*Rep.* 6.27). Ovid is, too, the human soul described in the *Consolation* that Cicero innovatively wrote for himself: 'As I say, divine, as Euripides dares to say, a god' (*ut ego dico, diuinus est, ut Euripides audet dicere, deus est*, *Tusc.* 1.26.65).[74]

Reading the poem's proem in this light yields a surprising reorientation: instead of reading that 'The spirit moves me to speak of forms transformed into new bodies', we might read that 'The spirit moves [me] into new bodies, that I might speak of forms transformed' (*in noua fert animus mutatas dicere formas / corpora*, 1.1–2). In the multi-fold mirror-game of this opening line—whose syntax 'changes shape before the eyes of the reader'[75]—Ovid invites us to imagine him moving, by figurative metempsychosis, into and through his poem's many bodies. Reflecting on his *Metamorphoses*, Ovid will imagine precisely this, that his poem's

---

[73] Prince contrasts with poet: the emperor, 'with peace bestowed, will turn his own spirit (*animum ... uertet*) to civil judgements, and, the most just author (*iustissimus auctor*), will move (*feret*) laws' (*pace data terris* <u>*animum*</u> *ad ciuilia* <u>*uertet*</u> / *iura* <u>*suum*</u> *legesque* <u>*feret*</u> *iustissimus auctor*, 15.832–3); by contrast, in a work-spanning zeugma that rivals Virgil's use of *condere* (*Aen.* 1.5 *urbem*, 1.33 *gentem*, 12.950 *ferrum*; cf. James (1995)), Ovid's spirit will 'move' him (*fert*, 1.1) to speak of the kinds of 'mutations' that, throughout the *Metamorphoses* but especially in its last book, are represented as forms of 'turning' (< *uerto*). For Ovid's opposition of laws and poetry, see *Am.* 1.15.5, *Trist.* 4.10.23–6.

[74] For Cicero's *Consolation*, see *Tusc.* 1.65, *Att.* 12.14.3; cf. Baraz (2012) 94. Ovid's description of Hercules' apotheosis (*parte sui meliore* <u>*uiget*</u>, *Met.* 9.269) may allude to *Tusc.* 1.65 *quae autem divina?* <u>*uigere*</u>, *sapere, inuenire, meminisse.*

[75] Feldherr (2002) 164; cf. Wheeler (1999).

many bodies, and their transformations, might constitute but one metamorphosis, one *imago*, writ large, of himself (*Trist.* 1.7.11–14):

> grata tua est pietas, sed carmina maior imago
> > sunt mea, quae mando qualiacumque legas,
> carmina mutatas hominum dicentia formas,
> > infelix domini quod fuga rupit opus.

Your pious devotion to me is dear to me, but my poems form my best portrait, which, such as they are, I ask that you read, those poems that speak of the changing forms of men, the work that their master's sad flight cut short.

In this sense, Ovid's *Metamorphoses*, 'fifteen books of changed forms' (*mutatae ter quinque uolumina formae*, *Trist.* 3.14.19), adapts the programmes of two other famous fifteen-book works: on the one hand, Ennius' *Annales* (originally in fifteen books), and, on the other, Varro's *Imagines* (Plin. *HN* 35.11; = *Hebdomades* (Gell. *NA* 3.10)), which distributed 700 portraits and descriptions of Greek and Roman figures into fifteen books. Ovid's *Metamorphoses*, however, invites us to collapse its multiplicity onto Ovid himself, much as another Ennian dream poem, *Epicharmus*,[76] has Jupiter become air, wind, clouds, rain, ice wind, then air again, on account of which, 'Jupiter are all of these things' (*Iupiter sunt ista*, Varro, *Ling.* 5.65). Ennius' grammatical inconcinnity reflects the paradox of his metempsychotic dream of Homer as himself; it also mirrors Ovid's figurative metempsychosis into and through his poem's many bodies. In the end, the *Metamorphoses*' many *corpora* are Ovid's *corpus*, which all will one day read in their hands, and scan in their skies: 'I shall be read', Ovid predicts, 'on the mouth of the people' (*ore legar populi*, *Met.* 15.878).

Conclusion

In the end, Ovid's movement spins, a meandering Byblical gyre, back into itself. The 5th century BCE sophist Gorgias famously noted, vis-à-vis Tragedy, that, 'He who deceives is more honest than he who does not deceive, and he who is deceived is wiser than he who is not deceived' (*ap.* Plutarch, *De Gloria* 5 ὅ τ' ἀπατήσας δικαιότερος τοῦ μὴ ἀπατήσαντος, καὶ ὁ ἀπατηθεὶς σοφώτερος τοῦ μὴ ἀπατηθέντος). We cannot say whether Ovid achieves the wisdom that attends genuine self-deception, but the conditional clause that brings his *Metamorphoses* to its ambiguous close must, in the end, prevent us from any tidy certainty that, as one scholar

---

[76] *ap.* Cic. *Luc.* 52 *nam uidebar somniare med ego esse mortuum* ('For I seemed to dream that I was dead').

has put it, 'Ovid's writing succeeds precisely in that aspect in which Byblis' must fail: though Byblis may not successfully write the ineffable, Ovid *can* (and in fact, does).'[77] Byblis does, it is true, fail to achieve her amatory desire. This paper has shown, however, that it is precisely this failure that transforms her into so potent an emblem of Ovid's literary art.

Dreaming, reading, writing, and reflecting critically on all three at once—*ecce poeta!*

The *envoi* to Ovid's *Metamorphoses* (15.871–9) is a vaunting boast of self-sublimation, wholly unlike Byblis' end. Still, the poem's last line, having learned courteous conditionality at Livy's feet (*Praef.* 13), refrains its ambitions: 'If there is any truth in the prophecies of poets, then I shall live' (*siquid habent ueri uatum praesagia, uiuam, Met.* 15.879). This logic is as circular, as intimate, as the perpetual flow of Byblis' fountain of tears, melted ice, bitumen, pitch, and ink: 'If bards have truth, then I, a bard, shall truly (I assure you) live forever.' Ovid believes he will be read by the people (*ore legar populi*, 15.878), his name, thereby, indelible (*indelibile*, 15.876); but what if, like Byblis' letter to Caunus, like Ovid's own *Ars Amatoria* in Augustus' hands (*Trist.* 2.237–40), this writer prove but 'read in part' (*lecta . . . parte, Met.* 9.575), his poem subject to the 'writing and erasure' Byblis emblematically enacts on her work (523–4)?[78]

Such, Ovid's poem knows, is the fate of fiction's dreamers, of humans and their histories, which is why it is so fitting that Byblis should have, in future times, gone on, not only to survive as the much-maligned prostitute of the *Ovide Moralisé*,[79] or to mutate, however disguised, into Petrarch's constrained lyrics,[80] or into the Christianized nymph of Thomas Gray's *Fons lacrimarum*. 'Une dixième muse vient de naitre: Byblis, Muse des arts du Livre et de l'Estampe', announced the editors of *Byblis* in 1922, laying the programme for their serial publication on the history of the art of printing, knowing well that their art, like the art of writing since its inception, always flows, with Byblis' spring, underneath the shadow of the dark holm-oak.[81] At one beginning of Roman literature, Homer cried in Ennius' dreams; at its new Ovidian beginning, literature begins with Byblis crying herself into Ovid's great dream of tales that flow so fluently from his spirit and so seamlessly into one another, 'these poems that tell of the changing forms of men' (*carmina mutatas hominum dicentia formas, Trist.* 1.7.13), that tell of 'bodies changed in ways not to be believed' (*in non credendos corpora uersa modos, Trist.* 2.64)—not to be believed, that is, except by its dreamer, and those who dream with him.

---

[77] Jenkins (2000) 451, echoing Farrell (1998) 323.
[78] Alison Sharrock *per litteras*; cf. Gibson (2006) 352–3.   [79] Possamai-Pérez (2009).
[80] Zak (2010) 64–6.
[81] Editor Pierre Gusman's classical credentials make it likely that *Byblis*' motto—'Liber Galliae Semper Florens'—and the title page and colophon's 'waxy begonia' (i.e. *begonia semperflorens*), reflect Lucretius' version of Ennius' vision of 'Homer always blossoming' (*semper florentis Homeri*, Lucr. 1.124).

Acknowledgements

My thanks to the Editors and to the readers for the Press for their many insightful suggestions and questions, as well as for saving me from several howlers; all remaining errors are my own. This paper is titled 'Ovid's Dream' to distinguish it from [ps.-?] Ovid, *Am.* 3.5, the so-called *Somnium Ovidii*.

6

Naso Deus

Ovid's Hidden Signature in the *Metamorphoses*

Mathias Hanses

In the *Wiener Studien* of 1899 and 1900, Austrian philologist Isidor Hilberg published a study that remains unique in its dedication to the modern search for ancient acrostics. On thirty-five densely packed pages, Hilberg lists several thousand 'intexts' he had discovered in Latin hexameter poetry, each entry mentioning only what he calls a *Zufallsakrostichon* and the relevant find spot. For example, the note 'deus Ov. met. 1, 29–32' (Hilberg (1899) 277) signals that the first letters of lines 1.29–32 in Ovid's *Metamorphoses* spell out the word *deus* when read vertically. Hilberg's efforts must have been tiring and time-intensive— or, as he puts it, 'lang und langweilig' ((1899) 269)—yet as the term 'fortuitous acrostic' suggests, he did not actually believe that his finds were anything other than accidents of poetic composition. Rather, the point of his collection was precisely to discredit those who believed that the words they read in the margins of Latin poetry created meaning in the text and/or were placed there intentionally by the poets. Accidents occur too frequently, he claimed, for them to be significant.

Hilberg's scepticism notwithstanding, the later twentieth and early twenty-first century's reader-centred criticism has been more willing to accept an intext as meaningful, provided only that it is possible to arrive at a successful interpretation of its interaction with the rest of the poem. Recent years have in fact seen so many convincing readings of ancient acrostics that it now seems safe to assume, in an admittedly somewhat circular move, that Greek and Roman poets wrote for an audience that expected to find such intexts in their poems.[1] Of course, the ancient practice of reading out loud or listening to recitations may have kept acrostics

---

[1] For acrostics in Ovid and other Latin poets, see esp. Fowler (1983); Courtney (1990); Barchiesi (1997a) 195; Carter (2002); Damschen (2004); Feeney and Nelis (2005); Hurka (2006); La Barbera (2006); Nelis (2006); Katz (2007), (2008), and (2016); Gore and Kershaw (2008); Grishin (2008); Castelletti (2008), (2012a), (2012b), (2014); Kubiak (2009); Somerville (2010); Colborn (2013); Danielewicz (2013); Kersten (2013); Smith (2013); Giusti (2015); Hejduk (2018); Kronenberg (2018b) and (2019). General introductions to the subject include Vogt (1967); Higgins (1987); Katz (2009) and (2013); and Luz (2010). I provide full bibliographies at Hanses (2014b) 609 n. 2 and Hanses (2016), to which can now be added the further, more recent items referred to in my notes throughout.

Mathias Hanses, Naso Deus: *Ovid's Hidden Signature in the* Metamorphoses In: *Metamorphic Readings: Transformation, Language, and Gender in the Interpretation of Ovid's* Metamorphoses. Edited by: Alison Sharrock, Daniel Möller, and Mats Malm, Oxford University Press (2020). © Oxford University Press.
DOI: 10.1093/oso/9780198864066.003.0007

hidden from many potential aficionados. Yet Greco-Roman poets frequently alert their audiences to the physicality of their books—that is, the presence of letters on a page—and recent studies reaffirm that many Greeks and Romans also read literature on their own and in silence.[2] Even those who voiced out every word would still have had to look at writing on a scroll. A large number of readers, including the most privileged intellectuals as much as those who had to rely on their recitation skills for their livelihood, would therefore have had the opportunity to detect hidden intexts in the compositions in question.

It is with these considerations in mind that I will seek in this paper to rehabilitate Hilberg's *deus* acrostic as a significant contribution to Ovid's *Metamorphoses*.[3] In particular, I will connect it to an additional, so-far undiscovered[4] intext in lines 1.452–5. Here, in the programmatic *primus amor Phoebi* passage that fully commits the *Metamorphoses* to distinctively Ovidian love stories, the poet has encoded his own *cognomen* in the letters at line end. Read vertically, they form the telestich *Naso*. A combination of these two intexts results in the authorial signature *deus Naso* or *Naso deus*, an apparent metapoetic suggestion that Ovid's accomplishments resemble those of a god. I suggest that this authorial signature can be read as a challenge to the Emperor Augustus, who was likewise broadcasting the immortality of his achievements, and that it invites comparisons with other forms of self-memorialization, like funerary monuments, literary *sphragides*, and even acrostic gravestones. At the same time, the intexts locate the poet within a tradition of using acrostics and similar forms of wordplay to demonstrate one's Hellenistic poetics. Important predecessors range from Virgil and Ennius to Nicander and, ultimately, to Aratus (as well as possibly to Homer). More generally speaking, the presence of not just an acrostic (*deus*), but also a telestich (*Naso*) in two of the *Metamorphoses'* most poetologically significant passages suggests that it is time to direct scholarly attention to the right-hand margin of the page. The recent resurgence of studies exploring the interaction between Greek and Latin literature and the material realities of the ancient world, including the physical arrangement of writing on papyrus, has already resulted in a great popularity for the study of acrostics. It is time to approach their equivalents at line end with similar enthusiasm.

Greek and Latin literature's original or, at least, its most influential acrostic occurs in Aratus' *Phaenomena* of the third century BCE. In his discussion of

   [2] See e.g. Knox (1968); Gavrilov (1997); and Winsbury (2009) 111–25, esp. 117–18, all responding to Balogh (1927).
   [3] Simon (1899) 227 and Damschen (2004) 97 n. 30 likewise note this acrostic, and the latter considers it deliberate, but they do not provide an interpretation.
   [4] After I had already written this article and it had undergone a first round of refereeing, it came to my attention that Matthew Robinson (2019) likewise discusses the *Naso* telestich. He does not, however, link it to the *deus* acrostic. The fact that we discovered the intext independently from one another and arrive at different, yet not incompatible interpretations, reassures me that its existence really is not fortuitous.

weather signs, the poet has encoded the programmatic term λεπτός—signifying an elegant style, literary craftsmanship, and a 'faint' or veiled sophistication[5]— multiple times into a passage describing different moon phases:

> λεπτὴ μὲν καθαρή τε περὶ τρίτον ἦμαρ ἐοῦσα
> εὔδιός κ᾿ εἴη, λεπτὴ δὲ καὶ εὖ μάλ᾿ ἐρευθὴς
> πνευματίη· παχίων δὲ καὶ ἀμβλείῃσι κεραίαις
> τέτρατον ἐκ τριτάτοιο φόως ἀμενηνὸν ἔχουσα
> ἢ νότῳ ἄμβλυνται ἢ ὕδατος ἐγγὺς ἐόντος.

Aratus, Phaen. 783–7

Faint and clear (moon) around the third day will be
an announcement of good weather. When she is faint and very red,
it's indication of wind. When she is rather thickish and with dull horns,
not having neat fourth-day light after the third,
then either it's the south wind that blunts her, or rain is near.

The adjective appears at least four times in the five lines in question (though more finds have been suggested).[6] The first λεπτή in verse 783 forms a so-called Γ-acrostic with the adjective's second occurrence in the letters at the head of each line. A third λεπτή traverses the passage diagonally at about a 45-degree angle. And a fourth instance in line 784 provides a connection between the content of the passage and the artistry displayed (both literally and figuratively) in the arrangement of its letters. Such echoes of an acrostic within the lines themselves have been termed 'verbal referents'[7] and are typically seen as confirming that the intext's placement is deliberate. Notably, Aratus' own model, the λευκή acrostic contained in the first five lines of Book Twenty-Four of Homer's *Iliad*,[8] lacks such a confirmation and is for this and other reasons typically considered accidental. In particular, it has been noted that at the time of the Homeric poems' first written fixation, the text may still have been presented in *boustrophedon* format and without adhering to strict line divisions.[9] This would have made an acrostic

---

[5] For Aratus as the term's possible originator and its use throughout the poet's oeuvre, see Cameron (1995) 321–8 and Volk (2010). For the term's history outside the *Phaen.*, cf. also Pfeiffer (1968) 136–8; Hopkinson (1988) 89–91; and Asper (1997) 242–3. For scepticism regarding its metapoetic meaning and significance, see e.g. Tsantsanoglou (2009) and Porter (2011).

[6] The acrostic was first noted by Jacques (1960) and further discussed (*inter alios*) by Levitan (1979); Kidd (1981) and (1997) *ad loc.*; and Bing (1990) and (1993). For the diagonal intext, see Hanses (2014b) and the responses by Danielewicz (2015) and Trzaskoma (2016). For further intexts in Aratus, see also Haslam (1992); Cusset (1995) and (2002); and Danielewicz (2005).

[7] So first Morgan (1993).   [8] Jacques (1960) 51.

[9] These realities make it less likely that Homer's acrostic was intended, but certainly not impossible. After all, as Damschen (2004) 105 points out, the intext might refer to the island where Achilles will be transported after his death and may hence be connected to the passage's melancholy content. Korenjak (2009) adds that even if the acrostic is fortuitous, it could at least have been *considered* meaningful by some ancient readers. Kronenberg (2018a) concurs and argues that Aratus might have seen the acrostic λευκή as anticipating the white light of dawn described at Hom. *Il.* 24.12–13. At (2018b) she traces the two acrostics' joint reception in Greek and Roman literature.

difficult to detect. By Aratus' day, however, and certainly by Ovid's, book rolls arranged hexameter verses in columns that adhered to the line divisions familiar to the modern reader.[10]

Homer's acrostic may be an accident, but a direct line of descent connects Aratus' intentional λεπτή acrostic to the intexts in Ovid's *Metamorphoses* that are at the centre of the present paper. Many of Aratus' imitators used acrostics to mark their own compositions as belonging in the same tradition of Hellenistic sophistication. Particularly relevant to my discussion are those cases where a poet used an acrostic to sign his composition, that is, to inscribe his own name into the text. These authors imitate not only the λεπτή passage but also a moment in Aratus' work where the poet plays on his own name.[11] Examples include Nicander, who twice signed his works with an acrostic,[12] and whose *Heteroioumena* served as a source for Ovid's *Metamorphoses*; the Roman poet Ennius, whose works apparently bore the hidden signature *Quintus Ennius fecit*;[13] and most importantly Virgil, who signed the *Georgics* with a reverse acrostic of his initials (<u>P</u>ublius <u>V</u>ergilius <u>Ma</u>ro) at 1.429–33.[14] Ovid was not only a successor of these poets, but also one of the *Phaenomena*'s Latin translators.[15] He would therefore have been keenly aware of the Aratean tradition when, as I argue, he worked his own signature as an intext into the *Metamorphoses*.

Let us move on, then, into the latter poem. The first book of Ovid's *Metamorphoses* features a series of creations, destructions, and successive re-creations. The world is formed from chaos and populated with living beings (1.5–88); humanity's gradual moral decline (89–150, 163–252) then causes the gods to send a flood (253–312), after which Deucalion and Pyrrha have to start over (313–415); and throughout, Ovid himself crafts the distinct literary cosmos that is the site of his countless transformations (1.1–4 and *passim*). The first divine agent to play an active role in this creative process is the unnamed *deus* or 'better nature' who settles the strife of conflicting elements that dominates the universe before the world's creation (*hanc deus et melior litem natura diremit*, *Met.* 1.21). He begins by separating aether, air, earth, and ocean and arranging them in their proper order. Before this intervention, there was no sun (*Titan*, 1.10); no pre-arranged spaces existed for earth and water (*tellus*, 1.12 and *Amphitrite*, 1.14); and, most significantly, 'the moon did not yet gain new horns by growing' (*nec noua crescendo reparabat cornua Phoebe*, 1.11).

---

[10] *P Berol.* inv. 7503 + 7804 = *BKT* 5.1.47–54 preserves a 1st-century CE manuscript of Aratus' *Phaenomena* and adheres to what we consider standard line divisions; see Martin (1956) 210–12. In the famous Gallus papyrus from the first century BCE or CE, line divisions likewise correspond to verses; see Anderson, Parsons, and Nisbet (1979). For the arrangement of late Republican and early Imperial Latin poetry into lines and columns, see most recently Schafer (2017).

[11] Aratus, *Phaen.* 1–2. See Bing (1990) and (1993). At Hanses (2014b) 609 n. 1, I suggest further plays on the name Aratus at *Phaen.* 383 and 532.

[12] Lobel (1928); Sullivan (2013).   [13] Cic. *Div.* 2.111–12 with Gore and Kershaw (2008).

[14] Brown (1963) 102–5; Katz (2008) and (2016); Somerville (2010); Danielewicz (2013).

[15] Galinsky (1975) 104; Cicu (1979); Damschen (2004) 106.

Students of Aratean wordplay are accustomed to paying special attention when poets refer to the moon and its 'horns'. Such references recall the λεπτή acrostic and therefore often alert the reader to the presence of an intext.[16] And indeed, it is at the very point where the demiurge is placing individual layers on top of each other—and preparing a place for the moon, as it were—that we encounter the *deus* acrostic:

> dissociata locis concordi pace ligauit:
> ignea conuexi uis et sine pondere caeli
> emicuit summaque locum sibi fecit in arce;
> proximus est aer illi leuitate locoque;
> densior his tellus elementaque grandia traxit
> et pressa est grauitate sua; circumfluus umor
> ultima possedit solidumque coercuit orbem.
> sic ubi dispositam quisquis fuit ille deorum
> congeriem secuit sectamque in membra redegit, ...

Met. 1.25–33

He bound the disparate parts in their places in harmonious peace:
the fiery and weightless energy of the vaulted sky
broke forth and made a place for itself at the highest top;
closest to it in lightness and location is the air;
denser than both is the earth, and it attracted the larger
elements and was weighed down by its own heaviness; flowing water claimed the
undermost places and surrounded the solid ground.
So the mass was arranged, and when he—whichever one he was of the gods—
had cut it and brought it, having been cut, into separate portions, ...

A variety of factors suggest that it is not by chance that the letters *deus* occur at the openings of lines 1.29–32. We might note, first of all, that Gregor Damschen (2004) has pointed to two further passages in the *Metamorphoses* that allude to the four elements and likewise bear acrostics and telestichs (*Met.* 12.235–44 and 15.194–8). Just as importantly, there is an additional occurrence of the noun *deus*, this time in the genitive plural, at the end of verse 1.32. Such verbal referents are familiar to us from the λεπτή acrostic, and they commonly occur in oblique cases. A famous parallel is provided by the oft-discussed *Mars* acrostic in Virgil's *Aeneid*:[17]

---

[16] For acrostics appearing in the vicinity of references to the moon, see Damschen (2004) 102–10; Meunier (2012); Klooster (2013); and Castelletti (2014). For signposting of intexts more generally, see Feeney and Nelis (2005); Somerville (2010); Hanses (2014b) and (2016).

[17] Hilberg (1899) 269 notes this acrostic but predictably considers it nothing more than an amusing coincidence. Fowler (1983); Morgan (1993) 143; Feeney and Nelis (2005); and others argue more convincingly that it is intentional. See also Horsfall (2000) *ad loc.* I submit at Hanses (2016) that Ovid

<u>m</u>os erat Hesperio in Latio, quem protinus urbes
<u>A</u>lbanae coluere sacrum, nunc maxima rerum
<u>R</u>oma colit, cum prima mouent in proelia <u>Martem</u>,
<u>s</u>iue Getis inferre manu lacrimabile bellum
[. . .] parant [. . .]

Virg. Aen. 7.601–5

<u>M</u>artial custom there was in Hesperian Latium, which from the first the
<u>A</u>lban cities held holy and which now the greatest in the world,
<u>R</u>ome, adheres to when at the beginnings of battles <u>Mars</u>
<u>s</u>tirs at their prodding, be it that they prepare to force lamentable war on the Getans . . .

In Virgil as in Ovid, the verbal referent occurs at line end. It therefore does more than suggest that the acrostic is not fortuitous. It also visually frames the passage on the right in a manner akin to the acrostic's own function as a border on the left. In our particular, Ovidian case, this framing function is further reinforced by the verbal referent's placement not just as the last word of any line, but at the end of the acrostic passage's fourth and final verse. The referent here marks the intext's completion and visually separates it from the lines that follow. Surely, then, the acrostic's placement is unlikely to be an accident.

Just as significantly, both the Virgilian and the Ovidian intexts foreground their respective passages' most prominent, divine actor. In the *Metamorphoses*, this interplay between the acrostic and the content of its constituent lines reaches a particularly striking level of sophistication. It has been pointed out that the language Ovid uses to describe the god's shaping of the world nods to other literary descriptions of an artist shaping (a representation of) the cosmos.[18] Ovid thereby calls attention to his own cosmogony's function as a metaphor or *mise en abyme* that reflects on the creative act of writing the *Metamorphoses*. In other words, the unnamed divinity stands in for the poet, and the poem *is* the cosmos whose creation and subsequent growth it describes over the course of fifteen books.[19] On this reading, the god creating the world of the *Metamorphoses* is the author himself, or at least resembles him closely.

The *deus* acrostic further reinforces this interpretation by highlighting that Ovid has been describing the unnamed god's careful ordering of the cosmos

---

plays on, and seeks to subvert, the *Mars* acrostic by working an *Amor* telestich into lines 3.507–10 of the *Ars Amatoria*.

[18] Esp. the forging of Achilles' shield in the *Iliad* (18.478–608), but also Hes. *Theog.* 116; Pl. *Ti.* 30a2–6; Ap. Rhod. *Argon.* 1.496–502; Lucr. 5.416–63; Cic. *Nat. D.* 2.98–104; Virg. *Ecl.* 6.31–40; the ecphraseis of the doors of the Sun's palace and of Arachne's and Minerva's tapestries in the *Met.*; etc. See Wheeler (1995).
[19] See Wheeler (1995) and Wickkiser (1999). On the *Metamorphoses* as forever suspended between immersing the reader in the world it describes and calling attention to the outside realities informing the text's production (including the physical object of the scroll), see Feldherr (2010), esp. 22–64.

specifically as a creation of horizontal strata (aether, air, earth, and ocean), each below the previous. The acrostic is itself the result of this kind of thoughtful grouping of layers underneath one another, as is the whole of the *Metamorphoses*. Readers would have been alerted to this similarity as they witnessed the acrostic gradually come into being with each additional line describing a new stratum of the cosmos.[20] The phrase *sic ubi dispositam* highlights the completion of this dual creation of universe and intext in line 1.32, the last of the acrostic. The god has added his signature, then, to his work in a manner that, I submit, prefigures Ovid's inclusion of his own name in the upcoming telestich. In doing so, he has drawn attention to his creation's arrangement into layers and to its resultant resemblance to lines of text on a physical page. Accordingly, the reader unrolling the scroll would have been provided with a visual illustration of the god/poet's activity as columns of verses continued to appear with the unfolding of the papyrus, and poem and cosmos came into being simultaneously.[21]

And yet, in spite of these striking resemblances between the demiurge and Ovid's own authorial persona, the god himself remains anonymous. The poem in fact emphasizes the divinity's namelessness in the very line that concludes the acrostic and confirms its intentionality via the significant placement of the verbal referent *deorum* at line end (*quisquis fuit ille deorum*, 1.32). Ovid thereby invites the reader to speculate on the demiurge's identity at the very point where the divinity's presence is most clearly highlighted within the text.

More than one identification is possible, of course, and probably intended. Early on, Ovid describes the demiurge as *deus et melior natura* (1.21, see above) and terminology familiar from Lucretius' *De rerum natura*—a work notoriously sceptical of the gods' interest in worldly affairs—occurs in the passage's vicinity (*semina rerum*, *Met.* 1.9). We may therefore be meant to envision the god as an allegory for the workings of nature, not as an actual being with a human appearance and personality. In a related reading, we could also understand Ovid's *deus* as a creator who intervenes in the cosmos only once and then remains entirely removed from its various stories. Yet alternatively, we may think of the passage as reasserting the gods' active participation in the universe and using Lucretius' own vocabulary against him. Potential candidates for the *deus'* identity would then include any number of divinities that have been seen as providing Ovid with

---

[20] It might have helped here if the acrostic had been made easier to detect by means of rubrication. There is, however, no material evidence that intexts were offset in red ink in the first centuries BCE and CE. Nevertheless, some scholars believe to have discovered metapoetical hints at the practice within the acrostics themselves, e.g. Habinek (2009) 131; Damschen (2004) 97 n. 28; Hanses (2014b) 612–13. See also Hanses (2016) 204. What we know for certain is that rubrication became a standard way of highlighting wordplay in later antiquity and the Middle Ages. See Levitan (1985) 254–5; Courtney (1990) 4; Ernst (1991); Heil (2007); and now Squire and Wienand, eds (2017).

[21] For the concept of poetic simultaneity underlying this image (i.e., the fiction that each line of text comes into being as the reader's eyes dart across it), see Volk (1997). Compare also the narratological approach adopted by Wheeler (1999) 8–33.

poetic inspiration, aiding in the creation of the *Metamorphoses*, and intervening in the poem's plots. Apollo would make for a logical candidate, in that he is the god typically invoked in the kind of Callimachean aesthetics that Ovid partially endorses in the poem's prologue.[22] In his earlier *Amores*, Ovid noted furthermore that Cupid had intervened in his creative process by modifying his composition's meter (*Am.* 1.1.1–4).[23] Since the *Metamorphoses* is to a large extent concerned with love and desires, this latter divinity would make sense as a possible creator-god as well.

Significantly, Apollo and Cupid make their first appearance in the *Metamorphoses* together, at 1.452–5, where they are engaged in a competition as to who is the better archer. Throughout the rest of the poem, this metapoetic contest plays out as a sustained tension between literary sophistication (Apollo) and emotionality (Cupid) as Ovid's tales continuously oscillate between the lofty and the licentious, the stern and the sensual.[24] It is at the moment of his two patron gods' first encounter that, I argue, Ovid has included his *cognomen* in the letters at line end:

> primus amor Phoebi Daphne Peneia, quem non
> fors ignara dedit, sed saeua Cupidinis ira.
> Delius hunc, nuper uicta serpente superbus,
> uiderat adducto flectentem cornua neruo ...

Met. 1.452–5

The first love of Phoebus was Daphne, daughter of Peneus. It was not an unknowing chance that created it, but Cupid's savage mania.
Him the Delian god, arrogant after the serpent's
defeat, had recently seen pulling the string and bending the bow of libido ...

The above passage makes for a particularly fitting location for Ovid to include his authorial signature in the text of the *Metamorphoses*. It is here, after all, that the poem for the first time turns to the illicit and often violently abusive sexual encounters between gods and humans that define Ovid's signature style. When read slowly and in sequence, the initial three words of line 452 enact this metamorphosis of the *Metamorphoses* in front of the readers' very eyes. The adjective

---

[22] At *Met.* 1.1–4 Ovid chooses the verb *deducere* to liken his poetic compositions to fine-spun textiles, even as he immediately undercuts these Hellenistic allegiances by promising a *perpetuum carmen* in the style of more traditional epic. For Apollo as the patron deity of Hellenistic poetry, see esp. Callim. *Aet.* 22, *Hymn to Apollo* 105–12 and Virg. *Ecl.* 6.1–5 with the discussions of Callimachean elements in Ovid's proem at Kenney (1976); Hopkinson (1988) 91–2 and Holzberg (1997) 123–6.

[23] For Cupid's role as an Ovidian 'muse', see esp. Gildenhard and Zissos (2000b). I have suggested elsewhere, at Hanses (2014a), that the god Mercury as he appears in Plautus' *Amphitruo* may likewise have served as one of the *Metamorphoses'* inspiring deities.

[24] Readers of Friedrich Nietzsche will be reminded of the antithesis between Apollo and Dionysus, a more (or even more) severe divinity than Cupid, in *The Birth of Tragedy* (1872).

primus announces an event that is novel to the poem; *primus amor* clarifies that we are dealing with the epic's 'original love story'; and it is only once we read the full phrase *primus amor Phoebi* that we have encountered the names of both of the *Metamorphoses'* patron gods (Amor/Cupid and Phoebus/Apollo) and launch into the first tale to fit the specific tastes of a former elegiac writer turned epic poet.

It is this artist's own name that has been inscribed in the right-hand margin to be discovered by a reader who pays equally careful attention not just to the letters' horizontal but also to their vertical arrangement. This same perceptive student of Ovidian verse might also notice within the same passage several oblique announcements of the presence of an intentional intext (which, again, is common in Greco-Roman wordplay). First of all, there is the recurrence of 'horns' at *Met.* 1.455, pointing back to Aratus' *Phaenomena* (785) and to the reference to the moon's hidden *cornua* at *Met.* 1.11. 'Horns' is also the technical term for the wooden knobs on either side of a papyrus scroll, so Cupid might be doing more than stringing his bow.[25] He could also be grabbing the book by the *cornua* either to unroll it, or to bend it into a more genuinely Ovidian composition, or perhaps rotating it the better to see the author's name.[26] And finally, if the reader still remains sceptical, the passage even says explicitly that what we see is not fortuitous. As Ovid puts it, *non fors ignara dedit* (1.452–3), the telestich has not appeared by accident. (Incidentally, line 1.452 ends in a monosyllable, *non*, which is relatively uncommon in epic hexameters and may suggest that Ovid sacrificed the standards of versification to the need to end the verse in the letter N. It is also worth noting that the vowels in the *Naso* telestich are the wrong quantities, *Nasō* instead of *Nāso*. Yet final syllables are *anceps* anyway. And while they would still have been pronounced according to each vowel's actual length, the telestich is a visual form of wordplay that does not rely on the reader to produce the sound *Nāso*, only to notice the letters at line end.)

The *Naso* telestich is meaningful, then, even when considered on its own merits. Yet we have also already observed some hints that it would derive further depth from being read in combination with that other moment of metapoetic creation that is the demiurge's ordering of the cosmos. Further support for this thesis comes from the fact that just before Apollo made his entrance, Ovid had narrated the repopulating of the earth after the deluge. This tale heavily emphasizes the same four elements that had featured prominently in the original creation of the world (1.416–37). What is more, line 1.454 includes two nods to the noun *deus*, one contained in the first and last syllables of the substantive adjective *De(li)us*, the other in the first and last syllables of the entire verse,

---

[25] For similar plays on *cornua*, see Barchiesi (1997a) 187; Wheeler (1999) 92–3; and Feldherr (2010) 26.

[26] Befitting this observation, Daphne is engulfed by *liber* ('bark' or 'a book') at the end of the episode (1.549).

Delius . . . superbus. Together, these two hidden allusions to the nameless demiurge suggest that it is here that we can unmask the creator-god's hidden identity.

Apollo or Cupid are possible solutions, but the poem has already foreshadowed that the demiurge may also be Ovid himself. It is fitting, therefore, that the lines bearing the *deus* acrostic describe the formation of the world, while the verses branded with the *Naso* telestich transform the cosmos into a distinctly Ovidian domain. As the universe continues to grow, line by line, the experience of gradually discerning the *Naso* telestich would have tied these two moments of creation together. After all, the second intext's gradual appearance on the right-hand side of the page would have suggested that it serves as a response, in a sort of intratextual dialogue, to its predecessor on the left. One possible answer, then, to the question of who created the world of the *Metamorphoses* is *Naso deus*, or Ovid the god. Apollo and Cupid each make their contributions, but it is *Naso deus* who has set them at odds with each other and supervises their ongoing contest.

Notably, Ovid had already been in the habit of signing his works with a combination of his *cognomen* and a noun or adjective defining his role in the text in question. The *Amores* and *Tristia* contain only the rather bland *Naso poeta* ('Ovid the poet', *Am.* 2.1.2 and *Trist.* 3.3.74), but he signs the *Ars amatoria* as *Naso magister* ('Ovid the teacher', 2.744 and 3.812), the *Remedia amoris* as *Naso legendus* ('Ovid the must-read', 71 and 72), and the *Epistulae ex Ponto* as *Naso tristis* ('Ovid the sad', 2.6.2), *Naso parum prudens* ('Ovid the hardly wise', 2.10.15), *Naso laesus* ('Ovid the injured', 3.5.4), and *relegatus Naso* ('exiled Ovid', 4.15.2).[27] In the *Metamorphoses*, no 'autograph' of this kind is present within the poetry itself, but a *deus Naso* or *Naso deus* intext would meet the requirements perfectly. Such a signature would hint at the author's role in the creation of a fictional cosmos where gods walk among humans and other animals.[28] What is more, it would raise the author to the status of a god, which could constitute more than merely a moment of tongue-in-cheek self-praise (though of course, it is that as well). It would also invite the reader to reflect on why, when, or how a human being might be elevated to divine status, or what kind of accomplishment would warrant such distinction. Is it the creation of a literary world such as Ovid's own or is it, say, the establishment of a new political system for which, as the poet's contemporaries would have been keenly aware, the Emperor Augustus had started to claim immortality? The answer could be either, neither, or both. But whatever it may be, the *Naso deus* signature, if real, might amount to an irreverent challenge to the Emperor's singular claim to divine status.[29]

---

[27] On Ovid's authorial signatures, see McKeown (1989) 321–2; Ingleheart (2010) 2–4; and Thorson (2014) 39–68.

[28] For the poem's reflections on the exact distinctions between these three categories, see Feeney (1991) 188–249.

[29] For Ovid's engagement with Augustan propaganda and the Emperor's claim to divine status, see esp. Hinds (1987a); Feeney (1991) 188–249; Barchiesi (1997a); Feldherr (2010) 65–124; and Ingleheart (2015).

It is precisely as this kind of marker of tensions between *Naso deus* and *diuus Augustus* that our intext would fit in well with Ovid's other authorial signatures, which essentially write his literary autobiography. He rises from first-time *poeta* to *magister* of love, after which there is no way around him: he is *legendus*. Then comes the inevitable fall, perhaps due to his love poetry's lack of respect for Augustus' legislation against adultery.[30] Having been *parum prudens* in offending the powers-that-be, he ends up a mere *poeta* again, *tristis* this time, *laesus*, and *relegatus*. It is at the apex of this career, right before his rise to fame turns into a descent to exile, that, I suggest, Ovid has labelled himself *Naso deus*. Perhaps, then, we are dealing with a self-aware nod at the authorial persona's misplaced arrogance and hubristic ignorance of his career's imminent collapse. Befitting this interpretation, the passage containing our telestich describes a *De(li)us superbus* in the act of over-estimating himself. Almost immediately after issuing his challenge to Cupid (who, significantly, is Augustus' distant cousin), Apollo emerges as entirely inferior to his powerful opponent. Yet as Ovid notes at the end of the *primus amor Phoebi* episode (*Met.* 1.558–63), Apollo is himself associated with Augustan propaganda. Cupid's victory could therefore also signify the emperor's defeat at the hands of a love poet. Consequently, what I posit is ultimately just one intext spelling out *Naso deus* could be understood as Ovid's claim to a poetic kind of immortality that even exile, death, or the metaphorical death that *is* exile cannot undo. He would be attaining divine status at the precise moment when he is forced to leave Rome, or perhaps even because of it. He may have to abandon his home, but his signature will forever remain inscribed in a work of art that will stand the test of time.

This latter reading finds further support in another passage with which the *Metamorphoses'* authorial signature engages in intratextual dialogue, that is, the *sphragis* or 'seal' that addresses the reader in the author's voice at the poem's end:

> iamque opus exegi, quod nec Iouis ira nec ignis
> nec poterit ferrum nec edax abolere uetustas.
> cum uolet, illa dies, quae nil nisi corporis huius
> ius habet, incerti spatium mihi finiat aeui;
> parte tamen meliore mei super alta perennis
> astra ferar, nomenque erit indelebile nostrum;
> quaque patet domitis Romana potentia terris,
> ore legar populi, perque omnia saecula fama
> (siquid habent ueri uatum praesagia) uiuam.

Met. 15.871–9

---

[30] See Ov. *Trist.* 2.207 and 2.211–12 with Stroh (1979) and, more recently, Ingleheart (2010) 2–4.

Now I have completed a work that neither the wrath of Jupiter nor fire
nor iron will be able to devour nor the passage of hungry time.
Whenever it wants, let that day that has power over nothing except
this body put an end to my uncertain lifespan;
still, by means of my better part I will forever be borne above
the lofty stars, and my name will be inerasable;
and wherever Roman power expands in subjugated terrain,
I will continue to be read by the mouth of the people, and through all ages
(if the prophecies of the seers contain any truth) through fame I will live.

Ovid here essentially declares his work a funereal monument, a testimony to his life and writings that will allow him to live on after his death. He does so by alluding to Horace's *Ode* 3.30 (*opus exegi* = *exegi monumentum, Carm.* 3.30.1), where Horace labels his own oeuvre more lasting than bronze or the pyramids. Propertius is active in the background of the passage as well. In poem 3.2, the elegist praises his compositions as superior not just to the pyramids but also to the Tomb of Mausolus (*Mausolei . . . sepulcri*, 21). Propertius thereby suggests that his and his contemporaries' concern ultimately is not with just any grave marker, even if it is impressive like the pyramids. Rather, the poets are issuing a challenge specifically to the Mausoleum of Augustus, which had towered over the Campus Martius since 28 BCE and would have easily been Rome's most visible funereal monument at the time of the *Metamorphoses*' composition. Ovid had made this connection all-but explicit by alluding to Augustus' *Res gestae* (eventually put on display by the Mausoleum) in his at-length treatment of Caesar's apotheosis, right before he placed his literary seal on the end of the *Metamorphoses* (15.745–870).[31]

The *sphragis* is an epitaph, then, stamped retroactively onto the tombstone that is Ovid's book and sure to guarantee his survival forever. It is in this latter respect that literature is superior to the Emperor's preferred form of self-memorialization (note that Ovid, unlike the catasterized Caesar, flies *above* the stars, *super . . . astra*, at 15.871–5). Even the most resilient stone monuments and bronze inscriptions are subject to the elements and to the teeth of time, but poems may live forever. They are safe from the wrath of Jupiter (*ira Iouis*), and even from Augustus himself, for as long as we remain interested in them.

It is with the suggestion that the superiority of Ovid's monument over the Emperor's consists in its literary nature that we return to our authorial signature.

---

[31] For the *sphragis* in general, see Kranz (1961). Wickkiser (1999) connects the seal of the *Metamorphoses* to the rest of the poem. Feldherr (2010) 65–85 explores how Ovid's *sphragis* interacts with the Emperor, his family, the Forum of Augustus, as well as the Mausoleum and *Res gestae* (for the related chronological problems, see 118–19, n. 26). Peirano (2014) discusses *sphragides* as literary epitaphs (but does not touch on the *Metamorphoses*). Ingleheart (2015) has similar thoughts on *Trist.* 3.3, related both to poetic self-memorialization through alternative funereal monuments, and to competition with the Mausoleum of Augustus.

The *sphragis* links back to the opening of Book One where we discovered the *deus intext*, in that the 'better part' that will persist after Ovid's death (*parte... meliore*, 15.875) recalls the 'better nature' (*melior natura*, 1.21) that had created the universe at the poem's beginning. The fire (*ignis*, 15.871) of Jupiter/Augustus that Ovid need not fear had likewise featured in the demiurge's creation of the cosmos (*ignea... uis*, 1.26).[32] Accordingly, when Ovid says that his 'name will be inerasable' (*nomenque erit indelebile nostrum*, 876) and that he 'will continue to be read' (*legar*, 878), he might not just be challenging Augustus, whose name—he implies—*is* erasable,[33] and pointing to the survival of the *Metamorphoses* in a general sense. Rather, he may be thinking specifically of his hidden signature, especially since the poem nowhere else explicitly mentions his name. Unlike Ovid's and Augustus' physical remains or the Mausoleum, the intext will remain visible forever and will not fall apart with the passage of time, provided people will continue to read the *Metamorphoses*.

Consequently, it is not just the *sphragis* at the end of Book Fifteen that serves as an epitaph for the poet. Rather, our intext fulfils this function as well, even more so in that it literally inscribes the dead author's name on an object that is meant to remind the onlooker of his existence. In fact, to include the deceased's name in acrostic form in a funerary inscription was common in the ancient world,[34] and Ovid's intext might recall this custom (although there is, of course, a notable disparity in length between the writings on a gravestone and the *Metamorphoses*).

For a particularly striking parallel, we can turn briefly to the funerary epigram of one 'famous seller of goat skins' (*notus... uendenda pelle caprina*), written like the *Metamorphoses* in dactylic hexameters. This epitaph spells out the man's full name in acrostic format: L. Nerusius Mithres (*CIL* 9.4796, *CLE* 437). In the first line, Nerusius invites the reader to 'consider who I, free now from cares, used to be' (*liber nunc curis fuerim qui, respice lector*), with a possible play on the fact that he (like Ovid) has turned into a text (*liber*) to be studied. Nerusius then continues in the first person and highlights that he has built himself a monument to recall his accomplishments (compare Nerusius' *struxi mihi marmora* with Ovid's *opus exegi*). Significantly, he wants to make sure that the same *fama* that will guarantee Ovid's survival (*fama... uiuam*, *Met.* 15.878–9) will continue to speak of him as well (*me fama loquetur*). Nerusius here employs a common trope of ancient epitaphs, which frequently invite the passers-by to recite the tomb's inscription. If the words are written in the voice of the deceased, this act can be seen as

---

[32] See Wickkiser (1999) for these and further parallels. Among the final book's many additional closural nods back to the poem's beginning are Pythagoras' speech (*Met.* 15.60–478), which likewise treats the four elements that were central to the *deus*' cosmogony, and the incomplete acrostic *incip* within the *sphragis* itself (*Met.* 15.871–75), noted by Barchiesi (1997a) 195.

[33] Note that Ovid had remarked earlier on that even the name of Rome could be extinguished were one to assassinate Augustus (*sanguine Caesareo Romanum exstinguere nomen*, 1.201).

[34] See e.g. Garulli (2013) and Mairs (2013).

bringing the dead back to life temporarily.[35] In Nerusius' as in Ovid's case, this would mean that the onlookers who pronounce the words will (perhaps unbeknownst to themselves) read out the names of the deceased as well. Their signatures are, after all, hidden as intexts in their respective compositions. Ovid may well be alluding to this reality when he expresses his own hope, resembling that of Nerusius, that he 'will be read by the mouth of the people' (*ore legar populi*, 15.878).

It is in its close similarity to funerary inscriptions, then, that the Ovidian intext invites contemplation on the respective merits of such markers of a persons' memory as were common in the highest and the lowest strata of Roman society. It asks the reader to compare the monument that is the *Metamorphoses* to a variety of alternatives ranging from the Mausoleum of Augustus to an acrostic gravestone like Nerusius'. Of course, contrary to Ovid's expectations, the Mausoleum of Augustus has been much reduced by the *edax uetustas*, but it still stands. And as if to complicate the point even further, Nerusius' tombstone was lost in the nineteenth century after close to two millennia of preservation (Bücheler reports in *CLE* that it 'appears to have perished', *uidetur periisse*), yet we nevertheless still know what it said.

It is likewise ironic (and probably intentionally so) that Ovid relies for his name's survival precisely on that one form of wordplay that requires written words to appear on a physical object. The rest of the poem could be enjoyed aurally or in any other medium, but for the authorial signature to be meaningful the text needs to exist on an item that is subject to decay. Ovid might be calling attention to this complicating factor precisely by inviting comparisons between pieces of literature and physical monuments. He could also be highlighting a possible solution in noting that his name will survive 'wherever Roman power expands in subjugated terrain' (*quaque patet domitis Romana potentia terris*, 15.877). He seems to envision countless reproductions ensuring that his poem— along with the hidden signature and unlike most actual funerary monuments— will outlast the onslaught of the elements. The steady transmission and continued recopying of texts across both time and space guarantees their survival in an almost disembodied state, nearly independent from any individual scroll (*nearly*, as is attested by the many texts that we did lose to the teeth of time). Ovid nods to this ethereal quality of literature but still has to acknowledge that even his personal form of immortality depends on his fellow Romans continuing to find new audiences for his work. If they stop caring (and reproducing his work), he may be forgotten.

If, then, we envision our Ovidian intext in this latter manner as an epitaph inviting contemplation of the book 'on' which it was written, it might actually

---

[35] On the dynamics inherent in reading funerary inscriptions out loud, see e.g. Svenbro (1988); Feldherr (2000); and Milnor (2014) 60–77.

make better sense to conceive of it not as an intext, but as a paratext. Paratexts are features that are in some sense external to a work, though still connected to it. They provide access to the text from their liminal status on its border.[36] Examples include an *incipit* at a book's beginning or a *sphragis* at its end. Our intext resembles such features—as do the no doubt countless, still undiscovered or undiscussed acrostics and telestichs that remain hidden in the *Metamorphoses*—in that it serves to contain or 'embrace' the book. If we are right to read *Naso* and *deus* together, then Ovid's signature would in fact enclose the text not just on one, but on two sides. Like an ancient *index*, *titulus*, or similar marker of a scroll's contents, it would also clarify not just the identity of the poem's author (*Naso*) but also, to a lesser extent, its content (*deus*). The intext may in this respect actually have a stronger claim to the title *sphragis* than the author's closural remarks so labelled by modern critics.[37] After all, the imprint of a signet ring or gem in wax is meant to attest to the identity of a text's author. Yet what we label a 'seal', that is, sections of text added to a poem at its beginning or end and stating or hinting at the author's name, is easily forged. By contrast, Ovid's hidden signature has actually stamped his name on the text. Unlike a physical label, it cannot rip off. And like a water mark, it is there for anyone to discover who knows what to look for, and for the author to prove, should the need arise, that the poem is his own.

Finally, but by no means least significantly, the paratext that is Ovid's obscured signature points to the *Metamorphoses'* place in the long tradition of hidden acrostics and telestichs in Greek and Roman poetry with which I began this discussion. It tells the reader, as it were, which shelf the poem belongs on. It goes with Virgil, Ennius, Nicander, Aratus, and even Homer, who perhaps unwittingly included an acrostic in his *Iliad* as well. It is precisely this latter comparison to an oral poem that throws the Ovidian signature's varied functions into sharpest relief. As I have intended to show, the intext encourages the reader to confront the precise nature of the *Metamorphoses'* materiality. The text is a scroll to unfold that uses the physical appearance of lines on the page as a metaphor for the creation of the universe it depicts. It is also a book that we, like Cupid in the *primus amor Phoebi* passage, can turn over, revisit, and re-examine for hidden intexts we may have missed on our first read. The original audiences of Homeric poetry would not have had this luxury.

Furthermore, the authorial marker written onto the text like a vase-painter's signature onto a physical artefact, or an acrostic on a gravestone, captures the poet at the very moment of being turned away from Rome, and yet of achieving divine status through the greatness of his composition. He is caught in transition, forever

---

[36] See e.g. Genette (1997), who more strictly speaking would have considered what I describe a 'peritext'; Jansen (2014b); and Peirano (2014).

[37] Compare e.g. Courtney (1990) 7–9 and Damschen (2004) 91–3.

at the margin of the text. In one of the *Metamorphoses*' so far undiscovered transformations, he has literally been turned into letters on the page.

In this respect, what I submit are an acrostic and a telestich combined into a single intext spelling out *Naso deus* invites us to reflect on the precise nature of Ovid's divinity or immortality. Even though the particular copy of the *Metamorphoses* that we are holding may be fraying at the edges and the ink containing the hidden words may be fading, the poem and its author's signature will probably still outlive us. Yet whether the *Naso deus* acrostic-*cum*-telestich will ultimately survive the Mausoleum of Augustus—or, for that matter, the memory of the *princeps* who relegated Ovid to the Black Sea—is far more doubtful. More likely, the two men will forever remain trapped in conversation, the greatness of the one very much depending on the accomplishments of the other.

To return, in closing, to the lines containing the telestich *Naso* (1.452–5), it is worth noting that they portray the god Cupid at a moment where he has just bent his bow (or has bent the book to use it *as* a bow) and is getting ready to let the metapoetic arrow fly. This is apt, since it is here, as I noted above, that the truly Ovidian part of the *Metamorphoses* is about to begin. But I also hope that the discovery of a meaningful telestich, a kind of intext that receives much less attention than the acrostic, will constitute a starting shot for modern-day Isidor Hilbergs to begin the serious exploration of hidden words at line end, and to examine how they contribute to the interpretation of Latin poetry.

Acknowledgements

The text of Ovid 's *Metamorphoses* is based on Tarrant (2004). Quotations from Aratus are taken from Kidd (1997). Virgil's *Aeneid* is cited according to Mynors (1969). In addition to the secondary literature cited throughout, my readings of each Ovidian passage rely on the commentaries of Bömer (1969) and (1986); Anderson (1997); Barchiesi and Koch (2005); and Hardie (2015b). All translations are my own. My sincere thanks go to the editors of this volume for including my contribution in their collection and for their many helpful comments. I am grateful as well to Erin M. Hanses for critiquing several drafts; to Joseph A. Howley for his bibliographical advice; and to the anonymous referees for useful suggestions that much improved this paper.

PART III

TRANSFORMATIONS OF
THE *METAMORPHOSES*

7

Latent Transformations

Reshaping the *Metamorphoses*

Monika Asztalos

In Ovid's stories one finds metamorphoses where the outward appearance is transformed while the inner being remains the same. In the poetic language of the *Metamorphoses* we sometimes find the reverse: when an expression is repeated, the appearance (word) is the same while the inner being (meaning) is not. But this is not spelled out by the poet; the readers have to participate and elicit what is hidden below the surface of the text. If they do not expect there to be more than meets the eye, they may find the repetitions offensive to good taste, the hallmark of a poet like Ovid. And if they happen to be textual critics, they may even judge them inauthentic.

Given that the originals of ancient literary works are all lost, readers are free to question the authenticity of any given passage. Editors sometimes exert that right with dramatic results: in modern critical editions passages deemed inauthentic, interpolations, are placed within square brackets.[1] This particular form of criticism is practised more often in poetry than in prose, and more often in some poets than in others. A larger number of lines have been bracketed in the *Metamorphoses* than in the *Aeneid*. To some extent this may be due to the transmission of the works, as Virgil's poems have been preserved in some manuscripts from late antiquity, and the text has remained relatively stable, but Ovid's *Metamorphoses* has suffered a different fate: no complete copy has survived from before the 11th century.[2] Still, the state of the transmission is only one factor that may determine to what extent the *Metamorphoses* is interpolated. The most important is the critic's expectations: it is in fact impossible to perform any kind of critical activity on any text without entertaining some idea about the kind of text one can expect from its author. So, what expectations have been determinative in the case of the *Metamorphoses*? Nicolaas Heinsius, the towering critic who published textual comments on the *Metamorphoses* in 1652, was particularly

---

[1] An interpolation is a part of a text that was not composed by the author but has, for one reason or another, found its way into the manuscript tradition.

[2] The complex textual tradition of the *Metamorphoses* has been elucidated by Tarrant (1983), and in his Oxford Classical Texts edition (2004). See Wahlsten Böckerman in this volume.

Monika Asztalos, *Latent Transformations: Reshaping the* Metamorphoses In: *Metamorphic Readings: Transformation, Language, and Gender in the Interpretation of Ovid's* Metamorphoses. Edited by: Alison Sharrock, Daniel Möller, and Mats Malm, Oxford University Press (2020). © Oxford University Press.
DOI: 10.1093/oso/9780198864066.003.0008

sensitive to what he considered offensive repetitions of words or superfluous pieces of information and questioned the authenticity of a number of lines on such grounds. Richard Tarrant, editor of the most recent OCT edition of the text, who has paid homage to his predecessor in a number of articles,[3] expects the same qualities in a text by Ovid: clarity, elegance and, in particular, economy of means. When those qualities seem to be lacking, the assumption is that early readers collaborated or competed with the poet by adding lines to the poem.[4] Adding lines, placing lines within square brackets, or removing brackets placed around a passage by previous editors are activities that contribute to a continual reshaping of the text of the *Metamorphoses*.

Below I will discuss three cases in which a repetition of a word or words provides a key to the interpretation of the story told. The first and third cases have been discussed in detail by critics questioning the authenticity of lines that contain repetitions. I will argue that repetition of words does not necessarily imply repetition of information but may, paradoxically perhaps, be the vehicle of a metamorphosis that is subtly hinted at by the poet. At the end of this contribution some reflections will be offered on the function of such latent transformations.

Echo Hiding in the Woods

My first case is the end of the story about the nymph Echo.[5]

> Spreta **latet siluis** pudibundaque frondibus ora
> protegit et solis ex illo uiuit in antris.
> Sed tamen haeret amor crescitque dolore repulsae;   395
> attenuant uigiles corpus miserabile curae
> adducitque cutem macies et in aera sucus
> corporis omnis abit. uox tantum atque ossa supersunt:
> uox manet; ossa ferunt lapidis traxisse figuram.
> [inde **latet siluis** nulloque in monte uidetur,   400
> omnibus auditur; sonus est qui uiuit in illa.]
>
> *Met.* 3.393–401

Having been rejected **she hides among the trees**; in her shame she covers her face with foliage, and from that time on she lives in unfrequented hollows.
But her love persists and grows with the pain of the rebuff. Her cares leave her no peace and reduce her wretched body. Wasting contracts her skin, and all bodily moisture disappears into the air. Only her voice and bones are left: her voice remains; they say that her bones have taken on the shape of stone.[6]

---

[3] Tarrant (1989a), (1999).   [4] See Tarrant (1989b) 158. See also Tarrant (1987).
[5] The text is as Tarrant (2004). I have added emphasis to the repetitions discussed.
[6] All translations are mine. Translations given after Tarrant's text are based on his interpretation. Lines bracketed by him are therefore not translated. At the end of my discussion of each of the three

When we first meet Echo, she is still a body, not merely a voice: *corpus adhuc Echo, non uox erat* (359). We are then told that Juno would often catch nymphs lying under her own Jupiter on a mountain (*sub Ioue saepe suo nymphas in monte iacentes*), but Echo detained her in conversation so as to allow her friends to get away. When Juno discovered her ruse she punished Echo with the particular speech impediment whereby she is bound to repeat mechanically the end of what a person within earshot has just uttered, something that leads to utter humiliation when that other person happens to be Narcissus, the object of her desire.[7] This is why she has become *resonabilis* (358, a word apparently coined for the occasion), resonant Echo.

Heinsius comments on 3.401: '... unless you think that this and the preceding lines should be removed. For what would be the point of repeating *Inde latet siluis*, when he had shortly before said *Spreta latet siluis*?'[8] In a review of Anderson's Teubner edition of *Metamorphoses* that appeared in 1977, Tarrant follows in Heinsius' footsteps and argues against the authenticity of the two lines,[9] which he would later bracket in his own Oxford Classical Texts edition. His first objection is: 'Lines 400–401 were first bracketed by Heinsius, followed not only by Merkel but also by several editors of more moderate tendencies.... Their most obvious weakness is the lame repetition, made worse by *inde*, of *latet siluis* from 393; this is not defended by the argument that between 393 and 401 Echo changes from a nymph to a voice: *latet siluis* is entirely apt for a person, quite unlikely for a disembodied voice.' But, as stated above, repetition of words does not necessarily imply repetition of meaning. In fact, our passage is immediately preceded by such a repetition in the exchange of words between Narcissus and Echo at 3.380 and 391–2:

> N. 'ecquis adest?' E. 'adest'.
> N. 'ante emoriar quam sit tibi copia nostri.' / E. 'Sit tibi copia nostri!'

A translation will reveal that there is a repetition of words without a repetition of information:

> N. 'Is there anyone there?' E. 'There is'.
> N. 'I would rather die than let you have me!' E. 'I wish you would have me!'

cases I give the Latin text as I think it should be established and a translation based on my own understanding of that text.

---

[7] *Met.* 3.356–69.

[8] [...] nisi hunc et praecedentem uersos tollendos censes. nam quid opus erat repeti *Inde latet siluis*, cum paullo ante dixisset *Spreta latet siluis*.

[9] Tarrant (1982) 356–7. In his commentary on *Metamorphoses* 3 (2006), based on Tarrant's edition, Barchiesi is non-committal with respect to the authenticity of 400–1 and does not offer any new arguments *pro* or *contra*.

Through this dialogue, only part of which is given here, Ovid has prepared the reader for a kind of wordplay that is particularly apposite in a story about Echo. For through the repetition of *latet siluis* Ovid produces an echo, playing with two of the different senses of the verb *latere*, 'to hide' and 'to be invisible'.[10] 'Having been rejected, she hides among the trees' (393), and 'From this point on she is invisible among the trees' (400).

Tarrant also objects that *omnibus auditur* can be taken in two ways: either 'she is heard on all of them' (*omnibus* sc. *in montibus*) or 'she is heard by all' (*omnibus* sc. *hominibus*) and that in either case, the text 'explicitly treats Echo as a universal phenomenon, whereas the rest of Ovid's account neatly evades the awkwardness of making a single nymph responsible for echoes in all parts of the world'.[11] I would argue that the text is not in need of bracketing but of emendation. I propose reading *nullique* for *nulloque* and *illo* for *illa*: *nullique in monte uidetur, omnibus auditur, sonus est qui uiuit in illo*, 'she cannot be seen by anyone on the mountain but she can be heard by all; she is a sound that lives on it'. It is almost inevitable, given what happens when texts are copied, that *nullique* should be replaced by *nulloque* before *in monte*. Ovid is elegantly connecting the end of the Echo-episode with its beginning: *in monte* at 363 is picked up by *in monte* at line 400, *corpus adhuc... non uox erat* at 359 is a stage on the way to the completion of the metamorphosis at 401, *sonus est*. In the beginning of the story we meet Echo living on a mountain with her fellow nymphs; we leave her still living on that mountain but now she is merely a sound.

After each *latet siluis* a clarification of the actual sense in which it is to be taken is made with the connective *-que* after the first word: *pudibundaque frondibus ora protegit* after the first *latet siluis* and *nullique in monte uidetur, omnibus auditur* after the second. The meaning 'she hides among the trees' is thus explicated by 'in her shame she covers her face with foliage'; the meaning 'she is invisible among the trees' by 'she cannot be seen by anyone, although she can be heard by all'. After each clarification, information is given about her habitat: when she hides among the trees she lives in unfrequented hollows; when she is invisible among the trees she lives on the mountain where we found her in the beginning of the story.

To return to Heinsius' rhetorical question: what is the point of repeating *Inde latet siluis*, when he had shortly before said *Spreta latet siluis*? The point, I would say, is that the second *latet siluis* is an echo of the first. It is the perfect conclusion to a metamorphosis intended to explain how Echo became an echo. With the conjectures proposed Ovid is still neatly evading the awkwardness of making Echo responsible for all the echoes in the world. Furthermore, *sonus est* connects the end with *resonabilis* in the beginning and should not be removed from the text. As for Tarrant's objection that '*latet siluis* is entirely apt for a person, quite unlikely for a disembodied voice', the objection is only valid if one assumes that the verb *latere* is used in the same sense ('to hide') on both occasions, which it is clearly not.

[10] *OLD* 1 and 3.   [11] Tarrant (1982) 356.

This is not a lame repetition but a metamorphosis of meaning that adds poignancy to the conclusion of the story.

My text and translation of lines 393–401 is as follows.[12]

> Spreta **latet siluis** pudibundaque frondibus ora
> protegit et solis ex illo uiuit in antris.
> sed tamen haeret amor crescitque dolore repulsae;   395
> attenuant uigiles corpus miserabile curae
> adducitque cutem macies et in aera sucus
> corporis omnis abit. uox tantum atque ossa supersunt:
> uox manet; ossa ferunt lapidis traxisse figuram.
> inde **latet siluis** nullique in monte uidetur,   400
> omnibus auditur; sonus est qui uiuit in illo.

Having been rejected **she hides among the trees**; in her shame she covers her face with foliage, and from that time on she lives in unfrequented hollows.

But her love persists and grows with the pain of the rebuff. Her cares leave her no peace and reduce her wretched body. Wasting contracts her skin, and all bodily moisture disappears into the air. Only her voice and bones are left: her voice remains; they say that her bones have taken on the shape of stone.

From then on **she is invisible among the trees**; she cannot be seen by anyone on the mountain although she can be heard by all: she is the sound that lives on it.

Pygmalion's Art

Tarrant's edition is as follows:

> interea niueum mira feliciter arte
> sculpsit ebur formamque dedit, qua femina nasci
> nulla potest, operisque sui concepit amorem.
> uirginis est uerae facies, quam uiuere credas   250
> et, si non obstet reuerentia, uelle moueri;
> **ars** adeo latet **arte** sua. miratur et haurit
> pectore Pygmalion simulati corporis ignes.
> saepe manus operi temptantes admouet, an sit
> corpus an illud ebur, nec adhuc ebur esse fatetur,   255
> [oscula dat reddique putat loquiturque tenetque]
> sed credit tactis digitos insidere membris
> et metuit pressos ueniat ne liuor in artus.
>
> *Met.* 10.247–58

---

[12] I have removed the brackets and substituted *nullique* for *nulloque* and *illo* for *illa*.

In this state of mind he successfully sculpted white ivory with an awe-inspiring artistic skill and gave it a beauty that no woman can possess by nature, and he fell in love with his own work. The outward appearance was that of a true virgin. One could have believed that she was alive and that she would wish to be touched if only her reverence[13] did not stand in her way. **To that extent is artificiality hidden through its own artistic skill.** Pygmalion stands in awe and experiences to the full a passion for what looks like a body. Often he brings his hands into contact with his work, examining if it is a body or ivory and does not yet admit it is ivory[14] but he believes that his fingers are sinking into the parts he has touched but fears that a bruise might appear on the limbs he has pressed.

The sculptor Pygmalion had become disillusioned about women. The Cyprian Propoetides had had the temerity to deny that Venus is a goddess, and when they were reported to prostitute themselves (the first to do such a thing) and Shame[15] abandoned them and they lost the ability to blush, Venus in anger turned them into stone. Disappointed that nature gave females so many moral flaws, Pygmalion decided to live unmarried (*sine coniuge*) and without a woman sharing his bed (*thalamique diu consorte carebat*). In this state of mind, he successfully sculpted white ivory with an awe-inspiring artistic skill (*mira arte*) and gave it a beauty that no woman can possess by nature. The outward appearance was that of a true virgin. One could have believed that she was alive and that she would wish to be moved if only her reverence (towards the personified *Pudor*, Shame) did not stand in her way. The sculptor himself is transformed from creator into viewer, standing in awe before his own creation. Filled with love for it he cannot believe that it is not real.

Then follows one of the most well-known lines in the entire poem: *ars adeo latet arte* (10.252). In the second occurrence of the word *ars* its meaning has been transformed: 'to that extent is the artificiality hidden through artistic skill'. There is, however, a textual problem: in the manuscripts *arte* is followed by the reflexive pronoun *sua*. What the transmitted text actually says is: 'to such an extent is artificiality hidden through its own artistic skill', *sua* referring implausibly to the artificiality. I propose the conjecture *suam* for *sua* and translate: 'to that extent is artificiality hidden through artistic skill. He stands in awe before his own.' In the lost original, a final *m* in *suam* could easily have been dropped before the *m* of *miratur*, a kind of error which occurs very often in manuscripts. If we read *ars adeo latet arte. suam miratur et haurit / pectore Pygmalion simulati corporis ignes*, there is an effective caesura *kata triton trochaion* after *arte*, which makes *suam*

---

[13] I.e., towards *Pudor*, the goddess Shame. See note 15.

[14] Or: and does not accept as true that it is still ivory.

[15] I would spell the Latin *pudor* with the capital *P* and take the text to mean that the goddess *Pudor* left the women in disgust. This would explain *reuerentia* at 251.

quite emphatic, as it should be.[16] Furthermore, *suam* provides a fitting direct complement to *miratur*. The first half-line is a statement about what artistic skill achieves (perhaps artistic skill in general, not necessarily Pygmalion's skill), that the artificiality of a work is hidden, while the second describes how Pygmalion, transformed from artistic creator to viewer, reacts to his own—but his own what? If we read *suam* sc. *artem*, he stands in awe before his own artistic skill or before his own work of art, if we take *ars* in yet another sense. Given the expression *mira arte* at line 247 one would assume that *artem* in one of the two senses is to be understood in *suam miratur*. But in whichever way it is taken, the reflexive *suam* is reported speech, and it is possible that the subject Pygmalion, who has by now fallen passionately in love, would wish to use the word *puellam* but does not dare to. We, the readers, are uncertain, but our uncertainty is paralleled by Pygmalion's uncertainty regarding what it is that he stands before and how he should label it, an uncertainty that is reflected also in the poetic language which itself has a wavering, unstable quality with multiple mirror effects.

What follows is a section in which the sculptor tries in vain to establish whether his work of art is just that, a work of art, or a true virgin (254–69). He does so by a number of tests, and each time he is unable to free himself from the impression that the virgin is real. Tarrant raises two objections to line 256: he sees in it 'a jumble of unrelated actions' and finds it 'highly unlikely that at an early stage of his courtship of the statue the timid lover that Ovid presents would confidently think that his kisses were being returned'.[17] But the actions are considered unrelated only because *tenet* is taken in the sense of 'to hold someone physically'. If taken in the sense of 'to hold the attention of someone',[18] the actions are related and reciprocal. The verbs *loquitur* and *tenet* are tied together formally by *-que*, and the point is that as Pygmalion speaks, the statue does not answer but looks attentive as if it could hear him. This is how the sculptor had made her. Pygmalion is presented not as a man courting the statue but as an artist who has the impression that his own work of art has been metamorphosed into nature and applies different tests to verify or falsify that impression, not necessarily in a certain order but repeatedly, *saepe* (254). He cannot convince himself that it is a statue: *nec adhuc ebur esse fatetur*; which I hesitate whether to translate 'does not accept as true that it is still ivory' or 'still (i.e. in spite of his repeated tests) does not accept as true that it is ivory'.[19] Perhaps the ambiguity is intended.

---

[16] One may compare the structure of the line with *Met.* 1.72, where the same caesura occurs before a form of *suus*, making the pronoun emphatically refer to what follows: *neu regio foret ulla suis animalibus orba.*

[17] Tarrant (2016) 101–2. Reed (2013) is non-committal and suggests that if the line is not an interpolation it should perhaps be moved to follow line 258.

[18] This is sense 22a in *Oxford Latin Dictionary*.

[19] I disagree with Tarrant's translation 'does not yet admit it is ivory' at line 255, since it implies that Pygmalion at some point in the future will admit it is ivory, something that he never does.

Pygmalion does not reach certainty but places the statue tenderly on a bed of down and calls it his bed-partner (*tori sociam*, which picks up *thalami consorte* at 246), and at the festival in honour of Venus he asks: *Sit coniunx, opto* (275), 'Let her be my wife, that is my wish' (*coniunx*, picking up *coniuge* at 245). But he is uncertain about how to refer to her: he does not have the temerity (*non ausus*) to say '*eburnea uirgo*' ('the virgin made of ivory'). Here *ausus* reflects *ausae* at line 238: the Propoetides had the temerity to deny that Venus is a goddess. Pygmalion does not have the temerity to assert that the sculpture is not a real virgin; presumably that would be a lack of reverence towards the goddess who had inspired in him such a passion. He settles hesitatingly (*timide*) for '*similis mea... eburnae*' ('my own... who resembles one made of ivory'). Not until line 280 do we find the words of Latin love poetry that the lover must have longed to utter: *ut rediit, simulacra suae petit ille puellae*: 'when he returned, he went straight away to the image of his own girl'. Until that moment, he has avoided the temptation to apply the expression *mea puella* to her. There is thus a hesitation on Pygmalion's part about what to call her: at 252 we have only *suam* (provided my conjecture is right); at 276 only *mea*; at 259–60 he brings gifts usually appreciated by girls (*puellis*) to her (*illi*), which is Ovid's way of showing that he treats her as his *puella* although the word is not used. At last he thinks of her as his own *puella*.

The testing situation is mirrored at 280–8, when Pygmalion has returned home from the festival. He then kisses the statue once and again (*iterum* 282) and touches her again and again (*rursus... rursusque* 288), but again he is in doubt, now hesitant to accept as true that it is a real virgin. The order of tests described in the first instance, feeling her body with his hands and kissing her, is now mirrored in that he first kisses her and then feels her body with his hands.[20] The first thing that she does upon receiving sensation is to feel his kisses and blush. The metamorphoses into stone of the Propoetides, abandoned by Shame and having lost the ability to blush, is now perfectly mirrored by the metamorphoses of a rigid material into a blushing young woman.

My text and translation of lines 252–8 is as follows:[21]

> ars adeo latet arte. suam miratur et haurit
> pectore Pygmalion simulati corporis ignes.
> saepe manus operi temptantes admouet, an sit
> corpus an illud ebur, nec adhuc ebur esse fatetur,　　　　255
> oscula dat reddique putat loquiturque tenetque
> et credit tactis digitos insidere membris
> et metuit pressos ueniat ne liuor in artus.

[20] The order is also an argument that line 256 is authentic.
[21] I have put a full stop after *arte* and substituted *suam* for *sua* at line 252; I have also removed the brackets around lines 256 and restored the transmitted *et* for which Tarrant substitutes *sed* at the beginning of line 257.

To that extent is artificiality hidden through artistic skill. Pygmalion stands in awe
before his own __ , and experiences to the full a passion for what looks like a body.
Often he brings his hands into contact with his work, examining if it is a body or ivory
and still does not accept as true that it is ivory /and does not accept as true that it is
still ivory.

He kisses it and it seems to him that his kisses are returned, he speaks to it and holds its
attention, he believes that his fingers are sinking into the parts he has touched and fears
that a bruise might appear on the limbs he has pressed.

The Aeginetan Plague

The third case concerns the devastating plague on the Island Oenopia having been
renamed Aegina. Tarrant's edition is as follows (*Met.* 7.523–32, 554–5, 561–2,
572–6, 615–8):

Dira lues ira populis Iunonis iniquae
incidit exosae dictas a paelice terras.
[dum uisum mortale malum tantaeque **latebat**   525
causa nocens cladis, pugnatum est arte medendi;
exitium superabat opem, quae uicta iacebat.]
principio caelum spissa caligine terras
pressit et ignauos inclusit nubibus aestus,
dumque quater iunctis expleuit cornibus orbem   530
luna, quater plenum tenuata retexuit orbem,
letiferis calidi spirarunt aestibus Austri.

  · · · · · ·

uiscera torrentur primo flammaeque **latentis**
indicium rubor est et ductus anhelitus aegre;   555

  · · · · · ·

nec moderator adest inque ipsos saeua medentes   561
erumpit clades obsuntque auctoribus artes;

  · · · · · ·

tantaque sunt miseris inuisi taedia lecti,
prosiliunt aut, si prohibent consistere uires,
corpora deuoluunt in humum fugiuntque Penates
quisque suos, sua cuique domus funesta uidetur.   575
[et, quia **causa latet**, locus est in crimine paruus.]

  · · · · · ·

'Iuppiter o ! ' dixi 'si te non falsa loquuntur   615
dicta sub amplexus Aeginae Asopidos isse
nec te, magne pater, nostri pudet esse parentem,
aut mihi redde meos, aut me quoque conde sepulchro.'

A dreadful plague befell the population as a result of the wrath of resentful Juno who detested the fact that the region had been named after a mistress.

In the beginning heaven weighed down the region with a dense darkness and clouds enclosing oppressive waves of heat, and while the thinned moon completed its circle by joining its horns and lessened it again four times, hot south winds breathed with deadly exhalations.

.   .   .   .

First the inwards are roasted. A sign of the hidden flame is redness and difficulty in breathing.

.   .   .   .

No moderator is at hand with assistance; the savage cause of ruin broke out against the medical men themselves, and the expertise harmed the experts.

.   .   .   .

And the miserable people are so disgusted with their own sickbeds that they jump out of them or if they do not have force enough to get up, they roll down onto the floor, and everyone runs away from his own home. Everyone thinks that his own home is deadly.

.   .   .   .

'O Jupiter,' I said, 'if it is true what they say, that you embraced Asopos' daughter Aegina, and if you are not ashamed to be my father, give my dear ones back to me or place me as well in the grave.'

In an episode in *Metamorphoses* 6, Arachne enters into a weaving competition with Athena. The motives she chooses are the metamorphoses of Jupiter in seducing women, one of them being Aegina, whom Jupiter had approached and conquered in the shape of fire (6.113). At 7.474 we learn that Aeacus, king of the island Oenopia, had renamed the island after his mother, Aegina. The distinction conferred upon Aegina, a *paelex* (mistress) in the eyes of Juno, was bound to provoke the wrath of the goddess, and she took her revenge by sending a plague that wiped out the entire population of the island except Aeacus and his three sons. Aeacus turned to Jupiter with a prayer that he should either let him die or give him his men back (615–8). He refers to a rumour saying that he is the result of a love affair between the god and the nymph Aegina. It is a tactful hint to Jupiter that he ought to turn his attention to what is happening in Aegina and stop his jealous and revengeful spouse—unless of course he is ashamed of his progeny and would be happy to see Aeacus and his family wiped out of existence. Jupiter repairs the damage by transforming hard-working ants on the island into strong and dutiful soldiers that are named Myrmidons. Tarrant argues against the authenticity of 7.525–7,[22] later bracketed in his own Oxford Classical Texts edition. Conte follows him in this.[23] I will deal with their objections below.

---

[22] Tarrant (1982) 357–8.   [23] Conte (2013) 49.

Met. 7.523–613 is Ovid's version of a narrative about a historic plague. The topos originates in Thucydides, Book 2, and enters Latin didactic poetry with Lucretius' description of a plague in Athens at the very end of his *De Rerum Natura*. Virgil includes a description of another historical plague in *Georgics* 3. Ovid's contribution to this topic has great similarities with those of his Roman predecessors. But this is not to say that the entire passage in the *Metamorphoses* is a description of the kind that one finds in *DRN* or *Georgics*.

Ovid immediately strikes an epic chord with *ira Iunonis* and *Iunonis iniquae*. Cf. *Iunonis ob iram* in *Aen.* 1.4 and *Iunonis iniquae* at the same position in *Aen.* 8.292. Lines 523–7 couch the story of the plague in an epic setting. The *malum* is not the evil (i.e., plague) but the cause of the evil,[24] and in this sense the word can stand for a person or god[25] and be translated 'enemy'. As long as the medical men thought they were dealing with a mortal enemy, *mortale malum*, not realizing that they were up against the wrath of an unforgiving goddess, they fought in vain. Their art was utterly defeated, *uicta iacebat*. Furthermore, the *causa nocens* in this particular epic setting is the injurious motive of Juno. One may recall *Musa, mihi causas memora*, 'Muse, tell me of the motives', of *Aen.* 1.8. And just like *malum*, the word *clades* can be used for someone who is the cause of ruin of a people.[26] So the *tantaeque causa nocens cladis* is the injurious motive of so great a cause of ruin, namely, Juno.

Tarrant, however, following Bömer, takes *malum* to refer to the disease, which inevitably leads to difficulties: 'The normal meaning of *mortale malum* would be "an evil with human causes, within human capability" (hardly "malum originibus naturalibus ortum", which is what it must mean here, in Bömer's words); *causa nocens* is even more peculiar.' Conte goes even further: '*causa nocens cladis* seems strange: *causa nocens* would be sufficient, just as *causa cladis* would be acceptable, but the group of three words has something badly amalgamated, and unpleasantly superfluous about it'. Against this I would say that if *causa cladis* meant 'the cause of the disease', the adjective *nocens* would indeed be superfluous. But its presence actually helps the reader to understand that the text is not about an impersonal cause but about the injurious motive of Juno, who turned out to be the bane of Aeacus when he lost all his men and with them the resources that gave him his power as an ally of the Athenians. Finally, Tarrant objects: '*quae uicta iacebat* is (as Heinsius saw) mere filler'. But in the epic setting this is the appropriate ending to a brief (very brief) story: it shows the inevitable outcome of a battle against a wrathful goddess.

Tarrant's main objection to *Met.* 7.525–7 is: 'where is the contrast implied by *dum uisum* . . . ? This only makes sense if at some point the true cause of the plague is discovered, which never happens in Ovid's narrative.' However, the story is not

---

[24] See *OLD* s.v. *malum* 7.   [25] *OLD* 7c.
[26] E.g. in *Aen.* 6.843: *duo fulmina belli, Scipiadas, cladem Libyae.*

concerned with discovery. Aeacus has explicitly told Cephalus that the wrath of Juno is behind the plague. Given that *causa nocens* refers to the injurious motive of Juno, to wipe out Aeacus' resources, the best way to understand *latebat* at line 525 is 'was hidden'. We know Juno from *Aen.* 1.36–7 as one whose feelings are hidden: *Iuno aeternum seruans sub pectore uulnus haec secum,* 'Juno forever preserving her wound inside said to herself...', and after her bitter monologue we read: *Talia flammato secum dea corde uolutans* (50), 'the goddess, turning over such thoughts in her inflamed heart'. At *Met.* 7.554–5, there is surely a reference to Juno's anger: *flammaeque latentis indicium rubor est,* 'the redness (of the sick people) is a sign of the hidden flame'. Shortly afterwards, at 561–2, we learn that 'no moderator was at hand with assistance; the savage cause of ruin broke out against the medical men themselves, and the expertise harmed the experts' (*nec moderator adest inque ipsos saeua medentes / erumpit clades obsuntque auctoribus artes*). The adjective *saeua* is characteristic of Juno: one may think of her *saeui dolores* ('savage pains') at *Aen.* 1.25. The verb *erumpo* is also epic: it is used in *Aen.* 1.579–81 when Achates and Aeneas long to break out from the cloud that had been their place of hiding, and in *Aen.* 10.890 and 11.609 when an aggressor breaks out from a distant place.

There is a clear sequence of events. While Juno's motives were still hidden, one fought with the weapons of medicine. To begin with, the innards of the patients are roasted and their bodies do not lose their heat by lying on the ground, but, on the contrary, the ground becomes hot below them (7.554–60). Juno tends to send punishments that correspond to the crimes, so if Jupiter seduced Aegina in the form of a fire, the inhabitants of the island named after her are aptly destroyed by a fire consuming them from the inside. But Juno is also consumed by a flame, and a sign of it is the redness of the sick and their difficulties in breathing. When savage Juno breaks out against the medical men, they give up. It is not far-fetched to see in the *moderator*, 'moderator' or 'ruler', at *Met.* 7.561 Jupiter himself, who often needs to be reminded that things are going very wrong because of his wife. He is the one who in the nick of time prevents Juno from continuing her warfare against the Trojans (12.791–842) and who was not there to assist his son Aeacus until his attention was turned to his wife's destructive behaviour.

Tarrant objects that lines 525–7 'ineptly anticipate 561–7 by introducing futile attempts at medical treatment before the plague has even begun'. This overlooks Aeacus' habits as a narrator. He enters the stage as an old slow-moving man (*tardus grauitate senili,* 7.478), a rambling narrator who likes to announce the outcome of a story before telling it. He does so at the very beginning of his story: *flebile principium melior fortuna secuta est; / hanc utinam possem uobis memorare sine illo! / ordine nunc repetam, neu longa ambage morer uos, / ossa cinisque iacent memori quos mente requiris* ('A lamentable beginning was followed by a better fate; would that I could tell you about the latter omitting the former! Now I shall go back and tell you what happened in the order of events, and so as not to detain you by wandering off in different directions: the men that you expect to find are dead, reduced to bones and ashes', *Met.* 7.418–21). In spite of his good intentions, he interrupts himself with a complaint: *et quota pars illi rerum periere mearum!* ('And how small a part of the things I lost do they not represent!').[27] At lines 525–7 he does it again: he announces the outcome of the story, the defeat of medicine, before beginning to tell it at 528. When he finally starts his story, he does so in a most appropriate manner with the word *principio*, but critics have seen problems with the position of that word at line 528. In Conte's view it 'should, obviously, be the opening of the whole narration', and this corroborates, in his opinion, the contention that lines 525–7 are an interpolation. Even Kenney, who finds nothing in lines 525–7 that is objectionable apart from their position and detects in the expression *exitium superabat opem* 'la giusta cadenza ovidiana',[28] thinks that the lines are, if not interpolated, probably misplaced, although he admits that it is not easy to find a place where they would fit. Such readings fail to notice the characteristic feature of Aeacus as a narrator.

This brings us to the second line deleted by Tarrant containing the expression *causa latet*, line 576, the conclusion to a description of how men leave their own homes believing that they are infested: their small abode is blamed. Tarrant finds *locus paruus* a bizarre locution and finds the whole line disturbingly flat. There is, I would say, an ironic contrast between the enormity of the disaster caused by a goddess and the small, insignificant homes that are blamed. But how is *causa latet* at this stage of the story compatible with Juno's wrath having come out of its hiding at line 562? It is compatible, but only if one takes it in a different sense: 'the cause is unknown'.

But what would be the point of using the combination of *causa* and *latere* in two different senses in this passage? I would suggest that it is to draw the reader's attention to a transformation of genre. The story about the plague is told in in two registers, the register of the *Aeneid* and that of the *Georgics*. In both works Virgil assumes the role of one telling of *causae* and *signa*. The section on diseases in *Georgics* 3 begins with the following line: *Morborum quoque te causas et signa docebo* (3.440), 'I will also teach you the causes and signs of diseases'.[29] And it is from that section that Ovid has taken many details in his account of the disease on Aegina. The *causa latet* at *Met.* 7.576 is perfectly understandable in this frame: the cause of the disease on Aegina is unknown to all common mortals, patients and medical experts alike.

---

[27] This exclamation is bracketed by Tarrant, perhaps because it represents a deviation from the intention that Aeacus has just announced. It is precisely because of the deviation that the line should be kept, since it reveals his inclination to wander off.

[28] Kenney (2011), whose commentary is based on Tarrant's edition, is referring to *Met.* 2.5, *materiam superabat opus*.

[29] Line 503: *haec ante exitium primis dant signa diebus*: The word *signum* is particularly important in *Georgics* 1 dealing with weather signs.

In the epic context, however, *causa* has a different dimension. Aeacus assumes the role of an epic poet when asked by Cephalus (who needs his support against Minos, currently waging war on the Athenians) to explain the absence of so many men whom he remembers from a previous visit. But Aeacus cannot hope for a Muse to reveal to him what is hidden to the human eye. Virgil's *Musa, mihi causas memora* ('Muse, tell me about the motives', *Aen.* 1.8–9) is a request beyond his power to utter. But he can put two and two together: the outburst of the plague was posterior to his renaming his island after his mother, and there were rumours that he was the outcome of a union between Jupiter and Aegina. In such a scenario, Juno's rage was a likely cause. What was revealed by the Muse in the *Aeneid* are causes of Juno's wrath that she has kept within herself. Such hidden motives are what Aeacus suspects.

There is an interesting connection between the two occurrences of the combination of *causa* and *latere* in the Aeacus episode and *Aen.* 5.1–7, an important new beginning for the Trojans after the Carthaginian parenthesis:

> Interea medium Aeneas iam classe tenebat
> certus iter fluctusque atros Aquilone secabat
> moenia respiciens, quae iam infelicis Elissae
> conlucent flammis. quae tantum accenderit ignem
> **causa latet**; duri magno sed amore dolores
> polluto, notumque furens quid femina possit,
> triste per augurium Teucrorum pectora ducunt.

Meanwhile Aeneas was keeping a steady course with his fleet, cleaving a path through the waves that were blackened by the northern wind, looking back on the city that was now lit up by the flames of ill-fated Dido. What cause lit such a huge fire is unknown, but the facts that pain is sharp when a great love has been profaned and that it is well-known what a furious female is capable of guides the thoughts of the Trojans during the dreadful omen.

The Trojans assume, correctly, that Dido killed herself and that they are watching her pyre, and they explain the size of the fire by the strength of Dido's feelings. But they are not aware of the plans and machinations of the gods that led to Dido's death. Only the poet himself can know that the pyre is a *triste augurium* that forebodes the critical situation described later on in *Aen.* 5 when Juno sends Iris to persuade the Trojan women to set their ships on fire. Iris, who is *haud ignara nocendi* ('not ignorant in the art of causing injury', 5.618), succeeds, and the fire seen by the Trojans leaving Carthage forebodes the fire that will be set on their fleet on Sicily.

To return to the Aeacus episode: *Met.* 7.523–7 is best characterized as an introduction in the epic register. At line 528 *principio* takes us straight into the didactic realm. It is not just the appropriate word in the beginning of an account of the plague as it appeared to ordinary humans, but rather it immediately sends the reader to the Latin didactic poems that contain excursions on particular plagues. Although in Lucretius' *De Rerum Natura*, the word *principio* at the beginning of a line is very common throughout his work, in Ovid's version it looks like an allusion to Virgil's *Georgics*, not, however, to the description of the plague in Book 3 but to the beginnings of Books 2 and 4. Each of these two books begins with an introduction to the matters that are going to be treated, and when the introductions are over, the accounts begin with *principio*, a didactic 'to begin with' (2.9 and 4.8). Ovid's account is written in the didactic register at 528–53, in the epic at 554–62, and again in the didactic until 615, where Aeacus addresses Jupiter and the epic register is resumed. The changes of register are more evident if one arranges the text in the following way, where E = epic register, D = didactic register:

E 1   Dira lues ira populis Iunonis iniquae
incidit exosae dictas a paelice terras.
dum uisum mortale malum tantaeque **latebat**   525
causa nocens cladis, pugnatum est arte medendi;
exitium superabat opem, quae uicta iacebat.
D 1   principio caelum spissa caligine terras
pressit et ignauos inclusit nubibus aestus,
dumque quater iunctis expleuit cornibus orbem   530
luna, quater plenum tenuata retexuit orbem,
letiferis calidi spirarunt aestibus Austri.

.   .   .   .   .   .

E 2   uiscera torrentur primo flammaeque **latentis**
indicium rubor est et ductus anhelitus aegre;   555

.   .   .   .   .   .

nec moderator adest inque ipsos saeua medentes   561
erumpit clades obsuntque auctoribus artes;
D 2   .   .   .   .   .   .
tantaque sunt miseris inuisi taedia lecti,
prosiliunt aut, si prohibent consistere uires,
corpora deuoluunt in humum fugiuntque Penates
quisque suos, sua cuique domus funesta uidetur.   575
et, quia **causa latet**, locus est in crimine paruus.

.   .   .   .   .   .

E 3   'Iuppiter o !' dixi 'si te non falsa loquuntur   615
dicta sub amplexus Aeginae Asopidos isse
nec te, magne pater, nostri pudet esse parentem,
aut mihi redde meos, aut me quoque conde sepulchro.'

E 1 A dreadful plague befell the population as a result of the wrath of resentful Juno who detested the fact that the region had been named after a mistress. As long as one seemed to deal with a mortal enemy and **the motive** of so great a cause of ruin **was hidden**, one fought armed with the art of medicine; but destruction proved stronger than the aid which was conquered and brought low.

D 1 In the beginning heaven weighed down the region with a dense darkness and clouds enclosing oppressive waves of heat, and while the thinned moon completed its circle by joining its horns and lessened it again four times, hot south winds breathed with deadly exhalations.

.   .   .   .

E 2 First the innards are roasted. A sign of the **hidden** flame is redness and difficulty in breathing.

.   .   .   .

No moderator is at hand with assistance; the savage cause of ruin broke out against the medical men themselves, and the expertise harmed the experts.

D 2   .   .   .   .

And the miserable people are so disgusted with their own sickbeds that they jump out of them or if they do not have force enough to get up, they roll down onto the floor, and everyone runs away from his own home. Everyone thinks that his own home is deadly, and since **the cause is unknown**, one's dwelling-place is blamed.

.   .   .   .

E 3 'O Jupiter', I said, 'if it is true what they say, that you embraced Asopos' daughter Aegina, and if you are not ashamed to be my father, give my dear ones back to me or place me as well in the grave.'

The frame, E 1 and E 3, is epic. The trigger of the disaster, Jupiter's infidelity with Aegina, is only referred to in these parts. Interestingly, Aegina is referred to as *paelex* in E 1. The narrator adopts Juno's perspective, for that is the word that would have come to her mind as she was silently musing over the wrong done to her. In a comment on 7.527, Bömer has noted that the terms *mederi* and *clades* return 'stichwortartig' at 561–2. They first appear in E 1 and return in E 2, the epic centre of the episode and the epicentre of the catastrophe. That medicine was of no avail is a detail found in the descriptions of a plague in all Ovid's predecessors (Thucydides 2.47.4, Lucretius 6.1179, Virgil *Georg.* 3.549–50), but Ovid brought it into the epic contexts of E1 and E2. That the sick suffer from heat is also found in the earlier accounts, but Ovid alone speaks of a hidden flame and of a *moderator* (E 2). There is a possibility to read E 2 metapoetically in that the hidden epic flame breaks out (*erumpit*) from the didactic surroundings. Looking at the arrangement above, we can see the structure of an epyllion.

We have in the Aeacus-episode one and the same story told in two registers. There is a transformation of meaning in the combination of *causa* and *latere* and as a consequence a transformation of poetic genre depending on whether Aeacus, the narrator, assumes the role of a didactic poet imparting knowledge to human beings or that of a narrator with some access to the gods and their motives. It is worth asking why both lines that contain this combination of terms have been considered inauthentic. The most important reason, I would suggest, is the expectation that the whole episode in 523–614 is nothing but Ovid's contribution to the topos 'description of a plague'. The expressions *mortale malum* and *causa nocens* are peculiar only if *malum* and *causa* are understood as a disease and its cause, and *quae uicta iacebat* is a mere filler only if its epic setting is not perceived.

Hidden Transformations

In the cases discussed repetitions of words do not involve repetitions of meaning. They carry latent transformations (notice that in all three cases Ovid uses the word *latere*), metamorphoses below the surface of the text waiting to be discovered. In the story of Echo, the second *latet siluis* creates an echo with an alteration of meaning, an imitation of the immediately preceding conversation between her and Narcissus. In the story of Pygmalion, changes occur in the artist himself before his work of art is metamorphosed: his uncertainty about the artificiality or reality of his own work, expressed in the vague and ambiguous *suam* (my conjecture), is replaced by certainty with the *mot juste* of Latin love poetry, *suae puellae*. In the episode regarding the plague in Aegina 7.523–642, there is a long stretch with no explicit metamorphosis until 7.622 where ants are turned into Myrmidons. But this long stretch contains a hidden metamorphosis: the repetition in *latebat causa/causa latet* hints at a transformation of literary genre. Readers embarking on the story about the plague in Aegina, Ovid's counterpart to Lucretius' and Virgil's descriptions of contagious diseases of a similar format, may expect a visit into didactic territory, but *causa* is a key term in both the *Georgics* and the *Aeneid*, and in the hundred lines between 7.523 and 7.621 Ovid's text is undergoing transformations back and forth between the languages and worlds of the *Aeneid* and the *Georgics*. In each of the three cases discussed the repetition draws attention to the poetic language itself.

8

The Bavarian Commentary and the Beginning of the Medieval Reception of the *Metamorphoses*

Ore legar populi, perque omnia saecula fama,
siquid habent eri uatum praesagia, uiuam.
(I shall have mention on men's lips, and, if the prophecies of bards
have any truth, through all the ages shall I live in fame.)

Met. 15.878–9[1]

Ouidius enodauit et enucleauit.
('Ovid elucidated and explained'.)

Clm 4610[2]

In the last lines of the *Metamorphoses* Ovid prophesies that he will win fame through all the ages. This, however, was not to be the case. For several centuries after the end of antiquity the *Metamorphoses*, the longest surviving Latin epic, a veritable sourcebook of mythology, with an anthology-like structure and a myriad of characters, seems to have been little read. The work came upon the medieval literary scene surprisingly late, for Ovid did not enter into the medieval mainstream until the late twelfth century, from which point on Ovid's texts gain momentum and start exerting a strong influence. However, it seems to be around a century earlier that his *Metamorphoses* makes its first slow start towards a larger audience. As the first comprehensive witness to the study of Ovid's text at this point in time stands one single commentary, the Bavarian commentary, also known by its manuscript name clm 4610.

The period when the *Metamorphoses* started finding readers again stands roughly halfway between our time and the time the text was composed. Even though the *Metamorphoses* might have had a difficult first millennium after

---

[1] All quotations from *Metamorphoses* are from Tarrant (2004), translations from *Metamorphoses* from Miller (1916).
[2] Clm 4610, 62ra. Wahlsten Böckerman (2016) 186. All translations in this paper are by the author, unless otherwise stated.

Robin Wahlsten Böckerman, *The Bavarian Commentary and the Beginning of the Medieval Reception of the Metamorphoses* In: *Metamorphic Readings: Transformation, Language, and Gender in the Interpretation of Ovid's Metamorphoses*. Edited by: Alison Sharrock, Daniel Möller, and Mats Malm, Oxford University Press (2020).
© Oxford University Press.
DOI: 10.1093/oso/9780198864066.003.0009

antiquity, not many would argue against it having had a very successful last five hundred years or so. Indeed, it still remains an influential text, constantly read, translated, and commented upon. Because of these many layers of inherited interpretations and explanations we risk taking much for granted as far as concerns the ways in which the work has been understood and studied throughout history. It is the aim of this paper, therefore, to take us back to the first documented readers of the *Metamorphoses* in order to investigate how they interacted with the text and how they devised their hermeneutic endeavour.[3]

In order to contextualize properly the commentary which is the centre of this paper, I will first present the fate of the *Metamorphoses* itself and what we know about its readers up to the twelfth century, and then briefly treat the medieval commentaries on the text. After this I will focus on the form and function of the commentary in clm 4610 as a means of analysing the Ovidian reader of the period.

The Fate of the *Metamorphoses* up to the Twelfth Century

Ovid became popular in his own lifetime and was much read throughout antiquity. He is, for example, mentioned by Seneca and during late antiquity we find works such as Claudian's *De Raptu Proserpinae*, which is greatly indebted to the *Metamorphoses*. On the other hand, the *Metamorphoses* does not seem to have been widely read from Late Antiquity until the eleventh century. There are no preserved manuscripts of the text before the ninth century, from when we have just two fragments.[4] It is only in the eleventh century that the text is starting to be copied and disseminated a bit more frequently. From this century we have twelve preserved manuscripts, most of them from the German lands. In the twelfth century production seems to increase dramatically, with more than double the amount of manuscripts preserved from this century compared to all three previous centuries together. In the late twelfth and the thirteenth centuries, Ovid really becomes established as an influential author among contemporary writers and in schools, whence the period is known through Ludwig Traube as *Aetas Ovidiana*.[5]

The information regarding preserved manuscripts of the *Metamorphoses* on its own does not tell us much if we do not put it in relationship to other texts. To get a clearer picture, we can make a comparison with the other curriculum authors:

---

[3] This paper is based on my PhD thesis *The Metamorphosis of Education: Ovid in the Twelfth-Century Schoolroom* (2016), which consists of an edition and English translation of the entire commentary in clm 4610 together with a contextualizing and analysing introduction. The present paper seeks to contribute to the discussion in books such as Clark, Coulson, and McKinley (2011, in Ginsberg 2011) which did not cover the earliest period.

[4] The following information is from Tilliette (2014) 70 and Munk Olsen (2014) 24–30.

[5] Traube (1911) 113. For a discussion of the concept, see Hexter (1986) 2.

Table 8.1 Number of preserved manuscripts and fragments for the curriculum authors from four centuries[6]

Century	9th	10th	11th	12th	Total
Virgil, *Aeneid*	37	25	47	85	194
Cicero, *De inventione*	5	9	33	128	175
Lucan, *De bello civili*	10	14	32	118	174
Horace, *Epistles*	6	15	37	95	153
Sallust, *The Jugurthine War*	2	7	37	94	140
Juvenal, *Satires*	7	23	36	52	118
Terence, *Comedies*	6	18	34	50	108
Statius, *Thebaid*	3	11	20	70	104
Persius, *Satires*	4	16	30	22	72

The numbers in Table 8.1 include both fragments and the complete texts of the works listed. Virgil's *Aeneid* is at the top of this league with a total of 194 preserved manuscripts, while Persius comes last with 72, which is still almost 30 per cent more than the preserved *Metamorphoses* manuscripts. All works show the same pattern of a steady, almost exponential, increase from century to century. These numbers tell us that, even though we are looking at preserved manuscripts and not the actual number of manuscripts available at the time, the pattern is broadly the same for all authors. This means that it is unlikely that there was a large quantity of Ovid's work in circulation in, for example, the ninth century, which has subsequently been destroyed or lost.[7] It should also be pointed out here that no great mystery need be ascribed to the scanty amount of preserved Ovidian manuscripts. He is not alone in this. If we take, for instance, Catullus and Lucretius, who, though famous today, were virtually unknown through the Middle Ages and survived in only one or two manuscripts, then Ovid, in comparison, suddenly seems to be quite well represented during the centuries.

Another means of examining the popularity of the *Metamorphoses* is by studying the text's impact on contemporary literature, but here, similarly, not much evidence is to be found until the late eleventh century. What can be extracted are brief mentions of Ovid by name. The earliest and most famous example is the case of Theodulf of Orléans, who in the eighth or early ninth century mentions 'talkative/chattering Naso' (*Naso loquax*) in his list-poem 'On the books I used to read'. This instance usually stands as a starting point where allusions to Ovid are concerned.[8] After Theodulf, allusions to Ovid pop up here

---

[6] This table is created from the information in Munk Olsen (2014) 24–30.

[7] Munk Olsen has limited his catalogue to the period from the ninth to the twelfth centuries. If we consult Reynolds (1983), we can add to this that the only authors that seem to have an older tradition than the ninth century are Persius, Terence, and Virgil, whose texts are extant in manuscripts from the fourth century onwards. Reynolds (1983) 293–5, 412–20, and 433–7.

[8] Dümmler (1881) 543, l. 17–20.

and there, but not very frequently.[9] Later on, in the eleventh century, the so-called Loire school displays a keen familiarity with Ovid. This little group, consisting of the learned churchmen Baudri of Bourgeuil, Marbode of Rennes, and Hildebert of Lavardin, seems to be of crucial importance for the establishment of a learned Ovidian discourse around 1100.[10] In all cases except for one or two mythologically themed poems by Baudri of Bourgeuil, however, most allusions to Ovid seem to be to other works, such as the *Heroides*, *Ars Amatoria*, or *Amores*, a fact which would suggest that the popularity of Ovid started with his shorter works and then came to include the *Metamorphoses*.

The poetry and prose of the period seems to mirror the manuscript situation for the *Metamorphoses* when it comes to the popularity of the work. It grows over time, but it is clear that by around 1100 Ovid has still not quite made his (second) breakthrough. He seems to have been read and appreciated in small circles, but is nowhere close to being the universal source for love poetry and mythological themes that he was to become from the thirteenth century and onwards.

The Commentaries

The commentary genre is of such importance in the Middle Ages that it may even be termed a 'commentary culture', since commenting was such a central feature of the broader field of medieval textual culture. Indeed, the commentary culture is still alive and strong today and especially within Classics, as well as other fields dealing with older texts.[11] During most of the medieval period virtually all older and even contemporary texts were at some point appended with a commentary. We must assume that before and parallel to the written commentary there existed oral commentary, but in its written form the commentary as a genre is almost as old as the written text itself. It really came into its own, however, with the ascendance of the codex in the fourth century. The codex format, the form of the book we are familiar with today, allowed for both the freestanding commentary and commentary written in the margins and between the lines, while earlier media, such as the papyrus roll, did not lend itself well to marginal commentary. The codex, then, allowed for the two principal formats of the medieval commentary, the freestanding commentary and the marginal commentary. The freestanding commentary, sometimes also referred to as a *catena* commentary, exists in a separate document, and has a distinct textual history, while the marginal commentary leads a life closely tied to its target text. The marginal commentary often

---

[9] For more on this see Wahlsten Böckerman (2016) 18–31.
[10] For more on this see Bond (1986).
[11] For many different stimulating perspectives on contemporary, and some historical, uses of the classical commentary see Gibson and Kraus (2002).

consists of longer commentary portions in the margins and short interlinear commentary in the main text. It is also often added to or altered as the text users see fit when copying the texts into a new manuscript.[12] Commentaries can often move between these two forms, a freestanding commentary can be composed from marginal commentary, or marginal notes may be added from a freestanding commentary.[13]

As far as commentaries on the *Metamorphoses* are concerned, we find that they share a history of dissemination similar to that of the text itself. The first ones appear late and they then start growing in number over time. In late antiquity, Servius refers to Ovid several times when commenting on Virgil, but we do not know of any ancient commentaries or biographies on Ovid except for possibly in the case of the so-called Pseudo-Lactantian *Narrationes*. This text has often been transmitted together with the *Metamorphoses* and consists of short prose summaries of the text with some minor interpretative commentary. The *Narrationes* has been ascribed to many different authors, of which Lactantius Placidus is the name most commonly mentioned, but this attribution cannot be found in any of the medieval manuscripts and is today considered spurious. The *Narrationes* has recently been dated to as early as the second century AD, while previous scholarship dated it to no earlier than the sixth century. The text as it survives is considered to be derived from a lost late antique commentary.[14]

The year 1100, or possible the decades just before that, is the starting point for our knowledge about the medieval commentaries on the *Metamorphoses*, for that was when the Bavarian commentary, known under the modern name clm 4610, was created. It is worth pointing out that some of the *Metamorphoses* manuscripts predating clm 4610 contain some marginal commentary. However, these commentaries are not substantial and based on paleographical evidence it is possible to conclude that most of them are written later than the main text. This means that most of the scattered marginal commentary found in the old *Metamorphoses* manuscripts is of the same age or of a later age than the commentary in clm 4610.[15] The same holds true if we compare it with the situation regarding Ovid's other works. There are some manuscripts, or fragments of manuscripts, of the other Ovidian works dated to the ninth through to the eleventh century, and some of them carry marginal commentary.[16] However, here as well there is nothing

---

[12] Although there are also several instances of marginal commentaries becoming canonized and copied with content and form intact, see for instance the *Glossa Ordinaria* on the Bible.

[13] The terminology surrounding commentaries can be complex and inconsistent. In this text I have striven to keep it as simple as possible and only use 'commentary' (modified by 'freestanding', 'marginal', or 'interlinear') throughout. For a discussion of historical and current commentary terminology see Copeland (2012) and Wahlsten Böckerman (2016) 32–5 and 61–2.

[14] Cameron (2004) 311. For a discussion of alternative dating of the *Narrationes* see Tarrant (1995) 83–115.

[15] For more on this see Wahlsten Böckerman (2016) 102–15.

[16] For a study of this and other commentaries on Ovid's other work see Hexter (1986).

substantial or of an earlier date than clm 4610. Therefore, the year 1100 stands at the beginning of our knowledge of complete commentaries on all of Ovid's works.

We may at this point also briefly consider what came after clm 4610 to understand its place properly. Besides clm 4610, the twelfth century also saw the birth of at least three other families of commentaries on the *Metamorphoses*. Two of these families are created by anonymous masters and seem to have been composed in the German lands and in France.[17] During the late twelfth century, the Orléans masters Fulco and Arnulf were both commenting on the *Metamorphoses*, as well as many of Ovid's other works. From this time on, just as with the manuscript for the *Metamorphoses* itself, the number of commentaries increases at a quick and steady pace. Arnulf wrote both an allegorical and a philological commentary and as far as we know his was the first in a long line of allegorical commentaries on the *Metamorphoses*. From the thirteenth century the allegorical tradition is represented by a commentary on Ovid by John of Garland and from the fourteenth century we know of Giovanni del Virgilio, a Bolognese scholar and correspondent with Dante. From the same century we also have the moralizing commentary *Ovidius Moralizatus* and the French *Ovide Moralisé*, a moralizing translation of the *Metamorphoses* more than three times longer than the original. While the allegorical tradition of commentating gained popularity from the thirteenth century onwards, there was also a continued tradition of philological commentary, witnessed mainly in the anonymous so-called Vulgate commentary, which, judging from the number of manuscripts in which it has been transmitted, remained popular for several centuries.[18]

As with the preserved manuscripts, focussing only on Ovid will not give a clear picture of the situation. To this end it may be effective to juxtapose the commentary tradition related to Ovid with that related to Virgil. Virgil is an exceptional author in that the success and popularity his works enjoyed during his lifetime was virtually uninterrupted up until (and far beyond) the high-medieval period. According to Suetonius, Virgil was the topic of lectures even in his own lifetime.[19] During the later centuries of antiquity and the early centuries of the Middle Ages, many commentators followed. Many of the earliest commentators on Virgil are known from the works of Suetonius and Aulus Gellius, author of the all-encompassing *Noctes Atticae*. In the fourth century, Aelius Donatus wrote his commentary and a generation or two after him, Tiberius Claudius Donatus (no relation to Aelius) wrote his *Interpretationes Vergilianae*, which is a line-by-line commentary on the *Aeneid* with a focus on rhetorical features.

---

[17] For more on these two families see Wahlsten Böckerman (2016) 116–38.
[18] For Fulco see Engelbrecht (2003); for Arnulf see Gura (2010); the Vulgate commentary is being worked on by Frank Coulson, Ohio State University; *Ovidius Moralizatus* and *Ovide Moralisé* are being worked on by Marek Thue Kretschmer, NTNU. All of these commentaries will be treated in a future article on Ovid in *Catalogus Translationum et Commentariorum* by F. Coulson.
[19] Ziolkowski and Putnam (2008) 627.

Servius, active in the late fourth and early fifth centuries, is without a doubt the single most important commentator, not only through his influence on Virgilian reception, but also through the use of his texts on other authors. Servius wrote commentaries on all of Virgil's works and they became the standard point of reference for centuries to come. Servius also appears as a character in the seven-book dialogue, the *Saturnalia*, of his contemporary Macrobius.[20] In this encyclopaedic work Virgil, mentioned more than seven hundred times, is not only the main focus when poetry is discussed, but also when most other human knowledge is considered.[21] The sixth century gives us the most famous allegorical commentator, Fulgentius, whose work *Expositio Virgilianae continentiae* differs sharply from, for instance, Servius, in that it makes an entirely allegorical reading of the *Aeneid*. While Servius and others make an occasional allegorical reading of a specific instance in Virgil, Fulgentius treats the entire story allegorically.

These are only a few of the early commentators on Virgil. They serve the purpose of showing how a large corpus of commentary text was created almost from the time of the author and then throughout history. When compared to Ovid, it illustrates the different fates of two ancient authors, but more importantly it tells us that, even though the medieval readers of Ovid might not have had any previous commentaries on his work to help them, they were in no way without other commentaries to give them an interpretative framework. Furthermore, the commentary genre is by its very nature eclectic. Besides other commentaries it draws also on many other types of texts. Most influential was Isidore of Seville and his twenty-book *Etymologies*, in which the medieval reader could find information about virtually everything, from grammar to weapons. In the case of Ovid there were also several compendia of mythographers, such as Hyginus (*Fabulae* and *De astronomia*), Solinus (*Collectanea rerum mirabilium*), and Fulgentius (*Mythologiae*) from the ancient and early medieval era, and later the so-called Vatican Mythographers. The collections of ancient myths, often retold in a brief and simple style, in these authors' works could often function as handy reference books for the commentators.

Codex Latinus Monacensis 4610—the Bavarian Commentary

We now finally arrive at the main focus of this paper—the Bavarian commentary, or clm 4610. The previous discussion has created a framework through which we can understand the position of clm 4610. We can see that although there are no known predecessors to clm 4610 as far as Ovidian commentaries are concerned, the commentary fits into a long tradition of commenting on ancient authors, and

---

[20] *Saturnalia* I.2.15.   [21] Ziolkowski and Putnam (2008) 636.

thus would have had plenty of texts to model itself on and to borrow from. The development of commentaries on Ovid corresponds with the increasing dissemination of Ovid's text (although the commentaries seem to come a bit later, which is perhaps not surprising). As the first in a long line of commentaries on the *Metamorphoses* it is of interest to find out what exactly this commentary is and what it says.

If we start with the material and historical context of clm 4610, we must note that not much is known about the manuscript. The manuscript clm 4610, which stands for *codex latinus monacensis* number 4610, is today at the Bayerische Staatsbibliothek, the Bavarian state library in Munich. It was originally one of several hundred manuscripts that came to the library from the Benedictine monastery Benediktbeuern during the *Säkularisation* in the early nineteenth century. During this time Napoleon raised the duchy of Bavaria to a kingdom and in the process confiscated the holdings of the monasteries in the region and transferred the books from their libraries to what was then Bibliotheca Regia Monacensis and later developed into the Bayerische Staatsbibliothek.

To speculate about the fate of the manuscript before the nineteenth century we must look to the manuscript itself. The manuscript contains owner markings in the form of the line *iste liber est Monasterii Benedictenpeuren* ('this book belongs to the monastery Benediktbeuern'), written in a gothic script in four different places in the manuscript.[22] The owner marks correspond to the first and last pages of the two booklets that make up the manuscript as it is preserved today and as it seems to have been bound since the late Middle Ages. These two booklets were originally two discrete texts created in different periods; only the second one concerns us, since it contains the commentary on the *Metamorphoses*.[23] The owner marks make it possible to conclude that the manuscript has probably been stored in the monastery for most of its existence, but we cannot say for sure whether it was created there or not. The script used in the commentary would suggest a south-German late eleventh- or early twelfth-century hand.

To contextualize the manuscript with this information briefly, we can note that this time and location places us in the Holy Roman Empire and the Duchy of Bavaria. The empire was not a stable, centralized unit, but rather a conglomerate of duchies and bishoprics, all of which struggled for power in relation to their neighbours, the emperor, and the pope. However, it was not the secular institution of the courts but rather the powerful network of monasteries and cathedrals that provided the institution for schooling and learning, and thus were also where most of the manuscripts of the period were created, used and stored. Relevant for this commentary is, of course, the Benedictine monastery Benediktbeuern, but also the close-by monasteries of St Emmeram, Tegernsee, and St Peter in Salzburg, all of

[22] On 1^r, 60^r, 61^r, and 84^r.
[23] For a detailed manuscript description see Wahlsten Böckerman (2016) 161–8.

them important centres of text production. The direct historical information that can be associated with the text is rather limited. Turning then instead to its formal characteristics we can state that the commentary in clm 4610 fills twenty-three folios and numbers, in total, *circa* 16,500 words, which comment on *circa* 460 passages from all fifteen books of the *Metamorphoses*. In the printed edition the commentary consists of around seventy-five pages, compared to the 481 pages of the *Metamorphoses*. From this we can instantly tell that the commentary will not cover every passage in its target text.[24]

When analysing the commentary, it is important to keep in mind the difference between discussing the possible functions of the different explanations in the text based on their form and content, and the purpose for which the actual manuscript clm 4610 might have been used. The latter question is much more difficult to answer since many scenarios are possible. The following three scenarios are the most likely with regard to the origin of the manuscript itself:

1. A schoolmaster's copy: a collection of notes made for or by a schoolmaster, from which the master lectured.
2. Lecture notes: notes taken down by students based on one or several masters' lectures.
3. Archival copy: Collection of notes taken perhaps from one or several free-standing commentaries, or extracted from marginal commentary, with the sole purpose of storing the information.

Ideally, we would want to have either some external evidence for its use or some textual evidence that would make its origin and use clear. The only textual evidence is the mention of one Manogaldus, who may be the same as Manegold of Lautenbach, an itinerant teacher of the late eleventh century. Manogaldus is mentioned five times throughout the commentary and, although he is the only contemporary source mentioned by name, he is not used any differently than older sources. I find it unlikely that the entire commentary can be attributed to him, but it may be that he lectured on the *Metamorphoses* during his lifetime.[25] Besides the mention of Manogaldus there is no more explicit textual evidence as to the manuscript's origin and therefore the best way of analysing the commentary and its relationship to Ovid is through the content and its function.

---

[24] As a comparison, Thilo's edition of Servius' commentary on the *Aeneid* covers 1305 pages (and the *Aeneid* is *circa* 2000 lines shorter than the *Metamorphoses*). Even considering the difference in format of editions and such factors, this clearly shows us the massive difference between the most well-known commentary on an ancient author and a latecomer such as clm 4610.

[25] For my take on the Manegold question see Wahlsten Böckerman (2016) 94–6. For more on Manegold and his neoplatonic views see Herren (2004) and Dronke (2016).

Function

The function of the commentary stands at the centre of this investigation. Previous researchers have been able to reach exciting results by this method. For instance, Suzanne Reynolds, in her *Medieval Reading: Grammar, Rhetoric and the Classical Text*, managed to build a model for medieval reading practices on a larger scale through analysing commentaries on Horace.[26] The aim of this study, however, is more limited. I simply strive to shine a light on certain features of the commentary and its users.

In my thesis my ambition to deal with the commentary in its entirety stemmed from what I call the 'Meiser sequence'. As stated several times above, although clm 4610 is the earliest known commentary on the *Metamorphoses*, it has not been well known to researchers. In modern times the commentary was first noticed by M. Haupt, who included a transcription of a small section of it in his article 'Coniectanea' from 1873, and less than ten years later Karl Meiser made a more thorough study of the text published in the article 'Ueber einen Commentar zu den Metamorphosen des Ovid'.[27] This article identifies which passages from the *Metamorphoses* are commented upon and also includes transcriptions of some extracts, as well as a discussion on some of its sources. With very few exceptions all scholars who have treated the commentary since have based their assumptions about the commentary and the early reception of Ovid on the short extracts in Meiser's article.[28] Excellent scholars such as Paule Demats and Michael Herren have based their theories solely on the selection made by Meiser.[29] More recently the always stimulating Peter Dronke has treated facets of clm 4610 in two separate books.[30] Dronke seems to have used Meiser but also consulted the manuscripts. This is ideal, but the aim of Dronke (and partly also that of Demats and Herren) is to investigate Christian-Platonic ideas, which is both a very broad field of investigation and, as far as clm 4610 is concerned, a fairly narrow one, since the commentary does not contain a lot of material in this area. Although these scholars achieved good results with the help of Meiser's extracts, it is my belief that the entire commentary should be made available and studied.[31] This is partly because after the entire commentary has been analysed and indexed the arguments of previous research might be strengthened or disproved (not the case thus far), but more so because it would serve the study of the reception of Ovid. With its relatively short length, but still commenting on the entire *Metamorphoses*, clm 4610 offers a unique opportunity to gain knowledge of how an entire

---

[26] Reynolds (1996).   [27] Haupt (1873); Meiser (1885).

[28] Exceptions to this rule are scholars dealing with the manuscripts related to the reception of Ovid, most well-known and prolific of whom is Frank Coulson, Ohio State University.

[29] Demats (1973) and Herren (2004).   [30] Dronke (2008) and Dronke (2016).

[31] For some recent argumentation on the benefits of making medieval readings of ancient literature available see Tarrant (2016) 155–6.

commentary, not more or less well-chosen parts of it, functions as a hermeneutic device on its own and in relationship to its target text. For this reason, I presented a complete critical edition with English translation of the commentary together with a thorough analysis of its context, form, and function in my dissertation. In the dissertation I made a careful analysis of the commentary text, cataloguing every explanation in the commentary, which allowed me to analyse their function in terms of categories of explanations.[32] I postulated ten categories sorted under four overarching categories. These categories managed to cover most of the *circa* 460 explanations to the *Metamorphoses* contained in the commentary. The categories are as follows:

Background: mythological background explanations

Grammar: grammatical explanations, paraphrase

Lexical: patronymics, lexicon, etymology

Interpretative: Euhemeristic, natural philosophy, narrative, plot.

In the following I want to see how these categories can be further put to work to make visible other patterns in the commentary than those identified in my thesis and what these can tell us.

Turning to the content we start with something outside the commentary proper, namely the so-called *accessus*, a prologue that introduces the commentary. As far as I know almost every medieval commentary was introduced by an *accessus*. They could even be collected into a volume of their own, as can be witnessed in the collection called *Accessus ad auctores*.[33] The *accessus* treats a set of standard headings, of which the heading 'intention of the author' (*intentio*), 'utility of the work' (*utilitas*), 'part of philosophy under which the work is classified' (*cui parti philisophiae*), and 'subject matter' (*materia*) are most common. The *accessus* is never explicitly followed up in the commentary, but rather works as an independent introduction and can even have a separate transmission history from that of the rest of the commentary text.[34] Two samples from the *accessus* in clm 4610 may give an indication of what attracted the readers of the high Middle Ages to Ovid:

---

[32] A short note on my terminology. When I speak of clm 4610, 'commentary' denotes the whole text, which in turn consists of two parts: lemma and explanation. Lemma, word or words from the commented upon text, is an established term, while the commentating text following the lemma has been given different names by different scholars. I have chosen the simple term 'explanation' in my thesis and that will also be the term used in this paper. For more on this see Wahlsten Böckerman (2016) 61–62, where also alternative terminology is discussed.

[33] Wheeler (2015).

[34] For more on the *accessus* see Minnis (1988) and Minnis and Johnson (2005).

Ouidius enodauit et enucleauit. Prodest nobis et ad ostendendam pulchram dictionum compositionem.

Ovid elucidated and explained. He also benefits us by showing beautiful composition.

Intentio Ouidii est omniumque fabulas scribentium, utpote Terentii, maxime delectari et delectando tamen mores instruere, quia omnes auctores fere ad ethicam tendunt.

The intention of Ovid and of all writers of stories, as well as that of Terence, is mainly to delight and by delighting to teach morals, since almost all authors strive towards ethics.[35]

These two examples tell us that Ovid explains the old stories and entertains us in a style which is worth emulating, while at the same time teaching us a moral lesson. These short lines cover three of the traditional headings of the *accessus*: 'intention of the author', 'utility of the work', and 'part of philosophy'. These are, however, general statements, which, as is explicitly stated in the second example, could be applied to many ancient authors.[36] These prologues to the commentaries have generally received far more scholarly attention than the long, difficult commentary texts they introduce, but in this study I prefer to keep the discussion regarding the *accessus* short and instead move on to the main commentary text.

The commentary text itself consists of around 460 distinct explanations to different passages in the *Metamorphoses*. The explanations are introduced by a so-called lemma, one or several words from the target text, which point to the relevant passage in the *Metamorphoses*. After the lemma follows the explanation proper. The explanations range from just a few words to several pages, although normally they are no longer than a paragraph or two. The area of interest for the explanations varies a great deal. At this point a small caveat is needed. When regarding the commentary as a whole it is important to remember that we cannot always expect to find coherent meaning in the text as it stands. Clm 4610 shows signs of being a copy or assemblage of other texts and it contains errors and distortions. This has to be kept in mind when analysing the text and trying to understand how it operates. This means that there are certain limitations to analysing the commentary as a whole as a representation of its original form, whatever that might have been. If one wanted to be entirely on the safe side one would say that the following is a reading of clm 4610 as a representation of certain cultural patterns around year 1100 when Ovid's *Metamorphoses* is concerned. In the following I will focus on three groups of explanations: those non-specific to the

[35] Wahlsten Böckerman (2016) 186 (clm 4610 62ra).
[36] For an example of the formulaic nature of the *accessus* see Wheeler (2015). The second example also echoes Horace's *pariter delectando ac monendo* from *Ars poetica* (l.333).

Metamorphoses, those specific, and an ad hoc selection with bearing on the future development of Ovid commentaries.

In the first group and in the commentary in general, the most frequent type of explanation revolves around giving the background or clarifying the details to the different stories in the *Metamorphoses*. The first example illustrates this type of explanation in its shortest form:

MONICHIOSQVE VOLANS. Monichius fuit gigas et dicitur iuuisse in con-structione murorum Athenarum.   (2.709)

AND FLYING [HE LOOKED DOWN ON] THE MUNYCHIAN [FIELDS]. Munychius was a giant and he is said to have aided in the construction of the walls of Athens.[37]

This explanation simply tells us who Munychius is and gives the reason for why the name is used in this instance. The next example shows a more detailed mythological background story:

ANDROMEDAN PENAS. Cepheus rex habuit coniugem Casiope<m>, que dixit se pulcriorem esse Iunone uel deabus marinis. Pro quo peccato belua exiens mare commedebat suum regnum. Iudicauit Iupiter, ut filiam suam Andromedam daret belue ad commedendum, et sic homines ulterius non commederentur.   (4.671)

THAT ANDROMEDA [SHOULD PAY] THE PENALTY. King Cepheus had a wife, Cassiope, who said she was more beautiful than Juno or the sea goddesses. For this sin a monster came from the sea and devoured his kingdom. Jupiter decided that Cepheus should give his daughter, Andromeda, to the monster to be eaten, and thus the people were no longer eaten.

The explanation is triggered by two words in the lemma and describes who Andromeda is as well as the background and the nature of her penalty. The phrase *uel deabus marinis* ('or some sea-goddesses') signals that there are two different versions of this story. In one version, Cassiopeia claims that she is more beautiful than Juno and, in the other, more beautiful than some sea-goddesses. The latter version can be traced to a mythographical compendium ascribed to the ancient author Hyginus.[38]

As noted above in the paragraph on Virgil and Ovid, the commentators rarely made up their explanations on the spot, but rather leaned on authorities and reused and rephrased (and sometimes misrepresented) earlier commentaries

---

[37] The reference to book and line in the *Metamorphoses* also refers to the relevant passage in the edition of the commentary, where each explanation is numbered according to which passage it comments upon.

[38] Hyginus, *fab.* 64 (ed. Marshall 1993).

and other sources. The next example illustrates the relation between clm 4610 and Servius:

TER CENTVM TONAT ORE DEOS non 'tercentum deos', sed tonat ter centum numina Hecates: unde [[et]] Hecate dicta est ηκατην, id est centum, potestates habens.   (Serv. *in Aen.* 4:510)[39]

[SHE] THUNDERS FORTH WITH HER MOUTH THREE TIMES A HUNDRED GODS, not 'three hundred gods', but she thunders forth thrice Hecate's hundred divinities: wherefore Hecate is named ηκατην, that is having a hundred powers.

HECCATEIA CARMINA M<ISCET>. Ideo Hecate dea inferni hoc nomine nuncupatur, quod sit centum potestatum.   (14:44)

SHE MIXES HECATEAN SONGS. Hecate, the goddess of the underworld, is known by this name because she is of a hundred powers.

Here clm 4610 explains Hecate in a manner closely modelled on Servius, but omits the etymological explanation. The two explanations are quite close, but not identical. Rather it is the case of a much younger commentary freely reusing older material. Servius' commentary on all of Virgil's work has been transmitted along with the text of Virgil from the earliest times and it is most likely that a medieval reader of ancient texts would have been quite familiar with Servius, as Virgil was probably the first pagan author they encountered. Servius is used as an explicit source, mentioned by name, four times in the commentary and used silently at least fifteen times, which is actually less than what one might have expected.[40]

The examples above belong to a group of explanations that are not specific to the *Metamorphoses*. That is to say, they are answers given to questions raised by reading the *Metamorphoses*, but the answers are almost a sort of 'medieval Wikipedia' kind of answers. They could have been drawn from a wide range of predecessors, compendia, and other types of texts which are difficult to identify. In the last example a parallel in Servius can be found and the manner of adaptation in the commentary can be studied. However, in most cases it is difficult to know whether the text in the commentary is a direct adaptation from Servius or whether it is derived from one or several intermediary sources. Because of the unspecific nature of these explanations and the fact that they can be derived from many other sources and periods we cannot use them to gain a direct understanding of the interpretative actions of the Ovidian reader around year 1100. If the commentary consisted only of this kind of explanations it would be difficult to trace any signs of a contemporary reader and that reader's relationship to Ovid (besides making a comparison between the selection and adaption of explanations with another

[39] Thilo (1881).
[40] For more on the commentaries' sources see Wahlsten Böckerman (2016) 92–101.

comparable text). However, the fact that they are found in the commentary at all still tells us what type of information was thought relevant at the time. To the category of mythological background information we can add explanations treating etymology, lexicon, and patronymics. All of these explanations are non-specific as to their origin. They could be derived from Isidore's *Etymologiae* or some other compendium or commentary. In total they make up the majority of the explanations in the commentary (the mythological background explanations alone number around 200).

Contrary to the type of explanations described above, it is also possible to identify a type including several different categories of explanations that in different ways are directly related to the *Metamorphoses*. These explanations are often answers that focus on the linguistic or narrative function of the *Metamorphoses*.

The following example belongs to a large group of grammatical explanations, which usually consist of short explanations to provide help in construing the sentence or in understanding certain features of the text on a purely linguistic level.

CIRCVMFLVVS HVMOR POSSEDIT VLTIMA et COHERCVIT SOLIDVM ORBEM, id est terram, quia nisi aqua circumdaret terram, terra esset solubilis et arenosa.   (1.30)

THE FLOWING WATER OCCUPIED THE LAST PLACE and ENCLOSED THE SOLID ORB, that is the earth, since if water did not enclose the earth, the earth would be soluble and sandy.

In this example the rearranged lemma itself constitutes the grammatical explanation and the explanation following *quia* ('since') belongs to a small category of explanations treating natural philosophy. The latter part could in this case be placed in the group of non-specific explanations, but the focus in this example is on the first category, the grammatical explanation. In the *Metamorphoses*, the passage reads as follows: *circumfluus umor ultima possedit solidumque coercuit orbem*. The explanation has simply moved the verbs so as to make their relation to their objects clearer. The commentary has also removed the enclitic *-que* ('and') and replaced it with a standard *et* ('and'). This short type of explanation is similar to the interlinear commentary or short marginal notes found in some *Metamorphoses* manuscripts. However, in the case of interlinear commentary, we can easily see how the teacher/student used the main text with the commentary as help, but in the case of the freestanding commentary, it is more difficult to imagine how exactly it was used. Did the master simply read it aloud while the students took notes, or are these explanations a model for schoolroom exercises?

Another group of explanations are of a more interpretative nature.

NVNC QVOQVE, VT ATTONITOS non solum MVTAVIT crines IN IDROS, sed etiam nunc fert idros IN PECTORE ADVERSO. Perseus pro constanti habebat, quod daturus erat Palladi caput Gorgonis. Ideo dicit quod iam ferebat 'in pectore', id est in lorica, que antiquitus tantum in pectore habebatur. Vel Ouidius non curauit ordinem.   (4.801)

AND NOW ALSO TO [SCARE] THE TERRIFIED SHE not only CHANGED her locks INTO SERPENTS, but she also now carries the serpents ON THE FRONT OF HER BREAST. Perseus knew for sure that he was going to give the head of the Gorgon to Pallas. Therefore Ovid says that she already carried it 'on her breast', that is on the cuirass, which in former times was carried on the breast only. Or Ovid did not care about the order of the stories.

This example makes direct mention of Ovid and is of an interpretative nature concerned with the plot of the *Metamorphoses*. This two-part explanation starts with a grammatical explanation of the lemma and then gives an explanation of how we must understand the sentence if we want to keep a working chronology in the stories. The commentator then states the consequence if we do not accept the explanation, namely that Ovid simply did not care about the order of the stories.

A small but very interesting group of explanations are explanations of a text-critical nature. They are similar in style to the previous example, but they relate to both the content of the *Metamorphoses* and the external life of the text, in which there were several different versions of the text available at the time.

FERT VTERO ET MATER QVOD VIX MIHI CONTIGIT VNI uel VNO. Si dixerimus, quod Iuno dicat 'uix mihi contigit uni' Iunoni, ut essem mater de Ioue, cum alie plures fuerint matres, tunc dicemus, quod Ouidius non caret peruertere fabulas. Vel 'contigit mihi in [i]uno', id est in Vulcano, quem de Ioue habuit, ut esset mater.   (3.269)

SHE CARRIES IN THE WOMB AND [WISHES TO BE MADE] A MOTHER, WHICH HAS BARELY HAPPENED TO ME ALONE (UNI) or WITH ONE (UNO). If we say that Juno says 'which has barely happened to me, Juno, alone' (uni) that I have been made a mother from Jupiter, although many others have been made mothers—then we will say that Ovid does not abstain from corrupting the stories. Or [Juno says] 'that has happened to me with one' (uno), that is with Vulcan, whom she had from Jupiter, so that she is a mother.

In this example, the lemma offers two alternatives, *uni* or *uno*. Both are extant in manuscripts of the *Metamorphoses* (although *uno* only as a correction or addition). Here the commentator argues for the plausibility of the different readings by adding further attributes to *uni* and *uno*. In the first case, he adds attributes to let us know that *uni* ('one', dative) must refer to Juno. In the second case the attributes explain that *uno* ('one', ablative) refers to Vulcan. The first alternative seems to be ruled out and the commentator argues (in a similar mode to the example above) that if this alternative is valid, then Ovid had the stories wrong. In contrast, the second alternative is backed up by a mythological background-type explanation, where we learn about Juno's child Hebe (not included in this quotation). This explanation shows signs of the medieval reader trying to harmonize all the ancient mythological information available to them to create a consistent ancient mythology.

The last three examples above belong to a group of explanations that, as opposed to the previous group, could only belong to the *Metamorphoses*. They are strongly associated with the text, usually interact directly with it, and sometimes even make direct mention of Ovid. This group is smaller than the non-specific group, but still contains a substantial number of explanations. It may be tempting to hear a schoolmaster's voice in these types of explanations, and later on, when commentaries with identified authors are concerned, this is probably exactly what we are witnessing. If we are looking for clues to the contemporary use and reading of the *Metamorphoses*, then these types of explanations will yield more of substance.

The last examples from the commentary will concern a type of explanation that can be sorted under the two broad groups discussed above (non-specific and text-specific explanations), but that I have chosen to discuss as a separate group as an ad hoc formation for the purpose of highlighting some connections between this commentary and the later development of Ovid commentaries.

The first example in this group concerns an allegorical explanation. The following is one of only two allegorical explanations in clm 4610:[41]

> INNICERE ANGVIPEDVM. Gigantes pedes habuisse dicuntur anguineos surgere a terra non ualentes, et significat illos, qui semper adherent terrenis. (1.184)

> [EACH] OF THE SERPENT-FOOTED [WAS IN ACT] TO LAY. Giants are said to have had snake-legs, not being able to rise from the ground, and this signifies those who always cling to earthly things.

The explanation reacts to the phrase *quisque anguipedum* ('each of the snake-legged ones') in the *Metamorphoses* and first explains that this is said about the giants, a common enough type of explanation, but then it goes on to say that this signifies those who always adhere to earthly things. This is a very short and compact allegorical explanation, and almost unique in the commentary, but it evokes a tradition that has been present since antiquity, used sparingly by Servius

---

[41] The other one is found in the explanation to 9:647 and concerns the mythological beast the Chimera.

in the case of Virgil, but completely by Fulgentius in his *Expositio Virgilianae continentiae*. This tradition was also to become much more frequent in commentaries on Ovid in later centuries. The first commentator to develop a more consistent allegorical interpretation on Ovid is the late twelfth century Arnulf of Orléans and his *Allegoriae*, illustrated by this example:

> Iactu Deucalionis lapides mutantur in viros. Iactu Pirre in feminas. Phisica ibi tangitur. In coitu enim viri et femine si superhabundat sperma viri creatur vir, si mulieris, creatur femina. Sed ad ostendendum hominis duriciam de lapidibus hoc dicit a materia prime creationis contractam.

> From Deucalion's throw the stones were transformed into men. From Pyrrha's throw, into women. This pertains to physics. For in sexual congress between man and woman, a man is created if male sperm abounds, a woman if female sperm abounds. But Ovid says this about stones to show the hardness of men caused by the substance of the first creation.[42]

Here Arnulf makes an allegorical interpretation of the passage in Book 1 of the *Metamorphoses* where Deucalion and Pyrrha repopulate the world.[43] Arnulf's allegories are few and short, but later on this mode of explanation becomes almost dominant, as can be seen in the fourteenth-century *Ovidius Moralizatus* by Pierre Bersuire.[44]

Akin to the allegorical explanation is the historicizing or euhemeristic explanation, of which a few can be found in clm 4610:

> FIDIBVSQVE MEI COMMISSA MARITI et cetera. Cadmus fecit Thebas. Amphion uero adauxit. Et dicitur etiam mouisse cum suis fidibus lapides ad muros faciendos. Sed secundum rei ueritatem non fuit aliud, nisi quia Amphion fuit homo sapiens et docuit rudes homines facere ciuitatem.   (6.178)

> ENTRUSTED TO MY AND MY HUSBAND'S LYRE et cetera. Cadmus founded Thebes, but Amphion enlarged it. And he is even said to have moved stones for the construction of the walls with his lyre. But in reality this was nothing other than that Amphion, being a learned man, taught the unskilled men to build the city.

Here the explanation consists of background information which is then challenged by the phrase *sed secundum rei ueritatem* ('but in reality'), which is then followed by the euhemeristic or historicizing explanation. This type is not very common and does not follow a consistent pattern. Some phenomena are

---

[42] Ghisalberti (1932) 202.
[43] See the discussion of precisely this issue of gendered creation in Feldherr's contribution to this volume.
[44] For a sample of Bersuire's work see van der Bijl (1971).

explained euhemeristically, while other similar phenomena are not. The euhemeristic explanation seems to work as a kind of alternative to or extension of the mythological background story, where, for some reason, the commentator has chosen not to take the text at face value but sought to find another meaning.

The two examples above could be said to pertain to the culture clash between ancient pagan culture and medieval Christian culture. The following two examples are a more explicit illustration of this clash:

> INDVITVR FACIEM TAVRI. Hic Ouidius plane Iouem deridet, non credens illum esse summum deum, sicut et alii philosophi non credebant, sed propter impera[re]tores sic locuti sunt dicentes Iouem esse summum deum.   (2.850)

> HE ASSUMED THE FORM OF A BULL. Here Ovid clearly makes fun of Jupiter. He does not believe that Jupiter is the highest god, just as other philosophers did not believe this, but on account of the emperors who said that he was the highest god, they said this.

> HANC LITEM D<EVS> ET M<ELIOR> NATVRA, id est uoluntas Dei, filius Dei, DIREMIT. Et sic quantum ad effectum, id est secundum <eos>, qui uidebant, non quod Deo aliquid accidat, ut sit 'melior'. Dictum est de Ihesu: 'Puer Ihesus proficiebat etate et sapientia apud Deum et homines'.   (1.21)

> THIS STRIFE GOD, AND THE BETTER NATURE, that is the will of God, the son of God, SETTLED. And thus with respect to the effect, that is according to those, who realised that nothing can happen to God, so that he would become 'better'. It is said about Jesus: 'The boy Jesus advanced in wisdom and age and grace with God and men.'

These explanations can be termed Christianizing, and as such are the only ones to be found in the commentary. Previous researchers, who only had access to a small selection from clm 4610, made quite a lot of these passages and saw it as a sign of the Christianization of Ovid.[45] However, in the *accessus* the commentator clearly places Ovid in a group of pagan philosophers.[46] These explanations are unique among *circa* 460 other explanations. This of course makes one wonder whether they were excerpted from a different material, or whether they were meant to serve as an example for possible interpretations of Ovid, but then not followed through in the rest of the commentary.

The first example does not mention Christianity explicitly, but rather only includes a critique of pagan religion in the form of Ovid's supposed mocking of Jupiter. The second example is explicitly Christian in that it mentions God and Jesus, and uses a quotation from the Bible (Luke 2:52). This explanation concerns

---

[45] Demats 1973 and Herren 2004 for varying views on this matter.
[46] Wahlsten Böckerman (2016) 184, clm 4610 62vb. See also Dronke (2016) on this matter.

the part of the first book of the *Metamorphoses* that treats the creation of the world. It reacts to the fact that the god/God is paired with the phrase *Melior natura* ('a better nature'), which is explained as the will of God. The explanation then states that *melior* ('better') should not be applied to God, who, of course, cannot be made better, but that this must refer to Jesus, who increased in wisdom as he grew older. This explanation is almost theological in its style and completely unique to this commentary.

With only a total of around fifteen explanations (and almost all of them euhemeristic), the group represented by these four examples cannot be considered representative for the commentary. They do, however, point to a future development of the Ovidian commentary. Towards the end of the twelfth century Arnulf wrote his allegories and from then on the Christianizing elements in Ovid commentaries started featuring strongly. The intellectual climate around 1200 and onwards, with the birth of the universities, the rise of scholasticism and also the fact that Ovid became an established author, was of course different from that around 1100. However, this alone does not answer the discrepancies between clm 4610 and later commentaries. If the features discussed in the third group had been entirely missing that would have been one thing, but they do exist, even if scattered through the text in a small number. Whether this indicates that there might originally have been more of this type of explanations, or whether they were the more or less unique creation of some master is difficult to tell. In both scenarios the presence of these few explanations would have been the choice of the commentator/compiler who made clm 4610 and would be a sign of the intellectual preferences or needs of their particular environment.

Conclusion

Let us begin the conclusion by summing up what we can say about Ovid's oldest documented readers, or, rather, about the first document witnessing a comprehensive reading of the *Metamorphoses*. We have seen that Ovid's poem was for a long time disseminated on a much smaller scale compared to many other ancient authors.

The commentary in clm 4610 seems to coincide with the increased copying of not only Ovid's text, but of ancient texts in general, and this also coincides with the so-called Renaissance of the twelfth century, or the Long Twelfth Century. The commentary is, as far as we know, the earliest preserved complete commentary on Ovid. This may be a pure coincidence, or there may not have been any substantial commentaries written on the *Metamorphoses* before year 1100. There were, however, plenty of other older texts available that an eclectic commentary like clm 4610 could sample.

When the commentary was analysed based on the original ten categories that I had postulated, I found that the following conclusions could be drawn: the commentary seems to prioritize familiarizing the reader with the world of the *Metamorphoses* by giving background information to the stories contained within. This strategy is continued by helping the reader to understand the actual text by giving grammatical help. A lesser function of the commentary is to enable the reader to generate a vocabulary based on the text, which it primarily does by using derivations and etymologies. Finally, the commentary provides a steady stream of interpretations ranging from euhemeristic to interpretations concerned with the narrative structure of the *Metamorphoses*. To this we now add the filter from the three groups discussed above. The first group, the non-specific explanations, shows the commentary at its most eclectic. This group also makes the commentary's ties backwards in time and tradition visible, its debt to famous commentators such as Servius, as well as unknown commentaries and compendia which must have worked as inspiration and sources for clm 4610. The second group, the text-specific commentaries, indicate an Ovidian commentary proper. Since they are so closely tied to the text of the *Metamorphoses* they could not very well have been copied from a commentary on another author. This means that even if the commentary in clm 4610 might be copied from one or several unknown sources, it is still in this document that we find the first proper readings of the *Metamorphoses*. The majority of these readings are quite elementary, but they also contain some rather advanced narratological or even text-critical explanations. This group would, in contrast to the previous group, represent the here-and-now of year 1100. This is also true for the third group, the special selection, but this group also specifically points forward to the future development of the Ovid commentaries. It is not a large group, but it raises the question of the development of allegorical, historicizing and Christianizing explanations.

Finally, the sampling and the eclectic nature of the commentary raise the question whether we can speak about a planned composition at all, or simply of a copy of random notes on Ovid. This question is difficult to answer definitively, but the different aspects of the content of the commentary still seem to point to a document with some sort of pedagogic propensity. Perhaps from our modern point of view, we may consider it an archaic database which allows us to extract pieces of what the high Middle Ages knew about the ancient world. The same analogy would then hold true for the *Metamorphoses*, which would be the primary store of information about the ancient world, supplied by the commentary but also supplying the source for extracting the code which is Ovid's language, and refining the readers' own code, which was by then the acquired language that was medieval Latin.

One thing is clear: although the prologue to the commentary claimed that 'Ovid elucidated and explained', it is obvious that the text's users around year 1100 needed large parts of the *Metamorphoses* to be just that—elucidated and explained. This elucidating and explaining would then continue non-stop until our own time and was in its own way the first step for Ovid to live, as he wanted, in fame throughout all the ages.

9

The *Metamorphoses* of Sin

Prudentius, Dante, Milton

Philip Hardie

The reception of Ovid's *Metamorphoses* is as varied and colourful as the poem itself. But certain aspects of that kaleidoscopic reception have attracted more attention than others. Ovid's *perpetuum carmen* provides the Renaissance and post-Renaissance imagination with the space and freedom to explore countless tales of Greek and Roman mythology in literature and art. The *Metamorphoses* is one of the major vehicles for the survival of the *pagan* gods. The anti-foundationalism of the Ovidian narratives has often helped to liberate writers and artists from the constraints of theological and ideological straitjackets. Ovid's dramatization of extreme cases of individual psychopathology has encouraged a turn inwards, and away from a focus on man's relationships and responsibilities within the structures of society and religion.

But the *Metamorphoses* is of course not blind to the 'serious' issues of society and religion that were a traditional preoccupation of epic. Ovid, the most poly-morphic of poets, offers many starting-points for poetry of faith and belief. In the Middle Ages the *Ovide moralisé* transformed the *Metamorphoses* into a manual of Christian doctrine and morality.[1] In this chapter I look at three Christian poets whose own deep religious convictions have never been in doubt, poets who are all also profoundly Ovidian: Prudentius, Dante, Milton. The Ovidianism of Dante and Milton has been the subject of numerous studies in recent years.[2] The eighteenth-century English scholar Richard Bentley labelled Prudentius, perhaps the greatest of the late antique Christian poets, 'the Virgil and Horace of the Christians', *Christianorum Maro et Flaccus*; but Prudentius can also turn on the

---

[1] Dimmick (2002) 279: 'The *Ovide moralisé* ... wants from the Bible ... a master narrative ... of sin and redemption, which centres, obsessively, on the Incarnation of Christ as the ultimate metamorphosis.' Desmond (2007) 74–5: 'As a Christian exegete dealing with the pagan deities, the *Ovide moralisé* translator elaborates on the Christian mysteries of the Trinity and the story of the Incarnation in order to restore a notion of divine ethics to Ovid's text.' In general on Ovid in the Middle Ages see the contributions in Keith and Rupp (2007); Clark, Coulson, McKinley (2011 in Ginsberg 2011).

[2] Dante and Ovid: Brownlee (1985); Barolini (1987/1989); Jacoff and Schnapp (1991); Sowell (1991); Levenstein (1996); Gildenhard and Zissos (2013) 200–3. Milton and Ovid: Harding (1946); DuRocher (1985); Rumreich (1989); Dufour (1999); Brown (2002) ch. 6; Green (2009); Kilgour (2012); Hardie (2015a).

Philip Hardie, *The Metamorphoses of Sin: Prudentius, Dante, Milton* In: *Metamorphic Readings: Transformation, Language, and Gender in the Interpretation of Ovid's Metamorphoses* Edited by: Alison Sharrock, Daniel Möller, and Mats Malm, Oxford University Press (2020). © Oxford University Press.
DOI: 10.1093/oso/9780198864066.003.0010

Christian Ovid when he wants.[3] In all three cases we will see that writing Christian metamorphosis is compatible with an Ovidian ingenuity and playfulness.

My three case studies in Ovidian reception are narratives of the transformation of human form into the shape of a snake or serpent. Prudentius and Milton narrate the metamorphosis of Satan himself from his anthropomorphic angelic shape into serpentine form. Dante witnesses the serpentine transformations of human sinners, the thieves in the seventh *bolgia* of the eighth circle of Inferno, but these too are satanic metamorphoses.

The Christian poets operate within a fixed theology of crime and punishment. Dante and Milton, at least, also narrate the metamorphoses of sin within a wider philosophy or theology of change and mutability. Crime and punishment, and the philosophy of mutability, are both themes in the *Metamorphoses*, but it cannot be said that Ovid presents a single message on either punishment or mutability. In the last book of the *Metamorphoses*, Pythagoras delivers a long didactic disquisition on the principle of mutability, but this Pythagorean and Heraclitean account of unending flux signally fails to account for most of the changes narrated in the *Metamorphoses*, which are one-way, 'terminal', metamorphoses.

Again, there are many stories of metamorphosis inflicted or undergone as divine punishment for a crime, but the reaction of the gods to mortal offences is more often than not morally ambiguous, and the reader is often reluctant to accept that the punishment fits the crime. This is notoriously the case for Actaeon, the justice of whose violent punishment by Diana is made a matter of debate by the narrator, *Met.* 3.253–5: 'Common talk wavered this way and that: to some the goddess seemed more cruel than was just; others called her act worthy of her austere virginity; both sides found good reasons for their judgment' (trans. F.J. Miller, Loeb).[4] The first narrative in the poem of the metamorphosis of a human being is one of the purest examples of a punishment fitting the crime: the bloodthirsty and wolfish Lycaon is transformed into the wolf that by nature and by name (Lyk-aon, from Greek *lukos* 'wolf'), he already was. This is an example of the *contrappasso* by which in Dante's *Inferno* and *Purgatorio* the punishment fits the crime. But this first 'regular' metamorphosis in Ovid's poem turns out not to have a programmatic value for the following narratives, any more than the Speech of Pythagoras in the last book has a summative value for all that has preceded.[5] Furthermore, the story of Lycaon is told by the first of the poem's internal narrators, Jupiter himself, whose view of the justice of Zeus does not entirely coincide with that of the primary narrator. And even Jupiter does not narrate

---

[3] Prudentius and Ovid: Salvatore (1985) ch. 2 'Ovidio cristiano'.

[4] Galinsky (1975) 13 on 'the clear link between the metamorphosis and the evasion of a concern with profound, moral, underlying problems, and the avoidance of a true moral solution': exemplified by the Erysichthon story, in which the 'grotesque depiction of Erysichthon's ravenous mania divert[s] us from serious concern with the problem of crime and punishment'.

[5] On the paradoxically non-programmatic nature of the Lycaon episode see Anderson (1989).

Lycaon's fate *as* a divine punishment; the metamorphosis, in Alessandro Barchiesi's words, 'proceeds by a kind of internal necessity, expressed through a series of physical and moral homologies between the man and the wild beast'.[6] The punishment directly imposed by Jupiter for the impiety of Lycaon and what Jupiter asserts (without evidence) to be a widespread criminality on the part of humanity is the grossly disproportionate destruction of almost the whole race of mankind by the Flood.

The story of Lycaon is also, as Barchiesi indicates, the first of the poem's multiple explorations of the boundaries between beast, man, and god. In the last books of the *Metamorphoses* there is an acceleration of narratives of apotheosis, transformations of humans into gods, that might be suggestive for the Christian teleological narrative of the redemption of mankind through the Incarnation of Christ, God's assumption of the nature of man, that allows man to regain his original godlikeness. Movement in the opposite direction, downwards from man to beast, becomes, in biblical terms, a 'fall', and a falling that is both physical and moral is emphasized in all three of my Christian serpentine metamorphoses.

The Ovidian model for human into serpent transformation is the metamorphosis of Cadmus and Harmonia at *Met.* 4.569–603.[7] Wearied by age and a long series of family disasters, Cadmus, the founder of Thebes, wonders whether he has been punished by divine anger for killing the serpent of Mars that infested the site of Thebes before the foundation of the city (*Met.* 3.28–98). If that is the case, says Cadmus, he prays that he himself may be stretched out in serpent form, a prayer that is instantly followed by his metamorphosis into a serpent. He undergoes a physical fall to the ground, *in pectusque cadit pronus* (579). As his body changes, he begs his wife Harmonia to touch him and clasp his hand, while he still has a hand that can be clasped. He is prevented from further human speech by the splitting in two of his tongue, and can utter only hisses instead of articulate complaints. Harmonia watches in consternation, her gaze fixed on Cadmus' individual body parts as they disappear one by one, and asks the gods that she too might be changed into the same serpent form (*cur non / me quoque, caelestes, in eandem uertitis anguem?* 593–4). No sooner has she spoken than she too is a serpent, sharing the shape at which she gazes. What had seemed to Cadmus to be a punishment for the 'crime' of ridding the site of the future city of Thebes of a terrifying and murderous serpent turns out to be the release of Cadmus and Harmonia from the years of misfortunes that have afflicted their Thebans, and it is the perpetuation, albeit in snake form, of the loving relationship of husband and wife, a *iuncta metamorphosis*: *et subito duo sunt iunctoque uolumine serpunt* ('and suddenly they are two snakes, and

---

[6] Barchiesi (2005) on *Met.* 1.232–9.
[7] On serpents and serpent-metamorphoses in the *Metamorphoses* see Genovese (1983).

they creep along with yoked coils', 600). Their end is comparable to the shared metamorphoses of other loving married couples, of Philemon and Baucis into trees in *Met.* 8, and of Ceyx and Alcyone into halcyon birds in *Met.* 11. Cadmus and Harmonia are harmless and peaceable serpents, preserving their nature as human beings. Cadmus falls, but this is a purely physical movement, without moral overtones. Nevertheless, this is the point when the city-founder, who has already left human society together with his wife by going into voluntary exile from Thebes, undergoes a descent in the chain of being from human to animal.

It is rather the serpent sacred to Mars, killed by Cadmus, that is a monster of Hellish destructiveness, an evil to be eradicated before human civilization can be planted in the virgin landscape:

silua uetus stabat nulla uiolata securi,	
et specus in media uirgis ac uimine densus	
efficiens humilem lapidum conpagibus arcum	30
uberibus fecundus aquis; ubi conditus antro	
Martius anguis erat, cristis praesignis et auro;	
igne micant oculi, corpus tumet omne uenenis,	
tresque uibrant linguae, triplici stant ordine dentes.	
quem postquam Tyria lucum de gente profecti	35
infausto tetigere gradu, demissaque in undas	
urna dedit sonitum, longo caput extulit antro	
caeruleus serpens horrendaque sibila misit.	
effluxere urnae manibus sanguisque reliquit	
corpus et attonitos subitus tremor occupat artus.	40
ille uolubilibus squamosos nexibus orbes	
torquet et inmensos saltu sinuatur in arcus	
ac media plus parte leues erectus in auras	
despicit omne nemus tantoque est corpore, quanto,	
si totum spectes, geminas qui separat arctos.	45

Met. 3.28–45

There was a primeval forest there, scarred by no axe; and in its midst a cave thick set about with shrubs and pliant twigs. With well-fitted stones it fashioned a low arch, whence poured a full-welling spring, and deep within dwelt a serpent sacred to Mars. The creature had a wondrous golden crest; fire flashed from his eyes; his body was all swollen with venom; his triple tongue flickered out and in and his teeth were ranged in triple row. When with luckless steps the wayfarers of the Tyrian race had reached this grove, they let down their vessels into the spring, breaking the silence of the place. At this the dark serpent thrust forth his head out of the deep cave, hissing horribly. The urns fell from the men's hands, their blood ran cold, and, horror-struck, they were seized with a sudden trembling. The serpent twines his scaly coils in rolling knots and with a spring curves himself into a huge bow; and, lifted high by more than half his length into the unsubstantial air, he looks down upon the whole wood, as huge, could you see him all, as is that serpent in the sky that lies outstretched between the twin bears.

> tum uero postquam solitas accessit ad iras
> causa recens, plenis tumuerunt guttura uenis,
> spumaque pestiferos circumfluit albida rictus,
> terraque rasa sonat squamis, quique halitus exit   75
> ore niger Stygio, uitiatas inficit auras.
> ipse modo inmensum spiris facientibus orbem
> cingitur, interdum longa trabe rectior adstat,
> inpete nunc uasto ceu concitus imbribus amnis
> fertur et obstantis proturbat pectore siluas.   80
>
> *Met*.3. 72–80

Then indeed fresh fuel was added to his native wrath; his throat swells with full veins, and white foam flecks his horrid jaws. The earth resounds with his scraping scales, and such rank breath as exhales from the Stygian cave befouls the tainted air. Now he coils in huge spiral folds; now shoots up, straight and tall as a tree; now he moves on with huge rush, like a stream in flood, sweeping down with his breast the trees in his path.   (trans. F.J. Miller)

Ovid's serpent is a close relative of destructive Virgilian serpents, in particular the two sea-serpents that kill Laocoon and his sons in *Aeneid* 2, in an act of bestial violence that foreshadows and motivates the destruction of the city of Troy—the fall of Troy. The Theban serpent is also related to the fire-breathing monster Cacus who infests the site of Rome until he is killed by the saviour Hercules in *Aeneid* 8, in another variant on the theme of the dragon-slaying hero.

Ovid engineers a kind of *contrappasso* between Cadmus' 'crime' in killing the serpent and his 'punishment' of transformation into a serpent, through the utterance of the mysterious voice that addresses Cadmus after killing the monster, 3.95–8: *dum spatium uictor uicti considerat hostis, / uox subita audita est: 'quid, Agenore nate, peremptum / serpentem spectas? et tu spectabere serpens.* ('While the conqueror stands gazing on the huge bulk of his conquered foe, suddenly a voice sounds in his ears. . . . "Why, O son of Agenor, do you gaze on the serpent you have slain? You too shall be a serpent for men to gaze on."') The reversibility of human hero and serpent victim, mirrored syntactically in the contrast of active and passive, nominative and accusative, will be important for both Dante's and Milton's versions of the serpent metamorphosis.

Prudentius *Hamartigenia*

deterior mox sponte sua, dum decolor illum
inficit inuidia stimulisque instigat amaris.
arsit enim scintilla odii de fomite zeli
et dolor ingenium subitus conflauit iniquum.
uiderat argillam simulacrum et structile flatu   190
concaluisse Dei, dominum quoque conditioni
impositum, natura soli pelagique polique
ut famulans homini locupletem fundere partum
nosset et effusum terreno addicere regi.
inflauit fermento animi stomachante tumorem   195
bestia deque acidis uim traxit acerba medullis;
bestia sorde carens, cui tunc sapientia longi
corporis enodem[8] seruabat recta iuuentam,
complicat[9] ecce nouos sinuoso[10] pectore nexus,
inuoluens nitidam spiris torquentibus aluum.   200
simplex lingua prius uaria micat arte loquendi,
et discissa dolis resonat sermone trisulco.
hinc natale caput uitiorum, principe ab illo
fluxit origo mali, qui se corrumpere primum,
mox hominem didicit nullo informante magistro.   205

Hamartigenia 186–205

He became afterwards corrupt of his own will because envy marked him with her
stain and pricked him with her sore stings. For the spark of hate was fed into a
flame by jealousy, and resentment suddenly kindled enmity in his heart. He had
seen how a figure fashioned of clay grew warm under the breath of God and was
made lord of the creation, so that earth and sea and sky had learned to pour forth
their rich produce in the service of man and yield it lavishly to an earthly ruler. He
puffed up his swollen spirit with the passion/ferment of his irritated mind, and the
bitter beast drew strength from the acid in his marrow; a beast formerly without
stain, when upright wisdom kept his tall young body free of knots. See!—with his
winding breast he enfolds new/strange coils, twisting his bright belly in curling
spirals. His formerly single tongue flickers with the art of varied speaking, and
divided by guile sounds with three-forked words. This is the original source of

---

[8] Of speech, 'clear, plain', e.g. Plin. *Ep.* 5.17.2 *scripta elegis erat fluentibus et teneris et enodibus, sublimibus etiam.*
[9] In a non-physical, mental sense at Cic. *Off.* 3.76 *si qui uoluerit animi sui complicatam notionem euoluere.*
[10] Of style, 'diffuse', full of digressions', e.g. Quint. *Inst.* 2.4.3 *narrandi…ratio…neque rursus sinuosa et arcessitis descriptionibus.*

vices, from that author/prince [of darkness] flowed the source of evil, who instructed by no teacher learned to corrupt first himself, and then mankind.

(trans. H.J. Thomson, Loeb, adapted)

In this passage from Prudentius' didactic-narrative poem on the 'Origin of sin' we see the moment of transformation in which the once beautiful Lucifer corrupts himself into the Satanic serpent, twisting and debasing the unknotted uprightness of wisdom (*sapientia ... recta*, 197–8) into the coils of pride and envy.

The passage is 'a mosaic of typical Virgilian phraseology on serpents',[11] prominent among which is the elaborate description of the 'malignant snake, in Calabrian pastures' (*malus Calabris in saltibus anguis*), which plagues the pastoral world in *Georgics* 3 (425–39). Prudentius also draws on details of Ovid's Theban pastiche of Virgil's malevolent serpents: Prudentius looks through Ovid to Ovid's own Virgilian models. The physical coiling and twisting is now unambiguously a moral perversion; and both physical and moral complication are mirrored in the discordant variety of speech issuing from the newly forked tongue. The three-pointed tongue of Virgilian and Ovidian snakes (*Geo.* 3.439 *linguis ... trisulcis* = *Aen.* 2.475; *Met.* 3.34 *tres uibrant linguae*) becomes the forked tongue of Satan, the source of lies and slander.[12] The Prudentian passage enacts the fall of language into figuration:[13] Lucifer's metamorphosis into the serpentine enemy of the shepherd is eased through a recurrent play on literal and metaphorical uses of words: *acerba, recta, enodis, complico, simplex, sinuosus*, some of which have a history of use as stylistic metaphors (see footnotes 8 and 10).

The synergy of metamorphosis and metaphor is highly Ovidian, as too are the hints of personification that play around the edges of Prudentius' metamorphosis narrative: Lucifer is impelled by both pride, *superbia*, and envy, *inuidia* (187), traditional motivations for Satan's attack on mankind. The *tumor*, 'swelling', of his pride is described some lines earlier in language that is echoed in the description of the personification of *Superbia* in Prudentius' *Psychomachia* (*Ham.* 168–70: cf. *Psychom.* 181–5). The serpent is a standard attribute, and sometimes embodiment, of *Inuidia*.[14] Ovid's Envy is found eating the flesh of vipers, and her sideways (*obliquus*) envious glance mirrors the sideways movement of snakes.[15]

---

[11] Mahoney (1934) 200.

[12] Cf. Giotto's envy with a snake coming out of her mouth to sting her own eyes: see Gellrich (2000) 110–11.

[13] Malamud (2011) 102–4 'Seeing and saying: Satan and the fall of language'; Malamud points out that the linguistic division brought about by the devil's sin is immediately followed by the poem's first extended simile, a postlapsarian staining of the transparency of language.

[14] Envy and snakes: see Meskill (2009) 53–5; Dunbabin and Dickie (1983) 24–5, 32–3.

[15] *Met.* 2.768–70 (Minerva) *uidet intus edentem / uipereas carnes, uitiorum alimenta suorum, / Inuidiam, uisaque oculos auertit*; 2.787 *illa deam obliquo fugientem lumine cernens*. For the sideways movement of snakes cf. Hor. *C.* 3.27.5–7 *rumpat et serpens iter institutum / si per obliquum similis sagittae / terruit mannos*; Lucr. 5.692–3 *annua sol in quo concludit tempora serpens, / obliquo terras et*

Satan is the author of a poetics of novelty, a *uaria ars loquendi* ('a varied art of speaking', 201), a *poikilia* valued negatively.[16] Prudentius himself is not immune to the temptations of varied and complicated poetic language. This passage is the kind of thing that Antonio Salvatore had in mind when he claimed that 'Prudentius shows himself to be even more of an *amator ingenii sui*, "in love with his own talent", even more intemperate than Ovid.'[17]

Dante *Inferno*

Dante exults in the power of his linguistic invention in the most extended passage of metamorphic narrative in the *Commedia*, the *bolgia* of thieves in *Inferno* 24 and 25. In a famous outburst (*Inf.* 25.94–9), Dante bids Lucan and Ovid fall silent in the face of his own virtuoso handling of the effects of snake bite and of serpentine metamorphosis, with reference to the Libyan snakes in book 9 of Lucan's *Civil War*, and to Ovid's accounts of the metamorphosis of Cadmus into serpent and of Arethusa into a fountain. Thumbing his nose at his poetic 'gods', Dante risks repeating the *hubris* of the most defiant of the thieves, Vanni Fucci, who finishes his threatening speech of prophecy to Dante by putting up two fingers to God. Dante tells us that this is the worst example that he sees in *Inferno* of the sin of pride (*Inf.* 25.13–15), the sin proper to Satan.

Dante achieves his unprecedented effects by grafting Lucanian snake bites on to Ovidian metamorphosis. The thieves are punished with the loss of their humanity as retribution for having deprived others of what properly belongs to them. There are three types of punishment. In the first (24.97–108) a snake punctures one of the thieves in the back of his neck. The result is instant combustion, and the man falls to the ground as a pile of ash. The dust instantly reforms itself as the man it was (who proceeds to reveal himself as Vanni Fucci), an event compared by the narrator to the death and rebirth of the phoenix.[18] In the second and third episodes more complicated fusions and exchanges of identity take place, in keeping with the Aristotelian and Thomist teaching that injustice involves a violation of one's relationship with others.[19] In the second (25.49–66), a six-

---

caelum lumine lustrans; Aen. 5.273–4 *qualis saepe uiae deprensus in aggere serpens, / aerea quem obliquum rota transiit.*

[16] ἁπλότης of literary style: Dion. Hal. *Ars rhet.* 9.14.   [17] Salvatore (1958) 268.

[18] Dante perhaps also remembers the bestiary lore that the snake rejuvenates itself by sloughing its skin, to which Virgil alludes in the simile at *Aen.* 2.471–5 comparing Neoptolemus, the son of Achilles who appears as if he were his father reborn, to a snake emerging from the earth after winter, *positis nouus exuuiis* 'renewed after sloughing its skin'. After Vanni Fucci has uttered his defiance against God, he is prevented from further speech of movement by other snakes that wrap themselves tightly about him (*Inf.* 25.4–9), possibly alluding to another episode in *Aeneid* 2, the serpents that wrap themselves around Laocoon and his sons (*Aen.* 2.212–24).

[19] Arist. *EN* 5.1; Aquinas *ST* II^a^-II^ae^ q. 58 n. 8 arg. 3; see Ginsberg (2011) 157.

legged serpent launches itself at a thief, clinging to him more closely than ivy, melding and melting the two figures into one appearance, annihilating the distinct human form in a betwixt and between, a both and neither that replicates the loss of individual identity in the fusion of Salmacis and Hermaphroditus in *Metamorphoses* 4. In the third, and climactic, metamorphosis (25.79–141), a small fiery black snake pierces the navel of a thief and falls back. Thief and snake stare at each other, both begin to emit smoke, and, in a minutely detailed account of the reciprocal metamorphosis, longer than any of Ovid's protracted narratives of transformation, they exchange not just looks, but also shapes, man turning into snake and snake into man, all the while keeping their gazes fixed on each other. The one rises up and the other falls down (121). The one looks at a serpent (as it changes into man), and the other is looked on as (he changes into) a serpent. Or, to quote Ovid's line with a change of punctuation and with a change of pronominal reference, *Met.* 3.98 (the mysterious voice addressing Cadmus as he looks on the body of the serpent that he has killed) '*serpentem spectas; et tu spectabere serpens*', 'a serpent is the object of your gaze; you too will be the object of gaze as a serpent'.

As well as exemplifying sin's descent from human to bestial, these transformations parody central metamorphic mysteries of the Christian faith. The phoenix-like reconstitution of the ashes of the first thief is a resurrection, of which the phoenix was a familiar symbol. The merging of the two shapes in the second metamorphosis parodies the doctrine of the two natures in the Incarnation of Christ. The resulting 'imagine perversa' 'seemed both two and none' (77–8): this instance of *uertere*, 'changing', is also a per-version—and perhaps also a 'perverse image' of the Incarnation. This fusion of physical and moral meanings of the vocabulary of metamorphosis is also seen a few lines earlier, 'two figures appeared mixed into one appearance, where two had been lost, *perduti*' (71–2). Ovid uses *perdere* objectively of the 'loss' of a previous shape through metamorphosis;[20] in *Inferno* 'perduti' inescapably also refers to lost souls.

As Dante passes through the *bolgia* of thieves, it seems that he is witness to single instances of transformations that will be repeated again and again. This at least seems to be a natural inference in the case of the first and third metamorphoses. Vanni Fucci will repeatedly turn to dust and rise again, and the fiery little snake and the human will repeatedly exchange shapes, although it is perhaps difficult to see how Agnello will disentangle himself from the alien who has grown into his human body. If that is so, repetition is what distinguishes the metamorphoses of sin from the metamorphoses of salvation—Incarnation, Resurrection, and the transcendence of the human, 'trasumanar', that Dante experiences in *Paradiso* 1 (64–72) as he gazes on Beatrice, an experience that he compares to that of Ovid's Glaucus when he tasted the magic herb that transformed him into a sea-god

---

[20] *Met.* 1.546 *mutando perde figuram*; 4.409 *nec qua perdiderint ueterem ratione figuram*; 13.405 *perdidit infelix hominis post omnia formam.*

(*Met.* 13.924–63). The thieves are condemned to sterile and demonic repetition, from which they can never escape to another level of being.[21]

Glaucus' account of his own metamorphosis into a sea-god concludes book 13 of Ovid's *Metamorphoses*. Earlier in the book there is an example of a ritual repetition, which is also a reflection of a metamorphosis. Every year the Memnon birds, whose bodies were a transformation of the glowing ashes that flew up from the funeral pyre of the Ethiopian hero Memnon, join in aerial battle, to fall again as they fell on their first appearance, as sacrificial offerings to their 'relative', the dead Memnon (13.615 *inferiaeque cadunt cineri cognata sepulto*). The image is one of annual gladiatorial games in honour of the dead man (*Parentalia*). Within the *Metamorphoses* the annual renewal of warfare by the resurrected birds foreshadows the periodic rebirth of the dying phoenix (*Met.* 15.391–407). The phoenix was to become a favourite image of positive rebirth and resurrection for both pagan panegyric of the Roman emperor, and for Christian celebration of the mysteries of the resurrection of Christ and of the general resurrection of the dead. The annual war between the opposing armies of Memnon-birds, a war between 'sisters' (*sorores, Met.* 13.608), is an image of civil war, to periodic repetitions of which, in one pessimistic view of Roman destiny, the Romans were condemned as punishment for the 'original sin' of Romulus' killing of his brother Remus. Dante compares the 'resurrection' of Vanni Fucci to the rebirth of the phoenix, but the description of the ashes and dust into which Vanni Fucci's body collapses and from which it is re-formed perhaps directs us rather to Ovid's Memnon-birds, which are formed from the black cinders (*atra fauilla, Met.* 13.604) of Memnon's pyre, and whose bodies fall every year as an offering to the ashes of their relative (*inferiaeque cadunt cineri cognata sepulto / corpora*, 615–6). Dust and ashes do not figure in Ovid's account of the phoenix's self-immolation and rebirth.

Milton *Paradise Lost*

Milton's Satan and his fellow devils undergo a serpentine transformation which becomes an annual event in something akin to ritual repetition: *Paradise Lost* 10.575–7 'Yearly enjoined, some say, to undergo / This annual humbling certain numbered days, / To dash their pride, and joy for man seduced.' Milton locates the first metamorphosis at a different point in the story from Prudentius, at the moment when Satan returns to Hell after engineering the Fall of Adam and Eve, in triumph, as he thinks, to report his victory to the assembled devils. After he

[21] See Kilgour (2007) 277–9 on the serpentine metamorphosis of Milton's devils and *Inferno* 24–5, with reference to the fixity of ritual repetition in the fallen world; Schwartz (1993), esp. ch. 4, on the difference between/proximity of ritual and Satanic repetition.

delivers his speech, glory turns to shame,[22] as he hears not applause, but 'A dismal universal hiss, the sound / Of public scorn'. His audience have turned into snakes, and Satan immediately experiences his own metamorphosis into a monstrous serpent, as 'supplanted down he fell' (513)—as Cadmus fell down flat on his chest (*in pectusque cadit pronus*, *Met.* 4.579). Satan's 'high capital' of Pandemonium turns into a snake pit, with a catalogue of serpents that alludes both to Lucan's Libyan snakes, and to Dante's transplantation to Hell of Lucan's catalogue.[23] Satan's fall into the shape of a snake is multiply determined: it is the fall that follows pride, to be commemorated in the 'annual humbling'; it is punishment for the fall of mankind, and it is a repetition of Lucifer's own original fall from heaven. Satan hears and looks at anthropomorphic bodies changed into serpents and himself changes into a serpent. This mutuality, another transform of the Ovidian line 'you gaze on a serpent, and you too will be gazed on as a serpent', is repeated when Satan and his audience crawl out of the hall of Pandemonium to face the rest of the 'heaven-fallen' devils, who are waiting to acclaim their triumphant chief, 538–41: 'They saw, but other sight instead, a crowd / Of ugly serpents; horror on them fell, / And horrid sympathy; for what they saw, / They felt themselves now changing; down their arms, / Down fell both spear and shield, down they as fast . . .', as they too experience the fall into serpent shape.

Satan falls from glorious hero into bestial monster. His transformation is also a *contrappasso* of a peculiarly fitting kind, 'punished in the shape he sinned' (516), as Milton puts it. To seduce Eve into eating the apple Satan had chosen as his disguise, from all the animals in Eden, the serpent. This is the last of a series of self-transformations performed by Satan as he tracks his human prey in Eden: he has taken on the shapes of lion, tiger, and toad (4.397–8 'himself now one, / Now other, as their shape served best his end'). Satan is a shape-shifter, as the Devil and demons traditionally are, able to change himself into any number of animal shapes, and back, at will. It is this freedom that is taken from him when he undergoes an involuntary transformation into serpent: 'a greater power / Now ruled him' (10.515–6).[24]

Previously, even the voluntary, and temporary, assumption of serpent form had offended Satan's sense of pride: 9.163–7 'O foul descent! That I who erst contended / With gods to sit the highest, am now constrained / Into a beast, and mixed with bestial slime, / This essence to incarnate and imbrute, / That to the highth of deity aspired.'[25] 'Incarnate' is a parodic foreshadowing of the Incarnation which the Son

---

[22] Cf. Hosea 4:7 'As they were increased, so they sinned against me: therefore will I change their glory into shame.'

[23] On Dante and Milton see Samuel (1966).

[24] On the metamorphoses of Milton's Satan see Dufour (1999).

[25] Cf. Phineas Fletcher *Purple Island* 7.11 'There turn'd to serpents, swoln with pride and hate, / Their Prince a Dragon fell, . . . Thus while the snake they heare, they turn to snakes; / To make them gods he boasts, but beasts and devils makes.'

has already promised to enter upon (3.227–41). God will be incarnated in man to redeem mankind and, eventually, lead man back up to heaven; the ethereal body of Satan will undergo incarnation in a beast to bring about the fall of man. His punishment will be a degradation to the level of a brute beast over which he truly has no control.

When we see Satan approaching Eve as the 'inmate bad' of the serpent, we see not bestial slime, but a gorgeous apparition, 9.495–510:

> So spake the enemy of mankind, enclosed
> In serpent, inmate bad, and toward Eve   495
> Addressed his way, not with indented wave,
> Prone on the ground, as since, but on his rear,
> Circular base of rising folds, that towered
> Fold above fold a surging maze, his head
> Crested aloft, and carbuncle his eyes;   500
> With burnished neck of verdant gold, erect
> Amidst his circling spires, that on the grass
> Floated redundant: pleasing was his shape,
> And lovely, never since of serpent kind
> Lovelier, not those that in Illyria changed   505
> Hermione and Cadmus, or the god
> In Epidaurus; nor to which transformed
> Ammonian Jove, or Capitoline was seen,
> He with Olympias, this with her who bore
> Scipio the heighth of Rome.   510

The Satan-serpent is lovelier than the serpents into which Hermione (Harmonia) and Cadmus were transformed in Illyria, a direct reference to *Metamorphoses* 4 (lovelier too than the serpent manifestations of Aesculapius, at *Met.* 15.669–74, and of Jupiter when he impregnated the mothers of Alexander the Great and Scipio). Is this a purely delusive beauty, because the bejewelled and erect shape of the serpent is now controlled by Satan, or is this a last glimpse of the innocent beauty of the serpent in prelapsarian Eden? Prudentius' description of Satan's fall through the transformation of his formerly beautiful and youthful upright body, corresponding to his once upright wisdom (*recta . . . sapientia, Hamartigenia* 197–8), is also a fall into figuration. Here in *Paradise Lost* we may have a last glimpse of serpentine ecphrasis before language is infected by the Fall, when words like 'maze' and 'redundant' have not yet acquired their negative moral overtones, and when an innocent serpent may still be 'erect' in a non-sexual sense.[26]

---

[26] On the infection of language at the Fall see Ricks (1963) 109–17 'Words, actions all infect'. 'Erect(ed)' of moral uprightness in *Paradise Lost*: 1.679–80 'Mammon, the least erected spirit that fell /

Whatever one's judgement on that, what is beyond doubt is that Milton's description is indebted to Ovid's description of the serpent of Mars on the site of Thebes, and also to Ovid's own Virgilian models, including the description of the sea-serpents that come from Tenedos at *Aeneid* 2.203–12. Milton had alluded to that passage at the beginning of his narrative, when Satan lies on the burning lake, talking to Beelzebub:

> Thus Satan talking to his nearest mate
> With head up-lift above the wave, and eyes
> That sparkling blazed, his other parts besides
> Prone on the flood, extended long and large   195
> Lay floating many a rood...

Compare the sea-serpents from Tenedos at *Aeneid* 2.203–11:

> ecce autem gemini a Tenedo tranquilla per alta
> (horresco referens) immensis orbibus angues
> incumbunt pelago pariterque ad litora tendunt;   205
> pectora quorum inter fluctus arrecta iubaeque
> sanguineae superant undas, pars cetera pontum
> pone legit sinuatque immensa uolumine terga.
> fit sonitus spumante salo; iamque arua tenebant
> ardentisque oculos suffecti sanguine et igni   210
> sibila lambebant linguis uibrantibus ora.

Suddenly there came over the calm water from Tenedos (I shudder at the memory of it), two serpents leaning into the sea in great coils and making side by side for the shore. Breasting the waves, they held high their blood-stained crests, and the rest of their bodies ploughed the waves behind them, their backs winding, coil upon measureless coil, through the sounding foam of the sea. Now they were on land. Their eyes were burning and flecked with blood. They hissed as they licked their lips with quivering tongues.   (trans. D. West)

Satan's eyes 'sparkling blazed', like the burning eyes of the Virgilian sea serpents, who carry their breasts raised up (*arrecta*) through the waves, as the head of the recumbent Satan is 'uplift above the wave', as Satan makes his first move towards lifting himself up from the abyss into which he has fallen. That this

---

From Heaven...'; 4.286–7 (Adam and Eve) 'Two of far nobler shape, erect and tall, / Godlike erect'; 7.506–10 (God plans the creation of man) 'a creature, who, not prone / And brute as other creatures, but endued / With sanctity of reason, might erect / His stature, and upright with front serene / Govern the rest...'; 11.508–9 'The image of God in Man, created once / So goodly and erect, though faulty since'. On Milton's use of Prudentius see Edwards (1995).

is not just a fall, but also a change we know from Satan's first words in the poem, addressed to Beelzebub, but equally applicable to Satan himself, 1.84–7 'If thou beest he; but O how fallen! how changed / From him, who in the happy realms of light / Clothed with transcendent brightness didst outshine / Myriads though bright…' 'How changed', an echo of the dreaming Aeneas' address to the mangled ghost of Hector at *Aeneid* 2.274–5 *ei mihi, qualis erat, quantum mutatus ab illo / Hectore…* ('Alas, what a sight he was, how much changed from that Hector of yore…').

Satan will succeed in lifting himself off the burning lake, and launching himself into a flight across the immensities of space that will take him to the newly created earth, but this ascent will lead him only to new descents, culminating in a change downward into the form of a serpent, condemned by God to go on its belly.

But like Dante, Milton does operate with a consistent model of constructive change, change upward from body to spirit, and change through time, change from Chaos, the realm of mere potency, to apocalyptic perfection, the realm of pure actuality.[27] Not the least marvellous of the metamorphoses of goodness, as opposed to the metamorphoses of sin, is the conversion of evil into good, as Adam exclaims after the archangel Michael has given him a prophetic account of the world down to the Last Judgement, 12.469–71: 'O goodness infinite, goodness immense! / That all good of evil shall produce, / and evil *turn* to good.'

Conclusion

In classical epic, snakes can be benign, as well as malign. Cadmus' gaze on the slain monstrous and hellish serpent of Mars is mirrored, in a mysterious way, in his own, and his wife's, metamorphosis into snakes, but the mirroring does not extend to the moral quality of the metamorphosed Cadmus and Harmonia: in serpent form they perpetuate the private virtue of mutual conjugal love, although the physical fall of the royal couple, and their retreat into the countryside, are emblematic of the public failure of Thebes, the self-destructive city founded by Cadmus. This is in contrast to the potential of Virgil's Troy, a city destroyed by outside enemies, to regenerate itself in cities to be founded in the future. That phoenix-like metamorphosis is made possible by the destruction wrought by the serpents that kill Laocoon and his sons, and it is foreshadowed in the image of the serpent rejuvenated that is applied to Neoptolemus, an Achilles redivivus, at *Aeneid* 2.471–5 *in malam partem*, but looking forward, *in bonam partem*, to the *Troia resurgens* that will eventually be Rome.[28] A snake of unambiguously good

---

[27] On positive change in *Paradise Lost* see Rumrich (1989).
[28] The reversal of the valence of the image of the serpent is the subject of the classic article of Knox (1950).

omen is that which appears from the tomb of Anchises at Aeneas' celebration of the anniversary of his father's death in *Aeneid* 5, 84–99. Whatever the precise nature of this calm and harmless snake (Aeneas himself is uncertain), it is clear that this sacred beast emblematizes the continuity of life out of death, a positive omen for the future of Aeneas and his descendants at a moment of renewed grief for the death of his father. At a point near the end of Ovid's *Metamorphoses*, the serpent of Aesculapius is brought to Rome to bring relief from a plague that is also an image of the disease of Thebes-style civil war from which Augustus had recently redeemed the Romans (*Met.* 15.622–744). This is a snake that reveals its divine majesty by raising itself up on high (*sublimis*) in the temple of Aesculapius (15.673–4). This is one of the 'lovely' serpents to which Milton compares the gorgeous apparition of serpentine Satan at *Paradise* Lost 9.503–10 (discussed above), in a list which concludes with the serpent-form in which Jupiter is said to have impregnated the mother of Scipio Africanus, 'her who bore / Scipio the heighth of Rome.'

Snakes may have positive meanings in Christian contexts. In obedience to the instruction of God, Moses raised up the brazen serpent on a pole in order to save the Israelites from the fatal effect of snake-bites (Numbers 21:6–9), an action taken by Jesus as a type of the redemptive lifting up on the Cross of the Son of Man (John 3:14–6). But in the Christian narrative poetry that has been the subject of this paper, deeply indebted to the traditions of classical epic, it is the negative aspects of the image of the serpent that predominate. The association that already existed in antiquity of serpents with malevolence was reinforced by the ease with which the serpent that creeps on the ground provides an image of Christian narratives of fall, both literal (Lucifer's fall from heaven, God's curse on the serpent in the garden that it should go on its belly), and figurative (the fall of Satan and of Adam and Eve from innocence into the original sin of pride and disobedience). Running through the series of Christian reworkings of the motif of serpentine metamorphosis is an emphasis on the gaze and on the visual, which can be traced back to the mutuality of spectatorship by which the mysterious voice in *Metamorphoses* 3 links Cadmus' slaying of the serpent of Mars and his own 'fall' into serpent form. Prudentius' Lucifer begins his descent into snake form when he gazes enviously at the newly shaped lords of creation, and his metamorphosis is vividly enacted as a spectacle before the reader's eyes. Dante and Milton both develop in strangely fascinating, and memorably vivid, ways the Ovidian specularity whereby the gaze on the serpent triggers serpentine metamorphosis in the person of the gazer. These are narratives that perhaps contain a warning to the reader, lest, as we read, and visualize the text, we find ourselves falling into a repetition of original sin, from which Christ, uniquely, has been able to redeem the descendants of Adam and Eve. Man's inability until that point in history to extricate himself from the tedious repetition of the original sin, and man's regrettable record of lapsing, even after the Incarnation, are perhaps registered in the demonic repetition that is so striking a feature of Dante's and Milton's accounts of serpentine metamorphosis. That repetition is also reflected in the series of rewritings of the classical epic stories of snakes in Prudentius, Dante, and Milton, each reflecting on his predecessors, in an accumulative chain of intertextuality that may be compared with the transhistorical migration of other famous passages in ancient epic, such as the simile, originally Iliadic, comparing to the leaves of trees the generations of man, the numberless souls of the dead, or the host of fallen angels;[29] or the bleeding tree, that goes back to the story of Polydorus at the beginning of *Aeneid* 3.[30]

---

[29] See Fowler (1997) on *Paradise Lost* 1.302–4.
[30] For a brief overview of the line that leads through Ovid, Dante, Ariosto, and Tasso to Spenser's Fradubio see W.J. Kennedy in Hamilton (2003) 318; see also Scott 1986.

10

Narcissus Revisited

Scholarly Approaches to the Narcissus Theme

Louise Vinge and Niclas Johansson

The story of Narcissus may have been told in Greece as far back as the second millennium BC, but it was Ovid's account of it, in the third book of *Metamorphoses*, that preserved it for posterity. As is well known, Narcissus did not remain fixed in the form that Ovid gave him: the story has been retold and reinterpreted in manifold ways during the 2000 years that separate us from the beginning of its written history. How does one approach the vast literary tradition constituted by a theme such as that of Narcissus? In this chapter, two scholars who published their respective studies on the Narcissus theme at a time distance of fifty years—one in 1967, the other in 2017—reflect on the scholarly frames and developments over five decades.

Louise Vinge

Half a century ago, I spent much time reading Ovid's *Metamorphoses* in various editions and translations, and mythographers from ancient times up to the eighteenth century, as well as a great many poems and dramas. This was in order to find out how the theme of Narcissus has been treated and understood through the ages. The result, a PhD thesis, was published in 1967 as *The Narcissus Theme in Western European Literature up to the Early 19th Century*. Looking back, I can see that I began my research under favourable conditions. In the early sixties, literary scholars were in a state of theoretical innocence. Structuralism had not had its breakthrough—this happened some years later, in the late 1960s. Nor had we learned to say 'intertextuality': the word was coined by Julia Kristeva in 1966,[1] but did not become prevalent in literary circles for some years. Theory of interpretation, hermeneutics, was not yet an issue—Hans Georg Gadamer's *Wahrheit und Methode, Truth and Method,* was published in 1960, but only by the end of the sixties did it reach literary studies in Sweden (although it was

---

[1] Kristeva (1969).

Louise Vinge and Niclas Johansson, *Narcissus Revisited: Scholarly Approaches to the Narcissus Theme* In: *Metamorphic Readings: Transformation, Language, and Gender in the Interpretation of Ovid's* Metamorphoses. Edited by: Alison Sharrock, Daniel Möller, and Mats Malm, Oxford University Press (2020). © Oxford University Press.
DOI: 10.1093/oso/9780198864066.003.0011

studied much earlier by theologians). Hans Robert Jauss, Gadamer's pupil, held his inaugural lecture, entitled 'Literaturgeschichte als Provokation der Literaturwissenschaft', 'Literary History as a Challenge to Literary Theory', in 1967,[2] and was quite soon discussed among us: 'history of reception' quickly became a household concept. Gender theories had barely been invented.

On the other hand, comparative literature was well established, thanks to René Wellek's version of structuralism, founded on the Prague school of linguistics. His learning and his approach to literary history and the history of criticism, together with his general openness, were well suited to the climate in which we worked. He did not, however, rank 'Stoffgeschichte' or 'Thematology' highly. 'Stoffgeschichte is the least literary of histories', he says in his *Theory of Literature*, 1949.[3] But there were others to defend it. Most important was Raymond Trousson, who presented his 'Plaidoyer pour la Stoffgeschichte' in *Revue de littérature comparée* 1964, the same year in which his large investigation *Le Thème de Promethée dans la literature européenne* was published.[4] That the time was ripe for studies of this kind was proven by a few others, among them Patricia Merivale, whose *Pan the Goat-God: His Myth in Modern Times* appeared in 1969. Jean Seznec's *The Survival of the Pagan Gods* (1953) has an important place in this wave of interest in classical mythology. Baroque studies flourished in those days, but also the systematizing work of Elisabeth Frenzel in Stoff-, Motiv- und Symbolforschung (1963) and *Stoff- und Motivgeschichte* (1974) was of great importance.

When I started, I had no idea whatsoever of the state of thematology or *Stoffgeschichte*. It all started with my previous work on the romantic poet Erik Johan Stagnelius, who made abundant use of classical mythology. Stagnelius saw the real world as a mirror of the ideal, all worldly beauty being an illusory reflection of the transcendent world in which the soul lived before its fall. What image could be more relevant to him than that of Narcissus, hopelessly enamoured of that unreachable beauty? On the last pages of my thesis, I could finally return to Stagnelius, and show that even the curious version in one of his poems, namely, that the boy believes that he sees a beautiful girl in the water, was not without precedents.

I organized all texts in chronological order and started each chapter with an overview of Ovid's position. The various editions, translations, and abridgements of the *Metamorphoses* were described, and the allegorical interpretations of Narcissus were analysed. After that, I took up the myth as it was treated or alluded to in poems and plays. A shortcoming of the literary histories I had read by then emerged: very few of them even mentioned the great popularity of the *Metamorphoses* in the later Middle Ages and the Renaissance.[5] I learned, and

---

[2] Jauss (1970).   [3] Wellek and Warren (1956) 250.
[4] See Trousson (1964b) and (1964a) respectively.
[5] See Böckerman in this volume on the poem's fortunes in the medieval period.

realized the importance of, the expression 'Aetas Ovidiana' for the twelfth century. The enormous *Ovidius moralizatus* and related texts from the fourteenth century in significant ways gathered ideas from much older explications of the myths and transmitted them to much later times. Not least, this tradition reflected a profound change in reading habits, as in some cases old verse editions in the vernacular were printed as prose texts. The material led me to conclude that the old ones were written to be read aloud, but the printed ones devised to be read silently.

The popularity of Ovid, the *Metamorphoses*, and the Narcissus story particularly, in the Renaissance was also evident in art history. G.F. Hartlaub's *Zauber des Spiegels* (1951) was an inspiring work. It was, however, a dry catalogue of paintings of mythological subjects, *Barockthemen*, compiled by Andor Pigler (1956), a Hungarian art historian who was one of the pioneers of iconography, that provided vital information about various paintings, painters, and their literary sources. While Erwin Panofsky was the leading light in the method of iconography and iconology, another scholar in the field was an eye-opener for me, namely, the American Jean H. Hagstrum. His book *The Sister Arts* (1958) had the subtitle *The Tradition of Literary Pictorialism* and contributed substantially not least to the understanding of the iconological importance of the mirror motif in the myth.

Combining image and text, emblem books were a source of Renaissance and baroque themes that had only begun to be explored systematically. Their importance had been pointed out to Swedish scholars by Axel Friberg in *Den svenske Herkules* ('The Swedish Hercules', 1945), but the real breakthrough in emblem studies came in the sixties with baroque scholars such as Albrecht Schöne and others.

The interpretations of Narcissus spanned a wide register: one of the more independent examples was the French twelfth-century *Narcisus* lai, where Echo is replaced by a princess who happens to see a handsome young man and falls in love so badly that she leaves all decency behind when trying to seduce him, but in vain. Her teenage torments are vividly described with irony and sympathy. The much more widely known *Roman de la rose* incorporated certain traits from the lai, and with curious effects transmitted those traits into the moralized Ovid.

The magnificent *Eco y Narciso* (1661) by Calderón gained a very special position through the extensive discussion about its meaning. Havelock Ellis, the English sexologist (1928), and the German romanist Ludwig Pfandl (1935) had both used the term 'narcissism' (which, by the way, was coined by Ellis) when discussing the play in the twenties and thirties. The French editor of the play, Charles V. Aubrun, and a number of other scholars—Edmond Cros, Werner Brüggemann, Angel Valbuena Prat, W.G. Chapman, and Pierre Groult—were much more interested in the relation of the play to the medieval and Renaissance allegorical interpretations of the myth. In fact, Calderón's transformation of the

Ovidian story in a sense prepared the way for psycho-analytical exploration. Liriope, for instance, Narcissus' mother, is a very active and weird figure. A witch rather than a nymph, she tries to protect her son from his fate by means of magic. The theme of illusion is essential to the play. Songs and music pervade the Arcadian landscape and give the drama an atmosphere of airy dreaminess. Profound psychological issues are at hand, so the interest from Havelock Ellis and the birth of 'narcissism' came naturally.

Ovid's tale of Narcissus and Echo was of course the most important text in the tradition, and structuring its motifs was a necessary preparation for understanding its reception. Especially important was the fact that the mirror scene has two parts or central motifs: the illusion, or error, is one, the recognition is another. How did new literary works built on the theme treat these motifs? Surprisingly to a modern reader, it turned out that what had interested most through the times up to the eighteenth century was not the recognition of the face in the water, but the mistake. That Narcissus at first does not understand that he sees himself, but thinks that he is looking at another person, a beautiful young man, or even a girl; that was the central aspect in the allegorical interpretations of moralists and emblematists. They developed the story as a warning for loving worldly pleasures, pride in physical beauty, vanity.

When the story was retold in *Narcisus*, in the *Roman de la rose*, or alluded to by Petrarch in a sonnet to Laura, on the other hand, there was a different lesson to be learnt from the tragic fate of Narcissus. He refused to love and was punished by Amor by the cruel means of having to love someone he could never have. What one should learn from this was that love conquers all and everything. *Amor vincit omnia* meant not that love between two lovers can conquer all obstacles, but that every living being is subjected to the power and force of love.

Finally, I reached the Romantics and Stagnelius, where I put an end to my study. I briefly sketched the importance of the myth to the symbolists with the help of Guy Michaud and, in the very last sentence, I did mention the term narcissism, which Freud used for 'the libidinal complement to the egoism of the self-preservative instinct'.[6]

Niclas Johansson

Out of the myriad research publications relating to Narcissus, Louise Vinge's study *The Narcissus Theme in Western European Literature up to the Early 19th Century* (1967) is probably the only work that is never passed over in any serious discussion of the theme. Yet, half a century has passed since its publication, and

[6] See Vinge (1967) 330.

innumerable scholars have continued the investigation of the self-enamoured ephebe. In the following, I will analyse the development of scholarly approaches to the Narcissus theme, with Vinge's study, rooted in the thematology of the 1960s, as a point of departure.

One of the main accomplishments of Vinge's study in relation to the status of knowledge at its time was to open up the full width of the history of the theme. There were studies that had focused on Ovid's own text, on the different ancient accounts of Narcissus, or on the general influence of Ovid on Western literature, but the wealth of the afterlife of Narcissus specifically had not been appreciated. It is therefore not surprising that when a scholar like Heinz Mitlacher in the 1930s, intrigued by Paul Valéry's handling of the theme, decides to dig deeper into its variations, he deems the two millennia separating himself from Ovid to more or less constitute a lacuna—with the exception of the twelfth-century *Narcisus* lai. He writes: 'Mit dem ausgehenden Mittelalter scheint dann die Narzißdichtung ins Stocken geraten zu sein [...] erst im 19. und 20. Jahrhundert kommt wieder der Aufschwung.'[7] This estimation is worth noting, because one of the most common approaches to Narcissus has been to take the shortcut from the *Metamorphoses* to the early twentieth century. For Mitlacher, Valéry provides the obvious acme of the Narcissus tradition; for most others, Freud is regarded as having the last word on Narcissus. To force the quick path between Ovid and Freud to reroute into a laborious detour through hundreds of texts in different genres and languages indeed seems to have been one of the motivations for Vinge's project. She writes in the introduction to her study:

> Even though our fundamental interest in a theme is decided by ideas of the times in which we live—should not an aim of the investigation also be to see whether we are right in putting the modern interpretations of the theme into older works which treat it? The interpretation which does not start out from a preconception of the nature of the theme or its 'true' or 'deepest' significance might at any rate more easily avoid the risk of depreciating the treatments of older times as superficial and meaningless. Instead of making such ideas a starting-point, the thematologist ought to regard it as his final task to study how a present-day conception of the significance is the result of a development.   (Vinge 1967: xi)

It is precisely the various vicissitudes of this development that are the result of Vinge's study.

In the end, however, she refrains from taking the detour all the way back to the present as she ends her investigation in the early nineteenth century. She suggests that the Narcissus tradition disintegrates in the nineteenth century in a way that

---

[7] Mitlacher (1933) 376 ['with the end of the Middle Ages Narcissus seems to stall as a poetic subject...Only in the 19th and 20th centuries does it see a recovery.']

obscures the relation between later treatments and the preceding tradition (largely due to the abstraction of the Ovidian framework).[8] After having inflated historical air into the narrow conjunction between Ovid and Freud, she thus leaves their reconnection pending, and she furthermore hints that there may be a definite break in the tradition which makes it difficult to pursue this type of research any further. I shall return to the two issues at stake here—the relation between Narcissus and narcissism, and the unity of the Narcissus tradition—as I broach the developments of subsequent research, but let me begin by introducing the context and operational procedure of Vinge's thematological study.

As Vinge observes above, the 1960s boom in thematological research occurred just before (or simultaneously with) several momentous developments in literary theory. And perhaps it was only because it did not engage in discussions about fusions of horizons, the meaning-constituting act of reading, how the elements in the text are determined through the systemic whole (or the arbitrary limitations of that whole), which ontological, ethnic or sexual biases function as preconditions for our understanding, etc., that it was able to embark on projects with a scope that few would attempt today.[9] On the other hand, some aspects of the approach would probably have been received more favourably a decade later. One often finds proponents of thematology such as Trousson defending it against accusations either of the dryness of its massive presentations of material, or of not paying sufficient attention to the study of sources and influences or to the expressive individuality of the artist.[10] With the shift in priorities brought about by structuralist poetics, intertextuality, and the 'death of the author', these accusations could easily be turned into so many reasons for praise.

Vinge's study is a large-scale mapping-out of the Narcissus theme over the centuries. It is explicitly not about 'the encounter with one's own self' or 'narcissism', but is instead given the following outer delimitation: 'such texts will be treated as mention the mythical figure Narcissus (Nárkissos) by name or which allude to him by obvious paraphrases [...], or such as contain a combination of motifs which are clearly recognisable as originating from the theme [...], or which quote older arrangements of the theme (most often Ovid's)'.[11] It is thus given a structural-intertextual definition rather than one which focusses on depth-meaning. Vinge carefully avoids any essentializing tendencies in general statements about the theme. As for the analysis of the theme, it generally follows the path laid out by Elisabeth Frenzel, which regards theme (or *Stoff*) as a high-level

---

[8] Vinge (1967) xv, 329–40.

[9] Indeed, Trousson (1965) 61–71 contends that the only satisfactory thematological study is one that takes a pan-European and historically all-encompassing perspective and covers the majority of the relevant texts in that universal frame. A few years before Vinge, Roland Derche (1962) 71–108 had published a thematological study with an even wider historical span, but limited to five texts (by Ovid, Calderón, Rousseau, Gide, and Valéry)—compared to probably around 200 in Vinge's study. Hardly more than a presentation of the texts, however, this study is of little interest for later research.

[10] Trousson (1965) 23–32, 45–59.   [11] Vinge (1967) xiv, xiii.

structural unit of content (as opposed to *Gehalt*) which, in a hierarchically descending order, is constituted by motifs, symbols, and traits.[12] Apart from these content-related categories, the study also takes into consideration narratological categories such as point of view and narrative ordering.

Ovid's narrative of Narcissus (*Met.* 3.339–512) is taken as the point of departure and provides the framework for an inner definition of the theme. The story is taken to fall into two major episodes—the *Echo* episode and the *reflection* episode—flanked by a few minor episodes and united by the motif of *reflection*, which is seen as the main motif of the theme. The motif of reflection is in turn subdivided into the *error* or *illusion* motif and the *recognition* motif, and it is seen to interact with other motifs such as those of *frustrated passion* and *crime and punishment*. Motifs like *homosexual love* and *hunger and thirst* are regarded as secondary in relation to that of frustrated passion. The *obliteration* motif is seen as foreboding the *death* motif, and the motif of *vengeance* connects the *Juno* episode to the surrounding Echo episode. The *leitmotif* of *metamorphosis*, finally, connects the Narcissus narrative to the surrounding work. In short: the predominant analytic procedure is that of a semi-formal division of the text into motifs and episodes and an ordering of them through vertical and horizontal relations of causality, premonition, illustration, contrast, etc.

This analysis is accompanied by a remarkable lack of attempts to interpret the meaning of the story as a whole, except in the negative. Vinge concludes: 'Ovid makes no moralising generalisations on the basis of this story. He tells a story which is at the same time curious and tragic without applying any didactic points of view.'[13] In this way, Vinge establishes a point of departure for her study which clearly strives toward semantic neutrality and instead focusses on providing something of proto-structuralist framework for the analysis of the inner structure of the theme. This approach corresponds well to the stated aim of achieving an unbiassed view of the development of the theme in that it refuses to allow a particular understanding of the source to colour the interpretation of its successors.

As Vinge then moves on to map out the long history of the theme, there are two operational procedures that stand out as the most important. On the one hand, she analyses the rearrangements of the motifs which constitute the inner structure of the theme. It is shown that certain motifs are left out and others added, that a certain motif is substituted for another motif, that some motifs are emphasized at the expense of others and that the ordering and the kind of relations between certain motifs are altered. On the other hand, she analyses the procedures by which the different authors attribute certain meanings to the theme. She pays attention to didactic or moralizing framings of it, of allegorical and other modes of

---

[12] Frenzel (1963) 21–43, Frenzel (1974) 7–30.   [13] Vinge (1967) 19.

interpretation, to views of myth that inform the understanding, to whether the theme is presented in a psychological, cosmological, or other framework. In both of these interacting procedures, there is a constant attention to the significance of shifts in genre, language, and historical context.

This type of study above all achieves a great overview of significant differences between different epochs, genres, and sub-traditions within a literary tradition originating from a common source. The source itself remains relatively obscure, and none of the subsequent texts are fully illuminated in their own right. What emerges is instead a schematic depiction of a historical structure united by the name 'Narcissus', and which rather distinctly represents relations between texts and groups of texts.

Since the publication of this study in 1967, much more has of course been said on the topic of Narcissus. As Vinge covers a vast scope, it is not surprising that later researchers have found things to add when it comes to Narcissus treatments in specific periods and particularly as regards its treatment in individual authors or texts.[14] They have rarely, however, fundamentally contradicted Vinge's view or forced alterations of the overall system, but have instead offered more in-depth perspectives on certain features. Scholars who have taken a larger scope, examined certain trans-historical connections, or attempted to say something more pointed about the essence of Narcissus, on the other hand, have often—explicitly or implicitly—levelled challenges at Vinge's thematological system. In an attempt at a schematization, I would say that one will find three different types of challenges against it: a) more formalized structural analyses, b) examinations of meaning-instability in the system, and c) displacements and ramifications of the unifying principle of the theme. Most subsequent inquiries into the Narcissus theme combine two or more of these features, and they do not always present them as challenges, but, for the sake of the clarity, I will try to isolate them and assess the impact they have on the perception of the history of the theme.

The first type of challenge directed at Vinge's kind of thematological system is a more rigid and abstract kind of system. We noted above that the thematological approach operates with a semi-formal analysis that with some accuracy could be termed proto-structuralist. In a 1980 essay, Trousson notes that a proper structuralist method is an interesting avenue for thematology:

> On entreprend alors de décomposer le thème en 'mythèmes' ou éléments signifiants, faisant apparaître les 'paquets de relations' qui forment les véritables unités

---

[14] Worth noting as regards Ovid's text are, among others, Rosati (1983), Gildenhard and Zissos (2000a), Vogt-Spira (2002) and Hardie (2002b). One could also mention Knoepfler (2010) regarding the earliest forms of the myth, Manuwald (1975) for a comparison between Konon and Ovid, Hadot (1976) regarding the ancient neo-Platonic interpretations, Walde (2002) regarding the Middle Ages, Knoespel (1985) regarding the Renaissance, and Matuschek (2002) regarding Romanticism, to take but a handful.

constitutives du thème; autrement dit, on en cherche l'"harmonie' par une lecture synchronique. Ainsi l'interprétation du signifié d'un thème se voit remplacée par l'étude de son organisation rationelle, et la succession diachronique des faits par un faisceau de relations synchronique.   (Trousson 1980: 6)[15]

The outline of an approach that follows this path as regards the Narcissus theme was sketched by Ezio Pellizer in 1987. Pellizer begins with an analysis of the first known written rendering of the Narcissus story, the one by Konon. Narcissus here turns down the persistent amorous advances of Ameinias and instead sends him a sword, with which Ameinias kills himself at Narcissus' doorstep while invoking the vengeance of Eros. When Narcissus later sees his image in the water and falls in love, he realizes that he suffers justly and kills himself, after which the narcissus flower grows from his blood.

Pellizer argues that the story can be reduced to a narrative programme in the modality of passionate love, where the negation of the seme of reciprocity generates variations of the seme of reflexivity. It is by way of a forced coincidence of self and other that one seme leads to the next: 'one attempts to short-circuit transitivity onto the other, and thereby to deny the difference in a sort of compression of the reciprocal into the reflexive'.[16] Pellizer then goes on to examine a few other Narcissus treatments, including the addition of the Echo episode by Ovid and that of a twin sister by Pausanias, and argues that they can be perceived as semantic isotopes of the original narrative programme. Pellizer writes:

It therefore seems possible to conclude that a story, subjected to variations in its enunciative modality (or simply narrated in a different cultural context) can generate, in itself, several of its own variants, simply by amplifying, along a homogeneous axis, the choice of relevant semantic traits.[17]

In this way, Pellizer regards the Narcissus theme in its entirety as a system with a specific inner logic which auto-generates new variations of itself. He explicitly speaks of 'the rules of the game that generates these representations' and argues that all manifestations of the theme are united by 'the definition of the correct orientation of passionate attitudes in interpersonal relations'.[18] He also asserts that the system is maintained through the long tradition 'leading from Conon to Pausanias, from Ovid through the medieval mythographers and Bocaccio to

[15] '[O]ne can then deconstruct the theme into "mythemes", or significant elements, revealing the "packages of relationships" which constitute the real constitutive unities of the theme; to put it otherwise, one can seek "harmony" through synchronic reading. Interpretation of the signified of the theme is thus replaced by study of its rational organisation, and the diachronic succession of the facts by a bundle of synchronic relations.'
[16] Pellizer (1987) 112.   [17] Pellizer (1987) 114.   [18] Pellizer (1987) 116–17.

Natalis Comes, from Calderòn [*sic*] to Scarlatti, and hence (why not?) to Sigmund Freud and his followers'.[19] Pellizer thus explicitly argues that 'the Narcissus theme' can be reduced to a semiotic matrix which produces all the theme's manifestations. Compared to Vinge's thematological analysis of the theme into interrelated motifs, Pellizer's is obviously both much more reductive and more formalized. It allows for a firmer grip on the coherence of the tradition and provides a way to articulate the semantic shifts from one version to the next. It aims at the inner logic of the theme and achieves a more systematic conception of it.

Yet, this formal abstraction is also its obvious disadvantage. Pellizer creates a closed system for which his analysis could hypothetically predict all possible outcomes. In doing so, he also encapsulates and fixates the meaning that the theme is allowed to harbour through an interpretation of its first written version. This means, first, that every understanding of the theme is highly dependent on Konon's text, and on the choice of analytic categories applied to it. Second, all traits of an individual Narcissus text which do not conform with the general matrix are regarded as secondary or inessential to the theme. Third, any significant historical shifts in the conception of theme will be disregarded. Therefore, this approach would not be able to account for the central significance of the iconic motif, of the role played by the prophetic structure introduced in Ovid, of the strand in the tradition which focuses on self-knowledge rather than self-love, of the shifts between moralizing, cosmological, psychological, and metapoetical interpretations, etc.

In short, the system that Pellizer creates only partially coincides with what we intuitively would call the Narcissus theme. The system is both narrower and wider than the theme. On the one hand, a theme can develop in any direction and any attempt at an a priori definition of it will always find that essential aspects of the theme elude its grasp.[20] On the other hand, Pellizer needs to rely on sources external to theme (in this case stories about Anteros and the androgyne) to establish the logic of the system, and thus builds a system that is not confined to the Narcissus theme. It is therefore not surprising that, when Pellizer eventually writes a broad history of the theme, he does not limit himself to the programme he had himself proposed.[21] His historical overview, which stretches from antiquity to modernity, is far less reductive and takes various aspects of the theme into account. It works much more as a complement to Vinge's study in that it does not contain a complete inventory, but rather focusses on certain aspects and certain groups of texts that have not been sufficiently appreciated in previous research. The structuralist approach projected in the earlier text here leaves its

[19] Pellizer (1987) 118.
[20] Claude Bremond (1993) has pointed out that this is a general problem for thematological research.
[21] Pellizer (2003).

traces not so much in the entirety of the enterprise as in how minor clusters of texts and motifs are treated. Connections are created between a few texts in the Narcissus tradition as well as with other themes, motifs, and mythological figures. In these more local clusters of texts, Pellizer's less formalized structural analyses allow the reader to discern a further depth of what is at stake in the different manifestations of Narcissus.

Similarly employing a less formalized structuralist approach in the intersection between the theme and a specific motif, Françoise Frontisi-Ducroux in a study of the motif of the mirror in antiquity dedicates two chapters to Narcissus.[22] By inscribing ancient treatments of the theme into the semiotic system established by Greek and Roman discourse on the mirror, Frontisi-Ducroux gives a convincing account of how the Narcissus theme sets important aspects the Greco-Roman gender system in play. As these examples show, the structuralist attempts at a more abstract and systematic formalization of the relations between different texts seem rather inapt for a broad outline of the theme in its entirety, but they can be highly rewarding when applied to local configurations of the theme, especially when they are interrelated with neighbouring motifs, themes, and characters.

The second type of challenge is the one which focusses on a semantic instability in the system. This challenge was very explicitly aimed at Vinge by John Brenkman in a 1976 deconstructive reading of Ovid, which has since been followed by many similar accounts with different emphases. Brenkman writes:

> The moment we are drawn into the logic of concepts like source and referent, we are tempted to assume that the 'original' text has a stable significance that later authors repeat. For example, the most comprehensive study of Narcissus texts [Vinge's] treats the Ovidian version as a collection of 'themes' variously realised or expanded in other authors. Ovid's narrative does not, however, supply a set of stable meanings that can serve to anchor another author's text's thematic organisation; it does not even provide a plot that another text could innocently recapitulate, and it situates its central characters, Narcissus and Echo, in a way that allows contradictory interpretations of their relation to one another.[23]

Just as in any deconstructive reading, Brenkman posits a construction that he attempts to undo. Despite the initial reference to Vinge's study, it is not there that he finds his target, but rather in the notion that literary theory always seeks a coincidence of meaning and literary form. This notion is elicited from Northrop Frye, from whom he quotes: 'The *mythos* is the *dianoia* in movement; the *dianoia* is the *mythos* in stasis.'[24] With this presupposition he offers an analysis of Ovid's narrative, which is certainly not dissimilar to Vinge's but which much more

---

[22] Frontisi-Ducroux (1997) 200–41.   [23] Brenkman (1976) 293.
[24] Brenkman (1976) 295–6.

clearly determines the semiotically governing elements of the text and which much more tightly locks these to an assumed meaning:

> It is clear that describing the narrative organisation (*mythos*) and its thematic unity (*dianoia*) will entail specifying the relation between Echo and Narcissus. Taken separately, their stories are related to one another through a displaced parallelism—a parallelism in that each character is pushed towards death when desire is not reciprocated by another, a displaced parallelism in that for Echo the other is another like herself, while for Narcissus the other is his mirror image. In both instances sexual union fails to occur, first because Narcissus withholds it and then because it is impossible. Their stories intersect in a way that gives meaning to this difference. Narcissus' imaginary capture is presented as the 'punishment' for his refusal to reciprocate the desire of others, and his encounter with Echo is obviously the narrative's most developed example of such a refusal. In short, the refusal to reciprocate is answered by the impossibility of having desire reciprocated.[25]

Brenkman's strategy is then to undo this interpretation by demonstrating how it depends on an authorial instance that tries—but fails—to control the production of meaning in the text. Brenkman's point of attack is the fact that the unifying interpretation hinges on the symmetrical relation between the Echo episode and the Narcissus episode—but that this symmetry is only made possible because Ovid intervenes to suspend Juno's punishment of Echo. Echo had been deprived of the ability to speak with her own voice, and the direct link between consciousness and voice had thus been broken. This poses a threat to the integrity and identity of her own self. Ovid, however, restores that link—and thereby reattaches significations to a consciousness—by staging the play of words where Echo is allowed to express her desire for Narcissus through words borrowed from him. In this way, the authorial instance reconstructs Echo as an integral character and allows her story to predetermine the significance of the Narcissus episode.

This predetermination happens on three levels. First, it makes Narcissus alone responsible for Echo's anguish and thus turns Narcissus' suffering into a punishment symmetrical to his crime. Second, it determines the significance of death as that which intervenes when sexual desire exceeds the possibility of satisfaction. Third, it converts the opposition between echo and reflection into an opposition between *speech* and reflection and thus establishes the hierarchy voice-consciousness/body/reflection, which regulates the relation between the two episodes.

Brenkman argues that this intervention on Ovid's part amounts to a semantic violence through which the narrative system attempts to suppress the meaning

---

[25] Brenkman (1976) 297.

produced by the text itself. Through a digression on Derrida's *La Voix et le phénomène*, Brenkman aligns this with the Western metaphysics of presence and its privileging of speech over writing.[26] By undoing this hierarchy, Brenkman argues that the text itself eludes the meaning that the narrative system attempts to impose on it. Narcissus' error is reinterpreted in the following way:

(1) Rather than being another like the self, the image is the other of the self. (2) The image is not responsive to the self, it affects the self. That is, the self-affection of Narcissus is such that the self is affected by its other, by the representation of itself in an external space. (3) Thus, when Narcissus discovers that he is not engaged in a dialogue, it is because the other is not a subject. It is a nonsubject that affects the self, a nonsubject without which the self could not appear to itself or recognise itself. (4) What then of the delay that Narcissus imagines between his own gestures and those of the image? Once again it is a question of reversing the terms and displacing their relation. If the image as other does not respond to the self but instead affects it, then the delay indicated by Narcissus' language becomes, when displaced, the anteriority of the other as the nonpresent nonsubject primordially affecting the self: not as a prior moment in linear time, but as *pure anteriority*, as *trace*.[27]

What Brenkman thus finds in Ovid's text is not a drama of how the refusal to reciprocate desire is rewarded with the denial of having one's own desire reciprocated, but an undermining of fundamental presuppositions for that interpretation: the integrity of selfhood and stability of meaning. The Ovidian text is 'a process of writing that squanders the security of a stable meaning'.[28]

Brenkman's reading of Ovid's text is undeniably interesting. The question for us, however, is what it does to our perception of the Narcissus theme. Brenkman frames his reading as an objection to Vinge's attempt to reconstruct a tradition from the Ovidian source. He writes: 'Only by unraveling the fabric of Ovid's Narcissus will it be possible to open a way into that larger network of writing that read and rewrite Ovid's narrative.'[29] Brenkman never returns to the question of what his reading implies for that network, and he makes no attempt himself to follow his conclusions beyond Ovid's own text. It seems to me that Brenkman's reading does indeed challenge the attempt to build a system like the one Pellizer proposes in his article more than a decade later. Pellizer's approach is dependent on a narrative system similar to the one that Brenkman deconstructs and would

---

[26] Derrida himself broaches the Narcissus theme in the essay 'Qual quelle' (Derrida (1972) 327–63) with a similar argument regarding the subject, but he only partly elaborates it through a reading of Valéry's 'Les Fragments du Narcisse'.

[27] Brenkman (1976) 321–2.   [28] Brenkman (1976) 327.   [29] Brenkman (1976) 293.

therefore be vulnerable to a criticism which exposes that system as contradicted by Ovid's text.

It is hard to see, however, that Brenkman's analysis would significantly disrupt Vinge's thematological project. We saw above that Vinge is reluctant to produce any specific interpretation of the general significance of Ovid's text. She explicitly does not ascribe to it the moral that Brenkman deconstructs. The very cautiousness with which she forebears to lock the source to a specific interpretation, but rather presents it in terms of an array of interrelated motifs, protects it from this type of criticism. Brenkman opposes a semantic closure of the source, which Vinge never proposed. In this light, Brenkman's analysis adds nuances to rather than disrupts the entire project. He allows us to see further possibilities when it comes to relating the motifs to each other and to contextualizing the significance of the theme. By opening up a wider spectrum of semantic possibilities in the 'source', Brenkman allows other features of later Narcissus texts to be traced back to Ovid. These other aspects—particularly the issues of the integrity of selfhood and the semantic stability of language—play a minor role in most of the theme's history—but they do come to the fore in the nineteenth and twentieth centuries.

Brenkman's reading has been followed by others which adopt a deconstructionist stance in relation to the Narcissus theme (but rarely with the same purity of Derridean method). John Hamilton, for example, proposes a reading of Ovid's Narcissus narrative that 'weniger zu konventionellen *Quellenforschung* führen, als vielmehr zu Erwägungen über das eigentliche Wesen der Quelle, sowohl in ihrem persönlichen (d.h. subjektiven) als auch in ihrem ontologischen Verständnis' [leads less to conventional *Quellenforschung* than to consideration of the actual nature of the source, both in its personal (that is, subjective) and in its ontological understanding].[30] Equating Narcissus with the tradition (the source) and Echo with the poet (the one who rewrites what has already been said), Hamilton then proceeds to a meditation on how original and copy presuppose each other and how 'jedes Subjekt dekonstituiert sich mittels seiner eigenen Konstitution' [each subject is deconstructed by means of its own constitution].[31] While Hamilton also remains within a Greco-Roman context, it is not least those who have turned to more modern times who have found this type of approach to the theme useful. So, for example, Gayatri Spivak (1993), who uses Ovid's text to attempt to reinstate Echo as the foreclosed framing of the male narcissistic subject in a psychoanalytic tradition, and Gray Kochhar-Lindgren (1993), who examines the dilemma of the entextualization of the human subject through the figure of Narcissus.

In a similar fashion, there have been a number of readings of Ovid's narrative— starting with Rosati and continuing with Hardie and von Glinski—that highlight its metapoetical dimension and aesthetic exploration of the nature of images, signs, and reading, and that thereby stress its relevance for romantic, symbolist, and even postmodern versions of Narcissus.[32] While readings such as these certainly deepen our understanding of the structure of Ovid's text and thereby add and reinforce certain connections in the history of the theme, they (and particularly Rosati) emphasize some of Vinge's conclusions, rather than challenge the system as such.

The third challenge to Vinge's thematological system comes not so much from any one reading, but from the sum of the diverse readings dedicated to Narcissus in one form or the other. The question is, what do they intend by 'Narcissus'? Where in the mass of all Western texts does one draw the line between 'Narcissus' and 'not Narcissus', lest the name be emptied of any pertinent reference? Let us look at how 'Narcissus' is conceived in three book-length studies on the subject from recent decades.

In a study of works by Freud, Jacques Lacan, Virginia Woolf, Michel Tournier, and John Fowles—none of which explicitly feature a character named Narcissus—Gray Kochhar-Lindgren focuses on '[t]he figure of Narcissus [which] haunts the twentieth century'.[33] What kind of entity is this Narcissus? Kochhar-Lindgren writes of

> the narcissistic mythos, a field of figural signification that includes not only the characters from Ovid's rendition of the narrative in *Metamorphoses*—Narcissus' parents Liriope and Cephisus, Tiresias, Echo, the spurned lovers of Narcissus, and Nemesis, who answers the prayer for his destruction—but also the more encompassing discourses of philosophy, psychoanalysis, and literature. A narrative that spans discourses in such a way is a myth, a narrative paradigm that creative interpretation rejuvenates at various cultural moments for various cultural reasons.[34]

This definition seems to offer no limits to 'Narcissus', but, reading between the lines, we understand that it is a myth, and as such a field of figural signification which crosses the discursive lines between philosophy, psychoanalysis, and literature and that is constantly transformed through creative interpretations. Kochhar-Lindgren further adds that a myth is something that 'attempts to fill with significance the gap between event and meaning, between sign and referent, and between signifier and signified'.[35] If we then turn to how Kochhar-Lindgren operates in his analyses, we find that, rather than analysing figurations of Narcissus (indeed, there are no explicit Narcissuses in his material), he continuously constructs Narcissus through his readings of different texts. Recurrent are formulations like: 'Whereas the threat of absolute solipsism marks the presence of

---

[32] Rosati (1983), Hardie (2002b) 143–72, von Glinksi (2012) 116–30.
[33] Kochhar-Lindgren (1993) 1.   [34] Kochhar-Lindgren (1993) 2.
[35] Kochhar-Lindgren (1993) 17.

Narcissus in philosophy, in literature, Narcissus' first and most abiding home, his sign is the self-reflexivity of narrative.'[36] Throughout his book, Kochhar-Lindgren paints a picture of Narcissus as a subject caught in a certain semiotic logic. What he does thereby is not so much to study the theme, or myth, as an *object*, but rather to continue what Hans Blumenberg (1986) has called the *work on myth*. Kochhar-Lindgren offers a renewed interpretation of the myth, informed by psychoanalytic narcissism, philosophical idealism, and literary auto-reflexivity. In this way, his text does not distance itself from the Narcissus theme as the object of research; it inscribes itself in the line of texts which constitute the Narcissus tradition and recreates its own image of Narcissus according to the mechanisms that govern all retellings of the narrative.

Steven Bruhm (2001), in a study that focuses both on texts that explicitly feature Narcissus and such that do not, takes a slightly different stance. His point of departure is the psychoanalytic notion of narcissism. But his intention is to 'use […] psychoanalysis against itself', to explore 'that rich overdetermination that makes Narcissus something more than narcissism'.[37] The figure of Narcissus is therefore focalized through the connection that psychoanalysis creates between narcissism and homosexuality, but that focus is widened in order to allow different figurations of Narcissus to disrupt the heteronormative logic that governs that association. It thus thematizes a 'Narcissus' which is not delimited to Freudian narcissism, but which yet is not synonymous with either Ovid's character or the sum of all rewritings of the theme. Bruhm is 'interested in a Narcissus who is framed by psychoanalysis but who at the same time exceeds it', and elaborates: 'Narcissus is the central unifying trope whose presence only bespeaks his absence, whose self-identification can only engender the slippages of desire, and whose mystifications within the masculine cannot belie the spectral traces, the vestiges of the penis as an organ of pleasure.'[38] What Bruhm does is to take one interpretation of Narcissus (if one allows that psychoanalytic narcissism can be regarded as an interpretation of Narcissus) and show how it is undermined by the assumption of a wider trope which forms around that interpretation. The 'Narcissus' that exceeds narcissism is a modern figure of male homosexuality, which psychoanalysis has tried to enclose through the concept of narcissism.

Negin Daneshvar-Malevergne (2009), finally, sets out to identify decadence as a '*figure narcissique*'. She begins by defining the *essence* of the myth and attempts to demonstrate its coincidence with a likewise essentialist definition of decadence. She writes in her conclusion:

> L'étude de l'émergence du mythe de Narcisse et du narcissisme dans la littérature fin de siècle française et anglaise implique donc la recherche d'un lien entre la décadence et les composantes et attributs de la légende de Narcisse. Leur examen

---

[36] Kochhar-Lindgren (1993) 6.   [37] Bruhm (2001) 17, 12.   [38] Bruhm (2001) 17–18.

approfondi nous révèle une similtude dans la logique, la structure et le système fonctionnel, bien plus, une affinité attestant le fait que la décadence et Narcisse ou narcissisme sont quasiment représentatifs voire originaire l'un de l'autre.[39]

What she aims at is thus more or less an identification of the respective *ideas* of Narcissus and decadence. In accordance with this aim, she touches only tangentially on explicit Narcissus treatments from the *fin de siècle*, mostly focussing instead on presenting a general view of decadence which coincides with her interpretation of Narcissus.

The understanding of Narcissus presented by Daneshvar-Malevergne is based on a wide reading, but it is also highly eclectic, incorporating psychoanalytic narcissism (usually read through the particular perspective of Christopher Lasch rather than Freud himself) as well as initiatory and mythic patterns from antiquity and based on such different and potentially conflicting authorities as Schelling, Cassirer, Eliade, Frazer, Vernant, Jung, Kerenyi, Bachelard, and Marcuse. What the synthesis of these various sources produces is a view of Narcissus as a figure of initiation, of death and rebirth—developed under a number of different facets— which corresponds to a view of decadence as a transition from one era to another.

Putting these studies by Kochhar-Lindgren, Bruhm, and Daneshvar-Malevergne next to each other, we can hardly avoid asking the following questions. Do they speak about the same thing? Do they have the same object of investigation? For one, 'Narcissus' is a mythic attempt to close a semantic gap in the constitution of the modern subject; for the second, he is the trope that connects narcissism and homosexuality; for the third, he is a pattern in the evolution of the *Zeitgeist*. This is a clear example of how the notion of Narcissus ramifies into different branches, which may have a common origin but which extend so far from it that the communication between them is disrupted. There is hardly any point in comparing their different views of Narcissus in the nineteenth and twentieth centuries, since the object 'Narcissus' does not provide a common denominator. They refer to the same mythological figure, but they do not study the same phenomenon.

While the definition of the exact delimitations of a literary theme is always open to discussion, for the Narcissus theme this problem escalates indefinitely around 1900 with the formation of the concept of narcissism. Since its coinage, narcissism has been taken as relative to the myth from which it etymologically derives. But it has also, since its conception, been given conceptual definitions independent of any relation to Narcissus. The originator of the concept, Havelock Ellis, spoke of a

---

[39] Daneshvar-Malevergne (2009) 302 [study of the emergence of the Narcissus myth and of narcissism in English and French *fin de siècle* literature, then, involves the search for a link between decadence and the constituent attributes of the legend of Narcissus. Close examination of them reveals similarities in logic, structure, and functional system, and, moreover, an affinity which attests to the fact that decadence and Narcissus/narcissism are almost representative of or even inherent in each other].

'Narcissus-like tendency', which he defined as an 'extreme form' of 'the phenomena of spontaneous sexual emotion generated in the absence of an external
stimulus proceeding, directly or indirectly, from another person'.[40] On the one
hand, then, narcissism refers to the Narcissus theme, but on the other, it has a
quite independent conceptual definition (which in this case, however, functions as
a sexological interpretation of Narcissus' condition). For Freud, who propelled
narcissism to fame, the reference to the theme is almost completely obliterated by
its conceptual definition as either *the libidinous cathexis of the ego* or *an early
autoerotic stage in the development of the libido*. Only twice does Freud mention
Narcissus, and in neither case does it have any significant importance for his
concept.[41]

Even so, the word 'narcissism' retains its relation to Narcissus, and the reference keeps being actualized by those who use it after Freud. From the early
twentieth century, it becomes almost impossible to draw a sharp dividing line
between the Narcissus theme and narcissism, whether the latter be understood as
Freud's concept, as the personality disorder described in *DSM-5* or according to
some other interpretation.[42] This is the background for the dispersion among the
studies of 'Narcissus' in modernity. The three studies we noted above all turn to
something they define as 'narcissism'—and which they regard as the essence of the
Narcissus theme. The problem is that they make different interpretations about
what the core of the theme is, and so come to speak about quite different things.

This problem can be generalized as the question: what is the unifying principle
of the Narcissus theme? I think there are three different kinds of answers to this
question. First, the unity can be *semantically* defined, i.e. by a certain meaning, be
it complex or simple, stable or unstable. Second, the unity can be *structurally*
defined, i.e. by some form of semiotic pattern or principle. Third, the unity can be
intertextually defined, i.e. by the relation between texts. Both in the three studies
mentioned above (by Kochhar-Lindgren, Bruhm, and Daneshvar-Malevergne)
and in the project proposed by Pellizer, the theme is defined by a combination
of semantic and structural features, whereas intertextuality, the relation between
texts, is left as a variable for the investigation to discover. Inversely, in Vinge's
thematological study, the theme is defined by a combination of structural and
intertextual features, whereas its meaning is left as a variable for the investigation
to discover. (This is precisely why Brenkman's criticism of Vinge misses the target:
she does not, as he supposes, define a stable meaning of the theme.)

Both approaches obviously have their advantages and disadvantages. Defining
Narcissus in semantic terms allows for a more in-depth analysis of a specific

---

[40] Ellis (1913) 1612. For a further discussion of the development of the concept of narcissism in
relation to the Narcissus theme, see Johansson (2017) 321–8, 342–53.

[41] Freud (1940–87) VIII:170, XII:6. *Diagnostic and Statistical Manual of Mental Disorders*. For an
extended discussion of the development of Freud's concept, see Johansson (2017) 333–401.

[42] Cf. American Psychiatric Association (2013) 669–72.

human-existential situation, condition, or dilemma. It is, however, not a viable approach if one wants to know how the meaning of the theme has developed through history, since the limits of its meaning are defined from the outset. It thereby also entails the possibility that we are not speaking of the same thing when we speak of Narcissus. The thematological approach, on the other hand, can be accused of dryness and of not penetrating deep enough into the depth-meaning that develops through the theme. But it serves very well to map out the broader network of texts that constitute the theme in a way that is both intuitively acceptable and based on a firm textual footing. This, I think, is the reason why thematology has not lost its relevance in spite of the major theoretical developments in recent decades. It provides the necessary reference points and framework that ensures that we know what we speak of when we speak of Narcissus and it fixes that to which bolder interpretations of Narcissus must be able to answer. In this capacity, thematology, it seems to me, has at least a descriptive role to play in all historically informed studies of a mythological theme.

Bibliography

Ahl, F. (1985) *Metaformations: Soundplay and Wordplay in Ovid and Other Classical Poets.* Ithaca, NY.

American Psychiatric Association (2013) *Diagnostic and Statistical Manual of Mental Disorders,* 5th edition, Washington.

Anderson, R.D., Parsons, P.J., and Nisbet, R.G.M. (1979) 'Elegiacs by Gallus from Qasr Ibrim', *JRS* 69: 125–55.

Anderson, W.S. (1972) *Ovid's Metamorphoses Books 6–10.* Norman, OK.

Anderson, W.S. (1989) 'Lycaon: Ovid's Deceptive Paradigm in *Metamorphoses* 1', *ICS* 14: 91–101.

Anderson, W.S. (1997) *Ovid's Metamorphoses: Books 1–5.* Norman, OK.

Arthur, M.B. (1982) 'Cultural Strategies in Hesiod's *Theogony.* Law, Family, Society', *Arethusa* 15: 63–82.

Asper, M. (1997) *Onomata allotria: Zur Genese, Struktur und Funktion poetologischer Metaphern bei Kallimachos,* Stuttgart.

Asper, M. (2011) 'Dimensions of Power: Callimachean Geopoetics and the Ptolemaic Empire', in Acosta-Hughes, B., Lehnus, L., and Stephens, S. (eds) *Brill's Companion to Callimachus.* Leiden: 153–77.

Bailey, C. (ed.) (1947) *Titi Lucreti Cari de rerum natura. Libri sex.* Oxford.

Balogh, J. (1927) '*Voces paginarum*: Beiträge zur Geschichte des lauten Lesens und Schreibens', *Philologus* 82: 84–109 and 202–40.

Balsley, K. (2010) 'Between Two Lives: Tiresias and the Law in Ovid's *Metamorphoses*', *Dictynna* 7: http://journals.openedition.org/dictynna/189.

Baraz, Y. (2012) *A Written Republic: Cicero's Philosophical Politics.* Princeton, NJ.

Barchiesi, A. (1994) *Il Poeta e Il Principe. Ovidio e Il Discorso Augusteo.* Rome/Bari.

Barchiesi, A. (1997a) 'Endgames: Ovid's *Metamorphoses* 15 and *Fasti* 6', in Roberts, Dunn, and Fowler (1997): 181–208.

Barchiesi, A. (1997b) *The Poet and the Prince.* Berkeley.

Barchiesi, A. (1999) 'Venus Masterplot: Ovid and the *Homeric Hymns*', in Hardie, Barchiesi, and Hinds (1999): 112–26.

Barchiesi, A. (2001) *Speaking Volumes: Narrative and Intertext in Ovid and Other Latin Poets.* London.

Barchiesi, A. (2002) 'Narrative Technique and Narratology in the *Metamorphoses*', in Hardie (2002a): 180–99.

Barchiesi, A. (2005) *Ovidio, Metamorfosi. Volume I: Libri I–II,* Fondazione Valla, Milan.

Barchiesi, A. (2006) 'Music for Monsters: Ovid's *Metamorphoses*, Bucolic Evolution and Bucolic Criticism', in Fantuzzi, M. and Papanghelis, T.D. (eds) *Brill's Companion to Greek and Latin Pastoral.* Leiden: 403–25.

Barchiesi, A. and Rosati, G. (2007) *Ovidio, Metamorfosi. Volume II: Libri III–IV,* Fondazione Valla, Milan.

Barkan, L. (1986) *The Gods Made Flesh: Metamorphosis and the Pursuit of Paganism.* New Haven.

Barolini, T. (1987/1989) 'Arachne, Argus and St John: Transgressive Art in Dante and Ovid', *Mediaevalia* 13: 207–26.

Beagon, M. (2009) 'Ordering Wonderland: Ovid's Pythagoras and the Augustan Vision', in Hardie P.R. (ed.) *Paradox and the Marvellous in Augustan Literature and Culture.* Oxford: 288–309.

Berger, A.-E. (1996) 'The Latest Word from Echo', *New Literary History* 27: 621–40.

Bettini, M. (2013) 'I Mostri Sono Buoni per Pensare', in Paris, R., Setari, E., and Giustozzi, N. (eds), *Mostri: Creature Fantastiche della Paura e del Mito.* Milan: 18–31.

Bing, P. (1990) 'A Pun on Aratus' Name in Verse 2 of the *Phaenomena*?', *HSPh* 93: 281–5.

Bing, P. (1993) 'Aratus and His Audiences', *MD* 31: 99–109.

Blanco Mayor, J.M. (2017) *Power Play in Latin Love Elegy and its Multiple Forms of Continuity in Ovid's Metamorphoses.* Berlin.

Bloom, H. (1975) *A Map of Misreading.* New York.

Blumenberg, H. (1986) *Arbeit am Mythos.* Frankfurt.

Bömer, F. (1969) *P. Ovidius Naso, Metamorphosen: Buch I–III.* Heidelberg.

Bömer, F. (1976) *P. Ovidius Naso, Metamorphosen: Buch IV–V.* Heidelberg.

Bömer, F. (1977) *P. Ovidius Naso, Metamorphosen: Buch VII–IX.* Heidelberg.

Bömer, F. (1986) *P. Ovidius Naso, Metamorphosen: Buch XIV–XV.* Heidelberg.

Bond, G.A. (1986) '*Iocus amoris*: The Poetry of Baudri of Bourgueil and the Formation of the Ovidian Subculture', *Traditio* 42: 143–93.

Boyd, B.W. (2006) 'Two Rivers and the Reader in Ovid: *Metamorphoses* 8', *TAPhA* 136.1: 171–206.

Boyd, B.W. (ed.) (2002) *Brill's Companion to Ovid.* Leiden.

Bradley. G.J. (2006) 'Colonization and Identity in Republican Italy', in Bradley, G.J., and Wilson, J.P. (eds) *Greek and Roman Colonization: Origins, Ideologies and Interactions,* Swansea.

Bradley, G.J. and Wilson, J.P. (eds) (2006) *Greek and Roman Colonization: Origins, Ideologies and Interactions.* Swansea.

Braswell, B.K. (1992) *A Commentary on Pindar Nemean One.* Fribourg.

Breed, B.W. (2006) *Pastoral Inscriptions: Reading and Writing Virgil's Eclogues.* London.

Bremond, C. (1993) 'Concept and Theme', in W. Sollors (ed.) *The Return of Thematic Criticism*, trans. A.D. Pratt, Cambridge: 46–59.

Brenkman, J. (1976) 'Narcissus in the Text', *The Georgia Review* 30: 293–327.

Brisson, L. (2002) *Sexual Ambivalence: Androgyny and Hermaphroditism in Graeco-Roman Antiquity*, trans. J. Lloyd. Berkeley.

Broderson, K. (2012) *Censorinus: Über den Geburtstag. Edition Antike.* Darmstadt.

Brown, E.L. (1963) *Numeri Vergiliani: Studies in Eclogues and Georgics.* Brussels.

Brown, S.A. (2002) *The Metamorphosis of Ovid.* London.

Brownlee, K. (1985) 'Dante's Poetics of Transfiguration: the Case of Ovid', *Literature and Belief* 5: 13–29.

Bruhm, S. (2001) *Reflecting Narcissus: A Queer Aesthetic.* Minneapolis.

Burrow, C. (1988) *Original Fictions*, in Martindale (1988): 99–120.

Buxton, R.G.A. (2009) *Forms of Astonishment: Greek Myths of Metamorphosis.* Oxford.

Calandra, E., Betori, A., and Lupi, A. (2016) 'Niobides en marbre dans la villa attribuée à Valerius Messalla Corvinus à Ciampino, Rome', *Comptes Rendus de l'Académie des Inscriptions et Belles Lettres* 1: 487–517.

Calvino, I. (1979) 'Gli indistinti confini', preface to *Ovidio. Metamorfosi*, a cura di P. Bernardini Marzolla, Turin: vii–xvi (= I. Calvino, *Saggi 1945-1985*, ed. M. Barenghi, Milan 1995, 904–16).

Cameron, A. (1995) *Callimachus and His Critics*. Princeton.

Cameron, A. (2004) *Greek Mythography in the Roman World*. New York.

Campbell, J.B. (2012) *Rivers and the Power of Ancient Rome*. Chapel Hill.

Carter, M.A.S. (2002) '*Vergilium vestigare: Aeneid* 12.587–8', *CQ* 52: 615–7.

Castelletti, C. (2008) 'Riflessioni sugli acrostici di Valerio Flacco', *GIF* 60: 219–34.

Castelletti, C. (2012a) 'A "Greek" Acrostic in Valerius Flaccus (3.430–4)', *Mnemosyne* 65: 319–23.

Castelletti, C. (2012b) 'Following Aratus' Plow: Vergil's Signature in the *Aeneid*', *MH* 69: 83–95.

Castelletti, C. (2014) 'Aratus and the Aratean Tradition in Valerius' *Argonautica*', in Augoustakis, A. (ed.) *Flavian Poetry and Its Greek Past*. Leiden: 49–72.

Celoria, F. (1992) *The Metamorphoses of Antoninus Liberalis: A Translation with a Commentary*. London.

Cicu, L. (1979) 'I Phaenomena di Ovidio', *Sandalion* 2: 117–28.

Citti, F., Pasetti, L., and Pellacani, D. (eds), (2014) *Metamorfosi tra scienza e letteratura*. Florence.

Clarke, B. (1995) *Allegories of Writing: The Subject of Metamorphosis*. New York.

Classen, C.J. (1981) 'Liebeskummer; eine Ovidinterpretation (*Met.* 9, 540–665)', *A&A* 27: 163–78.

Clay, J.S. (2003) *Hesiod's Cosmos*. Cambridge.

Colborn, R. (2013) 'Solving Problems with Acrostics: Manilius Dates Germanicus', *CQ* 63: 450–2.

Cole, T. (2008) *Ovidius Mythistoricus: Legendary Time in the Metamorphoses*. Frankfurt.

Coleman, R. (1977) *Vergil's Eclogues*. Cambridge.

Colpo, I., Ghedini, F., and Toso, S. (eds) (2011) *Tra testo e immagine: Riflessioni ovidiane*, in *Eidola: International Journal of Classical Art History* 8. Pisa.

Conte, G.B. (1986) *The Rhetoric of Imitation: Genre and Poetic Memory in Virgil and Other Latin Poets*. Ithaca.

Conte, G.B. (2013) *Ope ingenii: Experiences of Textual Criticism*. Berlin.

Contini, G. (1970) *Varianti e Altra linguistica; una Raccolta di Saggi (1938–1968)*. Turin.

Cooley, A.E. (2009) *Res gestae divi Augusti: Text, Translation, and Commentary*. Cambridge.

Copeland, R. (2012) 'Gloss and Commentary', in Hexter, R.J. and Townsend, D. (eds) *Oxford Handbook of Medieval Latin Literature*. Oxford: 171–91.

Corbeill, A. (2015) *Sexing the World: Grammatical Gender and Biological Sex in Ancient Rome*. Princeton.

Courtney, E. (1990) 'Greek and Latin Acrostichs', *Philologus* 134: 3–13.

Crabbe, A. (1981) 'Structure and Content in Ovid's Metamorphoses', *ANRW* 2.31.4.2274–327.

Curley, D. (2013) *Tragedy in Ovid: Theater, Metatheater, and the Transformation of a Genre*. Cambridge.

Curran, L.C. (1978) 'Rape and Rape Victims in the *Metamorphoses*', *Arethusa* 11: 213–42.

Cusset, C. (1995) 'Exercises rhétoriques d'Aratos autour du terme ἠχή', *RPh* 69: 245–8.

Cusset, C. (2002) 'Poétique et onomastique dans les *Phénomènes* d'Aratos', *Pallas* 50: 187–96.

Damschen, G. (2004) 'Das lateinische Akrostichon: Neue Funde bei Ovid sowie Vergil, Grattius, Manilius und Silius Italicus', *Philologus* 148: 88–115.

Daneshvar-Malevergne, N. (2009) *Narcisse et le Mal du Siècle*. Paris.

Danielewicz, J. (2005) 'Further Hellenistic Acrostics: Aratus and Others', *Mnemosyne* 58: 321–34.

Danielewicz, J. (2013) 'Vergil's *certissima signa* Reinterpreted: The Aratean *lepte*-Acrostic in *Georgics* I', *Eos* 100: 287–95.

Danielewicz, J. (2015) 'One Sign after Another: The Fifth *ΛΕΠΤΗ* in Aratus' *Phaen.* 783–4?', *CQ* 65: 387–90.

Davis, G. (2012) *Parthenope: The Interplay of Ideas in Vergilian Bucolic.* Leiden/Boston (Mnemosyne Suppl. 346).

Davis, T. (2016) *Ornamental Aesthetics: The Poetry of Attending in Thoreau, Dickinson, and Whitman.* Oxford.

De Jong, I.J.F. (2012) *Space in Ancient Greek Literature: Studies in Ancient Greek Narrative, Vol. III.* Leiden.

De Jong, I.J.F. (2014) *Narratology and Classics: A Practical Guide.* Oxford.

Demats, P. (1973) *Fabula: Trois études de mythographie antique et médiévale.* Geneva.

Dench, E. (2005) *Romulus' Asylum: Roman Identities from the Age of Alexander to the Age of Hadrian.* Oxford.

Derche, R. (1962) *Quatre mythes poétiques (Œdipe—Narcisse—Psyché—Lorelei).* Paris.

Derrida, J. (1972) *Marges de la philosophie.* Paris.

Derrida, J. (1988) 'Like the Sound of the Sea Deep Within a Shell: Paul de Man's War', trans. P. Kamuf, *Critical Inquiry* 14: 590–652.

Desmond, M. (2007) 'The goddess Diana and the ethics of reading in the *Ovide Moralisé*', in Keith and Rupp (2007): 61–75.

Dimmick, J. (2002) 'Ovid in the Middle Ages: authority and poetry', in Hardie (2002a): 264–87.

Doblhofer, E. (1968) 'Zwei sprechende Namen bei Ovid. Zur Interpretation von *Met.* 1, 384–394', *WS* 81: 98–102.

Dornseiff, F. (1922) *Das Alphabet in Mystik und Magie.* Leipzig.

Dougherty, C. (1993) *The Poetics of Colonization: From City to Text in Archaic Greece.* New York.

Dronke, P. (2008) *The Spell of Calcidius: Platonic Concepts and Images in the Medieval West.* Florence.

Dronke, P. (2016) *Sacred and Profane Thought in the Early Middle Ages.* Florence.

Ducci, E. (2013) *La Romanizzazione del Mito Greco nelle Metamorfosi di Ovidio*, PhD diss., University of Siena.

Dueck, D. (2012) *Geography in Classical Antiquity.* Cambridge.

Dufallo, B. (2013) *The Captor's Image: Greek Culture in Roman Ecphrasis.* New York.

Dufour, G. (1999) 'Les metamorphoses de Satan dans le *Paradis Perdu* de John Milton', *Imaginaires* 4: 53–70.

Dümmler, E. (1881) *Poetae Latini Aevi Carolini, Vol. 1.* Berlin.

Dunand, M. (1963) *Byblos, son histoire, ses ruines, ses légendes.* Beirut.

Dunbabin, K.M.D. and Dickie, M. (1983) '*Invida rumpantur pectora*: The iconography of Phthonos/Invidia in Graeco-Roman art', *JbAC* 26: 7–37.

DuRocher, R.J. (1985) *Milton and Ovid.* Ithaca.

Easterling, P.E. (2006) 'Sophocles: the first thousand years', *BICS* 87: 1–15.

Edwards, M.J. (1995) 'Chrysostom, Prudentius, and the fiends of *Paradise Lost*', *Notes & Queries* 42.4: 448–51.

Ellis, H. (1913) *Studies in the Psychology of Sex I.* Philadelphia.

Ellis, H. (1928) 'The Conception of Narcissism', in Ellis, H. (ed.) *Studies in the Psychology of Sex VII: Eonism and Other Supplementary Studies.* Philadelphia: 347–75.

Elsner, J. (2007) *Roman Eyes: Visuality and Subjectivity in Art and Text.* Princeton.

Engelbrecht, W. (2003) *Filologie in de Dertiende Eeuw: de Bursarii super Ovidios van Magister Willem van Orléans. Editie, Inleiding en Commentaar.* Olomouc.

Enterline, L. (2000) *The Rhetoric of the Body from Ovid to Shakespeare.* Cambridge.

Ernst, U. (1991) *Carmen figuratum: Geschichte des Figurengedichts von den antiken Ursprüngen bis zum Ausgang des Mittelalters.* Cologne.

Fabre-Serris, J. (2009) 'Sulpicia: An/Other Female Voice in Ovid's *Heroides*. A New Reading of *Heroides* 4 and 15', *Helios* 36: 149–73.

Fantham, E. (2004) *Ovid's Metamorphoses*. Oxford.

Farrell, J. (1998) 'Reading and Writing the Heroides', *HSPh*, 98: 307–38.

Feeney, D.C. (1991) *The Gods in Epic: Poets and Critics of the Classical Tradition*. Oxford.

Feeney, D.C. (1999) '*Mea tempora*: Patterning of Time in the *Metamorphoses*', in Hardie, Barchiesi, and Hinds (1999): 13–30.

Feeney, D.C. (2004) 'Introduction', in Raeburn, D. (trans.) *Ovid: Metamorphoses*. London.

Feeney, D.C. (2007) *Caesar's Calendar: Ancient Time and the Beginnings of History*. Berkeley.

Feeney, D.C. and Nelis, D. (2005) 'Two Virgilian Acrostics: *certissima signa*?', *CQ* 55: 644–6.

Feldherr, A. (1999) 'Putting Dido on the Map: Genre and Geography in Virgil's Underworld', *Arethusa* 31: 85–122.

Feldherr, A. (2000) '*Non inter nota sepulcra*: Catullus 101 and Roman Funerary Ritual', *ClAnt* 19: 209–31.

Feldherr, A. (2002) 'Metamorphosis in the *Metamorphoses*', in Hardie (2002a): 163–79.

Feldherr, A. (2010) *Playing Gods: Ovid's Metamorphoses and the Politics of Fiction*. Princeton.

Feldherr, A. (2016) 'Nothing like the Sun: Repetition and Representation in Ovid's Phaethon narrative', in Fulkerson and Stover (2016): 27–46.

Fetterley, J. (1978) *The Resisting Reader: A Feminist Approach to American Fiction*. Bloomington, IN.

Finley, M.I. (1979) *Ancient Sicily*. London.

Fitzgerald, W. (1995) *Catullan Provocations: Lyric Poetry and the Drama of Position*. Berkeley.

Fitzgerald, W. (2016) *Variety: the Life of a Roman Concept*. Chicago.

Fitzgerald, W. and Spentzou, E. (eds) (2018) *The Production of Space in Latin Literature*. Oxford.

Fletcher, K.F.B. (2014) *Finding Italy: Travel, Nation and Colonization in Vergil's Aeneid*. Ann Arbor.

Forbes-Irving, P.M.C. (1990) *Metamorphosis in Greek Myths*. Oxford.

Fowler, A. (1997) *Milton: Paradise Lost*. London.

Fowler, D.P. (1983) 'An Acrostic in Vergil (*Aeneid* 7. 601–4)?', *CQ* 33: 298.

Frame, D. (1978) *The Myth of Return in Early Greek Epic*. New Haven.

Frenzel, E. (1963) *Stoff- Motiv und Symbolforschung*. Stuttgart.

Frenzel, E. (1974) *Stoff- und Motivgeschichte*. Berlin.

Freud, S. (1940–87) *Gesammelte Werke: Chronologisch geordnet I–XVIII, Nachtragsband*. London.

Freud, S. (2010) *The Interpretation of Dreams: The Complete and Definitive Text*, trans. J. Strachey, New York.

Friberg, A. (1945) *Den svenske Herkules: Studier i Stiernhielms diktning*. Stockholm.

Frings, I. (2005) *Das Spiel mit den eigenen Texten. Wiederholung und Selbstzitat bei Ovid*. Munich.

Frontisi-Ducroux, F. (1997) 'Dans l'Œil du Miroir', in Frontisi-Ducroux, F. and Vernant, J.-P. (eds) *Dans l'Œil du Miroir*. Paris: 51–250.

Frontisi-Ducroux, F. (2003) *L'Homme-cerf et la Femme-Araignée. Figures Grecques de la Métamorphose*. Paris.

Fulkerson, L. (2005) *The Ovidian Heroine as Author: Reading, Writing and Community in the Heroides*. Cambridge.

Fulkerson, L. (2016) *Ovid: A Poet on the Margins*. London.

Fulkerson, L., and Stover, T. (eds) (2016) *Repeat Performances: Ovidian Repetition and the Metamorphoses*. Madison.

Gagliardi, P. (2003) *Grauis cantantibus umbra: Studi su Virgilio e Cornelio Gallo*. Bologna.

Gagliardi, P. (2011) 'Dafni e Gallo nell' *ecl.* 10 di Virgilio', *A&A* 57: 56–73.

Gale, M.R. and Scourfield, J.H.D. (eds) (2018) *Texts and Violence in the Roman World*. Cambridge.

Galinsky, G.K. (1975) *Ovid's Metamorphoses: An Introduction to the Basic Aspects*. Oxford.

Galinsky, G.K. (1997) 'The Speech of Pythagoras in Ovid's Metamorphoses 15.75–478', *PLLS* 10: 313–36.

Galinsky, G.K. (1999) '*Aeneid* V and the *Aeneid*', in Hardie, P.R. (ed.) *Virgil: Routledge Critical Assessments of Classical Authors. Vol IV*. London: 182–206.

Garulli, V. (2013) 'Greek Acrostic Verse Inscriptions', in Kwapisz, Petrain, and Szymanski (2013) 246–78.

Gavrilov, A.K. (1997) 'Techniques of Reading in Classical Antiquity', *CQ* 47: 56–73.

Gellrich, J.M. (2000) 'The Art of the Tongue: Illuminating Speech and Writing in Later Medieval Manuscripts', in Hourihane, C. (ed.) *Virtues and Vices: The Personifications in the Index of Christian Art*. Princeton: 93–119.

Genette, G. (1997) *Paratextes*. Paris.

Genovese, E.N. (1983) 'Serpent leitmotif in the *Metamorphoses*', in Deroux, C. (ed.) *Studies in Latin Literature and Roman History* 3. Brussels: 141–55.

Ghisalberti, F. (1932) 'Arnolfo d'Orleans: un cultore di Ovidio nel secolo XII', in *Memorie del R. Instituto Lombardo, Classe Lettere* 24: 157–234.

Gibson, R.K. (2006) 'Ovid on Reading: Reading Ovid', in Laird (2006): 346–79.

Gibson, R.K. and Kraus, C.S. (eds) (2002) *The Classical Commentary: Histories, Practices, Theory*. Leiden.

Gildenhard, I. and Zissos, A. (2000a) 'Ovid's Narcissus (*Met* 3:339–510): Echoes of Oedipus', *AJPh* 121.1: 129–47.

Gildenhard, I. and Zissos, A. (2000b) 'Inspirational Fictions: Autobiography and Generic Reflexivity in Ovid's Proems', *G&R* 47: 67–79.

Gildenhard, I. and Zissos, A. (2013) *Transformative Change in Western Thought: A History of Metamorphosis from Homer to Hollywood*. London.

Ginsberg, W. (2011) 'Dante's Ovids', in Clark, J.G., Coulson, F.T., and McKinley, K.L. (eds) (2011) *Ovid in the Middle Ages*. Cambridge: 143–59.

Giusti, E. (2015) 'Caesar Criss-Crossing the Rubicon: A Palindromic Acrostic in Lucan (1.218–22)', *CQ* 65: 892–4.

Giusti, E. (2018) 'Tiresias, Ovid, gender and trouble: generic conversions from *Ars* into *Tristia*', in *Ramus* 47: 27–57.

Gleason, M.W. (1995) *Making Men: Sophists and Self-Presentation in Ancient Rome*. Princeton.

Goldschmidt, N. (2013) *Shaggy Crowns: Ennius' Annales and Virgil's Aeneid*. Oxford.

Gore, J. and Kershaw, A. (2008) 'An Unnoticed Acrostic in Apuleius *Metamorphoses* and Cicero *De divinatione* 2.111–12', *CQ* 58: 393–4.

Gowers, E. (2005) 'Talking Trees: Philemon and Baucis Revisited', *Arethusa* 38: 331–65.

Granger, H. (2008) 'The proem of Parmenides' poem', *AncPhil* 28: 1–20.

Gransden, K.W. (1976) *Virgil: Aeneid, Book VIII*. Cambridge.

Green, M. (2009) *Milton's Ovidian Eve*. Farnham.

Griffiths, J.G. (1970) *Plutarch's De Iside et Osiride*. Cardiff.

Grishin, A.A. (2008) '*Ludus in undis*: An Acrostic in *Eclogue* 9', *HSPh* 104: 237–40.

Groves, R. (2016) 'From Statue to Story: Ovid's Metamorphosis of Hermaphroditus', *CW* 109: 321–56.

Gunderson, G. (2000) *Staging Masculinity: The Rhetoric of Performance in the Roman World*. Ann Arbor.

Gura, D. (2010) *A Critical Edition and Study of Arnulf of Orléans' Philological Commentary to Ovid's Metamorphoses*, PhD diss., Ohio State University.

Habinek, T. (2002) 'Ovid and Empire', in Hardie (2002b): 46–61.

Habinek, T. (2009) 'Situating Literacy at Rome', in Johnson, W.A. and Parker, H.N. (eds) *Ancient Literacies: The Culture of Reading in Greece and Rome*. Oxford: 114–40.

Hadot, P. (1976) 'Le Mythe de Narcisse et son Intérprétation par Plotin', *Nouvelle Revue de Psychanalyse* 13: 81–108.

Hagstrum, J.H. (1958) *The Sister Arts: The Tradition of Literary Pictorialism and English Poetry from Dryden to Gray*. Chicago.

Hamilton, A.C. (2003) *The Spenser Encyclopedia*. London.

Hamilton, J.T. (2009) 'Ovids Echographie', in Goebel, E. and Bronfen, E. (eds) *Narziss und Eros: Bild oder Text?*, trans. D. Hückman, Göttingen: 18–40.

Hanses, M. (2014a) 'Plautinisches im Ovid: The *Amphitruo* and the *Metamorphoses*', in Perysinakis, I.N. and Karakasis, E. (eds) *Plautine Trends: Studies in Plautine Comedy and Its Reception*. Berlin: 223–56.

Hanses, M. (2014b) 'The Pun and the Moon in the Sky: Aratus' *ΛΕΠΤΗ* Acrostic', *CQ* 64: 609–14.

Hanses, M. (2016) 'Love's Letters: An Amor-Roma Telestich at Ovid, *Ars amatoria* 3.507–10', in Mitsis and Ziogas (2016): 199–211.

Harder, A. (2012) *Callimachus: Aetia, 2 Vols*. Oxford.

Hardie, P.R. (1986) *Virgil's Aeneid: Cosmos and Imperium*. Oxford.

Hardie, P.R. (1993) '*Ut pictura poesis*? Horace and the visual arts', in Rudd, N. (ed.) *Horace 2000: A Celebration: Essays for the Bimillenium*. Ann Arbor: 120–39.

Hardie, P.R. (1994) *Virgil Aeneid: Book IX*. Cambridge.

Hardie, P.R. (1995) 'The Speech of Pythagoras in Ovid *Metamorphoses* 15: Empedoclean Epos', *CQ* 45: 204–14.

Hardie, P.R. (1997) 'Questions of Authority: The Invention of Tradition in Ovid's *Metamorphoses* 15', in Habinek, T. and Schiesaro, A. (eds) *The Roman Cultural Revolution*. Cambridge: 182–98.

Hardie, P.R. (1998) *Virgil*. Oxford.

Hardie, P.R. (ed.) (2002a) *The Cambridge Companion to Ovid*. Cambridge.

Hardie, P.R. (2002b) *Ovid's Poetics of Illusion*. Cambridge.

Hardie, P.R. (2006) 'Virgil's Ptolemaic Relations', *JRS* 96: 25–41.

Hardie, P.R. (2012) *Rumour and Renown: Representations of Fama in Western Literature*. Cambridge.

Hardie, P.R. (2015a) 'Milton as reader of Ovid's *Metamorphoses*', in Mack, P. and North, J. (eds) *The Afterlife of Ovid*. London: 203–19.

Hardie, P.R. (2015b) *Ovidio, Metamorfosi. Volume VI: Libri XIII–XV*, Fondazione Valla, Milan.

Hardie, P.R. (ed.) (2009) *Paradox and the Marvellous in Augustan Literature and Culture*. Oxford.

Hardie, P.R., Barchiesi, A., and Hinds, S.E. (eds) (1999) *Ovidian Transformations: Essays on Ovid's Metamorphoses and its Reception*. Cambridge.

Harding, D.P. (1946) *Milton and the Renaissance Ovid*. Urbana.

Harris, W.V. (2009) *Dreams and Experience in Classical Antiquity*. Cambridge, MA.

Harrison, S.J. (2007a) *Generic Enrichment in Vergil and Horace*. Oxford.

Harrison, S.J. (2007b) 'The Primal Voyage and the Ocean of Epos: Two Aspects of Metapoetic Imagery in Catullus, Virgil and Horace', *Dictynna* 4: http://journals. openedition.org/dictynna/146.

Hartlaub, G.F. (1951) *Geschichte und Bedeutung des Spiegels in der Kunst*. Munich.

Haslam, M. (1992) 'Hidden Signs: Aratus *Diosemeiai* 46ff., Vergil *Georgics* 1.424ff.', *HSPh* 94: 199–204.

Haupt, M. (1873) 'Coniectanea', *Hermes* 7: 294–7.

Heath, J. (1991) 'Diana's Understanding of Ovid's *Metamorphoses*', *CJ* 86: 233–43.

Heil, A. (2007) 'Christliche Deutungen der Eklogen Vergils: Die *Tityre*-Initiale im Codex Klosterneuburg CCl 742', *A&A* 53: 100–19.

Hejduk, J. (2018) 'Was Vergil Reading the Bible? Original Sin and an Astonishing Acrostic in the *Orpheus and Eurydice*', *Vergilius* 64: 71–101.

Henry, W.B. (2005) 'Elegy (*Metamorphoses*)', in *The Oxyrhynchus Papyri* vol. LXIX: 46–52.

Herren, M. (2004) 'Manegold of Lautenbach's Scholia on the *Metamorphoses*: Are There More?' *Notes & Queries* 51: 218–22.

Heslin, P.J. (2018) *Propertius, Greek Myth, and Virgil: Rivalry, Allegory, and Polemic*. Oxford.

Hexter, R.J. (1986) *Ovid and Medieval Schooling: Studies in Medieval School Commentaries on Ovid's Ars Amatoria, Epistulae ex Ponto, and Epistulae Heroidum*. Munich.

Higgins, D. (1987) *Pattern Poetry: Guide to an Unknown Literature*. Albany.

Hilberg, I. (1899) 'Ist die Ilias Latina von einem Italicus verfasst oder einem Italicus gewidmet?', *WS* 21: 264–305.

Hilberg, I. (1900) 'Nachtrag zur Abhandlung "Ist die Ilias Latina von einem Italicus verfasst oder einem Italicus gewidmet?"', *WS* 22: 317–18.

Hinds, S.E. (1987a) 'Generalising about Ovid', *Ramus* 16: 4–31.

Hinds, S.E. (1987b) *The Metamorphosis of Persephone, Ovid and the Self-Conscious Muse*. Cambridge.

Hinds, S.E. (1998) *Allusion and Intertext: Dynamics of Appropriation in Roman Poetry*. Cambridge.

Hinds, S.E. (2002) 'Landscape with figures: aesthetics of place in the *Metamorphoses* and its tradition', in Hardie (2002a): 122–49.

Hirschberger, M. (2008) 'Il Tema della Metamorfosi nel *Catalogo* Esiodeo delle Donne', in Bastianini, B. and Casanova, A. (eds) *Esiodo: Cent' Anni di Papiri*. Florence: 113–27.

Hollis, A.S. (2007) *Fragments of Roman Poetry c. 60 BC–AD 20*. Oxford.

Holst-Warhaft, G. (1992) *Dangerous Voices: Women's Laments and Greek Literature*. London.

Holzberg, N. (1997) *Ovid: Dichter und Werk*. Munich.

Hopkinson, N. (1988) *A Hellenistic Anthology*. Cambridge.

Hopkinson, N. (2000) *Ovid: Metamorphoses Book XIII*. Cambridge.

Hornblower, S. (2015) *Lycophron: Alexandra*. Oxford.

Hornblower, S. (2018) *Lykophron's Alexandra, Rome, and the Hellenistic world*. Oxford.

Horsfall, N. (2000) *Virgil: Aeneid 7*. Leiden.

Hubbard, T.K. (1998) *The Pipes of Pan: Intertextuality and Literary Filiation in the Pastoral Tradition from Theocritus to Milton*. Ann Arbor.

Hunter, R. (1999) *Theocritus, a Selection. Idylls 1, 3, 4, 6, 7, 10, 11 and 13*. Cambridge and New York.

Hunter, R. (2006) *The Shadow of Callimachus: Studies in the Reception of Hellenistic Poetry at Rome*. Cambridge.

Hunter, V. (1982) *Past and Process in Herodotus and Thucydides*. Princeton.

Hurka, F. (2006) 'Ein Akrostikhon in Ciceros *Aratea* (vv. 317–320)', *WJA* 30: 87–91.

Hutchinson, G. (2006) 'The metamorphosis of metamorphosis: P.Oxy. 4711 and Ovid', *ZPE* 155: 71–84.

Hutchinson, G.O. (2013) *Greek to Latin: Frameworks and Contexts for Intertextuality*. Oxford.

Ingleheart, J. (2010) *A Commentary on Ovid: Tristia, Book 2*. Oxford.

Ingleheart, J. (2015) '*Exegi monumentum*: Exile, Death, Immortality and Monumentality in Ovid, *Tristia* 3.3', *CQ* 65: 286–300.

Isager, S. (1998) 'The Pride of Halikarnassos', *ZPE* 123: 1–23.

Isotta, P. (2018) *La Dotta Lira. Ovidio e la Musica*. Venice.

Jacoff, R. and Schnapp, J.T. (eds) (1991) *Poetry of Allusion: Virgil and Ovid in Dante's Commedia*. Stanford.

Jacques, J.-M. (1960) 'Sur un acrostiche d'Aratos (Phén., 738–787)', *REA* 62: 48–61.

James, S.L. (1995) 'Establishing Rome with the Sword: *condere* in the *Aeneid*', *AJPh* 116: 623–37.

James, S.L. (2016) 'Rape and Repetition in Ovid's *Metamorphoses*: Myth, History, Structure, Rome', in Fulkerson and Stover (2016): 154–75.

Janan, M. (1988) 'The Book of Good Love? Design Versus Desire in Metamorphoses 10', *Ramus* 17: 110–37.

Janan, M.W. (1991) '*The Labyrinth and the Mirror*: incest and influence in *Metamorphoses* 9.', *Arethusa* 24: 239–56.

Jansen, L. (ed.) (2014a) *The Roman Paratext: Frame, Texts, Readers*. Cambridge.

Jansen, L. (2014b) 'Introduction: Approaches to Roman Paratextuality', in Jansen (2014a): 1–18.

Jauss, H.R. (1970) 'Literaturgeschichte als Provokation der Literaturwissenschaft', *Jahrbuch für Internationale Germanistik* 2.1: 25–8.

Jenkins, T. (2000) 'The writing in (and of) Ovid's "Byblis" episode', *HSPh* 100: 439–51.

Jenkyns, R. (1989) 'Virgil and Arcadia', *JRS* 79: 26–39.

Jidejian, N. (1968) *Byblos Through the Ages*. Beirut.

Johansson, N. (2017) *The Narcissus Theme from Fin de Siècle to Psychoanalysis: Crisis of the Modern Self*. Frankfurt.

Johnson, P.J. (2008) *Ovid Before Exile: Art and Punishment in the Metamorphoses*. Madison.

Johnson, S.F. (2016) *Literary Territories: Cartographical Thinking in Late Antiquity*. Oxford.

Jones, P.J. (2005) *Reading Rivers in Roman Literature and Culture*. Lanham.

Kachuck, A. (2015) *Solitude and Imagination: Cicero, Virgil, Horace, Propertius*. Princeton.

Kamen, D. (2012) 'Naturalized desires and the metamorphosis of Iphis', *Helios* 39: 21–36.

Kaster, R.A. (1995) *C. Suetonius Tranquillus: De grammaticis et rhetoribus*. Oxford.

Katz, J.T. (2007) 'An Acrostic Ant Road in *Aeneid* 4', *MD* 59: 77–86.

Katz, J.T. (2008) 'Vergil Translates Aratus: *Phaenomena* 1–2 and *Georgics* 1.1–2', *MD* 60: 105–23.

Katz, J.T. (2009) 'Wordplay', in Jamison, S.W., Melchert, C.H., and Vine, B. (eds) *Proceedings of the 20th Annual UCLA Indo-European Conference, Los Angeles, October 31–November 1, 2008*, Bremen: 79–114.

Katz, J.T. (2013) 'The Muse at Play: An Introduction', in Kwapisz, Petrain and Szymanski, (2013): 1–30.

Katz, J.T. (2016) 'Another Vergilian Signature in the *Georgics*?', in Mitsis and Ziogas (2016): 69–86.

Kay, T. (2016) *Dante's Lyric Redemption: Eros, Salvation, Vernacular Tradition*. Oxford.

Keith, A.M. (1999) 'Versions of Epic Masculinity in Ovid's *Metamorphoses*' in Hardie, Barchiesi and Hinds (1999): 214–39.

Keith, A.M. (2000) *Engendering Rome: Women in Latin Epic*. Cambridge.

Keith, A.M. and Rupp, S.J. (eds) (2007) *Metamorphosis: The Changing Face of Ovid in Medieval and Early Modern Europe*. Toronto.

Kenaan, V.L. (2004) 'Delusion and Dream in Apuleius' *Metamorphoses*', *CLAnt* 23: 247–84.

Kennedy, D.F. (1987) '*Arcades ambo*: Virgil, Gallus and Arcadia', *Hermathena* 143: 47–59.

Kenney, E.J. (1976) 'Ovidius Prooemians', *PCPhS* 22: 46–53.

Kenney, E.J. (2011) *Ovidio, Metamorfosi. Volume IV: Libri VII–IX*, Fondazione Valla, Milan.

Kersten, M. (2013) 'Ein Akrostichon im zweiten Buch De Bello Civili? Lucan. 2,600–608', *RhM* 156: 161–71.

Kidd, D. (1981) 'Notes on Aratus, *Phaenomena*', *CQ* 31: 355–62.

Kidd, D. (1997) *Aratus: Phaenomena*. Cambridge.

Kilgour, M. (1991) *From Communion to Cannibalism*. Princeton.

Kilgour, M. (2007) 'Changing Ovid', in Keith and Rupp (2007): 267–83.

Kilgour, M. (2012) *Milton and the Metamorphosis of Ovid*. Oxford.

Klooster, J.H. (2013) 'Horace, *Carmen* 4.2.53–60: Another Look at the *vitulus*', *CQ* 63: 346–52.

Knoepfler, D. (2010) *La Patrie de Narcisse*. Paris.

Knoespel, K.J. (1985) *Narcissus and the Invention of Personal History*. New York.

Knox, B.M.W. (1950) 'The Serpent and the Flame: the Imagery of the Second Book of the *Aeneid*', *AJPh* 71: 379–400.

Knox, B.M.W. (1968) 'Silent Reading in Antiquity', *GRBS* 9: 421–35.

Knox, P.E. (1986) *Ovid's Metamorphoses and the Traditions of Augustan Poetry*. Cambridge.

Knox, P.E. (1988) 'Phaethon in Ovid and Nonnus', *CQ* 38: 536–51.

Knox, P.E. (ed.) (2009) *A Companion to Ovid*. Oxford.

Kochhar-Lindgren, G. (1993) *Narcissus Transformed: The Textual Subject in Psychoanalysis and Literature*, University Park, PA.

Kofler, W. (2003) *Aeneas und Vergil: Untersuchungen zur poetologischen Dimension der Aeneis*. Heidelberg.

Korenjak, M. (2009) 'ΛΕΥΚΗ: Was bedeutet das erste "Akrostichon"?', *RhM* 152: 392–6.

Kraay, C.M. (1976) *Archaic and Classical Greek Coins*. London.

Kranz, W. (1961) 'SPHRAGIS: Ichform und Namensiegel als Eingangs- und Schlußmotiv antiker Dichtung', *RhM* 104: 3–46 and 97–124.

Krevans, N. (1993) 'Ilia's dream: Ennius, Virgil, and the mythology of seduction', *HSPh* 95: 257–71.

Kristeva, J. (1969) Σημειωτιϰή: *Recherches pour une Sémanalyse*. Paris.

Kronenberg, L. (2018a) 'Seeing the Light, Part I: Aratus's Interpretation of Homer's *LEUKE* Acrostic', *Dictynna* 15: http://journals.openedition.org/dictynna/1535.

Kronenberg, L. (2018b) 'Seeing the Light, Part II: The Reception of Aratus's *LEPTĒ* Acrostic in Greek and Latin Literature', *Dictynna* 15: http://journals.openedition.org/dictynna/1575.

Kronenberg, L. (2019) 'The Light Side of the Moon: A Lucretian Acrostic (*LUCE* 5.712–15) and Its Relationship to Acrostics in Homer (*LEUKE*, *Il.* 24.1–5) and Aratus (*LEPTE*, *Phaen.* 783–87)', *CPh* 114: 278–92.

Kubiak, D.P. (2009) '*Scitus arator*: Germanicus, *Aratea* 13', *SIFC* 7: 248–55.

Kwapisz, J., Petrain, D. and Szymanski, M. (eds) (2013) *The Muse at Play: Riddles and Wordplay in Greek and Latin Poetry*. Berlin.

Kyriakidis, S. (2014) 'From Delos to Latium: Wandering in the Unknown', in Skempis and Ziogas (2014): 265–90.

Kyriakidis, S. and De Martino, F. (eds) (2004) *Middles in Latin Poetry*. Bari.

La Barbera, S. (2006) 'Divinità occulte: Acrostici nei Proemi di Ovidio e Claudiano', *MD* 56: 181–4.

Labate, M. (1993) 'Storie di instabilità: l'episodio di Ermafrodito nelle *Metamorfosi* di Ovidio', *MD* 30: 49–62.

Lada-Richards, I. (2013) '*Mutata corpora*: Ovid's Changing Forms and the metamorphic bodies of pantomime', *TAPhA* 143: 105–52.

Lada-Richards, I. (2016) 'Dancing trees: Ovid's *Metamorphoses* and the imprint of pantomime dancing', *AJPh* 137: 131–69.

Lada-Richards, I. (2018) 'Closing up on animal metamorphosis: Ovid's micro-choreographies in the *Metamorphoses* and the corporeal idioms of Pantomime dancing', *CW* 111: 371–404.

Laird, A. (ed.) (2006) *Ancient Literary Criticism*. Oxford.

Lateiner, D. (1990) 'Mimetic syntax: metaphor from word order, especially in Ovid', *AJPh* 111: 204–37.

Lateiner, D. (2006) '*Procul este parentes*: mothers in Ovid's *Metamorphoses*', *Helios* 33: 189–201.

Lateiner, D. (2009) 'Transsexuals and Transvestites in Ovid's *Metamorphoses*', in Fögen, T. and Lee, M.M. (eds) *Bodies and Boundaries in Graeco-Roman Antiquity*. Berlin: 125–54.

Lee-Stecum, P. (2008) 'Roman *refugium*: Refugee Narratives in Augustan Versions of Roman Prehistory', *Hermathena* 184: 69–91.

Lee, A.G. (1953) *Metamorphoseon liber I*. Cambridge.

Lee, M.O. (1989) *Death and Rebirth in Vergil's Arcadia*. New York.

Lev Kenaan, V. (2008) *Pandora's Senses: The Feminine Character of the Ancient Text*. Madison, WI.

Levenstein, J. (1996) 'The pilgrim, the poet, and the cowgirl: Dante's Alter-*Io* in *Purgatorio* 30–31', *Dante Studies* 114: 189–208.

Levine, M.M. (1995) 'The Gendered Grammar of Ancient Mediterranean Hair', in Eilberg-Schwartz, H. and Doniger, W. (eds) *Off with Her Head: The Denial of Women's Identity in Myth, Religion, and Culture*. Berkeley: 76–130.

Levitan, W. (1979) 'Plexed Artistry: Aratean Acrostics', *Glyph* 5: 55–68.

Levitan, W. (1985) 'Dancing at the End of the Rope: Optatian Porfyry and the Field of Roman Verse', *TAPhA* 115: 245–69.

Lightfoot, J.L. (1999) *Parthenius of Nicaea: The Poetical Fragments and the Erōtika pathēmata*. Oxford.

Lightfoot, J.L. (2003) *Lucian: On the Syrian Goddess*. Oxford.

Liveley, G. (1999) 'Reading Resistance in Ovid's Metamorphoses', in Hardie, Barchiesi, and Hinds (1999): 197–213.

Liveley, G. (2003) 'Tiresias/Teresa: A "Man-Made-Woman" in Ovid's *Metamorphoses* 3.318–38.', *Helios* 30: 147–62.

Liveley, G. (2005) *Ovid: Love Songs*. Bristol.

Lobel, E. (1928) 'Nicander's Signature', *CQ* 22: 114.

Lomas, K. (2000) 'Between Greece and Sicily: an External Perspective on Culture in Roman Sicily', in Smith, C.J. and Serrati, J. (eds) *Sicily from Aeneas to Augustus: New Approaches in Archaeology and History*. Edinburgh: 161–73.

Loos, J.X. (2008) 'How Ovid remythologizes Greek astronomy in *Metamorphoses* 1.747–2.400', *Mnemosyne* 61: 257–89.

Loraux, N. (1993) *The Children of Athena: Athenian Ideas about Citizenship and the Division between the Sexes*, trans. C. Levine, Princeton.

Louÿs, P. (1898) *Byblis Changée en Fontaine*. Paris.

Ludwig, W. (1965) *Struktur und Einheit der Metamorphosen Ovids*. Berlin.

Lukacher, N. (1986) *Primal Scenes: Literature, Philosophy, Psychoanalysis*. Ithaca.

Luz, C. (2010) *Technopaignia: Formspiele in der griechischen Dichtung* Leiden.

Magnelli, E. (2014) 'Metamorfosi in poesia e poesia di metamorfosi in età ellenistica', in Citti, F., Pasetti, L., and Pellacani, D. (eds), (2014) *Metamorfosi tra scienza e letteratura*. Florence: 41–62.

Mahoney, A. (1934) *Vergil in the Works of Prudentius*. Washington.

Mairs, R. (2013) '*Sopha grammata*: Acrostichs in Greek and Latin Inscriptions from Arachosia, Nubia and Lybia', in Petrain, and Szymanski, Petrain (2013): 279–306.

Malamud, M.A. (2011) *The Origin of Sin: An English Translation of the Hamartigenia*. Ithaca.

Malkin, I. (1998) *The Returns of Odysseus: Colonization and Ethnicity*. Berkeley.

Manuwald, B. (1975) 'Narcissus bei Konon und Ovid', *Hermes*, 103.2: 349–72.

Marincola, J. (2013) 'Herodotus and Odysseus', in Munson, R.V. (ed.) *Herodotus: Volume 2. Herodotus and the World*. Oxford: 109–34.

Marshall, P.K. (ed.) (1993) *Hygini fabulae*. Stuttgart.

Martin, J. (1956) *Histoire du texte des Phénomènes d'Aratos*. Paris.

Martindale, C. (ed.) (1988) *Ovid Renewed*. Cambridge.

Matuschek, S. (2002) '"Was du hier siehst, edler Geist, bist du selbst": Narziß-Mythos und ästhetische Theorie ber Friedrich Schlegel und Herbert Marcuse', in Renger (2002): 79–97.

McAuley, M. (2015) *Reproducing Rome: Motherhood in Virgil, Ovid, Seneca, and Statius*. Oxford.

McKeown, J.C. (1989) *Ovid: Amores, Text, Prolegomena and Commentary in Four Volumes. Vol. 2*. Leeds.

McNelis, C. and Sens, A. (2016) *The Alexandra of Lycophron: A Literary Study*. Oxford.

Meinrath, D. (2014) *Leading (and Reading) by Example: Exemplarity in Ovid's Metamorphoses*, PhD diss., Princeton University.

Meiser, K. (1885) 'Ueber Einen Commentar Zu Den Metamorphosen Des Ovid', *Sitzungsberichte Der Königlich Bayerischen Akademie Der Wissenschaften. Philoso-Phisch-Philologische und Historische Klasse*. Munich.

Merivale, P. (1969) *Pan the Goat-God: His Myth in Modern Times*. Cambridge.

Meskill, L.S. (2009) *Ben Jonson and Envy*. Cambridge.

Metcalf, W.E. (2012) *The Oxford Handbook of Greek and Roman Coinage*. Oxford and New York.

Meunier, N.L.J. (2012) 'Ennius, les Astres et les Théories Anciennes de la Vision: à Propos de *Sol albus et radiis icta lux* (v. 84–85 Sk)', *RPh* 86: 101–21.

Miller, F.J. (1916) *Ovid Metamorphoses, Volume I: Books 1–8*, Loeb Classical Library, Cambridge, MA.

Miller, F.J. (1916) *Ovid Metamorphoses, Volume II: Books 9–15*, Loeb Classical Library, Cambridge, MA.

Miller, F.J. (1921) 'Some Features of Ovid's Style: III. Ovid's Methods of Ordering and Transition in the Metamorphoses', *CQ* 16: 464–76.

Miller, J.F. (2001) 'Tabucchi's Dream of Ovid', *Literary Imagination*, 3.2: 237–47.

Miller, J.F. (2012) *Empire and the Animal Body: Violence, Identity and Ecology in Victorian Adventure Fiction*. London.

Miller, J.F., and Newlands, C.E. (eds) (2014) *A Handbook to the Reception of Ovid*. Oxford.

Miller, P.A. (1999) 'The Tibullan Dream Text', *TAPhA* 129: 181–224.

Milnor, K. (2014) *Graffiti and the Literary Landscape in Roman Pompeii*. Oxford.

Minnis, A. (1988) *Medieval Theory of Authorship: Scholastic Literary Attitudes in the later Middle Ages*. Philadelphia.

Minnis, A. and Johnson, I. (eds) (2005) *The Cambridge History of Literary Criticism. Vol. 2, The Middle Ages*. Cambridge.

Mitlacher, H. (1933) 'Die Entwicklung des Narzißbegriffs', *Germanisch-romanische Monatsschrift* 21: 373–83.

Mitsis, P. and Ziogas, I. (eds) (2016) *Wordplay and Powerplay in Latin Poetry*. Berlin.

Moatti, C. (2015) *The Birth of Critical Thinking in Republican Rome*, trans. J. Lloyd, Cambridge.

Montarese, F. (2012) *Lucretius and His Sources: A Study of Lucretius' De Rerum Natura I.635–920*. Berlin and Boston.

Morgan, C. (2003) *Early Greek States Beyond the Polis*. London.

Morgan, G. (1993) 'Nullam, Vare...Chance or Choice in Odes 1.18?', *Philologus* 137: 142–5.

Morrison, A. (2011) 'Callimachus' Muses', in Acosta-Hughes, B., Lehnus, L. and Stephens, S. (eds) *Brill's Companion to Callimachus*. Leiden: 325–44.

Munk Olsen, B. (2014) *L'étude des auteurs classiques latins au XIe et XIIe siècles, T. 4, pt. 2. La réception de la littérature classique: Manuscrits et textes*. Paris.

Myers, S.K. (1994) *Ovid's Causes: Cosmogony and Aetiology in the Metamorphoses*. Ann Arbor.

Myers, S.K. (2009) *Ovid: Metamorphoses Book XIV*. Cambridge.

Mynors, R.A.B. (1969) *P. Vergili Maronis Opera*. Oxford.

Nagle, B.R. (1983) 'Byblis and Myrrha: Two Incest Narratives in the Metamorphoses', *CJ* 78: 301–15.

Nagle, B.R. (1988) 'Two Miniature Carmina Perpetua in the Metamorphoses: Calliope and Orpheus', *Grazer Beiträge* 15: 99–125.

Natoli, B.A. (2017) *Silenced Voices: The Poetics of Speech in Ovid*. Madison.

Nelis, D. (2006) 'Wordplay in Vergil and Claudian', *Dictynna* 3: http://journals.openedition.org/dictynna/220.

Newlands, C.E. (2018) 'Violence and resistance in Ovid's Metamorphoses', in Gale and Scourfield (2018): 140–78.

Nichols, A. (2018) 'Ctesias' Indica and the Origins of Paradoxography', in Gerolemou, M. (ed.) *Recognizing Miracles in Antiquity and Beyond*. Leiden: 3–16.

Nicolet, C. (1991) *Space, Geography, and Politics in the Early Roman Empire*. Ann Arbor.

Nietzsche, F. (1872) *Die Geburt der Tragödie aus dem Geiste der Musik*. Leipzig.

Norton, E. (2013) *Aspects of Ecphrastic Technique in Ovid's Metamorphoses*. Newcastle.

Nugent, S.G. (1990) 'This Sex Which Is Not One: De-Constructing Ovid's Hermaphrodite', *Differences* 2: 160–85.

O'Hara, J. (1996) 'Sostratus *Suppl. Hell.* 733: A Lost, Possibly Catullan-Era Elegy on the Six Sex Changes of Tiresias', *TAPhA* 126: 173–219.

O'Rourke, D. (2018) 'Make war not love: *militia amoris* and domestic violence in Roman elegy', in Gale and Scourfield (2018): 110–39.

Oliensis, E. (2009) *Freud's Rome: Psychoanalysis and Latin Poetry.* Cambridge.

Olstein, K. (1980) 'Pandora and Dike in Hesiod's *Works and Days*', *Emerita* 48: 295–312.

Ormand, K. (2005) 'Impossible Lesbians in Ovid's *Metamorphoses*', in Ancona, R. and Greene, E. (eds) *Gendered Dynamics in Latin Love Poetry.* Baltimore, MD: 79–110.

Otis, B. (1966) *Ovid as an Epic Poet.* Cambridge.

Otis, B. (1970) *Ovid as an Epic Poet.* Cambridge (2nd ed.)

Papaioannou, S. (2005) *Epic Succession and Dissension: Ovid, Metamorphoses 13.623–14.582 and the Reinvention of the Aeneid.* Berlin.

Papaioannou, S. (2003) 'Founder, Civilizer and Leader: Vergil's Evander and his Role in the Origins of Rome', *Mnemosyne* 56: 680–702.

Papaioannou, S. (2007) *Redesigning Achilles: 'Recycling' the Epic Cycle in the 'Little Illiad' (Ovid Metamorphoses 12.1–13.622).* Berlin.

Parry, H. (1964) 'Ovid's *Metamorphoses*: Violence in a Pastoral Landscape', *TAPhA* 95: 268–82.

Pavlock, B. (2009) *The Image of the poet in Ovid's Metamorphoses.* Madison, WI.

Peirano, I. (2014) ' "Sealing" the Book: The *Sphragis* as Paratext', in Jansen (2014a): 224–42.

Pellizer, E. (1987) 'Reflections, Echoes and Amorous Reciprocity: On Reading the Narcissus Story', in Bremmer, J. (ed.) *Interpretations of Greek Mythology*, trans. D. Crampton, London: 107–20.

Pellizer, E. (2003) 'Le Mythe de Narcisse', in Bettini, M. and Pellizer, E. (eds) *Le Mythe de Narcisse*, trans. J. Bouffartigue, Paris: 41–232.

Perkell, C.G. (1996) 'The "Dying Gallus" and the Design of *Eclogue* 10', *CPh* 91: 128–40.

Perutelli, A. (1978) 'L'inversione speculare: per una retorica dell'ecphrasis', *MD* 1: 87–98.

Pfandl, L. (1935) 'Der Narzißbegriff: Versuch einer Neuen Deutung', *Imago* 21.3: 279–310.

Pfeiffer, R. (1949) *Callimachus, I: Fragmenta.* Oxford.

Pfeiffer, R. (1968) *History of Classical Scholarship from the Beginnings to the End of the Hellenistic Age.* Oxford.

Pianezzola, E. (1999) *Ovidio. Modelli Retorici e Forma Narrativa.* Bologna.

Pigler, A. (1956) *Barockthemen: Eine Auswahl von Verzeichnisse zur Ikonographie des 17. und 18. Jahrhunderts.* Budapest.

Pintabone, D.T. (2002) 'Ovid's Iphis and Ianthe: When Girls Won't Be Girls', in Rabinowitz, N.S. and Auanger, L. (eds) *Among Women: From the Homosocial to the Homoerotic in the Ancient World.* Austin, TX: 256–85.

Porte, D. (1985) 'L'idée romaine et la métamorphose', in Frécault, J.M. and Porte, D. (eds) *Journées Ovidiennes de Parménie.* Brussels: 175–98.

Porter, J.I. (2011) 'Against λεπτότης: Rethinking Hellenistic Aesthetics', in Erskine, A. and Llewellyn-Jones, L. (eds) *Creating a Hellenistic World.* Swansea: 271–312.

Possamai-Pérez, M. (2009) 'Mythologie antique et amours incestueuses: le regard d'un clerc du Moyen Âge', *Anabases* 9: 173–84.

Poulet, G. (1961) *Les Métamorphoses du Cercle.* Paris.

Purves, A.C. (2010) *Space and Time in Ancient Greek Narrative.* Cambridge.

Quint, D. (1989) 'Repetition and Ideology in the *Aeneid*', *MD* 23: 9–54.

Raval, S. (2001) ' "A lover's discourse": Byblis in Metamorphoses 9', *Arethusa*, 34: 285–311.

Raval, S. (2002) 'Cross-Dressing and "Gender Trouble" in the Ovidian Corpus.' *Helios* 29: 149–72.

Reed, J.D. (2013) *Ovidio, Metamorfosi. Volume V: Libri X–XII*, Fondazione Valla, Milan.

Renger, A.-B. (ed.) (2002) *Narcissus: Ein Mythos von der Antike bis zum Cyberspace*. Stuttgart.

Reynolds, L.D. (ed.) (1983) *Texts and Transmission: A Survey of the Latin Classics*. Oxford.

Reynolds, S. (1996) *Medieval Reading: Grammar, Rhetoric and the Classical Text*. Cambridge.

Richlin, A. (1992) 'Reading Ovid's Rapes', in Richlin, A. (ed.) *Pornography and Representation in Greece and Rome*. Oxford: 158–79.

Ricks, C. (1963) *Milton's Grand Style*. Oxford.

Rimell, V. (2015) *The Closure of Space in Roman Poetics: Empire's Inward Turn*. Cambridge.

Rimell, V. and Asper, M. (eds) (2017) *Imagining Empire: Political Space in Hellenistic and Roman Literature*. Heidelberg.

Roberts, D.H., Dunn, F.M., and Fowler, D. (eds) (1997) *Classical Closure: Reading the End in Greek and Latin Literature*. Princeton.

Robinson, M. (1999) 'Salmacis and Hermaphroditus: When Two Become One', *CQ* 49: 212–13.

Robinson, M. (2019) 'Looking Edgeways: Pursuing Acrostics in Ovid and Virgil', *CQ* 69: 290–308.

Romano, A.J. (2009) 'The Invention of Marriage: Hermaphroditus and Salmacis at Halicarnassus and in Ovid', *CQ* 59: 543–61.

Rosati, G. (1983) *Narciso e Pigmalione: Illusione e spettacolo nelle Metamorfosi di Ovidio*. Florence.

Rosati, G. (2002) 'Narrative Techniques and Narrative Structures in the Metamorphoses', in Boyd (2002): 271–304.

Rosati, G. (2009) *Ovidio, Metamorfosi. Volume III: Libri V–VI*, Fondazione Valla, Milan.

Ross, D.O. (1975) *Backgrounds to Augustan Poetry: Gallus, Elegy and Rome*. Cambridge.

Rumrich, J.P. (1989) 'Metamorphosis in *Paradise Lost*', *Viator: Medieval and Renaissance Studies*, 20: 311–25.

Salvatore, A. (1985) *Studi Prudenziani*. Naples.

Salzman-Mitchell, P. (2005) *A Web of Fantasies: Gaze, Image, and Gender in Ovid's Metamorphoses*. Columbus.

Samuel, I. (1966) *Dante and Milton: the Commedia and Paradise Lost*. Ithaca.

Saunders, T. (2008) *Bucolic Ecology: Virgil's Eclogues and the Environmental Literary Tradition*. London.

Schafer, J.K. (2017) 'Authorial Pagination in the *Eclogues* and *Georgics*', *TAPhA* 147: 135–78.

Schiesaro, A. (2002) 'Ovid and the Professional Discourses of Scholarship, Religion, Rhetoric', in Hardie (2002a) 62–75.

Schmidt, E.A. (1991) *Ovids poetische Menschenwelt. Die* Metamorphosen *als Metapher und Symphonie*. Heidelberg.

Schmitzer, U. (1990) *Zeitgeschichte in Ovids* Metamorphosen. *Mythologische Dichtung unter politischem Anspruch*. Stuttgart.

Schwartz, R. (1993) *Remembering and Repeating: On Milton's Theology and Poetics*, Chicago.

Scioli, E. (2015) *Dream, Fantasy, and Visual Art in Roman Elegy*. Madison, WI.

Scott, S.C. (1986) 'From Polydorus to Fradubio: the History of a *topos*', *Spenser Studies* 7: 27–57.

Segal, C.P. (1969) *Landscape in Ovid's Metamorphoses: A Study in the Transformations of a Literary Symbol*. Wiesbaden.

Segal, C.P. (1994) 'Philomela's Web and the Pleasures of the Text', in de Jong, I.J.F. and Sullivan, J.P. (eds) *Modern Critical Theory and Classical Literature.* Leiden: 257–80.

Segal, C.P. (1998) 'Ovid's Metamorphic Bodies: Art, Gender and Violence in the *Metamorphoses*', *Arion* 5: 9–41.

Segal, C.P. (2005) 'Il corpo e l'io nelle *Metamorfosi* di Ovidio', in Barchiesi (2005): xvii–ci.

Seznec, J. (1953) *The Survival of the Pagan Gods: The Mythological Tradition and Its Place in Renaissance Humanism and Art,* trans. B.F. Sessions, New York.

Sharrock, A.R. (1991) 'Womanufacture', *JRS* 81: 36–49.

Sharrock, A.R. (1996) 'Representing Metamorphosis', in Elsner, J. (ed.) *Art and Text in Roman Culture.* Cambridge: 103–30.

Sharrock, A.R. (2002a) 'An A-musing Tale: Gender, Genre and Ovid's Battles with Inspiration in the *Metamorphoses*', in Spenztou, E. and Fowler, D. (eds) *Cultivating the Muse: Struggles for Power and Inspiration in Classical Literature,* Oxford: 207–27.

Sharrock, A.R. (2002b) 'Gender and Sexuality', in Hardie (2002a): 95–107.

Sharrock, A.R. (2015) 'Warrior Women in Roman Epic', in Keith, A.M. and Fabre-Serris, J. (eds) *Women and War in Antiquity.* Baltimore.

Sharrock, A.R. (2018) 'Till Death Do Us Part...Or Join: Love Beyond Death in Ovid's *Metamorphoses*', in Frangoulidis, S. and Harrison, S.J. (eds) *Life, Love and Death in Latin Poetry: Studies in Honour of Theodore D. Papanghelis.* Berlin: 125–36.

Sharrock, A.R. (forthcoming) 'Authors, Texts, Readings', in Gibson, R.K. and Whitton, C. (eds) *Cambridge Critical Guide to Latin Literature.* Cambridge.

Simon, J.A. (1899) *Akrosticha bei den augustischen Dichtern: Exoterische Studien, Zweiter Teil, mit einem Anhang: Akrostichische und telestichische Texte aus der Zeit von Plautus bis auf Crestien von Troies und Wolfram von Eschenbach.* Cologne.

Simpson, J. (1995) *Sciences and the Self in Medieval Poetry.* Cambridge.

Simpson, M. (2001) *The Metamorphoses of Ovid.* Amherst.

Skempis, M. (2014) 'Phenomenology of Space, Place Names and Colonization in the "Caieta-Circe" Sequence of *Aeneid* 7', in Skempis and Ziogas (2014): 291–324.

Skempis, M. and Ziogas, I. (eds) (2014) *Geography, Topography, Landscape: Configurations of Space in Greek and Latin Epic.* Berlin.

Skutsch, F. (1901) *Auf Vergils Frühzeit.* Leipzig.

Skutsch, O. (1985) *The Annals of Quintus Ennius.* Oxford.

Smith, A. (2013) '*Nomen inest*: A Declining Domicile and Caustic Acrostics in *Ex Ponto* III 3', *A&R* 7: 45–64.

Solodow, J.B. (1988) *The World of Ovid's Metamorphoses.* Chapel Hill.

Somerville, T. (2010) 'Note on a Reversed Acrostic in Vergil *Georgics* 1.429–33', *CPh* 105: 202–9.

Sourvinou-Inwood, C. (1987) 'Myth as History: The Previous Owners of the Delphic Oracle', in Bremmer, J. (ed.) *Interpretations of Greek Mythology.* London: 215–41.

Sowell, M.U. (ed.) (1991) *Dante and Ovid: Essays in Intertextuality.* Binghamton.

Spentzou, E. (2003) *Readers and Writers in Ovid's Heroides: Transgressions of Genre and Gender.* Oxford.

Spivak, G.C. (1993) 'Echo', *New Literary History,* 24.1: 17–43.

Squire, M. and Wienand, J. (eds) (2017) *Morphogrammata/The Lettered Art of Optatian: Figuring Cultural Transformations in the Age of Constantine.* Paderborn.

Stanivukovic G.V. (ed.) (2001) *Ovid and the Renaissance Body,* Toronto.

Stirrup, B.E. (1977) 'Techniques of Rape: Variety of Wit in Ovid's *Metamorphoses*', *G&R* 24: 170–84.

Straaten, M. van (1962) *Panaetii Rhodi Fragmenta.* Leiden.

Stroh, W. (1979) 'Ovids Liebeskunst und die Ehegesetze des Augustus', *Gymnasium* 86: 323–52.

Sullivan, M.P. (2013) 'Nicander's Aesopic Acrostic and Its Antidote', in Kwapisz, Petrain, and Szymanski (2013): 225–45.

Svenbro, J. (1988) *Phrasikleia: Anthropologie de la lecture en Grèce ancienne*. Paris.

Tabucchi, A. (1992) *Sogni di sogni*. Palermo.

Tarrant, R.J. (1982) 'Editing Ovid's Metamorphoses: Problems and Possibilities', *CPh* 77: 342–60.

Tarrant, R.J. (1983) 'Ovid', in Reynolds, L.D. (ed.) *Texts and Transmission: A Survey of the Latin Classics*. Oxford.

Tarrant, R.J. (1987) 'Toward a Typology of Interpolation in Latin Poetry', in *TAPhA* 117: 281–98.

Tarrant, R.J. (1989a) 'The Reader as Author: Collaborative Interpolation in Latin Poetry', in Grant, J.N. (ed.) *Editing Greek and Latin Texts*. New York: 121–62.

Tarrant, R.J. (1989b) 'Silver Threads Among the Gold': A Problem in the Text of Ovid's Metamorphoses', *ICS* 14: 103–17.

Tarrant, R.J. (1995) 'The *Narrationes* of "Lactantius" and the Transmission of Ovid's *Metamorphoses*', in Pecere, O. and Reeve, M.D. (eds) *Formative Stages of Classical Traditions: Latin Texts from Antiquity to the Renaissance*. Spoleto: 83–115.

Tarrant, R.J. (1999) 'Nicolaas Heinsius and the Rhetoric of Textual Criticism', in Hardie, Barchiesi, and Hinds (1999): 288–300.

Tarrant, R.J. (2004) *P. Ovidi Nasonis Metamorphoses*. Oxford.

Tarrant, R.J. (2016) *Texts, Editors, and Readers: Methods and Problems in Latin Textual Criticism*. Cambridge.

Thilo, G. (ed.) (1881) *Servii Grammatici qui feruntur in Vergilii carmina commentarii*, Vol. 1. Leipzig.

Thomas, R.F. (1983) 'Callimachus, the Victoria Berenices, and Roman Poetry', *CQ* 33: 92.

Thomas, R.F. (1986) 'Virgil's Georgics and the Art of Reference', *HSPh* 90: 171–98.

Thomas, R.F. (1988) *Virgil: Georgics*. Cambridge.

Thorson, T.S. (2014) *Ovid's Early Poetry: From His Single Heroides to his Remedia Amoris*, Cambridge.

Tilliette, J.-Y. (2014) 'Savant et poètes du moyen âge face à Ovide: les débuts de l'*aetas Ovidiana* (v. 1050–v. 1200)', in Picone, M. and Zimmerman, B. (eds) *Ovidius Redivivus: Von Ovid zu Dante*. Freiburg: 63–105.

Timpanaro, S. (1976) *The Freudian Slip: Psychoanalysis and Textual Criticism*. London.

Tissol, G. (1997) *The Face of Nature : Wit, Narrative, and Cosmic Origins in Ovid's Metamorphoses*. Princeton.

Traube, L. (1911) *Vorlesungen und Abhandlungen 2, Einleitung in die lateinische Philologie des Mittelalters*. Munich.

Tronchet, G. (1998) *La Métamorphose à l'œuvre*. Louvain and Paris.

Trousson, R. (1964a) *Le Thème de Promethée dans la littérature européenne*. Geneva.

Trousson, R. (1964b) 'Plaidoyer pour la Stoffgeschichte', *Revue de Littérature Comparée* 38: 101–14.

Trousson, R. (1965) *Les Études de Thèmes: Essai de Methodologie*. Paris.

Trousson, R. (1980) 'Les Études de thèmes: Questions de méthode', in Bisanz, A.J. and Trousson, R. (eds) *Elemente der Litteratur: Beiträge zur Stoff-, Motiv und Themenforschung. Elisabeth Frenzel zum 65. Geburtstag*. Stuttgart: 1–10.

Trzaskoma, S.M. (2016) 'Further Possibilities regarding the Acrostic at Aratus 783–7', *CQ* 66: 785–90.

Tsantsanoglou, K. (2009) 'The λεπτότης of Aratus', TiC 1: 55–89.

Van der Bijl, Maria S. (1971) 'Petrus Berchorius, Reductorium Morale, Liber XV: Ovidius Moralizatus, Cap. Ii.', Vivarium 9.1: 25–48.

Van Noorden, H. (2015) Playing Hesiod: The 'Myth of the Races' in Classical Antiquity. Cambridge.

Van Sickle, J. (1978) The Design of Virgil's Bucolics. Rome.

Vinge, L. (1967) The Narcissus Theme in Western European Literature up to the Early 19th Century, trans. R. Dewsnap, L. Grönlund, N. Reeves, and I. Söderberg-Reeves. Lund.

Vogt-Spira, G. (2002) 'Der Blick und die Stimme: Ovids Narziß- und Echomythos im Kontext römischer Anthropologie', in Renger (2002): 27–40.

Vogt, E. (1967) 'Das Akrostichon in der griechischen Literatur', A&A 13: 80–95.

Volk, K. (1997) 'Cum carmine crescit et annus: Ovid's Fasti and the Poetics of Simultaneity', TAPhA 127: 287–313.

Volk, K. (2008) Oxford Readings in Classical Studies: Vergil's Eclogues. Oxford.

Volk, K. (2010) 'Aratus', in Clauss, J. and Cuypers, M. (eds) A Companion to Hellenistic Literature. Malden: 197–210.

von Glinski, M.L. (2012) Simile and Identity in Ovid's Metamorphoses. Cambridge.

Wahlsten Böckerman, R. (2016) The Metamorphoses of Education: Ovid in the Twelfth-Century Schoolroom, PhD diss., University of Stockholm.

Walde, C. (2001) Die Traumdarstellungen in der griechisch-römischen Dichtung. Munich.

Walde, C. (2002) 'Narcissus im Mittelalter: Nach Ovid—vor Freud', in Renger (2002): 41–61.

Warner, M. (2002) Fantastic Metamorphoses, Other Worlds. Oxford.

Wellek, R. and Warren A. (1956) Theory of Literature. Harcourt.

West, M.L. (2007) Indo-European Poetry and Myth. Oxford.

Wheeler, S.M. (1995) 'Imago Mundi: Another View of the Creation in Ovid's Metamorphoses', AJPh 116, 95–121.

Wheeler, S.M. (1999) A Discourse of Wonders: Audience and Performance in Ovid's Metamorphoses. Philadelphia.

Wheeler, S.M. (2000) Narrative Dynamics in Ovid's Metamorphoses. Tübingen.

Wheeler, S.M. (ed) (2015) Accessus ad auctores: medieval introductions to the authors (codex latinus monacensis 19,475). Kalamazoo.

Whitaker, R. (1988) 'Did Gallus Write Pastoral Elegies?', CQ 38: 454–8.

White, H. (1982) 'Parthenius and the story of Byblis', Corolla Londiniensis, 2: 185–92.

Wickkiser, B.L. (1999) 'Famous Last Words: Putting Ovid's Sphragis Back into the Metamorphoses', MD 42: 113–42.

Williams, F. (1978) Callimachus' Hymn to Apollo. A Commentary. Oxford.

Wimmel, W. (1973) Hirtenkrieg und Arkadisches Rom. Reduktionsmedien in Vergils Aeneis. Munich.

Winsbury, R. (2009) The Roman Book: Books, Publishing and Performance in Classical Rome. London.

Wyke, M. (2002) The Roman Mistress: Ancient and Modern Representations. Oxford.

Zajko, V. (2009) 'Listening with Ovid: Intersexuality, Queer Theory, and the Myth of Hermaphroditus and Salmacis', Helios 36: 175–212.

Zak, G. (2010) Petrarch's Humanism and the Care of the Self. Cambridge.

Zeitlin, F. (1996) Playing the Other. Chicago.

Zernecke, A.E. (2013) 'The Lady of the Titles: The Lady of Byblos and the Search for her "True Name"', WO 43: 226–42.

Zetzel, J.E.G. (2002) 'Dreaming about Quirinus: Horace's *Satires* and the development of Augustan poetry', in Woodman, A.J. and Feeney, D.C. (eds) *Traditions and Contexts in the Poetry of Horace*. Cambridge: 38–52.

Ziogas, I. (2013) *Ovid and Hesiod: The Metamorphosis of the Catalogue of Women*. Cambridge.

Ziolkowski, J.M. and Putnam, M.C.J. (eds) (2008) *The Virgilian Tradition: The First Fifteen Hundred Years*. New Haven.

Ziolkowski, T. (2005) *Ovid and the Moderns*. Ithaca.

Zissos, A. (1999) 'The rape of Proserpina in Ovid *Met.* 5.341–661: Internal Audience and Narrative Distortion', *Phoenix* 53: 97–113.

Zissos, A. and Gildenhard, I. (1999) ' "Somatic Economies": Tragic Bodies and Poetic Design in Ovid's *Metamorphoses*', in Hardie, Barchiesi, and Hinds (1999): 162–81.

Index Locorum

Ovid (*cont.*)

General Index